THE STATE OF INTERPRETATION OF KEYNES

RECENT ECONOMIC THOUGHT SERIES

Editors:

Warren J. Samuels
Michigan State University
East Lansing, Michigan, USA

William Darity, Jr.
University of North Carolina
Chapel Hill, North Carolina, USA

THE STATE OF INTERPRETATION OF KEYNES

edited by

John B. Davis

of

Marquette University
Milwaukee, Wisconsin

Kluwer Academic Publishers
Boston/Dordrecht/London

Distributors for North America:
Kluwer Academic Publishers
101 Philip Drive
Assinippi Park
Norwell, Massachusetts 02061 USA

Distributors for all other countries:
Kluwer Academic Publishers Group
Distribution Centre
Post Office Box 322
3300 AH Dordrecht, THE NETHERLANDS

Library of Congress Cataloging-in-Publication Data
The state of interpretation of Keynes / edited by John B. Davis.
     p. cm. -- (Recent economic thought series)
  Includes index.
  ISBN 0-7923-9508-5 (alk. paper)
  1. Keynesian economics. I. Davis, John Bryan. II. Series.
HB99.7.S698   1994
330.15'6--dc20
                                      94-34751
                                          CIP

Printed on acid-free paper.

Printed in the United States of America

Contents

Contributing Authors

Edward J. Amadeo
Economics
Pontifícia Universidade Católica
 do Rio de Janeiro
Rio de Janeiro
Brazil 22453

Bradley W. Bateman
Economics
Grinnell College
Grinnell, IA 50112

Allin Cottrell
Economics
Wake Forest University
Winston-Salem, NC 27109

John B. Davis
Economics
Marquette University
Milwaukee, WI 53233

Robert W. Dimand
Economics
Brock University
St. Catharines, Ontario L2S 3A1
Canada

John E. Elliott
Economics
University of Southern California
Los Angeles, CA 90089

G. C. Harcourt
Faculty of Economics and Politics
Cambridge University
Cambridge CB3 9DD
Great Britain

Hans E. Jensen
Economics
University of Tennessee
Knoxville, TN 37996

Michael Syron Lawlor
Economics
Wake Forest University
Winston-Salem, NC 27109

Robert E. Prasch
Economics
University of Maine
Orono, ME 04469

Colin Rogers
Economics
University of Adelaide
Adelaide 5001
Australia

Jochen Runde
Girton College
Cambridge CB3 OJG
Great Britain

Claudio Sardoni
Dipartimento di Scienze
 Economiche
Università degli Studi di Roma
 "La Sapienza"
Rome
Italy

1 INTRODUCTION: THE INTERPRETATION OF KEYNES'S WORK

John Davis

By all accounts, interest in John Maynard Keynes's economic, political, and philosophical thinking has undergone a tremendous revival in the last decade. The proliferation of a wide range of scholarly papers, the appearance of a number of monumental biographies, and the completion of the thirty volume *Collected Writings* all mark a return of interest to what Keynes himself believed and said. Indeed this new interest in Keynes's work seems to have only been exceeded in the past by the attention devoted to Keynes after the publication of *The General Theory*, when Keynes's economic ideas revolutionized not only thinking about the economy as a whole, but also larger views about social responsibility toward unemployed labor and the role of the state in the economy. Coming almost a half century after Keynes's first impact, then, the question naturally arises, why this new interest in ideas that have long been a fundamental part of modern economics and Western social democracy? Why are Keynes's ideas now again a matter of central concern if, as has been said on many occasions, 'we are all Keynesians now'?

One widely accepted answer has to do with the inevitable perils of individual success. Keynes's thinking gave rise to the phenomenon of Keynesianism, which involved the reformulation and translation of the ideas and arguments of *The General Theory* into, first, the context of real world economic policies, and second, the reasoning structures of economists who often possessed very different theoretical inclinations and values. On the first score, Keynesianism arose in the post-war nineteen fifties when economic policy issues were no longer those that had dominated the earlier depression years when Keynes had written. Thus Keynesians thought that if massive unemployment was no longer an issue, Keynes's explanation of how one addressed unemployment could alternatively be applied to the question of how to stay close to full employment - 'fine-tuning' as it was often put. While this may have seemed straightforward for relatively uncomplicated times of rising output and low inflation, one thing this meant was that Keynes's deeper critiques of the nature of private investment went largely ignored. On the second score, economic theory - it is sometimes forgotten - was also undergoing other revolutions during the time Keynes wrote, revolutions if less easily named and associated with single individuals, still no less influential among the majority of economists. Perhaps the best label for the most important of these competing revolutions is Walrasianism. The general equilibrium conception of the economy as a whole, with its own agenda of normative arguments regarding the efficient allocation of resources, competed with Keynesianism, and was in good part responsible for re-directing much of what was accepted and acceptable in Keynes's thinking as Keynesianism.[1] From these two perspectives, then, it should come as no surprise that Keynes's successes - as would be those of any single thinker's - were necessarily mixed. Keynesianism from the beginning expanded and changed Keynes's ideas, and in so doing thus created future opportunities for the reinvestigation of what Keynes's himself had really said and meant. The return of interest to Keynes's own ideas, it might accordingly be said, just reflects the natural ebb and flow of thought we find in the history of ideas, where individuals of great stature periodically undergo re-examination in our efforts to evaluate their ideas in light of their influence.

This answer, however, while it tells us much about why interest would return to Keynes at some point, tells us little about why that interest developed in the last decade or so in particular. But here too there are elements of a plausible explanation. Mainstream macroeconomists today generally seem to agree that Keynesianism failed to respond effectively to two related challenges in the late nineteen seventies, one in the domain of real world economic policy-making and one in the domain of economic theory. With respect to macroeconomic policy, the consensus seems to be that Keynesianism - and thus Keynes's own thinking as well - possesses an inflationary bias, and is consequently more appropriate to depression-type economies than the sorts of economies we have today. In the world of economic theory, on the other hand, many macroeconomists believe that Keynes misunderstood the nature of expectations, and that an analysis of specifically rational expectations makes much of his thinking irrelevant. Against both of these charges, economists now classified as post-Keynesian have responded, first, that Keynes himself was quite sensitive to the problem of inflation, and second, that Keynes's emphasis upon uncertainty rather reflects a superior understanding of expectations requiring far less heroic and more realistic assumptions about individual behavior than does the rational expectations view. Nonetheless, in place of a once monolithic Keynesianism in policy and theory, there now exists debate between a number of different schools and orientations in macroeconomics. Post-Keynesians see this as the inevitable consequence of the original misinterpretation of Keynes's thinking in Keynesianism, and argue that once the post-war reconstruction boom had run its course, Keynesianism, with its view of investment and money conformable to Walrasianism, was bound to collapse. Only then, it follows, might Keynes's own thinking in *The General Theory* re-emerge to explain the nature of modern capitalist economies. The revival of interest in Keynes's thinking thus comes at the current time, because it took more than two decades for Keynesianism to be unmasked, and because Keynes's own thinking is uniquely able to explain current economic conditions.

I wish to amplify this account of new interest in Keynes's thinking in an effort to also say something about its intensity and depth. The account given above tells us both that a figure of Keynes's importance would at some point undergo re-examination, and that this re-examination began when it did because of the recent history of debate over macroeconomic policy and theory. But it stands in danger of underestimating the intensity of commitment to recovering Keynes's own thinking on the part of many contemporary scholars and policy-makers who argue that Keynes's thinking has become especially relevant to today's economic conditions. On the face of things, this seems a paradoxical claim, since Keynes - as his recent biographies so well demonstrate - was very much a figure of his times, and the economic world today is certainly different in many important respects from the time when he wrote. Thus extending the standard account of revival of interest in Keynes's thinking turns on sorting out the puzzling business of just what it was in Keynes that was, if not timeless, then at least makes our time much like his. I will argue that there are two things that fit this description, one concerning the recent path of world history and one concerning the on-going development of economics as a discipline. In connection with each I will also draw conclusions about promising and likely paths of development in future Keynes scholarship.

I turn first to recent world history. The general and particular effects of the astounding pace of change in the social political world in recent years are still beyond our full comprehension. For almost everyone, the nearly half century from the end of World War Two to the early nineteen nineties created a conception of world order - or disorder - that revolved around a planet-threatening deadlock between two geopolitical systems, simply put, capitalism and socialism. The future was always thought to be that only one system would survive, so that for many years this future was framed in terms of two well defined (opposed) strategies of political and economic development, one of which history would ultimately show to be correct. The world that is emerging at the end of the twentieth century, however, is evidently a far more pluralistic and more complicated one in terms of both political and economic power. Not only does world politics, between nations and peoples, seem to raise entirely new issues, but strategies of social economic development formerly thought coherent now encounter ethnic and religious resistance. At the same time, a new set of issues cutting across all societies threatens to overwhelm us, for example, the disruptive effects on local communities and peoples of an increasingly volatile international economic competition, the question of the sustainability of the world environment, and the destructive effects on world peace of ancient, fratricidal ethnic conflicts. Moreover, capitalism, the apparent victor or survivor of the past superpower conflict, depending upon one's point of view, still confronts a host of problems, not the least of which is persistent stagnation in world output along with the associated problems of unemployment and inadequate living standards for millions of people across the globe, a number made larger by the breakdown of traditional economies in the developing world by the extension of the world market.

Does this recall the times in which Keynes lived? His world was also a politically pluralistic one that was not to settle into massive ideological oppositions until the last decade of his life. The interwar world economy he knew and wrote about was in a state of transition in a manner much like today's world economy, where shifting economic power and changing conditions of production undermined industries and employment in economies once prosperous, while creating trade conflicts and currency fluctuations vis-a-vis new centers of economic development. Unemployment and material need were then too the chief effects of the world's economic problems. The existing centers of world power, and world government as well in the form of the United Nations, seem powerless today to control regional conflicts that resemble those that occurred in the nineteen twenties and thirties. And, though it might be said that today's goal of sustainable development makes modern environmental constraints a fundamentally new issue in contemporary economic development, that issue might well be recast in Keynes's terms as whether private investment can be maintained at a level sufficient for full employment, whatever the form of the constraints we face. Keynes, of course, had considerable doubts about what could be expected of a purely private system of investment, and his (not well known) long term policy recommendations explicitly called for greater public responsibility for the course and volume of investment. In the nineteen forties he extended the scope of this concern to the anticipated functioning of the post-war world economy in hopes of ameliorating tendencies toward world-wide stagnation through proposals for a system of international finance and balance of payments assistance. Today the principles behind this extension have come to underlie a network of international public agencies and organizations involved in national infrastructural investment and support for economic restructuring, so as to address the very problems Keynes foresaw from the perspective of his experience in the interwar period.

Through the accidents of world history, then, Keynes's concerns seem again to have become our concerns. Of course there are still many differences between his time and ours, and it would be naive to say that we can hope to find concrete solutions for all of the problems of today's world in strategies formulated in the nineteen thirties. What we may reasonably hope to learn from Keynes and the interwar period, however, is something about the general nature of a social and economic reasoning that works in a world in which power is diffused, but where the many of the problems facing the world ramify across nations and societies. Keynes tied his thinking to the institutions of his time - financial markets, business firms, government bodies, political parties, labor unions, banks, etc. - and then constructed an argument about an historical monetary economy in which expectations and conventions played central roles. He saw economics as a moral science that required a modelling of those relationships which the economist detected in actual economies, and then continually reformulated as experience and varying circumstances required. This type of approach - in contrast to the more abstract, formalistic methods of Walrasianism that impose one, general form of theory on all economies - is especially suitable to addressing concrete issues specific to particular social economies, and then investigating the extent to which the analysis generated can be applied across different national and local economies. Essentially, then, Keynes's method, practically attuned as it was to the specifics of his own time, is particularly suitable to a contemporary world in which national and regional differences in political systems and economic organization are important, but where various world-wide problems affect many societies in quite similar ways.

This suggests that one important theme in future research on Keynes's thought will be how Keynes's methodological thinking underlay his ability to incorporate expectations and conventions in his analysis of income determination. A convention for Keynes represents a structure or system of expectations regarding future events, where individuals employ money as a means of negotiating an uncertain future. Yet, though Keynes drew attention to the role of money in a fundamentally uncertain world, he did little more than point towards the nature of the behavior and form of social organization conventions involved. Standard economic theory adopts the simplest of assumptions about economic behavior in emphasizing atomistic individuals' self-interestedness, and Keynes, as a Marshallian, was at times drawn back to thinking in similar terms. But his view of the complexity of social institutions and their impact on individual decision-making, was nonetheless rich and insightful, and it was this grasp of what went on behind the economic magnitudes we observe that figured crucially in his thinking about the macroeconomy. Indeed, with his long term policy proposal for "a somewhat comprehensive socialisation of investment" as "the only means of securing an approximation to full employment" (CW, VII, p. 378), he demonstrated sensitivity to a particular combination of individual and social characteristics in intermediate-size organizations and institutions located between the state and the individual, which he believed were the key to a conception of a semi-public, semi-private process of investment. Still, little examination or development of the social theory presuppositions of Keynes's thinking has been done on this score, though it is arguably - for all its speculative character - one of the areas in which that thinking most comes into contact with our own time, and most challenged the underlying assumptions of standard economic theory.

Turning now to the issue of the on-going development of economics as a discipline, one arguably finds a set of changes afoot in the mainstream of the profession not unlike the recent developments in world history. In the nineteen seventies and eighties economists of the world were largely divided into two camps according to their support for the ideals of capitalism or socialism. Within western economics, this meant a division between mainstream neoclassical theory and a number of forms of what was often termed alternative theory: post-Keynesianism, neo-Ricardianism, Marxism, institutionalism and evolutionary economics, and social economics. But with the collapse of the eastern Soviet-type economies, the polar contest between neoclassicism and alternative theory in the west suddenly seemed less central. Voices on all sides became less strident, and economists in alternative camps allowed themselves to consider principles they had once condemned: generally those on the left giving more weight to the market process, and those on the right giving more weight to political intervention in the economy. In effect, then, a pluralism in economic theory arose to complement the diffusion of power and influence in the practical world. Though the classic opposition between the market and state management of the economy remained a fundamental dividing line between economists, other issues that bracketed this divide were increasingly debated in its place. In good part, I will suggest, this seems due to a process of evolution within neoclassicism that detached much new research from the simpler core propositions of the theory that had long motivated ideological debate.

Neoclassicism generally, as the dominant or mainstream approach for most western economists, seems to have suffered perils of success of a sort not unlike those Keynes's work experienced when developed as Keynesianism. In the universities where professional economists are trained, new doctoral research needs to be at least mildly innovative to be classified as original research. To a large extent, of course, this has always meant, in both economics and other disciplines simply the rather unreflective application of existing models and principles set out in the core of a theory to new topics. But it would be a mistake to think that research always only extends existing ideas, or that it never innovates upon them. And in fact, mainstream economic thought in the last two decades has raised a variety of new issues and areas that are not easily dealt with by traditional neoclassical theory: bounded rationality, experimental anomalies in expected utility theory, implicit contract analysis, perverse game theoretic results, new growth theory, path dependency, multiple selves analysis, information analysis, the development of new normative concepts, the analysis of odd markets (e.g., for government services, academic research, and health services), the new industrial economics, the new institutionalism, etc. In many instances the connection to traditional neoclassical models is reasonably clear, but in many other instances quite tenuous, since innovative theorists tend to add auxiliary assumptions to standard ones in attempting to expand a theory or capture the nature of new phenomena - this despite the fact that those producing new research typically still believe themselves to be operating within the neoclassical tradition.

What might be said to have happened is that neoclassical theory in the last two decades has undergone a process of evolution that has produced an internal differentiation between core and periphery research. The former remains largely wedded to older sets of traditional issues and is generally carried out by older economists, especially those attached to the model of Arrow-Debreu thinking, while the latter, which is often the province of more recently trained economists, involves new concepts and ideas that often implicitly and sometimes explicitly challenge the centrality of the core. Put in terms of the methodology of economics, the familiar Lakatosian notion that core notions (the 'hard' core) are never really threatened in the development of a scientific research program seems belied by recent experience. The new distinction between core theory and periphery theory in recent neoclassicism, in fact, seems to bring into question, first, the strength of the connections between core and periphery in neoclassical economics, and second, what the 'true' nature of the neoclassical core amounts to. Indeed, even investigating these issues is now complicated by the fact that the existence of many new perspectives on what constitutes the path of development of neoclassical theory makes the nature of core neoclassical theory appear differently to different researchers. This raises perhaps insoluble problems for explaining the core-periphery relationship and the 'true' nature of the core, so much so that it would not be surprising to find that when, say, a 'frontier' game theorist and 'frontier' new growth theorist debate their nominally shared theoretical heritage, they discover themselves in as much disagreement as formerly transpired between neoclassicists and alternative theorists.[2]

The likely path of debate within the mainstream of the economics profession, then, seems more difficult to explain than it once did. Previously, the development of neoclassical economics was seen to involve the continued extension of methodological individualist rationality theory to 'non-economic' domains of social life, for example, history, law, and the family, which other social sciences had long explained with other types of behavioral postulates. Indeed the expression, 'economics imperialism,' came to be widely associated with this stategy of extension and prospective path of development. But it seems that contact with other domains of social analysis also encouraged economists to experiment with introducing other views of behavior and decision-making into economics itself, as in the development of bounded rationality thinking, game theory, and the new institutionalism. A succession of such appropriations, however small, arguably produces theories, at least in some instances, in which the weight of explanation comes to rest on matters increasingly removed from standard concerns. Implicit contract theory is an interesting case. Initially theorists set out to explain worker-management agreements to monitor worker shirking and effort through accounts of workers as self-interested and risk averse. But soon a variety of additional motivational accounts of worker decision-making came forward to deal with the same phenomena, emphasizing social rather than individual characteristics of worker choice, such as whether a worker was an 'insider' or 'outsider.' In effect, in attempting to capture the complex character of contractual relations between firms and workers, often researchers incorporated behavioral assumptions which real world experience, but did not always fit the narrow mold of neoclassicism.

It may well be that mainstream economists are no longer as much concerned about maintaining proper neoclassical pedigree in their research as they once were. This might be explained by the fact that history has removed from front view many of the left and right issues that polarized economists in the west for many years between mainstream and alternative theory, so that with a reduced concern for avoiding what were once purportedly ideological topics and concepts, neoclassical economists are now more willing to experiment with ideas, whatever their source. While it might be too much to say that mainstream economists will henceforth begin to engage in wholesale borrowing of alternative theory concepts, it does not seem unreasonable to say that the once well-drawn dividing line between acceptable and unacceptable work in economics that correlated with mainstream and alternative theory will become more and more blurred. As mainstream economists - especially in applied work - choose from an increasingly eclectic and heterogeneous selection of theories and concepts, not only will the very notion of acceptable economic theorizing undergo a transformation, but the once monolithic character of neoclassicism - like that of Keynesianism - will likely undergo a breakup. One clear manifestation of this process of change is the proliferation of new hybrid sub-fields, especially as reflected in the recent explosion of new area and applied economics journals. Thus, health economics and environmental economics, to take two notable examples, might once have been thought insufficiently attached to the formal strategies of neoclassical analysis to be counted as proper areas of investigation for ambitious, young economists. Now these fields are occupied by many traditionally trained economists, who are either comfortable with making departures from standard principles as they believe justified by their subject matter, or who are pragmatically uninterested in the whole issue of whether their work is properly neoclassical. After all, one can now turn to the most competitive, prestigious economics journals to find papers on such topics as power, fairness, reputation, stereotypes, leadership, entrepreneurship, fads, and other such topics once thought beyond the pale.

Such developments, it can be argued, may well have as one effect the enhancement of Keynes's standing among economists. One unfortunate feature of a more narrow, more rigid economics profession is that economists tend to dismiss the whole of an individual's work if it is somehow thought to fall outside of mainstream concerns. Indeed, any monolithic profession suffering from defensiveness needs only the flimsiest of reasons to discount theories and work that have once been labeled non-traditional. Keynes, of course, made it clear from the outset in *The General Theory* that he was intent upon challenging customary thinking about the macroeconomy, or classical economics as he termed it, and thereafter insisted that understanding his work required a revolution in thinking. Though he also was a synthesizer of great talent, he seemed to think it especially important to emphasize that to understand the macroeconomy one needed to "escape from habitual modes of thought and expression" that "ramify ... into every corner of our minds" (CW, VII, p. viii). Such challenges, needless to say, are often not well received by those attached to the ideas under attack, and were it not for the severity of the times in which Keynes wrote, his message might well have gone ignored altogether. Indeed, it may be fair to say that what impelled many of Keynes's strongest critics in the nineteen seventies and eighties to criticize Keynesian arguments was less the purported failure of Keynesian policy and theory, something never systematically demonstrated, and more an inveterate hostility to the work of a former insider who could be so damning of cherished first principles. If this is true, then, in times of perforce greater charity towards variety of ideas in economic thinking and willingness to experiment, Keynes may come to appear a more acceptable critic, and his insights and talents as a economic theorist then be better appreciated than they have been for a number of years.

What does this imply about the future of Keynes scholarship? From the perspective of the recent development of economics as a discipline, the current revival of interest in what Keynes is thought to have said and meant, as distinct from what his ideas have come to mean in the form of Keynesianism, has two important dimensions. First, since Keynesianism involves a particular systematization of Keynes's thinking, a re-appreciation of Keynes's own ideas involves seeing how they are different from their Walrasian admixtures, and thus what advantages they possess over the Arrow-Debreu-type thinking coupled with Keynes's ideas in the neoclassical-Keynesian synthesis. Since much of the impulse behind the recent development of neoclassical theory is to pragmatically appropriate ideas and concepts that permit explanation of concrete phenomena,

Keynes's thinking, divorced of the systematization imposed upon it by subsequent Keynesians, may now become more accessible. Secondly, since revivals of past thinking naturally reflect a discipline's current concerns, it is fair to suppose that the elements of Keynes's thought that will receive the most attention are those thought likely to be the most valuable to the development of contemporary economics. Thus those who are the most convinced that Keynes's ideas merit new attention are apt to emphasize the elements in that thinking which they believe, given their own sense of the current state of development of economics, are most likely to be influential for a wider audience. At the same time, economists open to innovation in ideas are likely to be receptive to such themes.

Of course, the thought of other past economists may also for similar reasons come to command attention from younger, more innovative economists. Keynes enjoys one particular advantage in this respect. His intuitions and instincts as a practicing economist have now been well described to readers of his recent, excellent biographies (Skidelsky, 1983, 1992; Moggridge, 1992). This is of no little significance, since for many economists today a distorted image of Keynes as an individual had become part of the folklore of Keynesianism. The new biographies, however, show the concrete strategies of an innovative economist at work, and in this regard undermine the notion that Keynes's thinking needs to be fit to a formal, systematic apparatus of Keynesianism, while revealing Keynes's versatility and flexibility as a thinker in responding to changing circumstances. Thus though there have been many other fine economists who also possessed these attributes, Keynes, because of this special attention he has received, will undoubtedly become a prime example for economists and non-economists alike of an economist confronted with the task of finding solutions to real problems.

What, then, does this account of recent development in economics tell us about possible directions in Keynes scholarship? To the extent that the recovery of Keynes's own thinking involves a critical re-examination of the incorporation of Walrasian general equilibrium thinking in Keynesianism, economists interested in Keynes's own ideas may well conclude that special attention ought to be devoted to his distinct conception of equilibrium. Keynes, as Chick has emphasized, rejected the market-clearing concept of equilibrium as a balance of the forces of supply and demand, and rather thought of equilibrium as a point of rest in which forces leading to change are absent or countervailing (1983, p. 21). And, in contrast to the general equilibrium approach, Keynes retained the Marshallian partial equilibrium method, since it permitted him to explain investment causally in terms of factors held to be exogenous to the income determination process, such as the interest rate and long-term expectations. His analysis was thus structured around short and long periods, and amounted in his view to a theory of a "shifting equilibrium - meaning ... the theory of a system in which changing views about the future are capable of influencing the present" (Keynes, CW, VII, p. 293). Much in these ideas, it seems, resonates with contemporary investigations of the concept of equilibrium. In game theory in particular, economists have worked with Nash equilibrium concepts where each individual is doing the best possible in the circumstances. Games may also be sequential, allowing provisional solutions to be revised to accomodate stages of development in interdependent behaviors, and there are other refinements which are in the spirit of Keynes's more flexible approach to the concept of equilibrium.

Of course many of the more concrete issues facing much contemporary research in economics are quite different from those that Keynes encountered, even if the general climate of the world today resembles in important respects that of his day. Thus what may in the final analysis be the most instructive in Keynes's work for contemporary economics is how his general conception of economic method undergirds his particular views on equilibrium, expectations, and conventions. Economics is a moral science, Keynes wrote, that is,

> a science of thinking in terms of models joined to the art of choosing models which are relevant to the contemporary world .... The object of a model is to segregate the semi-permanent or relatively constant factors from those which are transitory or fluctuating so as to develop a logical way of thinking about the latter, and of understanding the time sequences to which they give rise in particular cases (CW, XIV, p. 296).

An essentially pragmatic view of economic method, then, was in Keynes's view necessary for clear thinking about a subject matter that took human motivation to be complex and the forms of economic organization to vary from one context to another. Contemporary economists seem more and more have a view of the subject matter of economics much like this one, and to the extent that the discipline continues to become pluralistic with many perspectives, Keynes's work should enjoy new study.

The essays and comments collected together in this volume were written on a set of themes meant to be representative of the current state of interpretation of Keynes's thinking. Some of the topics investigated have received much attention in the past, and some are of more recent interest. In the former category are topics on standard issues in the interpretation of Keynes's economics: the transition in Keynes's thinking from *The Treatise on Money* to *The General Theory*, the nature of the argument in *The General Theory*, and Keynes's economic policy views, with papers by Edward Amadeo, Michael Lawlor, and Bradley Bateman respectively. The latter category introduces themes of a wider nature, and includes two papers on Keynes's vision, one by Geoff Harcourt and Claudio Sardoni and one by Hans Jensen, and one paper on Keynes's philosophical thinking by John Davis. The strategy adopted in the selection of topics was to review the debates over Keynes's economics from fresh perspectives, and then go on to supply discussions of broader issues concerning the nature of Keynes as a thinker. Hopefully the collection as a whole will add to our general understanding of Keynes's work, and contribute to current revival of interest in Keynes.

Notes

[1] A very good illustration of this is the history of the rise of the ISLM analysis. See Young (1987) for an excellent account of how Keynes's thinking came to be represented in this standard piece of Keynesianism.

[2] See the 1991 centenary issue of the *Economic Journal* for an example of a spectrum of competing voices on the subject of where economics is coming from and where it is heading. Another symptom of the increasing detachment of new research from traditional principles is continuing flow of articles on the 'crisis' in economics.

References

Chick, V. (1983), *Macroeconomics After Keynes*. Cambridge, MA: MIT.

Clarke, P. (1989), *The Keynesian Revolution in the Making: 1924-1936*. Oxford: Oxford University Press.

Economic Journal (1991), Volume 101, Number 404.

Keynes, J. M. (1971-1989), *The Collected Writings of John Maynard Keynes*, Volumes I-XXX. Edited by D. Moggridge. London: Macmillan.

Moggridge, D. (1992), *Maynard Keynes, An Economist's Biography*. London: Routledge.

Skidelsky, R. (1983), *John Maynard Keynes*, Volume I, *Hopes Betrayed 1883-1920*. London: Macmillan.

Skidelsky, R. (1992), *John Maynard Keynes*, Volume II, *The Economist as Saviour*. London: Macmillan.

Young, W. (1987), *Interpreting Mr. Keynes: The IS-LM Enigma*. London: Polity.

2 CHANGES IN OUTPUT IN KEYNES'S *TREATISE ON MONEY*[1]

Edward J. Amadeo

1. Introduction

Volume XIII of Keynes's *Collected Writings*, published in 1973, contains an important document for the study of the transition from the *Treatise on Money* (TREATISE) to the *General Theory of Employment, Interest, and Money* (GENERAL THEORY): a note from five surviving participants of the Cambridge "Circus"[2] describing their relationship with Keynes, the nature of their criticism of the TREATISE, and their role in the development of the ideas leading to the GENERAL THEORY. The main criticism of the Circus was directed towards the assumption of a given level of aggregate output underlying the TREATISE's fundamental equations. The note attacks the assumption of given output as rendering the TREATISE somewhat irrelevant in light of the severe unemployment facing Britain in the 1920's and especially after 1929. The note also suggests that the Circus, by pointing out to Keynes the consequences of his assumption, played a fundamental part in the transition towards the GENERAL THEORY.

The survivors' view became the conventional view. Moggridge, the editor of Keynes's *Collected Writings*, was responsible for transforming the Circus survivors' view into the official view. Moggridge's arguments may be summarized as follows. First the specification of the fundamental equations is based on the assumption of given output[3] thus the book's conclusions are "not quite relevant to the conditions of 1930-31" (Moggridge, 1976, p. 89). Second, this assumption makes the equations inconsistent with the "verbal discussions concerning movements in output" (p.89) contained in the TREATISE itself. Third, Keynes came to realize the shortcomings of the assumption after the book was published through the comments of Hayek and Robertson and, most importantly the criticism of the Circus (p.88). Finally, the movement from the TREATISE to the GENERAL THEORY began after these criticisms with Keynes trying to "recast his analysis in terms of changes in output" (p.90).

The purpose of this paper is to argue that Keynes was, in fact, quite aware of the assumption of given output in the formulation of the fundamental equations and clearly considered changes in output (and unemployment) to be a relevant problem and that given the method of analysis used in the book, the specification of the equations is perfectly consistent with and, indeed, adequate for, the study of changes in output. This implies that the study of changes in output per se does not differentiate the TREATISE from the GENERAL THEORY: the method of analysis on which the study is based is the real differentia[4].

That Keynes considered changers in the level of output and unemployment a relevant problem is clear from his contributions to debates on policy issues in the 1920's. He opposed the return of Britain to the gold standard at prewar parity on the grounds that it would require a reduction in money wages which could only be achieved through "deliberate intensification of unemployment" (Keynes, 1931, p. 252). His 1929 pamphlet "Can Lloyd George Do It?" is yet another example of a discussion of changes in the levels of output and employment. In what follows, however, we shall concentrate on the consistency and adequacy issues rather than the relevance one.

Recently the notion that Keynes was unaware of the given output assumption has been challenged. Milgate (1983) has pointed out that Pigou, in a letter to Keynes in 1929, inquires if what he "argue[s] impl[ies] that changes in Bank rate cannot affect E [real income] or O [output]?" (JMK, XXIX, p.5). Likewise, Hawtrey, in his comments on the proofs of the TREATISE, argues that "Mr. Keynes's formula only takes account of the reduction in prices in relation to costs, and does not recognize the possibility of a reduction of output being caused directly by a contraction of demand without an intervening fall of price" (JMK, XIII, p. 152). Keynes read and made comments to Pigou's letter; he was also aware of Hawtrey's comments although he only answered them after the publication of the TREATISE.

Keynes was aware of the assumption before the book was published and there is obviously no dispute with Moggridge's first argument that the assumption permeated the specification of the equations. However, changes in output were the subject matter of a few chapters of the TREATISE. Kahn, himself an eminent participant of the Circus, admits that it was an error to conclude that changes in output were not discussed in the book. He writes: "I do not see how we could have attributed to Keynes the assumption of inelastic supply, and I am completely mystified by the questions: a) why we did not see this by ourselves; b) why it did not come out in the course of the discussions between Keynes and me" (Kahn, 1984, p. 108). It also was to "come out in the course of the discussions" between Keynes and Joan Robinson, and Keynes did not quite accept the criticism.

The fact of the matter is that Book III of the TREATISE -- in which the fundamental equations are formulated -- is based on the assumption that the level of output is given; Book IV, however, provides a discussion of credit cycles and has an explicit analysis of changes in output in which the equations play a central role.

The paper is organized as follows. After presenting some conceptual elements in section 2, we shall present a simple model for deriving the fundamental equations in section 3. This is followed by a discussion of how the equations can be used to study changes in output in section 4. Finally, section 5 provides a brief exposition of the steps needed to go from the TREATISE's model to that of the GENERAL THEORY.

2. Concepts and Definitions

2.1 'Supply' and 'Expenditure' Dimensions in Keynes's Economics

Two broad groups of concepts can be identified in Keynes's theory in the TREATISE and after. We shall refer to them as "expenditure" and "supply" dimensions. Most studies of the development of the theories of aggregate output and prices in the 1920's and 30's -- including the study of the transition from the TREATISE to the GENERAL THEORY -- concentrate on the expenditure dimension, that is, on the aggregate monetary aspects of the theories, definitions and determinants of income, saving and investment and the notion of monetary equilibrium [5]. Wicksell (1907, 1935) was the earliest champion of this dimension, laying down the framework for the study of "macroeconomics" as we refer to it today. He studied a "pure credit economy" in which the banking system acted as a creator of a means of exchange on demand; that is, one in which demand for credit could always be accommodated. This allowed current expenditure to be independent of current income or, more specifically, investment (I) to be independent of saving (S). Monetary equilibrium -- or expenditure equilibrium as we shall call it -- is characterized in the Wicksellian system by the equality of investment and saving. Wicksell's "cumulative process" is the result of a disturbance in the circular flow of income and expenditure or a discrepancy between investment and saving.

Keynes's work is best known for its expenditure dimension aspects. But there is also an important supply dimension in his contribution. It addresses the decisions to produce and employ taken by the "producer or manufacturer." The time horizon associated with these decisions being the "employment" or "production periods" (JMK, XXIX, p. 75). It corresponds to daily decisions based on "employment period expectations," 'daily' standing "for the shortest interval after which the firm is free to revise its decisions as to how much employment to offer " (JMK, VII, p. 47, n. 1). Equilibrium in this dimension is characterized by correct employment period expectations, that is, the equality between expected and actually realized results. Unlike the great majority of studies of Keynes's economics, we shall concentrate on the supply rather than expenditure dimension aspects of his work.

2.2 Methods of Analysis

Although economists often are not conscious of the particular method underlying their work, trying to make their method explicit and understand it may prove to illuminate the subsequent analysis. Some studies of Keynes's contributions emphasize the role of method, notably Hicks (1936, 1965) and Garegnani (1976, 1978, 1979).[6]

The taxonomy of methods presented here is defined by two attributes: first, the relevant time-unit and, second, the analytical object of study. As for the first attribute, we shall define two time-units: the "finite" and "equilibrium" periods. The finite period is a general concept which refers to any calendar or chronometric period; the choice of the particular time horizon depends on one's analytical purposes. Because it refers to an arbitrary cut in historical time, the finite period can correspond to either an equilibrium or a disequilibrium position. However, given its arbitrariness, it will more often than not be associated with a disequilibrium position, and, indeed, it seems safe to identify finite periods with disequilibrium positions.

In contrast, if we want to find a "period" necessarily associated with equilibrium, this can only be done by use of a purely logical period -- chronological ones will not do. Since this period is supposed to be associated with equilibrium by construction, let us label it the "equilibrium period." The actual length of time it takes for equilibrium to be achieved is not important here. Rather, attention is focused on the position of rest associated with a set of exogenously determined variables (data) and the parameters specifying the (expectational, behavioral, and technological) functional relations of the system.

The second attribute of the taxonomy presented here concerns the analytical objects of study, namely, the end-of-period position and the adjustment path. Independently of the period (finite or equilibrium), "statics" is used to designate the study of the end-of-period configuration of a system and "dynamics" the study of the adjustment path across a number of arbitrarily defined finite periods given any change in the data[7].

We shall now combine the two attributes and propose the following taxonomy of methods:

	Finite	Equilibrium
Statics	T	G
Dynamics		D

The choice of the letters "T," "G" and "D" here is not arbitrary. As we shall see, they refer to, respectively, the TREATISE, the GENERAL THEORY, and the drafts of the GENERAL THEORY.

The "static equilibrium" or "G" method corresponds to the conventional comparative statics method: it refers to the study of end-of-(equilibrium) period configurations associated with different sets of data. If we couple the equilibrium period with the study of the path of variables over time, this is an exercise in "equilibrium dynamics," the "D" method. The emphasis on the notion of equilibrium underlying the adjustment process and, hence, on stability conditions are the major feature of this method. The "finite static" or "T" method is appropriate for the study of immediate effects of a change in data; as we would expect, it will often picture the system in disequilibrium. A sequence of finite periods driven by changing expectations characterizes the method [8]. It will be appreciated that both the "sequence of T's" and "D" methods study a system over a series of finite periods; the difference between them depends on the role played by the notion of equilibrium and stability conditions (emphasized in the latter) and expectations (emphasized in the former).

We shall suggest in section 5 that Keynes, en route from the TREATISE to the GENERAL THEORY, followed a T-->D-->G path of methods, "T" standing for the TREATISE, "G" for the GENERAL THEORY and "D" for the drafts of the GENERAL THEORY [9].

3. A Model for the TREATISE

Equilibrium in the TREATISE corresponds to Marshall's "long periods," that is to say, to a position where capacity and capacity utilization as well as sectoral structure and technology adjust to demand. The definition of income in the book, according to which it is "identically the same thing [as]... the earnings of the factors of production (JMK, V. p. 111), provides clear evidence of the notion of equilibrium Keynes was assuming [10]. Normal profits or the normal remuneration of entrepreneurs, "themselves amongst the factors of production" (loc. cit.), enter the definition of income; this is not the case for unexpected or "windfall profits or losses" [11] resulting from differences between sale proceeds and the costs of production.

Equilibrium, however, is only a point of reference; the objective of the TREATISE is to study the causes of deviations from equilibrium and, once the system deviates, the repercussion effects (JMK, V, p. 120). We suggest that the appropriate finite time-unit for the study of disequilibrium positions in the book is the "employment" or "production" period as characterized in section 2. The following passage lends support to this view:

> "Insofar ... as production takes time ... and insofar as entrepreneurs are able at the beginning of a production period to forecast ...the demand for their product at the end of the production period, it is obviously the anticipated profit or loss on new business, rather than the actual profit or loss on business just concluded, which influences them in deciding the scale on which to produce and the offers which it is worth while to make to the factors of production" (JMK, V, p. 143; emphasis added)."

We consider the derivation of the fundamental equations from the perspective of the supply dimension, turning then to the expenditure dimension. Like in the GENERAL THEORY, in the TREATISE, profit maximization is assumed and, therefore, marginal cost is equated to the expected price. In the long-period, this assumption implies that producers equate average cost to the expected price or total cost to the expected sale proceeds:

1. $w/a(N^*) = w/e(N^*) = E[p]$

where $a(N)$ = the average cost function, $e(N)$ = marginal cost function, w = money wage and $E[p]$ = the expected price.

The level of output (X^*) to be produced during the current period is determined by the intersection of the cost curve and the expected price line, as depicted in Figure 1.

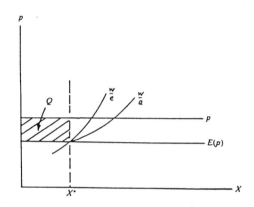

Assume that firms do not carry inventories from one period into another. If producers expectations happen to be incorrect, the expected and actual (or "market clearing") prices corresponding to X^* will differ, i.e., $E[p]$ and p will differ. Windfall profits or losses (Q) would, therefore, be given by

2. $Q = (p - E[p])\, X^*$

implying

3. $p = E[p] + Q/X^*$

4. $p = w/a(N^*) + Q/X^*$

According to equation 3, the actual price level can be decomposed into an expected and an unexpected (windfall) component respectively [12]. Equation 4 decomposes the price into the "income index" (or average cost) and an "profit index" [13].

We turn now to the expenditure interpretation of the fundamental equation. Here Keynes follows Wicksell quite closely. A developed banking system, creating credit on demand, makes investment independent of current saving. Or, put in a broader sense, it makes expenditure (Y) composed by investment (I) and consumption (C), independent of current income. It is assumed that saving (S) and consumption exhaust the value of income, as defined in the TREATISE. Profits, as given by the difference between expenditure (or aggregate sale proceeds) and income (or costs), are also equal to the difference between investment and saving:

5. $Q = I - S$

which, together with equation 4, gives rise to a second version of the fundamental equation:

6. $p = w/a + (I - S)/X$

In equilibrium, demand and income, in the expenditure dimension, and expected and actual prices, in the supply dimension, match. Windfall profits are zero. Or, as Keynes puts it in the TREATISE:

> "[T]he long-period or equilibrium norm of the purchasing power of money is given by the money rate of efficiency earnings [w/a]; whilst the actual purchasing power oscillates below and above this equilibrium level according as ... investment is running ahead of, or falling behind, saving" (JMK, V, p. 137).

In this section we have analyzed the immediate effect of an expenditure disturbance (I different from S) on the supply side or productive sphere of the economy leading to unforeseen results as represented by a discrepancy between expected and actual prices (p different from E[p]. This analysis was conducted, so to speak, "inside" the employment period to consider changes in output.

4. Changes in Output in the TREATISE

Keynes did not accept the criticism coming from the Circus that in the TREATISE the level of aggregate output was fixed. In a letter to Joan Robinson, he claimed the assessment was not quite accurate:

> "I think you are a little hard on me as regards the assumption of constant output. It is quite true that I have not followed out the consequences of changes in output in the earlier theoretical part [of the book].... But ... I have long discussions of the effects of changes in output; it is only at a particular point in the preliminary theoretical argument that I assume constant output" (JMK, XIII, p. 270).

The "preliminary theoretical argument" undoubtedly refers to book III of the TREATISE in which the fundamental equations are derived. Just as in the derivation developed in section 3 above, the study takes place during or "inside" the employment period. Producers choose the level of output at the beginning of the period based on their expected sale proceeds and information concerning the cost structure. Throughout the period they are faced with the actual demand. Although inventories may adjust, Keynes assumes that prices do the bulk of the "market clearing" adjustment. The derivation of the equations is an exercise in "finite statics" or, as Keynes puts it, the equations are "an instantaneous picture taken on the assumption of a given output." But, he continues, they represent an attempt "to show how... forces could develop which [involve] a profit-disequilibrium, and thus require a change in the level of output. ... [T]he dynamic development, as distinct from the instantaneous picture, was left incomplete and extremely confused" (JMK, VII, p. xxii).

The "dynamic development" is to be found in Book IV of the TREATISE ("The Dynamics of the Price Level") where Keynes sets as his task the explanation of the determinants of credit cycles. The idea is clearly to go "beyond" the employment period given a situation of profit-disequilibrium; in terms of our construction, the aim is to study the effects of $Q = (p - E[p])X^*$ being different from zero. In describing the "three types" of credit cycles (JMK,V, p. 252), Keynes clearly uses employment and prices.

The typical causality chain used to describe changes in output in Keynes's discussion of credit cycles begins with a change in the Bank rate which tends to make investment demand deviate from the current level of saving (I different from S). Producers, who are assumed to have been making their decisions over a period of relative normality, are taken by surprise by the expenditure shock. The effect in the supply dimension is measured by the difference between the expected and the actual prices, that is, $E[p] - p$, and as a result by the appearance of profits or losses. The latter will alter producers' expectations and plans and, therefore, their decisions concerning their future levels of output and employment. The following scheme synthesizes the causality chain characteristic of the TREATISE's model:

$$I > S ==> E[p] < p ==> Q > 0 ==> \text{ change in X}$$

The method employed in the TREATISE is perfectly consistent with and adequate for the study of changes in output. Profit-disequilibrium or the appearance of windfall profits or losses at the end of the period represents the bridge between two periods. As Keynes puts it when studying the expansionary effect on the consumption goods sector of an increase in investment demand.

> "[T]hose entrepreneurs who have liquid consumption goods emerging from the process of production are able to sell them for more than they have cost $[p > E[p] = w/a]$, ... and so to reap a windfall profit $[Q = (p-E[p]X^*]...$. [T]he almost inevitable result of profits on current output ... is to encourage manufacturers... to strain their efforts to increase their output" (JMK, V, p.258).

By emphasizing the role of supply dimension aspects in the TREATISE we have tried to show that the fundamental equations are an adequate tool to study changes in output.

5. Towards the GENERAL THEORY

From what has been said so far, it seems unreasonable to argue that the difference between the TREATISE and the GENERAL THEORY hinges on the study of changes in output per se. It hinges on the method underlying the theory of output determination. In the TREATISE the theory is cast in a finite or disequilibrium period analysis; in the GENERAL THEORY, in an equilibrium static analysis. In what follows we shall discuss very briefly the steps Keynes took in going from a disequilibrium to an equilibrium theory of output. The steps are unavoidably related to the expenditure and supply dimensions.

On the expenditure side, the essential step is Keynes's enunciation of the "psychological law" according to which consumption expenditure varies directly with income but to a lesser extent -- or that the propensity to consume is smaller than one. The law makes current income the central determinant of consumption and, at the same time, provides the system with an equilibrating adjustment process and stability condition for changes in output and prices [14].

As for the supply dimension, considerations about the role of employment period expectations in the adjustment process to changes in data are as important as the psychological law. The level of income based on which consumers make their expenditure decision is ultimately determined by producer's decision to produce and employ.

The latter, in turn, depends on expectations which may affect the path of variables over time and the stability conditions. In the GENERAL THEORY Keynes "omits reference" to employment period expectations and implicitly assumes that they are continuously fulfilled on the grounds that "in practice the process of revision of [these expectations] is a gradual and continuous one, carried on largely on the lights of realized results" (JMK, V. p. 50). In Keynes's 1937 lecture notes one reads that "the theory of effective demand is substantially the same if we assume that short-period expectations are always fulfilled" (JMK, XIV, p. 180).

To arrive at the GENERAL THEORY'S static equilibrium theory of output, Keynes, departing from the disequilibrium theory of the TREATISE, had to discuss the stability of the adjustment path of output, employment and prices. Indeed, this is precisely what one finds in the drafts of the GENERAL THEORY: the detailed study of the roles played by the propensity to consume and producer's expectations and decisions to fix the levels of output and employment given a change in autonomous expenditure. The following examples are meant to legitimize the suggestion that both supply and expenditure elements played a role in Keynes's preparation of the GENERAL THEORY.

According to a 1931 letter to Kahn, windfall profits respond to changes in investment ("dQ/dI [is] positive"), output [X] responds to changes in profits (dX has the same sign as Q) and finally, saving responds to changes in output ("dS/dX [is] positive"). Therefore, argues Keynes, "if, starting from equilibrium, an increase in I makes Q positive, X increases and S increases but Q/X gradually diminishes" (JMK, XIII, p. 347). The last statement, a progressive reduction in Q/X, as S increases --remember that in the TREATISE Q = I - S -- is the implicitly stability condition.

In a 1931-32 draft of the GENERAL THEORY, the study begins with "the case where there has occurred a decrease of disbursement leading to a decrease of profits" (JMK, XIII, p. 383). Keynes next studies the effects on the decision to produce of a reduction in profits and, then, the effect on earnings and expenditure; the latter refers essentially to consumption expenditure. At this point, the reasons for expenditure to fall less than earnings -- such as the "pressure of increasing poverty" which makes people save less -- come into the picture as an explanation of the contractionary process. Keynes concludes by arguing that

> "once we have reached the point at which income decreases less than earnings decrease with investment stable, the attainment of equilibrium presents no problem. For provided the spending always increase less than earnings increase and decrease less than earnings decrease, i.e. provided S and E have the same sign, and that investment does no change, any level of output is a position of stable equilibrium" (JMK, XIII, p.387).

It becomes quite clear from Keynes's writings that both supply and expenditure dimension elements were important to the study of the equilibrating path following a change in investment, and that the stability of this process was at center stage. Hence our suggestion that en route to the GENERAL THEORY from the TREATISE, Keynes made use of the "dynamic equilibrium" method. In this sense he took both an historical and analytical step between the two books.

Appendix: A Note on the Literature

Garegnani (1976, 1978, 1979) and subsequently Milgate (1982) have suggested that Keynes in the GENERAL THEORY makes use of the traditional (classical and early neo-classical) method of "long-period positions." We endorse this view, though a few remarks on terminology are needed. Garegnani's "long-period" is, in our terms, the "equilibrium period." Garegnani and the classicals assume that forces operating in a capitalist economy tend to continuously drive the system towards a "position of repose" (the long-period position) whenever it is shaken by a change in data : "deviations" from this position characterize the adjustment process which in our terminology takes place over a number of "finite periods."

Keynes, too, identifies the long-period with what we call here the equilibrium period when he writes that it "relates to a position towards which forces spring up to influence the short-period positions whenever the latter have diverged from [the long-period]" (JMK, XXIX, p.54). The concepts of "short" --in our terms, "finite" -- "and long" -- in our terms, "equilibrium" -- refer, respectively, to deviations from a position of rest and the position of rest itself.

Marshall (1890) employed the concept of "long" and "short" periods in a different manner. In his work, they refer essentially to the extent to which the productive structure responds (or accommodates) to changes in demand. In the "short-period" capacity utilization adjusts to demand whereas in the "long-period" capacity itself (besides the skill of labor and sectoral structure) adjusts. The notion of "short-period equilibrium" usually associated with the GENERAL THEORY's model actually corresponds to Marshall's usage of the term. Accordingly, the term "long-period equilibrium" characterizes the position of rest in growth theory.

The term "long-period" when applied to the GENERAL THEORY requires the following clarifying note: it refers to the usage of the term which identifies it with a general position of rest, not with Marshall's usage. Given the ambiguity of the term, we would rather refer to equilibrium to convey the notion of the position of rest.

It should also be made clear that Keynes's "forces spring[ing] up to influence the short-period positions whenever the latter have diverged from the [long-period]" corresponds to a process which, according to our taxonomy, would be cast into the "dynamic equilibrium" method. The method is supposed to describe the path of the system over a number of finite periods with emphasis given to the notion of equilibrium. An alternative approach to study the path of the system over time is the "sequence of static finite periods" method. Here, expectations play a major role in driving the variables and the notion of equilibrium is less emphasized. The method was developed by Hicks (1936, 1965) who calls it the "temporary equilibrium" method, following the influence of Lindhal (1939) and Hayek (1928) [15].

Notes

[1] I would like to thank Murray Milgate, Lance Taylor, Stephen Marglin, Amitava Dutt and Susan Vitka for their helpful comments. I am grateful to John B. Davis for encouraging me to write the paper and for his most useful editorial help. As usual, they are not responsible for my errors and misinterpretations.

[2] The Cambridge Circus was a seminar group composed of young economists created in 1931 to discuss Keynes's TREATISE. The survivors of the group who agreed on the note printed in the COLLECTED WRITINGS are Richard Kahn, James Meade, Piero Sraffa, Joan Robinson and Austin Robinson.

[3] As Moggridge notices, "Kahn realized clearly that the TREATISE equations were a limiting case --which was not really relevant to the conditions of 1930/1, when British unemployment averaged between 2 and 3 million" (Moggridge 1976, p.89).

[4] The claim that the study of changes in output does not differentiate the two books does not imply that it played the same role or had the same weight in the TREATISE and GENERAL THEORY. The central purpose of the GENERAL THEORY is to study the determinants of the levels of aggregate output and employment; the TREATISE's objective is to explore an alternative to the quantity theory of money as an explanation for the determinants of the price level in the short period; and to apply this alternative -- the fundamental equations -- to discuss "credit cycles." As we will argue presently, changes in output are consistently and adequately studied in Keynes's discussion of the "credit cycle" in the TREATISE.

[5] See, for example, A. Hansen (1951), Patinkin (1976, 1983) and B. Hansen (1981).

[6] References to the work of Garegnani and Hicks and a comparison with the taxonomy proposed here can be found in the appendix to this paper.

[7] We do not endorse the conventional view according to which there is a connection between dynamics and growth theory, on the one hand, and statics and employment theory, on the other hand. The comparison of both steady and stationary states is an exercise in "statics" according to the taxonomy. The study of adjustment processes and stability conditions in both growth and employment theories is a study of "dynamics." What differentiates the two theories in our view is not the method underlying them but the extent to which the productive structure is assumed to adjust to changes in demand: in employment theory, capacity utilization adjusts whereas in growth theory, capacity itself accommodates.

[8] There are some similarities between the "temporary equilibrium" method developed by Hicks (1965) and the sequence of finite periods described here.

[9] By "drafts of the GENERAL THEORY" we mean not only the drafts themselves but also other documents (letters, lecture notes, etc.) to be found in volumes XIII, XIV and XXIX of Keynes's *Collected Writings*.

[10] In a 1934 draft of the GENERAL THEORY Keynes noticed that in the TREATISE he took as the "meaning of income not the expectations which led to the current employment of the capital equipment actually in use, but the expectations which would have led to the original erection as well as the current employment of the equipment actually in use " (JMK, XIII, p. 425).

[11] "Profits" in the TREATISE are essentially unexpected; thus Keynes's recurrent reference to "windfall profits." He actually observes that "[i]t has been suggested ... that it might be better to employ the term windfalls for what I here call profits" (JMK, V, p. 113).

[12] The reader will recognize the Shacklelian flavor of this interpretation: "Keynes's...fundamental equation implicitly compares two states of the ... price-level. This equation takes an ex-post view of what we shall call a proper-named unit of time ...and shows both what the price level would have been in that interval had entrepeneurs' expectations, prevailing at its beginning,proved correct, and what in fact the price-level was. This realized price-level is thus also exhibited as the sum of two terms, the expected level and the unexpected divergence therefrom"(Shackle, 1967, p. 163).

[13] The income and profit indexes are closely associated with the TREATISE's concepts of "income inflation" and "profit inflation," respectively (JMK, V, p. 140).

[14] Patinkin (1976, 1983) considers the enunciation of this "psychological law" the central message of the GENERAL THEORY. As we shall notice, his analysis lacks a systematic discussion of the supply dimension aspects.

[15] See Milgate (1979) for a detailed study of the origins of the notions of intertemporal and temporal equilibria.

References:

Amadeo, E.J. (1989) *Keynes's Principle of Effective Demand*. Aldershot: Edward Elgar.

Eatwell, J. (1983) "The long period theory of employment," *Cambridge Journal of Economics*.

_____. (1983) *Keynes's Economics and Theory of Value and Distribution*. London: Duckworth.

Garegnani, P. (1976) "On a change on the notion of equilibrium in recent work on value and distribution," reprinted in Eatwell and Milgate [1983].

_____. (1978) "Notes on consumption, investment and effective demand I," *Cambridge Journal of Economics*, reprinted in Eatwell and Milgate [1983].

_____. (1979) "Notes on consumption, investment and effective demand II," *Cambridge Journal of Economics*, reprinted in Eatwell and Milgate [1983].

Hansen, A. (1951) *Business Cycle and National Income*. New York: W.W. North.

_____. (1981) "Unemployment, Keynes and the Stockholm School," *History of Political Economy*.

Harold, R. (1936) *The Trade Cycle*. New York: A. M. Kelley [1967].

Hayek, F. A. (1928) "Das intertemporale gleichgewichtssystem der preise und die bewegungen des geldwertes," *Weltwirtschaftliches Archiv*.

Hicks, J. R. (1936) "The General Theory -- a first impression," *Economic Journal*, 46.

_____. (1939) *Value and Capital*. Oxford: Clarendon Press, [1946].

_____. (1965) *Capital and Growth*. Oxford: Clarendon Press.

Kahn, R. (1984) *The Making of Keynes's General Theory*. Cambridge: University Press.

Keynes, J. M. (1973) *The Collected Writings of J. M. Keynes*, edited by D. Moggridge. London : Macmillan, Vols. V, VI, VII, XIII, XIV, XXIX; referred to in the text as JMK.

_____. (1930) *A Treatise on Money*, Vols. I and II, reprinted in JMK, Vols. V and VI.

_____. (1931) *Essays in Persuasion*. London: W.W. Norton.

_____. (1936) *The General Theory of Employment Interest and Money*, reprinted in JMK, Vol. VII.

_____. (1937) "The general theory of employment," *Quarterly Journal of Economics*, reprinted in J.M.K, XIV.

Lindhal, E. (1939) *Studies on the Theory of Money and Capital*. New York: A. M. Kelley, [1967].

Marshall, A. (1890) *Principles of Economics*. Macmillan, [1984].

Milgate, M. (1979) "On the origin of the notion "intertemporal equilibrium," *Economica*.

_____. (1982) *Capital and Employment*. New York: Academic Press.

_____. (1983) "Keynes and Pigou on the gold standard and monetary theory," *Contributions to Political Economy*.

Moggridge, D. E. (1976) *John Maynard Keynes*. New York: Penguin.

_____. (1973) "From the Treatise to the General Theory: an exercise in chronology," *History of Political Economy*, Vol.5, No. 1.

Patinkin, D. (1976) *Keynes's Monetary Thought*. Durham: Duke University Press.

_____. (1983) *Anticipations of the General Theory*. Oxford: Blackwell.

Shackle, G. L. S. (1967) *The Years of High Theory*. Cambridge: Cambridge University Press.

Wicksell, K. (1907) "The Influence of the Rate of Interest on Prices," *The Economic Journal*, 17.

_____. (1935) *Lectures in Political Economy*, Vol. II. New York: A. Kelley, [1978].

EDWARD AMADEO'S CONTRIBUTIONS TO THE INTERPRETATION OF KEYNES'S ECONOMICS

COMMENT BY ROBERT E. PRASCH

Introduction

Much like the long standing debate over the relationship between the major works of Adam Smith, an energetic discussion has emerged over the past twenty or so years regarding the relationship between the major texts of John Maynard Keynes. A subsection of the larger discussion is an investigation into the process which led Keynes to modify or abandon the framework of the *Treatise on Money* (1930) and write *The General Theory of Employment, Interest and Money* (1936).[1] Like the Smith scholarship, this debate is about much more than it initially appears to be. The actual discussion is, indirectly, about identifying and defining what is original and unique to *The General Theory*.

In the following paper I would like to locate Edward Amadeo's work in the context of a broader discussion which features three important strands of interpretation. The first strand is the view embodied in the work of Alvin Hansen and Don Patinkin. They have argued that Keynes's primary contribution was a theory of effective demand which was important for the determination of output in the short run (Hansen, 1936; Patinkin, 1982).[2] Neither economist saw Keynes' theory as providing the grounds for a critique of the idea that in the long run the amount of output could be uniquely determined by the theory offered in the Walrasian schema. There is a second view, associated with Pierangelo Garegnani, John Eatwell, and Murray Milgate, which argues that the Walrasian system is not an accurate depiction of the long period position underlying the Keynesian theory. They argue for the use of the Sraffian theory as the point of "long period" equilibrium (Garegnani, 1983; Milgate, 1982; Eatwell, 1983; Eatwell and Milgate, 1983). Finally, some scholars, such as G. L. S. Shackle and Jan Kregel, have argued that Keynes's emphasis on uncertainty indicates that he made a complete break with long period theories in *The General Theory* and that his theory is best understood as a theory of short term dynamics (Shackle, 1974, 1967 ch. 11; Kregel, 1980). They have argued that *The General Theory* is about the dynamics of an economy which must, and by its nature necessarily is, operating in the short term.

Each of these well developed viewpoints evoke different answers to what might otherwise be a relatively simple exegetical exercise in Keynesian economics.[3] The quest outlined above is magnified by the fact that Keynes did not provide a clear statement as to what he thought the linkage was. We do know from the preface to the *Treatise on Money* that he was somewhat unsatisfied with that book as it went to print. He made the point that his ambivalence was tied to the fact that his thinking was in transition throughout the writing process (Keynes, 1971, p. xvii). We have another hint in the preface to *The General Theory* where he states that "The relation between this book and my *Treatise on Money*, which I published five years ago, is probably clearer to myself than it will be to others; and what in my own mind is a natural evolution in a line of thought which I have been pursuing for several years, may sometimes strike the reader as a confusing change of view" (Keynes, 1964, p. vi). In his recent contributions to this discussion, Amadeo has offered an interesting, and I believe important, interpretation of this transition.[4]

Critique of the "Conventional View"

Amadeo starts his paper with his contention that he will refute what he claims is the "conventional view" of the transition from the *Treatise* to *The General Theory*. He indentifies this conventional view as that of Donald Moggridge (Moggridge 1973, 1976) in which it is claimed that the criticism of the members of the Cambridge "Circus" brought Keynes's attention to the narrow, even irrelevant, status of the theoretical apparatus of the *Treatise* due to its dependence on an assumption of fixed output. Moggridge claimed that this criticism, combined with the criticism of intellectual adversaries such as Hawtrey, Robertson, and to a lesser degree Hayek, resulted in a need to rework the *Treatise*, and in particular, a need to answer questions related to the level of output and the factors which cause a change in that level.

Now, it is true that Moggridge's view is important. Indeed, since he is the person most closely associated with the project of assembling *The Collected Writings of John Maynard Keynes* for publication, one is, and should be, inclined to take his writing on Keynes very seriously. However, having said that, I am not inclined to agree that Moggridge's view of the role of the "circus" in the transition ever represented the conventional view. It might be more accurate to say that it was, at one time, an important view. For example, Lawrence Klein in his widely read book *The Keynesian Revolution*, argued that at the time of the *Treatise* Keynes was still very much under the sway of the classical school. In his words, "Keynes, being a good classical economist, implicitly accepted the above theory of the level of output. Hence in his fundamental equation we can assume that output is given, $0=0$" (Klein, 1966, p. 20). Another important writer who argues for the importance of Cambridge based criticism is Don Patinkin. It is his view that the insular nature of the Cambridge school contributed to Keynes's implicit assumption that the feedback of his colleagues, and perhaps a few outsiders at Oxford or the LSE, would represent an extensive circulation of his ideas (Patinkin, 1976, pp. 20-21; Patinkin, 1993, pp. 12-13).[5]

This "conventional" view of the importance of the "Circus" to the evolution of *The General Theory* is only partially shared in a recent book by Peter Clarke. Clarke focuses on the positive contribution of the Circus in providing the theory of the multiplier and gives less weight to their critique of the assumption of fixed output in the "Widow's Cruse." After all, as Clark points out, this assumption had been widely noted and commented upon (Clarke, 1988, pp. 244-54). On the other hand, Robert Skidelsky directly challenges the Moggridge view when he concludes that "Despite much 'pooled memory' to the contrary, the Circus seems to have played a relatively minor role in the development of the *General Theory*" (Skidelsky, 1992, p. 447).

I believe that the sample of quotations offered above indicate that the Moggridge view, while clearly shared by some important interpreters, cannot really claim to be the "conventional view." Indeed, it may be significant that in Moggridge's recent biography of Keynes the role of the Circus is portrayed as one of a number of factors which led Keynes to reconsider his monetary theory (Moggridge, 1992, pp. 531-33).

The Supply Dimension of Keynes's Thought

Having disputed this relatively minor point, I wish to move on to the substantive issues raised by Amadeo's contribution to this volume. This is Amadeo's rearticulation and clarification of what he calls the "supply dimension" of Keynesian economics. In recent years, with the eclipse in popularity of the Hansen- Klein interpretation of *The General Theory*, there has been a renewed interest in the all but forgotten chapters on the price level and the employment function in *The General Theory*. Over the last fifteen years this change in emphasis has generated some excellent work on the supply characteristics of Keynes. The long running, and most interesting, debate between Don Patinkin and his critics in the pages of *History of Political Economy* come to mind in this regard (Patinkin, 1976, 1977b, 1978, 1987, 1989; Roberts, 1978; Fusfeld, 1985, 1989; Littleboy and Metha, 1987; Davidson, 1989).

Amadeo, in his own way extending this discussion, argues that it is within Keynes's changing conception of time that the methodological changes most clearly emerge. In Amadeo's view, the fundamental equations of the *Treatise* featured a conception of time in which profit-seeking firms begin by finding themselves in the Marshallian long period.[6] He defines this as ."..a position where capacity and capacity utilization as well as sectoral structure and technology adjust to demand." Amadeo is quick to point out that in the *Treatise* this long period is only a point of reference. The goal is ."..to study the causes of deviations from equilibrium and, once the system deviates, the repercussion effects." This change occurs as market conditions, unknown at the beginning of the market day, impose a degree of "windfall profit" on the firm. The firm makes its future production decisions on the basis of the amount of "windfall profit." Amadeo calls this approach the "finite static" method. To Amadeo this method ."..is appropriate for the study of [the] immediate effects of a change in data; as we would expect, it will often picture the system in disequilibrium.

A sequence of finite periods driven by changing expectations characterizes the method." He argues that Keynes, in leaving the *Treatise*, has changed his focus in *The General Theory* to a study of the conditions characteristic of an underemployment equilibrium.[7] In developing the notion that within Keynes's theory there is an implicit "long period" formulation, Amadeo aligns Keynes with the conventional idea of equilibrium as an exercise in comparative statics. It follows that within *The General Theory* there is in fact a coherent notion of the level of output and the price level that will prevail in the long period. In arguing for his conclusion with regard to the temporal structure of Keynes' work Amadeo is, as he notes, in keeping with the arguments presented in Garegnani (1983) and Milgate (1982).

The Meaning and Significance of the Supply Versus Expenditure Discussion

Garegnani, (1983), Milgate (1982), and Eatwell and Milgate (1983) have argued that the major flaw of Keynes's economics was his neglect of a clearly articulated long period formulation. They are convinced that this failure inhibited the progress of economic theorizing since it left an opening for the neoclassical synthesis to emerge as a plausible interpretation of Keynesian economics. They argue that the synthesis effectively blunted the critical message implicit in Keynes and stifled the emergence of a well defined alternative to the neoclassical school.

According to authors such as Garegnani, Milgate, or Eatwell the neoclassical synthesis was designed to allow for "Keynesian" effective demand failures to occur in the short period while repositioning the general equilibrium model as the only acceptable theory for describing a long run equilibrium. Keynes's theory is then effectively presented as a special, albeit very important, case in a more general long run theory of general equilibrium. In such a case Keynes, the primary critic of A. C. Pigou, is himself reduced to providing little more than a rearticulation of Pigou's theory of unemployment.

Critics of the neoclassical synthesis argue that there are two fundamental problems with it as an interpretation of the historical record. First, Keynes himself thought that his theory was incompatible with the theory of Pigou. For instance, he repeatedly contrasted their positions in *The General Theory*.[8] Second, in the era after the Cambridge Capital Controversy, Post Keynesians are no longer convinced that the general equilibrium project can even claim to be a coherent theory. The critics conclude that to maintain the synthesis view is to make the Keynesian theory either trivial or incoherent (Eatwell, 1983; Eatwell and Milgate, 1983).

However, to criticize the synthesis tradition is not the same thing as providing an alternative. Milgate, in his 1982 book, *Capital and Employment*, acknowledges that there is not enough material in Keynes for a fully developed long period Keynesian theory. He argues that the most fruitful approach would be to merge the long period classical theory of Sraffa (1960) with the effective demand theory of output in Keynes (1964). While Amadeo concurs with Eatwell (1983) and Milgate (1982) on the importance of establishing a distinct long period formulation for Keynes, he makes his unique contribution when he begins to describe what such a formulation might look like.

While Amadeo follows Milgate and Eatwell in assigning importance to finding a Keynesian long period, he is convinced that careful textual exegesis, one that incorporates the *Treatise*, can uncover a distinct long period supply dimension within Keynes's theory. This solution answers the challenge raised by Garegnani, Milgate, and others without committing us to an arrangement wherein Keynes and Sraffa must be merged. In my opinion this task, to the extent that Amadeo has completed it, represents a substantial contribution to intellectual history. If Amadeo is correct, it may be that Keynes's economics has its own unique long period formulation. In establishing this insight Amadeo has also, depending on your point of view, refuted or transcended the Shacklian notion that pervasive uncertainty makes a coherent long period discussion impossible or irrelevant (Shackle, 1967 ch. 11, 1974).

In his work Amadeo has suggested a new, and potentially important, alternative interpretation of Keynes.[9] This new alternative is not simply the positing of a research paradigm but goes a long way towards resolving some of the historical questions surrounding a number of the neglected chapters in Keynes's opus. Some notion of cost and price appears to be buried in chapters 4, 6, 17, 20, & 21 of *The General Theory*. By accepting Amadeo's interpretation of the temporal structure of Keynes's theory we can reenvision the theory as simultaneously a theory of price and the level of output.[10] A corollary of this new work on the "supply dimension" is that Keynes's economics can be freed of the charge that it did not desire, or was theoretically incapable of providing, a coherent theory of inflation.

To What Extent is Keynes's Economics Consistent With Classical Political Economy?

Reestablishing the Keynesian theory of aggregate supply (or the employment function as Keynes might have preferred given his objections to the theory of index numbers as they were then practiced) does not imply that the theory resembles the classical long period view. This fact is explicitly acknowledged by Milgate. In his words, ".. it is necessary to find compatible theories of value and distribution with which to supplement Keynes's principle of effective demand. It is here that the theoretical system of the old Classical Economists seems to offer the greatest promise of success" (Milgate, 1983, pp. 187-8).

While a merger of the Sraffian and Keynesian doctrines may be an interesting project in its own right, I am not convinced that Keynes would have thought that his theory was consistent with Sraffa's. I think this is the case for a number of reasons. The first argument can be derived from a note Keynes wrote to George Bernard Shaw a year before the publication of *The General Theory*:

...I believe myself to be writing a book on economic theory which will largely revolutionise- not, I suppose, at once but in the course of the next ten years- the way the world thinks about economic problems. When my new theory has been duly assimilated and mixed with politics and feelings and passions, I can't predict what the final upshot will be in its effect on action and affairs. But there will be a great change, and, *in particular, the Ricardian foundations of Marxism will be knocked away* (Keynes, "Letter to G. B. Shaw, 1/1/35," 1973, pp. 492-3, italics added).

Now let us consider the particulars of this statement. He is speaking to a Socialist, one who, through his past publications, has indicated that he has a sustained interest in economics. We also know that at this time Sraffa's book, *Production of Commodities By Means of Commodities*, is already in draft and has privately circulated in Cambridge (Sraffa, 1960, Preface). We also know that Keynes is familiar with Sraffa's work. I would suggest that both correspondents knew that only one person in England was working on the "Ricardian foundations of Marxism." This letter, and the identity of the person it is being sent to, indicate that there is a subtext to the statement that both parties could have been expected to recognize. I believe this letter indicates that Keynes considered his theory to be inconsistent with the work of his friend and colleague Piero Sraffa.

Second, I would point to Keynes's directed effort, in the first two chapters of *The General Theory*, to depict the classical and neoclassical economists as jointly flawed. There are also the numerous technical and polemical points against Ricardian economics throughout *The General Theory* (Keynes, 1964, pp. 18, 32, 190-2, 244, 340). Let us recall that Keynes was aware of Sraffa's interests and research during the years prior to the publication of *The General Theory*. Finally, there is Keynes's 1933 characterization of Malthus as the "First Cambridge Economist." One could discount the importance of this essay as one inspired by a mood that predates the increasing influence of Sraffa on Cambridge economics, but I do not think that there is any evidence that Keynes had a change of heart on this manner either before or after 1936 (Keynes, 1963).

I could be convinced by Amadeo that Keynes had a rough alternative to the neoclassical theory of long period equilibrium in mind when he wrote *The General Theory*. But we should understand that such a proposition still leaves us a long way from establishing that what Keynes envisioned was the classical theory as it was then being reformulated by Sraffa.[11]

In Amadeo's hands the discussion of the change between the *Treatise* and *The General Theory* focuses on the nature of time and the properties of underlying equilibria. This is an interesting approach but it does suggest a challenge to other important interpretations which have received attention in the literature. For example there are authors who doubt that the notion of equilibrium can be made to be consistent with Keynes's economics (Shackle, 1967 ch. 11, 1974).[12] Besides this strain of anti-equilibrium writing there is a related literature which contends that the change which took place in Keynes's research was a focus on the characteristics of a "monetary economy" as opposed to a "real-exchange" economy (Dillard, 1954; Skidelsky, 1992, pp. 442-3).

Amadeo has tried to create some room in his presentation of the long period equilibrium for these alternative interpretations. However, he wants to discourage us from placing these concerns at the center of the analysis.[13] It is my guess that scholars who focus on the parts of Keynes which emphasize expectations or the "monetary theory of production" would find the focus of Amadeo's research misplaced. Keynesian "fundamentalists" argue that the message of *The General Theory* is that the economy is necessarily in the short period. They point, not to long periods, but to institutions and conventions as providing the basis for any short term stability which is observed in the economy (Kregel, 1980). Scholars of this persuasion are not likely to be brought around by Amadeo's careful arguments but hopefully they will, like the present writer, find them both carefully constructed and very suggestive.

Notes

[1] Even as we make these comments we should recall that some important interpreters argue that these books actually constitute one argument and should be treated as such (Shackle, 1974). However, the text does reflect the view that there has been an important, and moreover, identifiable evolution in the period between these two texts.

[2] For an overview and history of this interpretation of Keynes see Young (1987).

[3] It is well known that the inventors of new processes or commodities are not completely certain, at the time of the invention, what the full implication of their innovation will be with regard to the "circular flow" of the economy. For instance, the inventors of the combustion engine or television did not envision our contemporary uses for their respective technologies. The reason is that the meaning and function of new technologies is partly defined by the public's ongoing use of them. So it is with ideas. I believe that the more original or innovative aspects of Keynes's own work only came to him slowly and in the process of ongoing learning and discussion. Hence multiple intentions may have been there at the start and it may have been difficult for Keynes himself to comprehend the full implications of his thought. We, through our applications and ongoing ruminations on his ideas, can more fully define and understand them. In this sense, I would be inclined to disagree with Leland Yeager's assessment that *The General Theory* was an unsuccessful book (Yeager, 1993, p. 70). It may not have been fully worked out, but new ideas are rarely born in their totality.

[4] In addition to the the chapter included in this volume, I would like to broaden my comments to include Amadeo (1989).

[5] Having attributed these thoughts on the importance of the "circus" to Patinkin, I wish to note that he has stated that the debates with Hawtrey, Robertson and Hayek should receive more weight in the ."..received version of the transition" (Patinkin, 1977a, p. 6).

[6] In some of the recent literature on Keynes great emphasis is placed on the exact meaning of equilibrium and what it means to be in equilibrium (Garegnani, 1983; Milgate, 1982). A sympathetic guide to the complexities of these issues is provided in a most helpful series of articles by Fernando Carvalho (Carvalho, 1983/4, 1987, 1990). These definitions and distinctions are crucial to Amadeo's article and reflect the ideas he developed in Amadeo (1989).

[7] By arguing that Keynes (1964) embodied a theory of unemployment equilibrium, Amadeo and the Sraffian school both share one of the important conclusions of the "synthesis" tradition (See Hansen, 1936; Lerner, 1936; Harrod, 1936).

[8] I might add that Pigou was also convinced that Keynes' theory was incompatible with his own. See his review in *Economica* (May 1936). Eventually Pigou did moderate his view of *The General Theory* although he continued to disagree with it on several points (Pigou, 1951, pp. 4, 21, 64-65).

[9] This conclusion will not be shared by all readers. For instance, Don Patinkin has concluded that on matters related to the conditions of supply Keynes was simply confused. As Patinkin has forcefully stated, "And that is my main point: that the obscurity with which the aggregate supply curve is presented in the *General Theory* is a sign not of profundity, but of obscurity: not, as some would have us believe, of a deep underlying analytical framework in which everything falls into place, but of the same confusions and imprecisions which manifested themselves in the 1933 drafts of the book and which continued to live on in Keynes' mind furtively, below the surface, through the final version as well" (Patinkin, 1982, p. 150).

[10] Of course, other attempts to formulate a theory of price out of the raw materials of *The General Theory* have been made. One of the earliest, and perhaps most interesting, is Townshend, (1937). We should note in passing that Don Patinkin, in a passage consistent with his view that the supply dimension in Keynes is a muddle, sees chapters 17 and 21 to be "problematic" (Patinkin, 1976, p. 22).

[11] Now having argued that the theoretical links between Sraffa and Keynes are weak is not equivalent to an assertion that a research project designed to forge such links is misguided or uninteresting. The point is that such a project would represent the construction of a new theory. It would not, if the evidence that I have provided is convincing, constitute a historical exercise.

[12] In an interesting restatement of the anti-equilibrium argument Nina Shapiro argues that it is not uncertainty *per se* that undermines the notion of equilibrium, but the existence of capital accumulation. She argues that because Keynes was unable to articulate a consistent theory of capital accumulation, he could not see that his long period fragments were inconsistent with the rest of his theory (Shapiro, 1978).

[13] "It should be added that the emphasis on uncertainty and changes in expectations, as well as the relative unimportance ascribed to the notion of equilibrium, implies a certain lack of definiteness of results not always desirable in economic theorizing." (Amadeo, 1989, pp. 141-2).

References

Amadeo, Edward J. (1989) *Keynes's Principle of Effective Demand*. Brookfield, VT: Edward Elgar.

Carvalho, Fernando J. C. (1983-84) "The Concept of Time in Shacklean and Sraffian Economics." *Journal of Post Keynesian Economics*. 3:2 (Winter), 158-69.

—————————. (1987) "Alternative Analyses of Short and Long Run in Post-Keynesian Economics." In Randy Albelda, Christopher Gunn and William Waller (eds.). *Alternatives to Economic Orthodoxy*. Armonk, NY: M. E. Sharpe.

_____. (1990) "Keynes and the Long Period." *Cambridge Journal of Economics*. 14, 277-290.

Clarke, Peter. (1988) *The Keynesian Revolution in the Making, 1924-1936*. Oxford: Clarendon Press.

Davidson, Paul. (1989) "Patinkin's Interpretation of Keynes and the Keynesian Cross." *History of Political Economy*. 21: 3, 737-741.

Dillard, Dudley. (1954) "The Theory of a Monetary Economy." In Kenneth Kurihara (ed.). *Post Keynesian Economics*. New Brunswick, NJ: Rutgers University Press, 3-30.

Eatwell, John. (1983) "The Long-Period Theory of Employment." *Cambridge Journal of Economics*. 7, 269-285.

_____ and Murray Milgate. (1983) "Introduction." In John Eatwell and Murray Milgate, (eds.) *Keynes's Economics and the Theory of Value and Distribution*. New York: Oxford University Press, 1-17.

Fusfeld, Daniel R. (1985) "Keynes and the Keynesian Cross: A Note." *History of Political Economy* 17: 3, 385-388.

_____. (1989) "Keynes and the Keynesian Cross: Reply to Don Patinkin." *History of Political Economy* 21: 3, 545-547.

Garegnani, Piero. (1983) "On a Change in the Notion of Equilibrium in Recent Work on Value and Distribution" in John Eatwell and Murray Milgate (eds.) *Keynes's Economics and the Theory of Value and Distribution*. New York: Oxford University Press, 29 - 145.

Hansen, Alvin. (1936) "Mr. Keynes on Underemployment Equilibrium." *Journal of Political Economy*. (October), 667-686.

Harrod, R. F. (1947) "Keynes and the Traditional Theory." *Econometrica* (1937), reprinted in Seymour E. Harris, *The New Economics*. New York: Alfred A. Knopf.

Keynes, John Maynard. (1963) *Essays in Biography*. Geoffrey Keynes (ed.) New York: Norton.

_____. (1964) *The General Theory of Employment, Interest, and Money*. New York: Harcourt, Brace, Jovanovich.

_____. (1971) *Treatise on Money: The Pure Theory of Money*. Volume V in The Collected Writings of John Maynard Keynes. London: Macmillan.

_____. (1973) *The General Theory and After: Part 1, Preparation*. Volume XIII of The Collected Writings of John Maynard Keynes. Donald Moggridge (ed.) London: Macmillan.

Klein, Lawrence R. (1966) *The Keynesian Revolution*. 2nd ed. New York: Macmillan.

Kregel, Jan. (1980) "Markets and Institutions as Features of a Capitalistic Production System." *Journal of Post Keynesian Economics*. Vol. 3, #1, (Fall), 32-48.

Lerner, Abba P. (1947) "Mr. Keynes' 'General Theory of Employment, Interest and Money'." *International Labor Review* (1936), reprinted in Seymour E. Harris, *The New Economics*. New York: Alfred A. Knopf.

Littleboy, Bruce and Ghanshyam Mehta. (1987) "Patinkin on Keynes' Theory of Effective Demand," *History of Political Economy*. 19:2, 311-328.

Milgate, Murray. (1982) *Capital and Employment: A Study of Keynes's Economics*. New York: Academic Press.

Moggridge, Donald E. (1973) "The Cambridge Circus, 1930-1," in Volume XIII of *The Collected Writings of John Maynard Keynes*, 337-343.

––––––––––––. (1976) *John Maynard Keynes*. New York: Penguin.

––––––––––––. (1992) *Maynard Keynes: An Economist's Biography*. New York: Routledge.

Patinkin, Don. (1976) *Keynes' Monetary Thought: A Study of its Development*. Durham, NC: Duke University Press.

––––––––––––. (1977a) "The Process of Writing *The General Theory*: A Critical Survey." In Don Patinkin and J. Clark Leith (eds.) *Keynes, Cambridge and The General Theory*. London: Macmillan, 3-24.

––––––––––––. (1977b) "The Aggregate Supply Function: A Correction," *History of Political Economy*. 9:1, 156-159.

––––––––––––. (1978) "Keynes' Aggregate Supply Function: A Plea for Common Sense" *History of Political Economy*. 10:4, 577-596.

––––––––––––. (1982) *Anticipations of the General Theory? and Other Essays on Keynes*. Chicago: University of Chicago Press.

––––––––––––. (1987) "Keynes' Theory of Effective Demand: A Reply" *History of Political Economy*. 19:4, 647-658.

––––––––––––. (1989) "Keynes and the Keynesian Cross: A Further Note." *History of Political Economy*. 21:3, 537-547.

––––––––––––. (1993) "John Maynard Keynes (1883-1946)." In Walter Allan (ed.) *A Critique of Keynesian Economics*. New York: St. Martin's Press, 1-57.

Pigou, Arthur C. (1936) "Mr. J. M. Keynes' General Theory of Employment, Interest and Money. *Economica*. Vol. III:10, (New Series), 115-132.

––––––––––––. (1951) *Keynes's General Theory: A Retrospective View*. London: Macmillan.

Roberts, David. (1978) "Patinkin, Keynes, and Aggregate Supply and Demand Analysis." *History of Political Economy*. 10:4, 549-576.

Shackle, George L. S. (1967) *The Years of High Theory: Invention and Tradition in Economic Thought, 1926-1939*. Cambridge: Cambridge University Press.

Shackle, George L. S. (1974) *Keynesian Kaleidics: The Evolution of a General Political Economy*. Edinburgh: Edinburgh University Press.

Shapiro, Nina. (1978) "Keynes and Equilibrium Economics." *Australian Economic Papers*. 17, (December), 297-223.

Skidelsky, Robert. (1992) *John Maynard Keynes: The Economist as Savior, 1920-1937*. London, Macmillan.

Sraffa, Piero. (1960) *Production of Commodities By Means of Commodities*. Cambridge: Cambridge University Press.

Townshend, Hugh. (1937) "Liquidity-Premium and the Theory of Value."
    Economic Journal. 47, (March), 159-169.
Yeager, Leland. (1993) "The Keynesian Heritage in Economics." In Walter
    Allan (ed.) *A Critique of Keynesian Economics*. New York: St. Martin's
    Press, 59-71.
Young, Warren. (1987) *Interpreting Mr. Keynes: The IS-LM Enigma*. Boulder,
    CO: Westview Press.

3 THE OWN-RATES FRAMEWORK AS AN INTERPRETATION OF THE *GENERAL THEORY*: A SUGGESTION FOR COMPLICATING THE KEYNESIAN THEORY OF MONEY

Michael Syron Lawlor*

...It is my belief that the far-reaching and in some respects fundamental differences between the conclusions of a monetary economy and those of the more simplified real-exchange economy have been greatly undersestimated by the exponents of the traditional economics; with the result that the machinery of thought with which real-exchange economics has equipped the minds of practitioners in the world of affairs, and also of economists themselves, has led in practice to many erroneous conclusions and policies. The idea that it is comparatively easy to adapt the hypothetical conclusions of a real wage economics to the real world of monetary economics is a mistake. It is extraordinarily difficult to make the adaption, and perhaps impossible without the aid of a developed of theory of monetary economics. (Keynes, 1933, p. 410)

---

*Department of Economics, Wake Forest University, Box 7505, Winston-Salem, NC, 27109. Ph.: (919) 759-5564. Internet: lawlor@ac.wfunet.wfu.edu. For useful comments and advice, I would like to thank, without implicating, Bobbie Horn, Dudley Luckett, Sandy Darity, T.K. Rymes and Allin Cottrell. John Davis provided editorial suggestions that much improved the final presentation.

1. Introduction

In 1947, Keynes' biographer, pre-publication critic, and collaborator R. F. Harrod, summed up the *General Theory* as follows:

> The theory of interest is, I think, the central point in his scheme. He departs from old orthodoxy in holding that the failure of the system to move to a position of full activity is not primarily due to friction, rigidity, immobility or to phenomena essentially connected with the trade cycle. If a certain level of interest is established which is inconsistent with full activity, no flexibility or mobility in the other parts of the system will get the system to move to full activity. *But this wrong rate of interest, as we may call it, is not itself a rigidity or inflexibility. It is natural, durable, and in a certain sense, in the free system inevitable.* That is why he lays what may seem an undue emphasis on the doctrine that interest is essentially the reward not for saving but for parting with liquidity. Given the complex forces affecting liquidity preference, such and such is the rate of interest that will naturally and necessarily and, so long as underlying forces remain unchanged, permanently obtain. Yet that rate of interest may be inconsistent with the full activity of the system (1947, pp. 69-70, italics added).

Such an extensive quotation is justified by two remarkable qualities of the statement. First, Harrod's statement, when fully digested, can be seen to embody a viewpoint at odds with almost all major conceptions of the meaning of Keynes' theory of employment. As a moment's reflection over the quotation will reveal to the modern economist, this "central point in his scheme" is not compatible with any standard "Keynesian" exposition of underemployment equilibria. In the "Keynesian" case, the *definition* of unemployment is its correspondence with some sort of "rigidity" in an otherwise smoothly operating general equilibrium system. Among some old Keynesians, the rigidity was explained as the interest rate becoming stuck in the "liquidity trap" by a pessimism so severe that no amount of inducement could satisfy the public's craving for liquid balances. When this case was recognized as both theoretically and empirically implausible (see Keynes' own view in Keynes, 1936, p. 207), attention shifted to inflexibility in the labor market. By the logic of the neoclassical synthesis, deviations from full employment had to be due to some non-clearing rigidity in the labor market. It was the final recognition of this point that led to both the breakdown of the Keynesian consensus and the most modern 'Keynesian' theory, New Keynesian Economics, which attempts to formulate microfoundation explanations for "rationally" explaining why the labor market might not clear[1].

Notwithstanding these analyses, Harrod tells us Keynes concluded that "no flexibility or mobility in the other parts of the system will get the system to move to full activity." What might Harrod be driving at with his assertion that Keynes' central point is a "wrong rate of interest," that this rate "is not itself a rigidity or inflexibility," but is "natural, durable and in a certain sense...inevitable?" That question is answered by recourse to the second remarkable quality of Harrod's statement, which is that in a concise, shorthand way, he expresses the central concerns of Keynes' own post-*General Theory* restatements of his revolutionary new theory. In these papers (1937a,b,c), Keynes addresses himself almost entirely to monetary concerns, trying to elaborate his theory of employment via his theory of the interest rate. A variety of different approaches and points are raised in these papers, including Keynes' views on uncertainty, expectations and the role of money and interest in his theoretical explanation of unemployment equilibria. Taken as a whole, Keynes' post-*General Theory* defense of his position reveals his feeling that his monetary theory of the interest rate clearly distinguishes him from his predecessors and contemporaries, and was generally being misunderstood by his interpreters. The implication of both Harrod's statement and Keynes' own emphasis on monetary matters in defending his theory, is that *a complete understanding of Keynes' theoretical attempt to explain unemployment is fundamentally related to his views on money and interest.*

It is the purpose of this essay to try to elucidate that part of Keynes' monetary theory that is implicit in Harrod's statement and explicit in Keynes' 1937 defense[2] by analyzing a neglected view of Keynes' monetary views, "the own-rates of interest" framework, put forth in chapter 17 of the *General Theory*. In so doing I hope to be able to show that the state of the debate over Keynes' monetary theory concerns the degree to which the monetary analysis of the *General Theory* constitutes a break from the received tradition. Better yet, it is probably more appropriate to say that the state of the debate **still** concerns this question, since as Harrod's quote illustrates the question is hardly a new one.

Recently, though, the publication of Keynes' *Collected Writings,* and the theoretical disarray in modern macroeconomics have given rise to renewed efforts to interpret Keynes' own writings and those of his contemporaries and predecessors. Various historical and analytical issues are brought forward by this literature (see Rogers, 1989 and Cottrell, 1994) . Among these is the issue of identifying just what historical tradition of monetary theory the *General Theory* sought to depart from. Initial work on detailed historical analysis of this issue has now begun, but there is still much to be learned about what Keynes considered orthodox monetary theory. Bridel (1987) has shown that the Cambridge theorists of Keynes' day were actually quite sophisticated in their saving-investment analysis. In particular they paid a large amount of attention to the role of expectations in analyzing the business cycle. Laidler (1991) has recently detailed the extent of Marshall's, largely invisible, influence in this regard as well. In another paper (Lawlor, forthcoming), I have investigated the historical and intellectual context for Keynes's views on financial markets. Marshall's influence looms large in this story as well, but so do many now neglected antecedents to the *General Theory* in the pre-1930's literature.

Yet Keynes was also influenced greatly by Wicksell. His *Treatise* is in fact self-consciously Wicksellian. Colin Rogers (1989) has shown well the extent to which this Wicksellian tradition can be used as a foil against which to contrast Keynes's more "monetary" theory of the rate of interest. Leijonhufvud (1981) also skillfully makes the point that the monetary theory of the *General Theory* constitutes its greatest departure from the Wicksellian tradition that had dominated, and continues to dominate, the theory of aggregate fluctuations. For Leijonhufvud, though, this break with the natural/market rate analysis is seen as a strictly retrograde move on Keynes's part. Allin Cottrell and I (Cottrell and Lawlor, 1991) have critiqued Leijonhufvud on this point, resurrecting the analysis of chapter seventeen of the *General Theory* to support the argument for the theoretical advance Keynes made on the Wicksellian tradition.

In this essay I will attempt to document the largely theoretical analysis of that paper using detailed textual analysis. The emphasis will be on the radicalness which Keynes' monetary views in the *General Theory* represent for the Wicksellian tradition. The goal will be to show that it is possible to interpret the incomplete, often misunderstood, but always tantalizing Chapter 17 of that work as an alternative framework in which to understand the importance that Keynes attached to the influence of expectations, conventional psychology and liquidity in the determination of asset values and so rates of interest. The method will be historical, attempting to link up the argument at all points with the ideas contained in works historically relevant to Keynes' own - either that of students, colleagues or contemporary theoretical adversaries. It is hoped that this will then shed new light on the meaning of Harrod's view that the interest rate was the key to Keynes' system by showing that the framework of analysis discernable in a careful reading of chapter 17, dubbed here for lack of a better term the "own-rates" framework, offers new insight into the possibilities of a monetary analysis alternative to the traditional ones.

The essay proceeds as follows. We start with a very brief highlighting of the issues raised by Sraffa in his critical review of Hayek's *Prices and Production* in 1932, the immediate source for Keynes of the idea of "own-rates of interest." The importance of this discussion is to establish the firm historical basis of the own-rates framework in a critique of Wicksellian theorizing such as Hayek then represented. We then proceed to document the creative use made by Keynes of Sraffa's concept in the *General Theory*. The paper ends with an attempt to interpret various parts of the rest of the *General Theory* in this framework.

2. Sraffa and Commodity Rates of Interest

"...Mr. Piero Sraffa, from whom nothing is hid" (Keynes, 1972 (1933), p. 97).

The central piece of evidence in support of the theme that the "own-rates" theory of interest represents both a substantial critique of the Wicksellian "natural-rate" doctrine, and also the foundation of a new approach to the place of money in economic theory is an obscure twelve-page review of Hayek's *Prices and Production* (Hayek, 1931) by Piero Sraffa in the *Economic Journal* for 1932. The place of this review in our theme is but a part of its larger historical setting in the development of interwar business cycle theory in general, and the transition of ideas in Cambridge economics from the *Treatise on Money* to the *General Theory* in particular. Sraffa's review represents a confluence of both of these intellectual tides by bringing to bear the latest (as of 1932) thinking of the theoretical debates of the "Cambridge Circus" on the system of thought propounded by Keynes' greatest rival to preeminence in business cycle theory at the time, F.A. von Hayek. That Sraffa's role in this whole debate should be so obscure yet (as we shall see) so powerful is further testament to the mysteriousness of his legendary academic career as a maieutic gadfly. Many interesting issues in monetary theory are raised by the exchange between Sraffa and Hayek.[3] For now we want only to establish the origin of Keynes's "own rates" concept, and to highlight it's corrosive relation to the Wicksellian natural rate doctrine.

Sraffa's review begins with a general methodological criticism of Hayek's approach to monetary theory which clearly defines both his and Keynes' own approach. His criticism revolves around the conception, common to the whole Wicksellian tradition, that in order to investigate the properties of, and policies toward, monetary influences on production, one should begin with a hypothetical "barter" state and compare this ("natural," "real" etc.) system with an actual money system. As Sraffa indicates, the error of this method arises from the tendency to take the "real" barter state as the "natural" condition of equilibrium and to consider any deviation from this state as "distortions" caused by the "artificial" interference of the banks. In Hayek's case, this tendency shows up as a polemic for a predetermined policy conclusion:

> The starting-point and the object of Dr. Hayek's inquiry is what he calls "neutral money"; that is to say, a kind of money which leaves production and the relative prices of goods, including the rate of interest, "undisturbed," exactly as they would be if there were no money at all (Sraffa, 1932a, p. 42).

For Sraffa, Hayek falters from the start by making a state which is exactly as if "there were no money at all" the object of his inquiry into *monetary* theory and policy. His objections center on two heads. First, such a method could only serve as a policy inquiry into money if it took as its starting point various real monetary economies and then compared the results of disturbances to this system with the results in the nonmonetary economy. "This would bring out which are the essential characteristics common to every kind of money, as well as their differences, thus supplying the elements for the merits of alternative policies" (p. 43). Sraffa claims that Hayek ignores this point in his single-minded pursuit of "the wholly different problem of proving that only one particular banking policy (that which maintains constant under all circumstances the quantity of money multiplied by its velocity of circulation) succeeds in giving full effect to the 'voluntary decisions of individuals'..." (p. 43).

But Sraffa has a further objection to the use of a barter state as the starting point of theoretical monetary analysis. He claims that by reducing a monetary system to a hypothetical barter state, the analysis ignores those very functions of money that define the problems of a monetary economy:

> The differences between a monetary and a non-monetary economy can only be found in those characteristics which are set forth at the beginning of every textbook on money.

> That is to say, that money is not only the medium of exchange, but also a store of value
> and the standard in terms of which debts, and all other legal obligations, habits, opinions,
> conventions, in short all kinds of relations between men, are more or less rigidly fixed
> (p. 43).

Since Hayek's starting point of a hypothetical "neutral" barter state considers only money which is "used purely and simply as a medium of exchange," his inquiry can easily ignore the "most obvious" effects that a monetary policy will have in a real money economy, where

> when the price of one or more commodities changes, these relations [described above]
> change in terms of such commodities; while if they had been fixed in commodities, in
> some specified way, they would have changed differently, or not at all (pp. 43-44).

Thus, by confining him to his hypothetical world, Hayek's method "amounts to assuming away the very object of the inquiry."

In essence, the problem is that while imagining a system in which there is no money deprives us of our practical foundation in knowledge of a money economy, the opposite method of defining a money economy which we understand and then removing various aspects of money to define its "moneyness" builds on the concrete, not the speculative[4].

Yet, having made these methodological criticisms, Sraffa goes on to internally critique Hayek's use of the method of money neutrality. Two issues, in particular, will form the basis for Sraffa's idea of own rates of interest. They are the concept of intertemporal transactions in the hypothetical moneyless barter state, and the notion of a "natural-rate" of interest that equilibrates the flow of savings supplied by the public with the demand for investment funds by the entrepreneurial sector. Explicitly at issue here is the whole Wicksellian scheme of monetary analysis of which Hayek was a devoted follower and also the issues that will later appear in Keynes' *General Theory* as the "essential properties" of interest and money. The common thread in both treatments is that taste for the concrete as the starting place of analysis that is the hallmark of both Sraffa's and Keynes' approach, here embodied in the idea of own-rates of interest.

> Dr. Hayek's theory of the relation of money to the rate of interest is mainly given by
> way of criticism and development of the theory of Wicksell. He states his own position
> as far as it agrees with Wicksell's as follows: -- "In a money economy, the actual or
> money rate of interest may differ from the equilibrium or natural rate, because the
> demand for and the supply of capital do not meet in their natural form but in the form
> of money, the quantity of which available for capital purposes may be arbitrarily changed
> by the banks" (Sraffa, 1932a, p. 49).

For Sraffa, the conception of the relation between the theory of money and the theory of prices (or conversely, the conception of the difference between a barter and a monetary economy) implied by this Wicksellian theme represents the heart of the problem with the "natural-rate" doctrine:

An essential confusion, which appears clearly from this statement, is the belief that the divergence of rates is a characteristic of a money economy: and the confusion is implied in the very terminology adopted, which identifies the "actual" with the "money" rate, and the "equilibrium" with the "natural" rate. If money did not exist, and loans were made in terms of all sorts of commodities, there might be at any one moment as many "natural" rates of interest as there are commodities, though they would not be "equilibrium" rates. The "arbitrary" action of the banks is by no means a necessary condition for the divergence; if loans were made in wheat and farmers (or for that matter the weather) "arbitrarily change" the quantity of wheat produced, the actual rate of interest on loans in terms of wheat would diverge from the rate on other commodities and there would be no single equilibrium rate (1932a, p. 49).

This is a complicated passage full of issues which can only be understood in the context of the rest of Sraffa's critique. First, it is important to note the attention to terminology because Sraffa's use of terms is a crucial aspect of his difference with Hayek. The Hayekian analysis revolves around the specification of a barter-like "neutral" monetary policy where neutrality is defined as a state which leaves "the relative prices of goods, including the rate of interest, 'undisturbed,' exactly as they would be if there were not money at all" (Sraffa, 1932a, p. 42). Further, Hayek had defined the rate of interest which would achieve this result as the natural or equilibrium rate.

Utilizing this long-period "equilibrium" conception and taking at face value Hayek's argument that the "natural-rate" is indeed the rate that would obtain in a barter-like state, Sraffa asks a very obvious question: what would loans and interest rates look like if money did not exist, and how would they be different from rates of interest in a money economy? His answer: if we were really in a barter state, the only meaning that loans, savings, or investment could have would be defined in physical terms, money being nonexistent by definition. Thus, "natural" rates of interest would be rates defined in "real" or physical terms. The ratio between the amount of a physical commodity today to the amount it trades for at some future date would be the physical analog to rates of interest. This is the germ of the conception of own-rates of interest. As to how such barter-rates differ from interest rates on money, Sraffa only hints that the essential difference is not captured by the Wicksellian schema. It would be left to Keynes in 1936 to fully draw out the implications of this idea for a monetary economy. Sraffa's role is mainly critical. But in these critical "years of high theory" at Cambridge, it was "escaping the old ideas" that formed the major hurdle.

Furthermore, Sraffa claims that his barter rates are not as hard to imagine as we might think. "In order to realize this, we need not stretch our imagination and think of an organized loan market amongst savages bartering deer for beavers. Loans are currently made in the present world in terms of every commodity for which there is a forward market." It is at this point that Sraffa provides a practical illustration of the concept of the "natural" or "commodity"-rate which measures the intertemporal equivalents, in physical terms, between spot and future market transactions.

When a cotton spinner borrows a sum of money for three months and uses the proceeds to purchase spot, a quantity of raw cotton which he simultaneously sells three months forward, he is actually "borrowing cotton" for that period. The rate of interest which he pays, per hundred bales of cotton, is the number of bales that can be purchased with the following sum of money: the interest on the money required to buy spot 100 bales, plus the excess (or minus the deficiency) of the spot over the forward price of the 100 bales (p. 50).

This simple idea is Sraffa's interpretation of barter rates of interest. They are simply interest rates on a loan defined in terms of intertemporal equivalents of the physical unit being loaned. This is what Keynes would later mean by "the marginal efficiencies of a good in terms of itself" (1937a) and "own-rates of interest" (1936 p. 223). It is Keynes' eventual use of the concept that is our main focus, but it will be instructive to follow Sraffa a bit further since his use of the concept is much more directly concerned with its implication for the Wicksellian natural-rate doctrine.

Armed with a concrete conception of what a rate of interest means in barter terms, Sraffa goes on to compare this conception with the Wicksellian scheme. In such a world, equilibrium (in Sraffa's sense) means that "the spot and forward price coincide, for cotton as for any other commodity; and all the 'natural' or commodity rates are equal to one another, and to the money rate." But, if supply and demand get out of long-period equilibrium for any reason, the spot and forward prices diverge, and the "natural" rate of interest on that commodity diverges from the "natural" rates on other commodities. In other words, "equilibrium" rates are not "natural" if by equilibrium we mean prices equal cost of production and by "natural" we mean barter-like (moneyless) intertemporal loans. Thus, Hayek's (and Wicksell's) attempt to equate the equilibrium rate with the putative natural rate represents an "essential confusion." For, as Sraffa comments in the exchange which followed the review, Hayek's policy prescription of equating the money rate with the natural rate can have no meaning in Hayek's own preferred situation of an expanding economy: "The only meaning (if it be a meaning) I can attach to this is that his maxim of policy now requires that the money rate should be equal to all these divergent natural rates" (Sraffa, 1932b, p. 251).

In a sense, Sraffa has here caught Hayek in a trap of his own making and no amount of squirming can release him, short of abandoning some part of his Wicksellian scheme. In *Prices and Production* Hayek had explicitly set out to conduct an investigation of the effect of monetary influences on *relative* prices. He also claimed to have rejected any reliance on "vague" concepts of averages such as the price level. He was thus led to found his polemic for a neutral monetary policy on the cyclical influence of money on relative investment flows in an accumulating economy. His policy prescription was to eliminate these "forced savings" influences by setting the money rate of interest equal to the "natural" rate. Here, Sraffa has shown that if you really want to define natural rates in barter-like terms, that it is a necessary relative price effect that these rates will "naturally" diverge in an economy in which accumulation is going forward. The basis of Sraffa's argument is that any new accumulation is directed to different employments by divergences of market prices from the "natural" price, a good Marshallian argument. "It will be noticed that, under free competition, this divergence of rates is as essential to the effecting of the transition [to a more capitalistic economy] as is the divergence of prices from costs of production; it is, in fact, another aspect of the same thing" (Sraffa, 1932a, p. 51).

Consequently, a theoretical investigation, within the framework of a natural rate that reflects a barter state of savings and investment, into the relative price effects of credit- (read bank-) induced forced savings must deal with the fact that "there may be as many 'natural' rates as there are commodities" (Sraffa, 1932a, p. 50). Hayek must either give up a unique "natural" rate as a guide to policy, abandon the whole Wicksellian conception, or fall back on one of his hated aggregates to deliver himself from this quandary. Sraffa points out that within the Wicksellian framework, one way out would be to use as a policy guide "... a 'natural' rate of interest which, if adopted as a bank-rate, will stabilize a price-level (i.e., the price of a composite commodity): it is an average of the 'natural' rates of the commodities entering into the price-level, weighted in the same way as they are in the price-level itself" (p. 51). By this method, Wicksell could salvage his own system (although the "natural" rate would now be non-unique, changing with every change in the components of the price index) and could meet Hayek's criticism of the falling price-level effects. But Hayek himself cannot fall back on such a solution since he has already rejected the conception of an average price level as vague and useless.

It is at this point that we come full circle to the starting methodological position and we see that Sraffa's own view is that we should abandon the whole Wicksellian scheme. Having shown the only logically consistent meaning that can be attached to the theoretical and policy conclusions of the Wicksellian framework, Sraffa implies that the whole effort is a misguided one from the start.

> It appears, therefore, that these non-monetary economies [i.e., those defined by his composite "natural" rates] retain the essential feature of money, the singleness of the standard; and we are not much the wiser when we have been shown that a monetary policy is "neutral" in the sense of being equivalent to a non-monetary economy which differs from it almost only by name (Sraffa, 1932a, p. 51).

In other words, the distinction between monetary effects and real effects is not illuminated by the Wicksellian approach of defining the "natural" state of saving and investment in hypothetical "barter" terms, where barter means uninfluenced by the arbitrary actions of the banks. As Sraffa had commented at the start, the Wicksellians are not actually defining a barter state, so much as a hypothetical "real" system, where money can only serve as a medium of exchange ("being entirely unaware that it may be doubted whether under a system of barter the decisions of individuals would have their full effects...."). Thus, by ignoring the more important distinctions between a monetary and nonmonetary economy, "those characteristics which are set forth at the beginning of every textbook on money," the Wicksellian approach provides a misguided framework for a monetary theory.

In effect, what Sraffa has done here is to repeat his standard procedure of accepting a theoretical framework and then pushing it to its furthest logical extremes to see what insights it might yield[5]. In the case of the "natural rate" view of monetary theory, what he found was a gaping emptiness beneath a thin skin. There is no unique natural rate that will stabilize the price level and ensure against forced savings in an accumulating economy. The essential properties of interest and money are ignored when we use a state in which money serves none of its multifarious cultural, conventional roles as the starting point of monetary theory. And the central problems of savings, investment and business cycles are not elucidated by this artificial distinction since "with or without money, if investment and saving have not been planned to match, an increase in saving must prove to a large extent 'abortive'" (Sraffa, 1932a, p. 52). This last sounds like the "Circus" speaking, in its echo of the *General Theory*. And it is to the *General Theory* that the constructive use of the idea of own-rates leads us.

3. From Sraffa to Keynes: The State of Monetary Theory, 1935

As a bridge over the uncharted, and perhaps forever unknown, question of what personal role was played by Sraffa in the eventual form of Chapter 17 of the *General Theory*, we can utilize the thoughts of a Cambridge student of the early thirties, a disciple of Keynes', Adam Smith Prizeman and eventually Professor of Economics at the Benares Hindu University, Mr. Bhalechandra P. Adarkar. Adarkar's *The Theory of Monetary Policy* (1935) provides an interesting contemporary survey of the major monetary theories of the thirties and constructive work on the usefulness of this body of theory for practical monetary management.

Besides the fact that Adarkar provides a concise discussion of the complete range of interest rate theory at the time, he forms an important intellectual link in our study by virtue of his knowledge of Keynes' monetary theory in the transition period from the *Treatise on Money* to the *General Theory*. Keynes' influence is clearly stated in Adarkar's preface:

> It will not be difficult for the reader, however, to discern the intellectual genealogy of this effort and he will at once perceive how deeply indebted I am to J.M. Keynes, that leader of modern monetary thought, in much that I have to say in the following pages (p. viii).

From this, we can feel confident that Adarkar's view will reflect the Cambridge school's view on monetary matters. For our purposes, two chapters are especially interesting: Chapter seven on "Mr. Sraffa's Commodity Rate," and chapter eleven titled "Is Barter Theory Relevant?"

In the latter of these two, Adarkar sets out to investigate "the question as to what extent the theory of a non-monetary economy is likely to be useful in the understanding of monetary phenomena." He notes that the concept has been much used by modern writers on monetary problems, but that "the attitude of most writers in this matter has been altogether dubious, if not misleading." "Cassell, Wicksell and Hayek" are explicitly mentioned as cases where "hypothetical considerations of a non-monetary character have been introduced in monetary theory in connection with our problem [the idea of a natural rate]." His approach to the question is to consider a number of different conceptions of barter since these "hypotheses...are not *in parti materia* but relate to distinct concepts of the non-monetary economy" (1935, p. 86). Adarkar distinguishes between two conceptions of a barter economy. The first is a Robinson Crusoe economy used by Bohm-Bawerk and Rosher to illustrate capital accumulation. This economy is not really barter so much as exchangeless, and here the acts of investment and saving actually occur in physical terms. More interesting for our purposes is what Adarkar calls "an advanced social economy, in which there is exchange but no *medium* of exchange, in which goods are exchanged against goods" (p. 87).

Hayek's ideal barter state is identified with this money-less economy where "only those investments can be carried out which are justified by the available real savings...[which] avoids the disparity between savings and investments, resulting from our adherence to money" (p. 89). But the assumption that such a moneyless state would be more stable than a monetary system, Hayek's thesis, is questioned by Adarkar. He points out that "relative valuations of goods, services and other forms of wealth are liable to fluctuate therein as much as they do in a money economy." In fact, he thinks that such a nonmonetary economy would be *less* stable since all of the factors making for disruption, "*viz.*, psychology, natural and physical phenomena, discoveries and so forth are present," but the monetary factor, "the only one that implies some sort of control," is "absent" (p. 88). As we will see, this closely reflects Keynes' own ideas about a barter state.

Due to this instability, and because focusing on barter phenomena encourages us "to forget that what we are primarily concerned with is money itself and its mysterious interactions on the processes of production, distribution and consumption," Adarkar finds such nonmonetary systems of little use in either monetary theory or policy. Interestingly for our thesis, he connects this rejection with an abandonment of the whole natural-rate doctrine utilizing Sraffa's review of Hayek. He says that even if we accept the automaticity of savings and investment in the barter state, "it does not help us to ascertain the *ideal* rate of interest that should be adopted under the *money* system." Relying on Sraffa's example, he points out that even in the barter state, the natural rate is not unique but varies with the number of commodities considered. "Moreover, even if we succeed in constructing such an average 'barter' rate, we have no reason to suppose that rate, *because it secured the savings-investment equalization, under barter, would do so here also*;... It is for this reason, among others, that we have to reject the very ingenious concept of the 'natural rate'..." (p. 90).

Is barter theory relevant? To a Keynes' disciple of 1935:

> There is no need, however, to suppose that a return to barter would mean the elimination of all the economic problems arising from changes in relative valuations. True, money sometimes distorts the vision and puts false appearances on the realities of economic life and thus necessitates our probing deeper, viewing kaleidoscopically what is happening in the realm of realities. But this is not the same thing as to visualize the modern money economy as a mere disfigured replica of its cruder ancestor (Adarkar, 1935, p. 91).

In chapter 17 of *The General Theory*, Keynes lifts Sraffa's barter rates (redubbed by Keynes as own-rates) out of that "disfigured replica of its crude ancestor" and sets them down in a modern money economy. So far, we have established the corrosive effect that Sraffa's commodity-rates approach represents to the whole Wicksellian natural-rate, loanable funds framework. We need now to pick up the development of its more constructive uses in illustrating Keynes' liquidity preference theory. Once again, Adarkar proves a useful bridge in that in the same book in which he disparaged the usefulness of the natural-rate doctrine, he also reviewed "Mr. Sraffa's Commodity Rate" (1935, pp. 41-44). Working without the benefit of the *General Theory* and missing entirely the ironic critique implied by Sraffa's use of own-rates, Adarkar finds little use for the concept in his own concern with monetary policy. He seems to have thought that Sraffa was in fact proposing that his average commodity rates be adopted as a policy guide. Nevertheless, the very naivete of his criticisms, coming as they do from a student of the Keynes of the *Treatise*, provides a useful transition to Keynes' own use of the concept.

Adarkar's chapter is mainly focused on the possible use of Sraffa's average commodity rate as a standard by which the banking authorities might set the money rate. To this task, he finds it inadequate due to its instability. What is particularly interesting, though, is that Adarkar critiques the bare concept of the commodity rates from the standpoint of the rich institutional detail about monetary markets of Keynes's *Treatise on Money*. Again, he foreshadows many of the issues that will appear in Keynes' own use of this concept.

Adarkar points out that Sraffa's commodity rates bear a strong resemblance to Fisher's attempt to reckon "real" rates of interest "for each separate commodity by correcting the money rate for a change in its new spot price" (Adarkar, 1935, p. 42). But the difference between them, he notes, is that Fisher wanted to consider the difference between two spot prices separated in time while Sraffa's rate is completely calculated on current market evaluations as reflected in simultaneously existing spot and future prices. Thus, Fisher's real rate "is a *de facto* affair, on which monetary policy could only hold a *post mortem*"; but Sraffa's rate "is a living fact on which we could rely for active guidance in that if disequilibrium arises, the forward prices indicate it" (p. 42).

It is this forward-looking aspect of Sraffa's commodity rates that peculiarly adapts them to Keynes' preferred mode of monetary theory: uncertainty about the future. And, of course, what Sraffa implied in his review was that precisely those functions of money which relate to uncertain intertemporal situations were the ones Hayek and the natural rate theorists were ignoring at the peril of relevance to a "real monetary economy." Adarkar, although still confused about Sraffa's use of the concept, details the implications such psychological aspects of money hold for commodity rates.

First, he mentions that in a risky market the equilibrium position of spot and future prices will not exactly coincide due to the "cost of hedging." "As Mr. Keynes has shown (1930, vol. 2, p. 143), in equilibrium the spot price exceeds the forward price, the 'backwardation' amounting to as much as 10 percent in the case of seasonal crops" (p. 43). In the *General Theory*, this normal backwardization is subsumed under one element of his conception of own-rates, the liquidity premium. Adarkar further notes that a true reckoning of such rates must take into account "costs of warehousing, insurance [and] deterioration" of the stocks held over; "the *speculative* element" in spot and forward dealings; and the "current ideas and expectations of businessmen as to the probable course of future production" (p. 44). Each of these influences, we will see, also has a counterpart in Keynes' own-rates framework. While for Adarkar these influences made it "questionable whether we could depend upon such data to discover the norms and equilibria of industry," in Keynes' hands these concerns will constitute a "monetary theory of production" based on both real and monetary influences. It may be that one implication of this theory is that there are no "norms and equilibria" by which we can regulate the economy through monetary policy, as was the goal of the natural rate theorists. But in terms of explicating Keynes' central concern with interest and money in defining unemployment equilibriums theoretically, Adarkar foreshadows Keynes' own argument, to which we now turn.

4. Keynes: The Theory of Interest and the Theory of Employment

Chapter 17 comes 222 pages into a complicated *theoretical* attempt to define unemployment equilibria as the normal case of a capitalist economy. As many of his pre-publication correspondents and post-publication critics have commented, its discussion runs on a more general plane of reasoning from the more closely argued model that precedes it[6]. Yet, it obviously must be understood as a part of that greater work. For this reason, it is prudent to preface our detailed investigation of chapter 17 with a brief look at Keynes' argument up to that point.

Keynes' theory of the equilibrium positions of the economic system was "general" in its insistence on the possibility of a range of outputs and employments being consistent with the normal functioning of the system. Keynes felt that his essential conclusion was that a less-than-full employment equilibrium was the normal case within this possible range. In arriving at this conclusion, he felt that the fundamental analytical breakthrough in his own thinking had been the realization of "the psychological law that when income increases, the gap between income and consumption will increase" (1973b, p. 85). It was from this simple idea that he derived his fundamental building blocks of the multiplier and the theory of effective demand. Keynes thought that the neglect of aggregate effective demand, or "demand for output as a whole," had made the classical theory irrelevant except in the special case of full employment. His analysis of their argument in chapter 2 attributes this neglect to a reliance on the second classical postulate and Say's Law. For Keynes, the way to exhibit such a range of equilibria was to throw out the second postulate and to supply the missing equation for effective demand.

Because saving is not necessarily directed to productive use, the level of aggregate demand fluctuates. The result is uncertainty over future levels of activity. To Keynes, this meant his aggregate demand theory would have to deal with saving and investment activity in an uncertain environment. Hence, the fascinating discussions of expectations for which *The General Theory* should be, and in some circles is, famous.

Keynes situated the main effect of this uncertainty in the investment activity of business. Having cut the strict productivity moorings from beneath the classical theory of interest, it was necessary for Keynes to provide an alternative formulation. Thus, the last element in his system was the liquidity preference theory of interest. This filled the gap in a manner consistent with his analysis of the psychological uncertainty of investment behavior.

In brief, given short-period conditions, output and employment depend upon aggregate effective demand, which is wagged up and down by fluctuating investment behavior (the consumption function being stable). A complex of productivity, monetary and expectational conditions, all packed into the portmanteaux of the liquidity preference function and the marginal-efficiency-of-capital schedules, determines investment behavior and thus output and employment. According to Keynes, when it is realized that output and employment are not givens, but are uniquely correlated with the level of effective demand, the *practically* obvious existence of involuntary unemployment can be *theoretically* explained. It is only in the context of this argument that his definitions of involuntary unemployment and full employment can be understood.

Keynes left it to chapter 17 to fully draw out his theory of interest and money for reasons clearly set out in the first paragraph of that chapter:

> It seems, then, that the rate of interest on money plays a peculiar part in setting a limit to the level of employment, since it sets a standard to which the marginal efficiency of a capital-asset must attain if it is to be newly produced. That this should be so, is, at first sight, most perplexing. It is natural to enquire wherein the peculiarity of money lies as distinct from other assets, whether it is only money which has a rate of interest, and what would happen in a non-monetary economy. *Until we have answered these questions, the full significance of our theory will not be clear* (Keynes, 1936, p. 202; my italics).

5. The Essential Properties of Interest: Own Rates in a Monetary Economy

In synthesizing a general theory of interest and money that is compatible with his general theory of employment, Keynes draws on Sraffa's commodity rates as an exploratory tool, now following out the implications of this notion for what Sraffa termed "real monetary economies." Methodologically, this involves Sraffa's subtle admonition to Hayek about starting from concrete situations as well as Adarkar's less subtle references to the failing of commodity rates to capture the full institutional detail of a monetary economy. Though we have gone far afield from Keynes, coming back to roost in chapter 17 will provide (at least) one way to understand Harrod's comments about Keynes' central concern with a "wrong rate of interest" that is "not itself a rigidity or inflexibility," but is "natural, durable, and in a certain sense, in the free system inevitable" (1947, p. 70). To use Keynes' own words, "Until we have answered these questions the full significance of our theory will not be clear."

In chapter seventeen of the *General Theory* Keynes immediately gets down to concrete cases, introducing commodity-rates as a natural definition of interest on both money and other types of assets:

> The money rate of interest--we may remind the reader--is nothing more than the percentage excess of a sum of money contracted for forward delivery, e.g. a year hence, over what we may call the "spot" or cash price of the sum thus contracted for forward delivery. It would seem, therefore, that for every kind of capital-asset there must be an analogue of the rate of interest on money. For there is a definite quantity of (e.g.) wheat to be delivered a year hence which has the same exchange value today as 100 quarters of wheat for "spot" delivery. If the former quantity is 105 quarters, we may say that the wheat-rate of interest is 5 percent. per annum; and if it is 95 quarters, that it is *minus* 5 percent. per annum. Thus for every durable commodity we have a rate of interest in terms of itself...." (p. 222).

Footnoting Sraffa, Keynes works through an example, similar to Sraffa's cotton spinner, of the wheat-rate of interest. He defines such commodity rates as "own-rates" and notes that "there is no reason why their rates of interest should be the same for different commodities," since the relations of spot and future prices for different commodities are "notoriously different" (p. 223). Thus, in the most general context of the own-rates conception, "the money rate of interest has no uniqueness compared with other rates of interest, but is on precisely the same footing" (p. 225).

Yet, although as an intertemporal market equivalent there is no difference between a money transaction and a wheat transaction, Keynes implies that the money rate is unique for two interrelated reasons. The money rate is the standard in which all other future values are contracted for and estimated, and there are peculiar reasons why the money rate may be less flexible downward than other rates. If we can show why these two properties adhere to money rather than other assets, we will have some justification for using money as the standard in which to measure the marginal efficiency of capital, and for using the money rate as the marginal efficiency which "rules the roost" in the sense of providing a rate which other assets must attain to be newly produced. In other words, it is the fact that money is just another asset *and* that it is a peculiar asset that warrants attention on the money rate as the regulator of investment.

In order to get to the rest of the differences and similarities between the range of observed assets and their own-rates of interest, Keynes introduces a scheme of attributes which defines the relative desirability of different assets, essentially a demand equation for assets. This scheme addresses Adarkar's comments (based on the *Treatise*, remember) on the specific failings of the commodity-rates in a monetary economy as well as illustrating Keynes' liquidity preference theory. It is through this abstraction that Keynes relocates the own-rates from the Wicksellian world to his own.

Taking "various commodity-rates of interest over a period of (say) a year" and measuring each rate "in terms of itself" as the standard of intertemporal value, Keynes finds "three attributes which different types of assets possess in different degrees." These are:

(i)   Some assets produce a yield or output q, measured in terms of themselves, by assisting some process of production or supplying services to a consumer.

(ii)   Most assets, except money, suffer some wastage or involve some cost through the mere passage of time (apart from any change in their relative value), irrespective of their being used to produce a yield; i. e., they involve a carrying cost c measured in terms of themselves....

(iii)   Finally, the power of disposal over an asset during a period may offer a potential convenience or security, which is not equal for assets of different kinds, though the assets themselves are of equal initial value. There is, so to speak, nothing to show for this at the end of the period in the shape of output; yet it is something for which people are ready to pay something. The amount (measured in terms of itself) which they are willing to pay for the potential convenience or security given by this power of disposal (exclusive of the yield or carrying cost attaching to the asset), we shall call its liquidity-premium ℓ (pp. 225-226).

In Keynes' scheme, an asset's own-rate of interest will be defined by "its yield *minus* its carrying cost plus its liquidity premium." Recalling Adarkar's specific complaints about commodity rates, we can now see that in Keynes' definition, we have so far taken account of "costs of the stocks held over" with c, "current ideas and expectations of businessmen as to the probable course of future production" with q (and to some extent ℓ), and "the speculative element" with ℓ. But Adarkar's further concern with the relation of pure commodity rates to the Fisher effect is also addressed by Keynes. It is worthwhile to look at this relationship a bit more closely since it sheds light on the important and interesting question of the relation of interest rates and inflation in the own-rates framework.

Keynes claims that so far as the relationship between spot and future prices on different commodities reveals a multitude of own-rates, any of these commodities which are held for investment purposes could conceivably be used as the standard in which to measure the marginal efficiency of capital assets (recalling that his concern is with explaining investment demand):

> For we can take any commodity we choose, e.g. wheat; calculate the wheat-value of the prospective yields of any capital asset; and the rate of discount which makes the present value of this series of wheat annuities equal to the present supply price of the asset in terms of wheat gives us the marginal efficiency of the asset in terms of wheat (p. 224).

According to Keynes, the choice of standard is arbitrary so long as "no change is expected in the relative value of two alternative standards." We are very close here to the Fisherian doctrine of the effect of expected inflation on current interest rates. The relative value of two alternative standards is just Fisher's "appreciation of money" where we are, as Keynes says (p. 227), "taking money (which need only be a money of account for this purpose, and we could equally well take wheat) as our standard of measurement...." In this situation, it is possible to correct for differences in both different standards over time or in relative changes with respect to one particular standard. In the case of choosing a standard, all "own-rates" would move up and down "when one of the alternative standards is expected to change in value in terms of the other." The influence of Sraffa may even be echoed here in the attention given to the possibility of an invariant standard of value. Basically, there are two problems involved. First, there is the question of which good to use as the standard in which to measure all relative own rates (including the all important marginal efficiency of capital) today. As Keynes said above, this choice is arbitrary in the sense that we can value any expected stream and current price in terms of any standard we choose, e.g. wheat. "If no change is expected in the relative value of two alternative standards, then the marginal efficiency of a capital-asset will be the same in whichever of the two standards it is measured, since the numerator and denominator of the fraction which leads up to the marginal efficiency will be change in the same proportion" (Keynes, 1936, p. 224).

But, secondly, if one of the standards is expected to change in value (appreciate), "the marginal efficiencies of capital-assets will be changed by the same percentage, according to which standard they are measured in." Keynes illustrates his conception of the effect such an appreciating standard will have on the structure of own-rates by a simple example where "wheat, one of the alternative standards, is expected to appreciate at a steady rate of a percent, per annum in terms of money." According to Keynes, in this simple case a will provide an additive adjustment factor to the marginal efficiency of an asset to distinguish rates determined in one standard or another with the ranking of asset values remaining unaffected:

> The marginal efficiency of an asset, which is x percent, in terms of money, will then be x-a percent, in terms of wheat. Since the marginal efficiencies of all capital-assets will be altered by the same amount, it follows that their order of magnitude will be the same irrespective of the standard which is selected.

Keynes' simple example of a standard appreciating at a steady rate skirts a great complication here, in that the real problem will arise when different assets appreciate at different rates and these rates of appreciation are ex-ante uncertain. In other words, relative rates of appreciation are not all to be expected to be the same in terms of any particular standard. Fisher was well aware of this problem when he noted: "There are, therefore, theoretically just as many rates of interest expressed in terms of goods as there are kinds of goods diverging from one another in value" (1930, p. 42). His solution--not surprisingly, coming from the master of the theory of index numbers--was to express his "real rate" of interest by adjusting the money rate with *ex post* changes in a cost of living index.

Keynes himself was no fool when it came to index number problems (see *Treatise*, book II), and perhaps his collaboration with the meticulous and cautious Sraffa, who by this date was already concerned with the difficulties of aggregate conceptions of capital, made him justifiably wary of aggregate indices of all kinds. This wariness (as well as Sraffa's influence?) shows up in the present context in his comment on defining a standard:

> If there were some composite commodity which could be regarded strictly speaking as representative, we could regard the rate of interest and the marginal efficiency of capital in terms of this commodity as being, in a sense, uniquely *the* rate of interest and *the* marginal efficiency of capital. But there are, of course, the same obstacles in the way of this as there are to setting up a unique standard of value.

In accordance with this rejection of a composite standard, Keynes includes an appreciation factor "a" in his equations for own-rates which take into account "what the changes in relative values during the year are expected to be" in order to "determine the expected returns on different types of assets which are consistent with equilibrium" (p. 227). By this method, Keynes avoids the problems of a "unique standard of value," while retaining price expectations in his demand for asset scheme. The "a" terms also serve the function of converting the diverse commodity own-rates into a single (but not unique) standard of value. Thus, where

$$q_i - c_i + \ell_i$$

defines the commodity own-rate in real terms for commodity i, the same rate measured in money terms will yield the "money rate" of commodity i,

$$q_i - c_i + \ell_i + a_i.$$

A question immediately arises which can only be dimly seen at this stage. What has become of the Fisher effect here? Essentially, it has been dethroned from Adarkar's strictly algebraic *post mortem* of interest rates that have already happened and replaced with a living, current expectation[7]. In the process, Keynes has also abandoned any attempt to theoretically define an index measure of the different expected appreciation rates of different assets by different people. There will, nevertheless, be a market effect of these expectations in terms of different own-rates being brought into equality in money terms by the additive "a" terms. But, as we will see, since Keynes' views on financial markets place great weight on the diversity of opinions about the future course of asset values, this effect is not well-captured by an index number approach. What will be important will be the "shifting" of these market valuations which will reflect a change at the margin of opinion (i.e., some of Keynes' "bears joining the bull brigade").

From the standpoint of the Fisher effect, the main element of this expected appreciation will reflect uncertainty about the future ability of the monetary standard to fulfill its role as the most liquid asset. As we will see when we get to Keynes' views on the essential properties of money, this will involve Fisher's interest in the stability of prices in money terms to some extent. But the effect of instability will not be a strictly additive factor in valuing interest, but a complicated matter of social convention. By this view, Keynes' ultimate Fisher effect is more drastic than Fisher's own. For Keynes, a lack of confidence in the socially conventional standard is more qualitative than quantitative. If instability detracts from money's role as the liquidity standard, some substitute for liquidity will be set up by the organic methods of market evolution. But a full understanding of these issues requires more detail of the own-rates framework.

6. The Structure of Own-Rates in Asset Market Equilibrium

Returning to the development of the own-rates framework of asset market equilibrium, it is useful to digress a bit and consolidate the argument so far. What we have seen is that the bare concept of a commodity rate introduced by Sraffa implies that, from the most general standpoint, the money rate of interest is not unique. Just like a money transaction, any intertemporal market rate implies an own-rate of exchange between spot and future quantities. To be absolutely clear about this deceptively simple idea, it is convenient to resort to some algebra. In this context, we will start from (and then elaborate on) the useful algebraic formulation of own-rates of interest by Joseph Conard (1959, pp. 119-154). Although Conard is led astray in his discussion by failing to account for Keynes' views on uncertainty, his formal discussion of the concepts of commodity rates and money rates is the clearest exposition in the literature.

Conard begins his investigation by defining own-rates as a case of the Fisherian "rate of return over cost" (p. 120):

$$\frac{\textit{Expected future value - present value}}{\text{present value}}$$

In this framework, "real" or "commodity" own-rates (which we will designate as r_c) are defined in quantities (Q) of the physical commodity

$$r_c = \frac{Q_2 - Q_1}{Q_1}. \tag{1}$$

Denominated in a standard of value, the same rate will become a money-denominated own-rate in value terms (which we will define $r_{c,m}$):

$$r_{c,m} = \frac{P_2Q_2 - P_1Q_1}{P_1Q_1}. \tag{2}$$

By this method, Conard shows that Keynes' "a" terms, the difference between real own-rates and money own-rates, are inherently complex

$$a = r_{c,m} - r_c \tag{3}$$

$$= \frac{P_2Q_2 - P_1Q_1}{P_1Q_1} - \frac{Q_2 - Q_1}{Q_1} \tag{4}$$

$$= \left(\frac{P_2 - P_1}{P_1}\right) \left(\frac{Q_2}{Q_1}\right) \tag{5}$$

So the "a" that transforms a real own-rate into a money own-rate is the expected proportionate price change times the ratio of the intertemporal quantity equivalents.

We can use this formulation to clarify a number of issues. First, recall that Sraffa (1932a, p. 50) had defined the commodity rate as being equal to the money rate "plus the excess (or minus the deficiency) of the spot over the forward price." This is the definition referenced to Sraffa by Keynes that he used in working out his wheat example. It provides a clear link between the abstract concept and market phenomena. Using Conard's framework, we can specify this link more clearly. The relationship postulated by Sraffa is

$$r_c = r_m - \left(\frac{P_2 - P_1}{P_1}\right) \tag{6}$$

where: r_c = the commodity own-rate
r_m = the money own-rate
P_2 = the future price of the commodity
P_1 = the spot price of the commodity

It is noteworthy in this context that Keynes defines equilibrium in the asset market as the situation where all own-rates, defined in a common standard, are equal. "Thus in equilibrium the demand-prices of houses and wheat in terms of money will be such that there is nothing to choose in the way of advantage between the alternatives" (p. 227). Using money as the standard, this means that all money own-rates and the money-rate itself will be equal in equilibrium; or, for all commodities i,

$$r_c^i + a^i = r_m. \qquad (7)$$

In terms of the above definitions,

$$r_m = \frac{M_2 - M_1}{M_1}$$

$$r_c^i = \frac{Q_2^i - Q_1^i}{Q_2^i} \qquad (8)$$

$$a^i = \frac{P_2^i - P_1^i}{P_1^i}\left(\frac{Q_2^i}{Q_1^i}\right),$$

by which we get a more precise version of the Sraffa formula:

$$r_c^i = r_m - \left(\frac{P_2^i - P_1^i}{P_1^i}\right)\left(\frac{Q_2^i}{Q_1^i}\right) \qquad (9)$$

This not only confirms the Sraffian lineage of Keynes' concept (Sraffa's definition can be fit into Keynes's framework), but it also makes clear that Keynes' definition of equilibrium in this context is strictly a current, short-period affair. To see this, recall that Sraffa, using the long-period as his definition, defined "'equilibrium' rates as the situation where spot and forward prices coincide...and all the 'natural' or commodity rates are equal to one another, and to the money rate" (Sraffa, 1932a, p. 50). But here, Keynes has defined his "equilibrium" as an equality between all own-rates measured in money terms which, as the above formula makes clear, could easily be a disequilibrium in the long period sense. This may be one way of understanding Keynes' insistence that the difference between a monetary and a real economics entails a specification of the "line of division between the theory of stationary equilibrium and the theory of shifting equilibrium--meaning by the latter the theory of a system in which changing views about the future are capable of influencing the present situation. *For the importance of money essentially flows from its being a link between the present and future*" (1936, p. 293).

In this view, Keynes' "shifting equilibrium" is defined by a monetary equilibrium on the asset market where all own-rates *consistently measured* are equal, but spot and forward prices still diverge according to current expectations of productivity, carrying costs and liquidity. Alternatively, Sraffa's equilibrium commodity rates are part of the theory of "stationary equilibrium." In a formal sense, this is captured by Sraffa's view that equilibrium requires all own-rates *measured in quantity terms* to be equal, and all spot and future prices to coincide. This is why the details of Keynes' "a" terms are so important. It is the movements of the prices on spot and future markets that guarantee his equilibrium position will exhibit a market configuration of equal *expected* money-denominated own-rates for every asset. But to see why Keynes' equilibrium *shifts* with "changing views about the future," we need to investigate Keynes' second question of Chapter 17. What is it about money as an asset that makes it unique?

In terms of his schema of attributes of assets, Keynes distinguishes money by its high liquidity premium and low carrying cost;

> ...it is an essential difference between money and all (or most) other assets that in the case of money its liquidity-premium much exceeds its carrying cost, whereas in the case of other assets their carrying cost much exceeds their liquidity premium (p. 227).

The full implications of the special character of money, though, only become apparent in terms of Keynes' argument about the relationship between his shifting equilibrium on the asset market and the level of employment. His argument, at its most general level, focuses on the role of interest rates as a determinant of new investment spending. In the own-rates context, investment is disaggregated into individual capital-assets which are both newly produced and traded on second-hand markets. At any given time, the outstanding stocks of both physical and pecuniary assets will be valued by the market in accordance with the demand for each asset's individual attributes of productivity, carrying cost and liquidity. Given that the stocks are slowly adjusted, the price established on the second-hand market will determine, when compared with the "normal supply price," in what directions and amounts investment flows proceed.

The definitions of equilibrium and the movements implied between equilibrium positions are very poorly specified by Keynes. At some junctures, his argument involves defining instantaneous stock equilibriums and at others discussing short-period flows of production of investment goods, and at yet others he seems to be talking about secular levels of capital accumulation. In fact, to make sense of his argument, it is necessary to bring in a number of elements that define a very complicated picture only hastily sketched by Keynes.

An analytical interpretation of this framework is possible if we center our attention on Keynes' equilibrium own-rates as a market phenomenon around which his complicated short-run analysis operates[8]. By this interpretation, a stock equilibrium configuration of asset returns can serve as a focus of both liquidity preference theory in general and of money's special qualities as an asset.

To begin, we have Keynes' assertion that equilibrium in the asset market will be characterized by a state where all own-rates, measured in a single standard, will equal each other (1936, pp. 227-228). It is in this context that he defines the "a" terms for each asset as the expected rate of appreciation of that asset in terms of the standard. Lerner (1952, pp. 173-179) and Conard (1959, pp. 120-134) show that when reduced to any common standard, the rate of interest on all assets will be driven to equality since any deviations (abstracting from risk and term differences) would provide arbitrage opportunities that would drive the prices of the assets into such an equilibrium. Thus, in the context of asset market equilibrium, the "a" terms can be seen as the *necessary* positions of supply and demand equilibrium in spot and forward markets that ensure that all assets yield an equal return when consistently measured. This is clearly shown in the form given to the a's above where they are defined by the difference between spot and future prices:

$$a^i = \frac{P_2^i - P_1^i}{P_1^i} \left(\frac{Q_2^i}{Q_1^i}\right) \qquad (10)$$

It is Keynes' scheme of motives for holding different assets that provides the underlying economic forces which drive the demands for various commodities. Productivity, costs and liquidity considerations shift these demands between the various stocks of assets; but, on the market, the price configuration given by the relationships of the money rate and the spot and forward money prices is driven toward an equilibrium defined by the a's. Conard (1959) provides clear examples of this in the form of a variety of assets, each of which has different commodity own-rates, but all of which yield an equal rate when measured consistently in any of the standards. Abba Lerner (1952) provides a similar analysis in his insightful interpretation of the own-rates theory and concludes:

> The wheat rate of interest and the money rate of interest are not automatically equal by definition: they are only brought into approximate equality in equilibrium by arbitrage in perfectly competitive markets.

To use Keynes' example where there are 3 assets--money, houses and wheat-- we get 3 individual money-rates of own-interest all measured in money as the standard. The wheat rate is due to its predominant physical characteristic of high carrying cost and is primarily held for an expected rise in its price:

$$r_{w,m} = a_1 - c_1 = \frac{Q_2^w - Q_1^w}{Q_1^w} + \frac{P_2^w - P_1^w}{P_1^w} \left(\frac{Q_2^w}{Q_1^w}\right) \quad (11)$$

The house rate is due primarily to its productive capacity to generate services, q:

$$r_{h,m} = a_2 + q_2 = \frac{Q_2^h - Q_1^h}{Q_1^h} + \frac{P_2^h - P_1^h}{P_1^h} \left(\frac{Q_2^h}{Q_1^h}\right) \quad (12)$$

The money rate is defined by the unique character of money that "its yield is *nil*, and its carrying cost negligible, but its liquidity premium substantial[9]" (p. 226).

$$r_{m,m} = l_3 = \frac{M_2 - M_1}{M_1} \quad (13)$$

Using this framework, the asset market equilibrium condition is defined by

$$r_{w,m} = r_{h,m} = r_{m,m}$$

or

$$a_1 - c_1 = a_2 + q_2 = l_3$$

or,

$$\frac{Q_2^w - Q_1^w}{Q_1^w} + \frac{P_2^w - P_1^w}{P_1^w} \left(\frac{Q_2^w}{Q_1^w}\right) =$$

$$\frac{Q_2^h - Q_1^h}{Q_1^h} + \frac{P_2^h - P_1^h}{P_1^h} \left(\frac{Q_2^h}{Q_1^h}\right) = \frac{M_2 - M_1}{M_1}$$

7. Stocks of Assets and Flows of Activity: The *General Theory* viewed through the Own Rates Equilibrium Construct

Many writers have commented on the stock equilibrium quality of Keynes' analysis, by which we mean that equilibrium is defined for a market evaluation of an existing quantity of capital, money bonds etc. Kenneth Boulding was so taken with this aspect of Keynes' approach that he proposed *A Reconstruction of Economics* (1950) based on the sole use of stock rather than flow equilibrium theory. G.L.S. Shackle (1967, p. 145) has commented that this use of stock analysis is particularly evident in Keynes' interest rate theory:

> One more of the great changes in outlook of economic theoreticians stands largely to Keynes' credit, and again it is largely a case where an idea or practice of Marshall's was radically deepened and enlarged. Marshall had compared the existing with the desired total stock of money, and proposed to regard the latter as proportional to national income. This was perhaps the first turning of the tide against the neoclassical emphasis on flows in contrast with stocks. Keynes' theory of the interest-rate fused method and meaning inseparably in a purely "stocks" analysis. It is the essence of the liquidity-preference theory that stocks and not flows are in command, and in stating this theory Keynes showed a "stocks" analysis at work.

It is interesting that Shackle mentions Marshall in this context since, as we have seen above, the very definition of "equilibrium" own-rates by Sraffa and Keynes, respectively, hinges on the choice of defining them in the Marshallian long period (for Sraffa) or short period (for Keynes)[10]. But actually the better distinction to be drawn in this context is between a monetary and non-monetary economy. Consequently, Sraffa, who in critiquing Hayek's method of neutral money was explicitly operating on the terrain of a non-monetary economy, looked to flows of resources between industries to eventually equalize all own-rates and the money rate by equalizing the spot and future prices of every commodity in a long period equilibrium. But Keynes, more alive to the financial realities of a complex money economy, relies on the arbitraging of wealth owners and speculators to drive the relation of spot and future prices of the outstanding stocks of assets into a configuration *today* that reflects current expectations about the desirability of each in the never realized *future*. As we will see, the importance of money in this scheme will revolve around its use as the link between these current expectations and the level of own-rates on the market today. It will be through the own-rate on money defined by its liquidity premium (along with the expected return on capital) that all of Keynes' fascinating discussion of long-term expectations and non-Benthamite opinions about the future will enter into the framework of the asset-holding equilibrium of chapter 17. Two more elements of the framework of analysis must first be dealt with.

Although Keynes defines asset equilibrium on the market by a configuration of prices on spot and forward markets (as just shown), this is in a sense only the observable surface phenomenon around which the really interesting aspects of his story are centered. In fact, the major virtue of the own-rates analysis of

Keynes' interest rate theory may be that it does provide such a manageable focusing device for the complex considerations he wanted to discuss in his interest rate theory, the same complexities that we have argued are ignored in the latter-day "Keynesian" vision. It is not idle to speak of the market equilibrium rates as a "centering" device in this context since the complete story involves movements that occur both beneath this market equilibrium, in the form of individual decisions about expected asset values, and above this equilibrium in the form of flows of newly produced assets that respond to the market-determined prices. Before continuing, it is necessary to briefly discuss both.

Keynes' analysis of the interest rate in chapters 13 and 15 of the *General Theory* is addressed to the determination of the rate of interest on money in modern financial conditions. At the root of the argument is the question of how (in what form) a given level of savings out of income (the determination of which he had already distinguished from financial markets *per se*, by his aggregate demand analysis)[11] will be held. In the simplest terms, Keynes formulates the decision as one between holding savings in the form of "immediate, liquid command" over goods and services versus being "prepared to part with immediate command for a specified or indefinite period, leaving it to future market conditions to determine on what terms he can, if necessary, convert deferred commands over specific goods into immediate command over goods in general" (p. 166). The extent to which wealth holders prefer one type of asset over another is the definition of their current state of *liquidity preference*. Defining this preference as a demand for *money* (in excess of that required for active circulation) and the rate of interest on money as the price of parting with this liquidity, money interest becomes the "'price' which equilibrates the desire to hold wealth in the form of cash with the available quantity of cash."

But a further question remains. Why is it that anyone would want to hold wealth in a form that yields a rate of return less than other financial instruments? Why does such a thing as liquidity preference exist? Keynes argues that the fundamental condition giving rise to a liquidity preference is "the existence of *uncertainty* as to the future of the rate of interest." This, of course, is the source of the famous "bootstrap" critique of Keynes whereby it is uncertainty over the future rate that determines the current rate of interest (Robertson, 1940, pp. 35-36; Hicks, 1946, pp. 163-164). From the standpoint of the complexity of the own-rates structure, this is shown to be a specious argument in that all of the multifarious elements of productivity, costs and time preference that the bootstrap critique considers left out of Keynes' argument are present here. Yet, in another sense, the "bootstrap" formulation goes to the heart of the expectational context for the existence of a liquidity premium: uncertainty over future prices[12]. But this should not be a criticism in the world Keynes was interested in describing. As Keynes repeatedly emphasizes, in his world actors *are* uncertain about the future, and the expectations that they hold about the future are just what the bootstrap critique implies: "hoist on their own petard."

What we are driving at is the central theme that Keynes emphasized as the distinguishing feature of his *General Theory* in the 1937 *Q.J.E.* article (Keynes, 1937c), namely the "conventionality" of expectations in an uncertain environment. As Keynes emphasized in that article, this conventional quality of expectations enters into the economic scheme with particular force through asset valuations, both financial and real capital. In terms of the own-rates structure, both types of expectations about profitability of investments and movements of financial prices will influence the equilibrium configuration through various q's, a's and l's. But expectations will be especially relevant to the discussion of the peculiarities of money since "...*uncertainty* as to the future course of the rate of interest is the sole intelligible explanation of the type of liquidity preference...which leads to the holding of cash" (p. 201).

Since our emphasis is on the use of the own-rates theory as a tool in understanding the monetary character of Keynes's theory, two elements that are laid out in chapters 12, 13 and 15 of the *General Theory* are worth emphasizing for the insight they lend to our understanding of chapter 17. Keynes emphasized in these discussions that the interest on money, arising as it does out of a desire for liquidity in the face of uncertain expectations about the future course of capital asset values, rests on a *conventional* judgment of what the future course of interest will be. For this reason, financial markets: (1) are "made" by the simultaneous existence of a variety of opinions; and (2) are subject to precipitous swings when the fabric of the conventional judgment is weakened. A few lengthy quotations from Keynes (1936) demonstrate the importance of these points:

> ...the rate of interest and the price of bonds have to be fixed at the level at which the desire on the part of certain individuals to hold cash (because at that level they feel "bearish" of the future of bonds) is exactly equal to the amount of cash available for the speculative motive. Thus, each increase in the quantity of money must raise the price of bonds sufficiently to exceed the expectations of some "bull" and so influence him to sell his bonds for cash and join the "bear" brigade (p. 171).

> ...It is interesting that the stability of the system and its sensitiveness to changes in the quantity of money should be so dependent on the existence of a *variety* of opinion about what is uncertain (p. 172).

> ...Changes in the liquidity function itself, due to a change in the news which causes revision of expectations, will often be discontinuous, and will, therefore, give rise to a corresponding discontinuity of change in the rate of interest. Only, indeed, in so far as the change in the news is differently interpreted by different individuals or affects individual interests differently will there be room for any increased activity of dealing in the bond market (p. 198).

Now the tie-in between these two crucial aspects of liquidity preference theory--the necessity of a diversity of opinions and the liability of reevaluations in conventional judgments to effect sea changes in interest rates--and the own-rates theory has two consequences. First, the argument about the diversity of opinions provides the link between the equilibrium market structure of the own-rates when measured in a common standard with the scheme of individual judgments as to the expected productivity, liquidity and appreciation of various assets. In other words, in order to "make a market" for the variety of individual assets, it is necessary that individual estimates of the q's, a's, and l's differ among individual investors. This is what we meant earlier by the individual decisions that go on *beneath* the structure of the equilibrium market configuration of asset prices.

Thus, by this argument the asset market equilibrium configuration implied by the own-rates structure is "built up" from a sophisticated microfoundation. The sophistication lies in the explicit recognition of the social level influences on individual behavior, in the form of the market opportunities available to wealth holders and the social conventions underlying their future expectations. Further elaboration of this kind of (neglected) microfoundations would involve the role of different classes or "ideal types" of transactors on the markets, each with different goals and constraints. Two strong-type examples of this are evident in the Cambridge tradition of dividing bond holders up into two groups: widows and orphans and freewheeling speculators. R.F. Kahn (1954) makes much of this in his view of liquidity preference theory and notes that it links up the Keynes of the *General Theory* with the "two views" of the *Treatise*. More recently, work on the social foundations of the idea of rational expectations has come back to this point (Frydman, 1982; Frydman et al., 1982). Interestingly for us, the focus has been on the possible *instability* of a rational expectations equilibrium in its resemblance to the "Holmes-Moriarity problem" which is formally the same problem as Keynes' famous beauty contest (see O'Driscoll and Rizzo, 1985, pp. 84-85). In the own-rates equations for asset demand, this underlying conception of individual evaluations would actually imply a different equation for each different asset for each different agent. With n assets and m traders, we would get mn own-rate equations in the most general case. The market equilibrium rates would be equivalent to evaluations of the marginal traders only.

The second implication of these views of Keynes' is that this underlying variety of opinion, making up both sides of the market for the total stock of existing assets, can move rapidly between various evaluations of the future (Keynes' "bearishness and bullishness" of the *Treatise*) because of alterations in the skein of conventional judgments upon which such evaluations exist. Keynes goes so far as to suggest that if all opinions about the future course of prices were unanimous and held with certainty, that a complete revaluation of assets could occur without any change in holdings whatsoever:

> If the change in the news affects the judgment and requirements of everyone in precisely the same way, the rate of interest (as indicated by the price of bonds and debts) will be adjusted forthwith to the new situation without any market transactions being necessary (p. 198).

The confluence of these two points is the determination of the shifts in Keynes' "theory of shifting equilibrium" to which we previously equated the "own-rates" theory. Assets are held in expectation of gain based on conventional judgments of the future by different individuals. This precarious equilibrium is liable at any time to "shift" when the foundation of current opinion about the future is disturbed. The magnitude of the shift will depend on the extent to which it is shared and the length of time it takes for a new convention to be established. Thus, our asset market "equilibrium" is seen to be simultaneously a fragile balancing of individual opinions, and one firmly based in the economic motives of personal gain (here, though, only personally defined) by investors and speculators seeking their own advantage.

The macroeconomic importance of this asset equilibrium, now shown to constitute a market element with an underlying microstructure, is the effect that the level of the shifting stock equilibrium has on "flows" of investment and hence employment. It is here that the last element of Keynes' "vision" of chapter 17 comes in. These flows are the other side of the spectrum of which the own-rates form the center. For the result of the "highly conventional" phenomenon of asset market equilibrium has a very real effect in governing the desirability of investments in labor-employing projects. As Harrod's statement implied, it is for perfectly natural reasons that the rate of interest is "wrong." If in an uncertain world there is no reason to expect asset prices to reflect purely real employment opportunities, then the interest rate:

> ...may fluctuate for decades about a level which is chronically too high for full employment: --particularly if it is the prevailing opinion that the level established by convention is thought to be rooted in objective grounds much stronger than convention, the failure of employment to attain an optimum level being in no way associated, in the minds either of the public or of authority, with the prevalence of an inappropriate range of rates of interest (Keynes, 1936, p. 204).

This was the conclusion of Keynes' basic theoretical model of employment developed in the *General Theory* of which the liquidity preference function was an integral part. In chapter 17 with the use of the "own-rates" theory, Keynes shows that it may be that it is the very nature of money that causes this situation. In so doing, he addresses the further points of discussion in our Wicksellian theme: the nature of money, what a nonmonetary economy would look like, and whether there is such a thing as a "natural" rate of interest, which would avoid this problem altogether.

With our notion of asset market equilibrium in mind, we can follow Keynes into his discussion of the uniqueness of money in Sections II and III of chapter 17. It is interesting to note that he addresses the question to a situation that was firmly established as the starting point of business cycle theory in the Wicksellian literature of his time. In particular, recall that Hayek (and Mises before him) wanted to discuss the natural rate in the context of an economy in which accumulation was going forward. Likewise, for Wicksell the goal was to try to use the marginalist method to explain this situation, using the tools of a long period value theory where factors all earned an equal rate of return. Keynes' innovation was to bring the financial side into this scheme and let his asset market equilibrium configuration determine equal "financial" rates of return at any given time. This is consistent with his severing of the savings-investment link that formed the basis of the Wicksellian story, where the interest rate equated *real* flows of savings with *real* flows of investment at the natural rate. Starting from this conception, the Wicksellian and loanable funds theorists would investigate the consequences of an upward shift in the investment schedule which set off new investment at the existing market rate of interest. In Wicksell, Mises and Hayek, the result of such a shift depended on whether the market rate was allowed to move to a new higher "natural rate" that would equilibrate saving and investment. According to this story, it was because the banking system could hold the rate beneath the natural rate, that we get "forced savings," an intertemporal misallocation of resources and an eventual crisis (see Leijonhufvud, 1981, pp. 151-160).

Keynes bases his analysis of the employment-generating effects of the own rates equilibrium on a similar situation. He asks what would be the limiting factor that brings the production of new capital goods to a standstill? In his scheme, where the secondhand markets for goods continually revalue the whole stock of assets, the flow of new capital goods is determined by a comparison of the market-established rate of return on the existing stock with the expected marginal efficiency of new projects. In price terms, Keynes describes the comparison in terms of a "demand price" for capital goods which is fixed by discounting expected future streams of income from an investment back to the present using the market rate of interest (determined by the own-rates equilibrium). This demand-price is then compared to a supply-price which represents the marginal cost of producing that asset. If the demand-price exceeds the supply-price, new capital goods will be produced:

> Now those assets of which the normal supply-price is less than the demand-price will be newly produced; and these will be those assets of which the marginal efficiency would be greater (on the basis of their normal supply-price) than the rate of interest (both being measured in the same standard of value whatever it is). (Keynes, 1936, p. 228)

Once in this Wicksellian situation of accumulation, where does the process stop? For Keynes, it stops when some asset's own-rate refuses to decline as accumulation goes forward and so holds up the market equilibrium rate of interest. The importance of *declining* own-rates is impressed upon Keynes by his capital theory. Basically, he assumed a declining marginal efficiency of capital assets as production of them expanded in the short run. The best discussion of this process is found in chapter 11 where the "Marginal Efficiency of Capital" is explicitly addressed:

> If there is an increased investment in any given type of capital during any period of time, the marginal efficiency of that type of capital will diminish as the investment in it is increased, partly because the prospective yield will fall as the supply of that type of capital is increased, and partly because, as a rule, pressure on the facilities for producing that type of capital will cause its supply price to increase (p. 136).

To link this disaggregated, expectations-based view of capital with the asset market that the own-rates represent, Keynes further emphasizes in chapter 16 that the failing of technical capital theory lies in ignoring the fact that a capital-asset is just another potential rate of return to investors in a modern economy. The classical argument that it is the physical productivity of capital that sets the pace of investment

> ...overlooks the fact that there is always an alternative to the ownership of real capital-assets, namely the ownership of money and debts; so that the prospective yield with which the producers of new investment have to be content cannot fall below the standard set by the current rate of interest (pp. 212-213).

This reasoning is the basis of Keynes' contention that the source of the return on capital is not that it is productive, but that it is scarce:

> ...the only reason why an asset offers a prospect of yielding during its life services having an aggregate value greater than its initial supply price is because it is *scarce*; and it is kept scarce because of the competition of the rate of interest on money (p. 213).

All of this attention to Keynes' theories of money interest and capital serves not only to link up the own-rates framework with the larger work of which it is a part, but also prepares our way toward understanding Keynes' attribution of uniqueness to money as an asset. In a way that Keynes does not explicitly point out, his argument for the uniqueness of money assets is an integral combination of his capital theory and liquidity preference theory. As we will see, the uniqueness of money is that it is only a very imperfect capital-asset; but that its peculiarities from a capital theory standpoint are just those qualities which make it desirable as a *liquid* asset. Perfectly in accordance with Keynes' views on money and capital, then, the own rates theory brings the analysis of financial and real assets under one framework[13].

In the simplest terms, the marginal efficiency of each capital-asset, d, will be defined by that rate of interest which, when used to discount a future stream of expected returns from an investment, will just equal the current supply-price of that capital asset. If the present supply price of capital-asset i is given, then solving the following for d will yield the marginal efficiency of that capital asset.

$$P^{s^i} = \sum_{j=1}^{n} \frac{R^i_j}{(1+d)^j}$$

where: P^{si} = the present supply price of capital asset i;
R^i = the expected future stream of returns for each period j;
d = a rate of discount.

In terms of the own-rates, this d will equal the expected own-rate for capital asset i:

$$d = q_i - c_i + a_i + l_i$$

Then in equilibrium, those traders at the margin of preference between the different assets will determine an equilibrium value of r where for all assets (i = 1, ..., n)

$$r = q_i - c_i + l_i + a_i$$

By Keynes' simplified example, we can reduce this to our 3 assets (wheat, houses and money) where the equilibrium interest rate (measured in money terms) becomes

$$r = a_1 - c_1 = q_2 + a_2 = l_3.$$

In this context, the importance of the declining own-rates as accumulation proceeds revolves around which rate will hold up the decline of the others. Since they must "necessarily equal" on the market, the downwardly rigid rate will provide the level to which the others fall[14].

> As the stock of the assets, which begin by having a marginal efficiency at least equal to the rate of interest, is increased, their marginal efficiency (for reasons, sufficiently obvious, already given) tends to fall. Thus, a point will come at which it no longer pays to produce them, *unless the rate of interest falls* pari passu. When there is *no* asset of which the marginal efficiency reaches the rate of interest, the further production of capital assets will come to a standstill (p. 228).

8. The Essential Properties of Money

The question Keynes is led to consider by this reasoning is, which of the own-rates will be the stubborn one that holds up the decline? Keynes thought there were certain "peculiarities" of the money rate which made it the own-rate that is reluctant to fall as output increases. The uniqueness of money as an asset revolves around the employment-generating effects that we have ascribed to the own-rates market equilibrium, and which we have seen flow from Keynes' views on capital. It is because capital-assets can be produced that they ultimately fall in value (their own-rates decline) as accumulation proceeds. The first unique characteristic of money is that it cannot be so readily produced in response to changes in its price:

> Thus, the characteristic that money cannot be readily produced by labour gives at once some *prima facie* presumption for the view that its own-rate of interest will be relatively reluctant to fall; whereas if money could be grown like a crop or manufactured like a motor car, depressions would be avoided or mitigated because, if the price of other assets was tending to fall in terms of money, more labour would be directed into the production of money (pp. 230-231).

But since this zero elasticity of production is also satisfied by any other pure rent factor fixed in supply, this cannot be the sole uniqueness of money. "The second *differentia* of money is that it has an elasticity of substitution equal, or nearly equal, to zero; which means that as the exchange value of money rises, there is no tendency to substitute some other factor for it." Keynes' argument here is that since the only reason money is held is for its liquidity value, that a change in the relative value of money will not have an adverse effect on its desirability as an asset. This is because the liquidity premium of a unit of money is only *increased* by an increase in its relative value (a decrease in prices). "This follows from the peculiarity of money that its utility is solely derived from its exchange value, so that the two rise and fall *pari passu*, with the result that as the exchange value of money rises, there is no motive or tendency, as in the case of rent-factors, to substitute some other factor for it." If, like other rent factors, the desirability of the money-asset fell as its price rose, then an increased demand for it would "slop over into a demand for other things." Then the demand for money as an asset would at least indirectly reach a point of calling forth new employment. Since this is not the case, there is the possibility that money could become "a bottomless sink for purchasing power" (p. 231).

From the standpoint of capital theory, then, the two peculiar qualities of money are that demand for it cannot call forth new production directly as in the case of capital goods proper, or even indirectly through substitution of other factors as in the case of pure rental items. For these two reasons, the avenues by which movement in capital-asset own rates is accomplished, by new production, are closed off to the money asset.

But what of other liquid goods (e.g. wheat) of which it may not be possible to immediately increase the supply in response to an increased demand? Why couldn't the wheat rate of interest hold up all the other rates? This is where Keynes' second attribute of assets to hold, carrying-costs, comes in. Recall that Keynes had earlier defined money by its quality of possessing the highest excess of liquidity-premium over carrying-cost. The importance of the low carrying-cost of money is that it sharply distinguishes money from all other potentially liquid assets (as opposed now to productive ones). Here, the distinction rests not on the supply side but on the demand side. In the case of all other liquid assets, the advantages offered through holding increased stocks of them are sharply limited by the cost of holding them for any appreciable time. Thus, "although a larger stock might have some attractions as representing a store of wealth of stable value, this would be offset by its carrying-costs in the shape of storage, wastage etc." But this is not so in the case of money where "the readiness of the public to increase their stock of money in response to a comparatively small stimulus is due to the advantages of liquidity (real or supposed) having no offset to contend with in the shape of carrying-costs mounting steeply with the lapse of time" (p. 233).

Keynes uses this argument to explain why he thinks the effect of falling prices on the "effective supply" of money will not offset the position of money as a bottomless sink of purchasing power. In essence, he is anticipating what would become the "real balance" effect made so much of by Patinkin. He asks if it might not be the case that the stagnating influence of the high money-rate would be offset by an "effective" increase in the supply of cash? The increased cash that resulted from falling prices (a reduction in the wage-unit) would operate via two avenues:

> a reduction in the wage unit will release cash from its other uses for the satisfaction of the liquidity motive; whilst, in addition to this, as money-values fall, the stock of money will bear a higher proportion to the total wealth of the community (p. 232).

Keynes disputes the argument that these effects would satisfy the increased demand for liquidity and thus negate the dominant position of the money rate in setting the pace of investment. First, he claims that the important reaction to a fall in the wage unit concerns "the *difference* between these [capital assets' own-rates] and the money rate of interest." It could be that the decline in wages would be even worse in creating an expectation of further declines and thus decreasing the marginal efficiency of capital. Secondly, he cites his frequent point that "the fact that wages tend to be sticky in terms of money, the money-wage being more stable than the real wage, tends to limit the readiness of the wage unit to fall in terms of money." And in fact, due to the major place of wages in the expectations of future demand that hold up the marginal efficiency of capital, this stickiness is beneficial on the whole. Thirdly, "the most fundamental consideration in this context" is the characteristic of money's high liquidity-premium over carrying-cost which makes it possible to absorb extra quantities of money without facing as great an increase in opportunity costs as other assets. As we will see, these qualities of wage stickiness and low carrying cost are Keynes' explanation for money's liquidity. Thus, both the capital theory aspects and the liquidity characteristics of money combine to give the money rate its "sting":

> The significance of the money-rate of interest arises, therefore, out of the combination of the characteristics that, through the workings of the liquidity-motive, this rate of interest may be somewhat unresponsive to a change in the proportion which the quantity of money bears to other forms of wealth measured in money, and that money has (or may have) zero (or negligible) elasticities both of production and of substitution (p. 234).

The effect on employment, then, operates through the level of equilibrium set by the necessary equality of the money-rate and all other own-rates, and the pace of investment demand this rate calls forth. When the money-rate is reluctant to fall, all other own-rates fall to its level and no further. "The money-rate of interest, by setting the pace for all the other commodity-rates of interest, holds back investment in the production of these other commodities without being capable of stimulating investment in the production of money, which by hypothesis cannot be produced." From the asset market view, the very existence of the social convention of money becomes Keynes' culprit for unemployment:

"Thus in the absence of money...the rates of interest would only reach equilibrium when there is full employment" (p. 235).

This is the point at which the capital theory argument for the importance of money as the asset which holds up the own-rates of all other assets joins the liquidity preference discussion of the essential properties of money. Ultimately, Keynes' attribution of importance to the money-rate rests on the qualities of money as an asset "which constitutes money as being in the estimation of the public, *par excellence* 'liquid'." In section IV, Keynes brings the argument full circle by considering "how far those characteristics of money as we know it, which make the money rate of interest the significant rate, are bound up with money being the standard in which debts and wages are usually fixed" (p. 236).

His consideration proceeds in two steps. "In the first place, the fact that contracts are fixed and wages are usually somewhat stable in terms of money unquestionably plays a large part in attracting to money so high a liquidity premium." It is because future debts and costs will be payable in money that money can perform its liquidity function, by definition. If the future standard of payments was not expected to be stable, then money would not be liquid[15]. But this very stability is dependent upon the low elasticity of production of the money-asset which caused the trouble with its rate of interest. It is also true, Keynes claims, that the low carrying-cost of money is important to its role as the standard of deferred payments. "For what matters is the *difference* between the liquidity-premium and the carrying costs." Even if the public attached as high a liquidity premium to wheat by fixing contracts, in wheat terms the carrying-costs would nevertheless be so high that "the wheat rate of interest would still be unlikely to rise above zero" (p. 237).

The importance of the low carrying cost on money is the link between this consideration of money as the medium of exchange and a standard of deferred payments and its function as a store of value. Consequently, Keynes secondly considers the "subtle" fact that

> The normal expectation that the value of output will be more stable in terms of money than in terms of any other commodity, depends of course, not on wages being arranged in terms of money, but on wages being relatively *sticky* in terms of money (p. 237).

If this were not the case, and wages were "expected to be more sticky in terms of some one or other commodities other than money," then two requirements would have to be met by those commodities if they were to take our money's place as the dominant own-rate. First, they would have to have a constant cost relative to real-wages for any scale of output. Secondly, they would have to have a sufficiently low carrying-cost to allow any "surplus over the current demand at cost-price...[to be] taken into stock without cost." The first requirement guarantees that the good's relative value would remain stable over the short and the long run as production ebbs and flows. The second requirement ensures that any old stock of the commodity would not affect its value. If such a commodity could be found, it "might be set up as a rival to money" in its role as the most stable of all stores of value (p. 238).

Keynes did not think it was "probable that any such commodity exists," but from our theoretical vantage point it is interesting to note that these very requirements are strictly met by a fiat standard which Keynes always had in mind when he spoke of money. In that case, the cost of production is fixed (at nearly zero) and invariant to scale, and the costs of holding are as close to zero as possible (in its own terms). Keynes saw a duality of meaning between the predominating fact that money is the standard of payment and its peculiar qualities as an asset:

> I conclude, therefore, that the commodity, in terms of which wages are expected to be most sticky, cannot be one whose elasticity of production is not least, and for which the excess of carrying-costs over liquidity-premium is not least. In other words, the expectation of a relative stickiness of wages in terms of money is a corollary of the excess of liquidity-premium over carrying-costs being greater for money than for any other asset (p. 238).

9. Money, Prices and Conventions: The Social Context for Monetary Analysis

As Keynes says, "Thus we see that the various characteristics, which combine to make the money-rate of interest significant, interact with one another in a cumulative fashion." All of the qualities of money can now be seen as dependent on each other. Moreover, the centrality of the money-rate, resting as it does on the very properties which make money liquid, illustrates the essential unity of Keynes' monetary, capital and investment theory. Even further, the fact that the liquidity function of money ensures that wages and payments will be most stable in money terms provides a theoretical justification to the traditional "Keynesian" concern with the fixed money wage case. In recent years, this assumption has become the very symbol of ad-hoc theorizing with which economics should have no truck. While, in fact, Keynes' complete theory of unemployment does not rest on rigid money-wages[16], his discussion of money shows why he thought it was such an important case to treat.

The quality of sticky money wages is an assumption much closer to the reality of a money economy than the opposite assumption of Pigou-effects and real-balance-effects where money prices freely adjust to keep relative prices the same. Keynes emphasized this point in chapter 17 with reference specifically to Pigou and his "presumption in favour of real wages being more stable than money-wages." Keynes point out that with change in employment (scale of output) and the high carrying-cost of wage goods, the stickiness of real wages would

> ...cause a violent oscillation of money prices. For every small fluctuation in the propensity to consume and the inducement to invest would cause money-prices to rush violently between zero and infinity. That money-wages should be more stable than real wages is a condition of the system possessing inherent stability (p. 239).

In terms of our set-up of the own-rates market equilibrium, Keynes is emphasizing that the "a" terms would have to fluctuate wildly if prices were assumed to be the sole adjustment factor that equated own-rates to a fixed liquidity premium. In other words Pigou's mistake ("in fact, experience...and logic") is in assuming the operation of a "real balance" effect that would automatically readjust the nominal stock of money to provide the desired liquidity without affecting interest rates. Such a rapid and complete adjustment to changing conditions of money demand would imply much less price stability than we in fact observe or than is compatible with the stability of the system. This argument clarifies Keynes' frequent assertion that even if wages and prices were perfectly flexible in a depression, that the effect on expectations of such instability (operating through expected q's of capital assets in our own-rates) would make matters even worse.

But if real relative values are not the source of stability to the system, we are led to ask what does the amount of observed stability (is there any?) in the interest rate depend upon? This question is not taken up by Keynes, but its fascination led one of Keynes' students, Hugh Townshend[18], to call for an amendment to the theory of value based on Keynes' analysis of a money economy. Townshend thought that chapter 17 represented "the most general theory" of Keynes' book (1973b, p. 258). "Thus, it would seem that Mr. Keynes' doctrine of liquidity-preference really involves a generalization of the classical (marginal) theory of value" (1937, p. 160). Specifically, the generalization that Townshend envisioned depended on extending value theory into the determination of "money prices" in an economy where goods are not just produced for immediate consumption but are also held for future security. In this context, the structure of relative prices will not be strictly determined "at the margin of production" (as in the classical theory) but will depend to some extent (depending on the degree of "moneyness" or liquidity of a good) on the psychologically determined liquidity premiums that attach to monetary assets. The psychological impacts of these liquidity premiums are explicitly referred to by Townshend as involving the distinction between the "exchange of existing assets (at the margin of exchange) and the production of new assets (at the margin of production)" (p. 160).

Emphasizing the role of expectations in this generalized theory of value, Townshend sees the stability of the system of money prices so determined to depend on the existence of a stable *convention*. Here is the answer we are seeking to the necessary practical role of sticky money prices in lending stability to the system. Townshend shows us the extent to which Keynes followed out that subtle method of basing even his most highly abstract conclusions on an observed reality of the economy rather than a purely hypothetical system:

> Since in fact money-values do not fluctuate wildly in the short period (save in abnormal conditions with which we are not here concerned), they must be kept reasonably stable by some characteristic of our real world of which a realistic theory of prices must take account. It would seem that this characteristic must be either a *conventionality* of outlook causing stability of expectations as to the money-prices of durable assets of certain kinds,

or else *conventional* maintenance of some degree of stability of the money-price of the only other exchangeable value, viz. labour--that is to say a conventionally stable wage-unit (pp. 161-162).

Townshend dismisses the contention that the quantity of money along with its velocity of circulation can stabilize prices since to a greater or lesser extent any money stock can support any price level. This is because there need not be much actual exchange to revalue the stock of existing assets if the opinions about their future value are unanimous enough. But since such upheavals of prices do not continuously occur, the stability must depend on a convention:

...since the quantity of money does not determine "the"--or, rather, any--price level, no prices would be determinate at all, unless at least one money-value--the price of *something*--were determined by habit or convention.

The implications for economic theory are that no prices are strictly determinate since nothing is "*absolutely* determined by convention" (except perhaps in a command economy) and that economic theory can only provide "*approximately* true" propositions about relative prices "which is the best we can hope for in an undetermined and shifting price-world" (p. 162). For Townshend, this casts a pall over any attempts at "dynamic theorizing." If we can only base our value theory on the shifting sands of a liquidity convention, then our theory can only be specified for the duration of each individual convention and no longer[19]. This notion provides some rationale for Keynes' simplest model where money-wages are fixed and only the shortest short-period equilibrium is investigated.

Townshend's fascinating writings extend Keynes' views on interest and money in novel directions. But for our purposes, they also bring us back to the extent to which the own-rates theory represents a challenge to the Wicksellian framework for monetary theory. First, the emphasis on the conventional basis of interest and prices serves to illustrate that Sraffa's injunction on the use of barter theory as the starting point of monetary economics was much more than just polemical tactics. As Townshend makes clear, the very notion of a structure of prices in a world where expectations of the future influence actions today has to start from some basis in the facts of the situation:

All exchange values are relative (ratios). If all possible sets of values in a community are to be comparable numerically, there must be a money of account--a common denominator to which the ratios are reducible. In a capitalist community--that is to say, one in which some people employ hired labor for future profit--people will also hold durable assets for future security. Even if there is no legal tender money, assets so held--whether goods or paper claims--will possess liquidity-premiums; and some claims and/or other assets will come to oust other assets...for the purpose of liquid holdings. We then have, in *all* essentials for the purpose of a theory of value, a monetary economy.... The generally accepted claims or goods will modify the values which they are used to measure and are already real money for the purposes of the theory of value. Thus the textbook conception of a barter as non-monetary economy has no place in a discussion of value. *The theory of value in a capitalist economy is the theory of money-prices* (Townshend, 1937, pp. 166-167, italics added).

In other words, if the essence of money involves its role as a link between the present and the future, a link that grows out of its acceptance as the social numeraire, then money can only fulfill its role if it is assumed that money will be worth something at that future date. Keynes has shown us that this sort of expectation, which the money rate of interest is based upon, ultimately rests on an agreed upon convention of the stability of money prices. In the Wicksellian framework, where the operative forces of the case are looked for in a strictly "real" side of the economy, all of this is ignored. For Wicksell and Hayek, the barter-like "natural" rate of interest is the starting point of investigation. But if Keynes is right about money, there is nothing at all natural about such a barter rate in a money economy.

This friction between Keynes' theory and the whole natural rate, loanable funds framework is finally drawn out in the last two sections of chapter 17. In these, he explicitly addresses himself to the question of what a nonmonetary economy would resemble and what meaning can be given to the idea of a *natural* rate of interest.

Recall that Sraffa had shown, and Adarkar had recognized, that the nonmonetary state in which the "natural" rate was supposed to rule could not really be conceived of in barter terms. As Sraffa commented in his review of Hayek, "It may be doubted whether under a system of barter the decisions of individuals would have their full effects" (1932a, p. 43). What the Wicksellians really wanted to define was a hypothetical state in which the social contrivance of a medium of exchange existed, but where none of the accompanying intertemporal allocation problems that follow from the use of money in an uncertain environment encumber the decisions of individuals. To the natural rate theorists, this could be accomplished by simply controlling the money supply.

Starting from a much richer conception of the social functions of money, Keynes conceived of such a "so-called 'non-monetary economy" in a much different way. The only meaning he could give to the idea was a situation in which no asset possessed that fundamental quality of possessing a liquidity-premium in excess of its carrying cost.

> There exists nothing, that is to say, but particular consumables and particular capital equipments more or less differentiated according to the character of the consumable which they can yield up, or assist to yield up, over a greater or shorter period of time: all of which, unlike cash, deteriorate or involve expense, if they are kept in stock, to a value in excess of any liquidity premium which may attach to them (p. 239).

Even in this case, Keynes' liquidity motive would enter in the relative evaluation of assets by wealth holders. Here, the liquidity would depend on the variety, stability and marketability of the goods which each asset is capable of assisting in the production of[20]. The rate of interest, then, would still be dependent upon the liquidity preferences of the public, illustrating the fact that money is a purely social-specific device.

> There is, clearly, no absolute standard of "liquidity" but merely a scale of liquidity--a varying premium of which account has to be taken.... The conception of what contributes to "liquidity" is a partly vague one, changing from time to time and depending on social practices and institutions (p. 240).

But if no exclusively liquid good exists, would interest rates be low enough to ensure full employment growth and accumulation? Keynes does not specifically say, but implies that if such a money-to-hold did not officially exist, that one would have to be invented! It is as if liquidity preference is a human desire so strong that it creates its own object. As an example, Keynes mentions "that in certain historic environments the possession of land has been characterized by a high liquidity-premium in the minds of owners of wealth." In the absence of a good money, land would make a suitable liquidity standard due to its low elasticities of production and substitution and due to the fact that its output is at least as stable and marketable as any other. Keynes speculates that this might account for the unusually high mortgage rates, in excess of the net productivity of land found in many agricultural economies.

If it were the case that some readily marketable good is socially "set up" as the liquidity standard in a nonmonetary economy, this answers the question of the efficiency of such a natural state. For land in these situations can be every bit as inhibiting of production and accumulation as money is today:

> That the world after several millennia of steady individual saving, is so poor as it is in accumulated capital assets, is to be explained, in my opinion, neither by the improvident propensities of mankind, nor even by the destruction of war, but by the high liquidity premium formerly attaching to the ownership of land and now attaching to money (p. 242).

It was this very conception of a liquidity premium being a *necessary* social convention where wealth holding is a private matter, that Joan Robinson focused her attention on when she came to discuss "Own Rates of Interest" (1961). Already in her later classical political economy stage, this former Keynes student conceived of the problem of liquidity-premiums keeping up the rate of interest as a class-distribution issue. Defending Keynes against Kaldor's (1960) argument that land could not serve such a purpose because "the rise in the purchase price of land can lower its yield to any extent," and thus diminish its attractiveness, Robinson makes the important point that this ignores the fact that the liquidity premium is altogether different from a mere explicit return. As Keynes emphasizes, liquidity premiums are of the nature of his long-term expectations in the sense that they reflect uncertainty, not risk[21]. This is why he defines them as a "potential convenience or security..."for which there is "...nothing to show...at the end of the period in the shape of output; yet it is something for which people are ready to pay something" (1936, p. 226). Robinson takes up the idea of non-pecuniary yields from land as the liquid asset and fashions it into an historical explanation of the transition from a feudal state, represented by landed wealth, to a capitalist one, represented by capital wealth. Her argument adds "the pleasure of gentlemanlikeness derived from owning land" to the argument, but essentially applies Keynes' idea that some asset will always be set up as the liquidity standard by social convention. In an interesting twist on Keynes' main premise that the interest rate on money holds up the pace of investment, Robinson speculates that, in the transition to capitalism, the traditional attribution of liquidity (and social distinction) to land holding may serve to hold up (primitive?) accumulation.

What she has in mind is an "'historic environment' when the capitalist wealth-owners exist side by side with gentlemen, whose extravagance and misfortune from time to time forces them to pledge their ancestral estates." In this example, which corresponds closely to Keynes' hypothetical land-monetary economy,[22] the vent for savings in non-productive land holdings may impede the rate of investment in productive industry:

> Now, so long as land is known to be safe and sound while all industrial investment has a high risk premium, and when, as Keynes assumed, the return to be expected in each round of I [investment] is less than the last, lending to a gentleman will be a formidable rival to financing industry (Robinson, 1961, p. 590).

Robinson (1961) notes that this situation will be even worse in a social environment in which capitalists derive a further non-pecuniary "pleasure of gentlemanlikeness...from owning land." Also echoing Keynes, she thinks the problem could be long lasting if "capitalist wealth is diverted to purchasing land at second hand which...[if land yielded no non-pecuniary returns] would be more readily available to find an outlet in financing new investment." Besides providing an interesting theoretical slant on the classical political economists' marked antagonism to the profligate ways of the landed aristocracy, the main point to be taken from Robinson's essay is that Keynes' framework is malleable enough to fit many social and historic environments; and that liquidity preference theory itself is empty without such social detail.

10. Conclusion

In order to bring our discussion back to our original starting point of the antagonism of Keynes' monetary views with the Wicksellian natural rate tradition, it is appropriate to point out that Keynes ends his own chapter on "The Essential Properties of Interest and Money" by explicitly dissenting from that view. Attributing the idea to Wicksell, Keynes notes that his own *Treatise on Money* used the idea of a natural rate "which preserved equality between the rate of savings...and the rate of investment." In doing so he had, "however, overlooked the fact that in any given society there is, on this definition, a *different* natural rate of interest for each hypothetical level of employment." In other words, savings always equals investment and the rate of interest, by determining the level of investment, just determines the level of employment for which the equality of saving and investment is defined.

> Thus it was a mistake to speak of *the* natural rate of interest or to suggest that the above definition would yield a unique value for the rate of interest irrespective of the level of employment. *I had not then understood that, in certain conditions, the system could be in equilibrium with less than full employment* (1936, pp. 242-243, italics added).

Keynes identifies the old Wicksellian concept as "merely the rate of interest which preserve the *status quo*" a rate which we really have no interest in defending. Declaring that it is not even a useful analytic category, he proposes to replace it with a *neutral* or *optimum* rate of interest. This more general concept would identify the rate of interest "...which is consistent with *full* employment, given the other parameters of the system" (p. 243).

With this concept in mind, we can see that Keynes' difference with the Wicksellian framework is not a mere choice over analytical frameworks (as Hicks (1937) would have it), but it is every bit as fundamental to his innovations on classical theory as the theory of aggregate demand. Just as in that case, the ultimate significance of Keynes' interest rate theory is its allowance for *equilibria* consistent with less than full employment. Rejecting the idea of a "natural" rate which would equilibrate the system at full employment is just a corollary to rejecting the full employment assumptions built into Say's Law. By his analysis of the social role of money as the liquidity standard, Keynes has shown that money as a social institution (whether a free-money or a state-money) has important (negative) externality effects. Harrod's comment about a "wrong" rate of interest that is "natural, durable, and in a certain sense, in the free system inevitable," can now be seen as an insight stemming directly from Keynes' essential properties of interest and money.

By channeling the richness of Keynes' vision of the financial aspects of a modern money economy into a framework which identifies these equilibria, the own-rates theory provides an interpretive device that highlights the radical nature of Keynes' theoretical revolution. And from the standpoint of further work in macroeconomics, the lesson of this view is that trying to join Keynes to Wicksellian rootstock creates a graft that will not take. Keynes' monetary theory is not a simple afterthought, or appendage that can easily be thrown overboard to pursue orthodox concerns. That is, not unless we are willing to revert to a full-employment paradigm where unemployment can only arise from a friction or rigidity, incompatibly thrust into an otherwise smoothly operating system. This is the error we have seen that led the "Keynesian Revolution" to the impasse it faces today. Such a full employment framework is just the sort of propaedeutic world that Keynes was warning us against when he wrote:

> Or we can pass from this simplified propaedeutic to the problems of the real world in which our previous expectations are liable to disappointment and expectations concerning the future affect what we do today. It is when we have made this transition that the peculiar properties of money as a link between the present and the future must enter into our calculations. But, although the theory of shifting equilibrium must necessarily be

pursued in terms of a monetary economy, it remains a theory of value and distribution and not a separate "theory of money." Money in its significant attributes is, above all, a subtle device for linking the present to the future; and we cannot even begin to discuss the effects of changing expectations on current activities except in monetary terms. We cannot get rid of money even by abolishing gold and silver and legal instruments. So long as there exists any durable asset, it is capable of possessing monetary attributes and, therefore, of giving rise to the characteristic problems of a monetary economy (1936, pp. 293-294).

Notes

[1] See Lawlor (1993) for an analysis of the historical antecedents to New Keynesian Economics in pre-Keynesian Cambridge economics.

[2] Little notice has been taken in the literature on interpreting Keynes of the degree to which his immediate post-*General Theory* writings utilize the "own-rates" framework which we will be analyzing in this paper. There is not space to go into the matter in detail here. But the interested reader, upon comparing this essay with Keynes's responses to his critics in 1937 (especially Keynes 1937a, and 1937b, which explicitly use the language and analysis of chapter 17, but the much discussed 1937c also can be interpreted in light of this framework), should readily see the continuity between these and his analysis in chapter 17 of the *General Theory*. It is also worth noting at this point that Keynes uses the framework in a rather catholic manner in the first of these two papers, emphasizing it as a general metatheory within which a variety of interest rate 'theories' can be interpreted. This argument is precisely the analytical standpoint from which Allin Cottrell and I depart in our use of the framework (Cottrell and Lawlor, 1991). For a more complete historical treatment see Lawlor (forthcoming).

[3] See Lawlor and Horn (1992) for a more complete analysis of the "Sraffa-Hayek" exchange.

[4] In general, of course, it is naive to make prescriptive methodological claims such as this. Methodology is much more useful as an interpretive device than as a formula for theory building. Yet there runs throughout the doctrinal history of the particular economic debate we are investigating - the debate over the proper grounding and meaning of interest - a persistent and peculiar tension between theory and reality. Thus for instance we have numerous examples of discussions highly abstracted from reality, often running in terms of either Robinson Crusoe productivity parables (see White, 1982 for an extensive historical survey) or introspective self-examinations of the motives to abstain from consumption (Bohm-Bawerk, Mises, and Fisher, for example). Yet these theories of interest, more than perhaps any other component of orthodox theory in the post 1870's era, were continually beset with internal contradictions. As a result dissenters from orthodoxy, including many acute observers from Veblen (1909) and Marx (1894, Part V, esp. ch. 22) down to Clower (1967), have often noted that, in fact, economic theory has so far provided no generally accepted grounds upon which to base the theory of interest. But alternatively, there has also been a long tradition of 'realistic' monetary analysis which never exhibited much interest in these theoretical machinations by which, chided Veblen (1909, p. 250), "..the whole 'money economy,' with all the machinery of credit and the rest, disappears in a tissue of metaphors to reappear theoretically expurgated, sterilized, and simplified into a 'refined system of barter,' culminating in a net aggregate maximum of pleasurable sensations of consumption." Much of this latter 'realistic' literature has emanated from attempts to understand monetary policy and central banking. Two prime examples would be Bagehot (1877) and Goodhart (1989). Goodhart (p. 222) makes his position in this regard quite clear: "Theoretical analysis of the determination of interest rates has not been helped by economists' frequently resolute refusal to look at the way markets function in reality."

Our argument here is that Keynes, who was acutely aware of the functioning of real financial markets, was making an attempt in the *General Theory* to bring this knowledge to bear in conducting an analysis, at the highest level of abstraction, of the essential properties of interest and money. He was thus naturally alive to the kinds of methodological issues Sraffa was raising against Hayek.

[5] The same method was employed by Sraffa, for example, in his critique of the Marshallian Supply concept (Sraffa, 1926).

[6] In fact, many interpreters of Keynes' *Theory*, both hostile and sympathetic, have found the argument of chapter 17 to be not only highly abstract--*but unintelligible*. For instance, the man generally credited with "bringing Keynes to America," Alvin Hansen, had this to say in his famous *Guide to Keynes* (1953, p. 159):

> Chapter 17, on the properties of interest and money, ties in with the subject matter of money and liquidity preference.... But the topic is elevated to a very abstract plane. Immediately after the appearance of the *General Theory* there was a certain fascination about Chap. 17, due partly no doubt to its obscurity. Digging in this area, however, soon ceased after it was found that the chapter contained no gold mines...in general, not much would have been lost had it never been written.

With expositors like this, it is no wonder Keynes' monetary views suffered such eclipse. This attitude carried over to Hansen's most famous student, P.A. Samuelson, who also must be credited with a large part of the "Keynesian" version of Keynes. In an evaluation of Keynes as an economist (1947b) in which Samuelson relegates the own-rates theory to the category of "Mares' nests of confusions" (p. 149), and in which he explains why "liquidity preference...cannot be of crucial significance," he draws the following remarkable conclusion about Keynes as an economic theorist:

> ...Keynes seems never to have had any genuine interest in the theory of value and distribution. It is remarkable that so active a brain would have failed to make any contribution to economic theory (p. 155).

One supposes this view of Keynes' contribution goes a long way toward explaining the easy cooptation of "Keynesianism" by orthodox neoclassical theory.

As an example of hostile reviews, one that takes a particularly venomous line on chapter 17 is H. Hazlitt's (1959) "The Failure of the 'New Economics'." Hazlitt's volume has much to recommend itself as a curative to anyone considering putting a vituperative attack into print. It reserved a large quota of its venom (and exclamation points!) for Chapter 17:

> "Chapter 17 of the *General Theory*, 'The Essential Properties of Interest and Money,' is dull, implausible, and full of obscurities, non-sequiturs, and other fallacies" (p. 236).
> "Of all of the confusions in the *General Theory*, this is one of the most incredible" (p. 237).

[7] Keynes's interesting, but cryptic comment to the effect that he considered Irving Fisher to be the "great-grandparent" of his interest rate theory (Keynes, 1937b, p. 203n) takes on new significance in light of chapter 17. When, coming directly from chapter 17 of the *General Theory*, one reads Fisher's analysis of "appreciation and interest" (Fisher, 1907 and 1930) there is noticed a very striking degree of similarity between the two - in aims, methods and even language. I have analyzed this issue in more detail in another place (Lawlor, forthcoming).

[8] We will thus be consciously avoiding any discussion of secular trends in capital accumulation (i.e. the justly infamous "stagnationist thesis"). These comments of Keynes's, surfacing in obiter dicta throughout the *General Theory* (including in chapter seventeen) are, by our interpretation, both wrongheaded and not logically deducible from his general

theoretical arguments (see note 14). On the other hand, the hypotheco-historical accounts of the operation of asset markets and their role in the rate of investment (as in, for example, the "land as money" model Keynes put forth in ch. 17) will be briefly touched on below. Here the point is to illuminate the social context which defines the central problematic of chapter 17: the emergence and consequences of a liquidity premium.

[9] In the following expression the term

$$\frac{M_2 - M_1}{M_1}$$

is the own-rate on money, which, since money is the unit of account, is the same in quantity and value terms. It corresponds directly to the idea of interest rates in general as intertemporal market equivalents represented by simultaneous spot and future prices. In the case of money it might be conceived, for example, as a bond for which M_1 is paid today in exchange for M_2 a year hence. "The money rate of interest - we may remind the reader - is nothing more the percentage excess of a sum of money contracted for forward delivery, e.g. a year hence, over what we may call the "spot" or cash price of the sum thus contracted for forward delivery" (1936, p. 222). Note also that the money rate of interest does not contain an "a" term, since it is the standard against which the appreciation of all other assets are measured.

[10] T. K. Rymes reminds me that Shackle is possibly referring to the original Marshallian stock equilibrium analysis in Marshall's "Essay on Money" written in 1871 (Marshall, 1975). I have investigated the role of this essay in forming a part of the intellectual context for Keynes's monetary analysis in another place (Lawlor, forthcoming).

[11] The role of Keynes' intricate analysis of the circulatory route of cash in different uses in the economy was laid out in the *Treatise* (1930, book 1, ch. 3). Although it is suppressed in the *General Theory*, this analysis is essential to a complete understanding of liquidity preference theory. See Shackle (1967, ch. 15) for an insightful blending of the two strands of the theory of cash balances.

[12] In the context of a demand for money function, Tobin (1958, pp. 65-86) shows that there is a further distinction to be made over a definite expectation of a changed future rate (that is held with "certainty") versus a situation of no certain expectation of a change, but a general subjective "uncertainty" over its future value. He is able to show that both situations can lead to a typically shaped liquidity preference function. I am grateful to Allin Cottrell for this point, whose analysis (Cottrell, 1993) of this work of Tobin in light of Keynes's own theory of probability is very illuminating.

[13] This intricate fusion of capital theory and monetary theory is the core of Shackle's (1967, ch. 11) unique blending of Keynes' views on money and uncertainty in the *General Theory* with his crucial restatement in 1937c. Shackle makes no use of the own-rates paradigm, but I think our discussion to this point might clarify his argument for some readers. For instance, the following eloquent passage nicely complements our view with that grace of expression that is Shackle's hallmark:

> Writers on Keynes's theory of investment incentive give all their attention to the concepts of the marginal efficiency of capital and the interaction of a quantity so named with the interest-rate on loans of money. To do so is to study the formal configuration of the engine without asking about its thermal source of power. The marginal efficiency of capital is nothing but a formal sum waiting for the insertion of numerical values in place of its algebraic symbols. The essential problem of why at any time the investment flow has the size it has is contained in the question what is the source of these numerical values, by which psychic alchemy is the list of incongruous ingredients chosen and fused into an answer to the unanswerable. Keynes's whole theory of unemployment is

ultimately the simple statement that, rational expectation being unattainable, we substitute for it first one and then another kind of irrational expectation: and the shift from one arbitrary basis to another gives us from time to time a moment of truth, when our artificial confidence is for the time being dissolved, and we, as businessmen, are afraid to invest, and so fail to provide enough demand to match our society's desire to produce. Keynes in the *General Theory* attempted a rational theory of a field of conduct which by the nature of its terms could be only semi-rational. But sober economists gravely upholding a faith in the calculability of human affairs could not bring themselves to acknowledge that this could be his purpose. They sought to interpret the *General Theory* as just one more manual of political arithmetic. In so far as it failed this test, they found it wrong, or obscure, or perverse. The same fate had overtaken his *Treatise on Probability* (1967, p. 129).

Notice that Book IV of the *General Theory*, under the heading "The Inducement to Invest," includes the following chapters (in order): "The Marginal Efficiency of Capital, The State of Long-Term Expectations, The General Theory of the Rate of Interest, The Classical Theory of the Rate of Interest, The Psychological and Business Incentive to Liquidity, Sundry Observations on the Nature of Capital, The Essential Properties of Interest and Money, and The General Theory of Employment Restated." The implication, of course, is that investment is explained by the interaction of money, capital and interest, all bound together in an expectational framework. "The essential problem of why at any time the investment flow has the size it has is contained in the question what is the source of these numerical values, by which psychic alchemy is the list of incongruous ingredients chosen and fused into an answer to the unanswerable" (Shackle, 1967, p. 129). We are arguing here that Chapter 17 provides just such a psychic alchemy.

[14] It will be immediately clear from this that Keynes's whole argument about the importance of the money rate of interest in determining investment flows depends on the assumption that the own-rate on capital goods, or the marginal efficiency of capital will *decline* as production increases during the upturn in activity. The question arise in this context (see Eatwell (1983)): is the own-rates analysis as Keynes uses it subject to the capital critique? Would the well-known possibility of capital reswitching and reversal undercut Keynes' argument just as they have the typical neoclassical parables about capital accumulation?

I wish to present an argument against this view. My argument rest on two points. One, that it is improper to identify Keynes's MEC with the marginalist theory of distribution, and two, that his discussion is, properly speaking, only applicable to a short-period argument. Briefly I will try to elaborate on both of these points.

First, as P. H. Wicksteed (1914) long ago pointed out, there is a fundamental distinction to be made between the marginalism of neoclassical capital theory and the margin of Ricardian rent theory. While the latter runs in terms of an apriori ranking of *different* units - e.g. grades of land ranked by fertility - the former runs strictly in terms of *identical* units combined in varying proportions. In the Ricardian case the decline in fertility as the margin is pushed out is a matter of apriori definition. In the neoclassical case the varying proportions enter as a functional determinant of a declining productivity relation - i.e., productivity varies inversely with the capital intensity associated with various 'quantities' of capital. And as Sraffa made clear at the beginning of his *Production of Commodities* (Sraffa, 1960, p. v-vi), the classical margin is not subject to the same critique as is neoclassical marginalism.

The point of all of this is that Keynes's marginal efficiency of capital is more analogous to the Ricardian conception than the neoclassical one (as Pasinetti (1974, pp. 29-53) has noted). In its aggregate form (as in chapter 11 of the *General Theory),* it represents a ranking of different types of capital good according to *expected* yields and current supply prices. "This gives us the marginal efficiencies of particular types of capital-assets. The greatest of these marginal efficiencies can then be regarded as the marginal efficiency of capital in general."

Secondly, as Keynes's comments on capital (both in chapters 11 and 16) make clear, he seems to have been aware of the difficulties of making aggregate notions of capital definable and he was certainly no marginal productivity theorist. Thus a modern reader of chapter 11 cannot help but wonder over the conversations Keynes might have had with Sraffa when, for instance, we see Keynes warning:

> There is, to begin with, the ambiguity whether we are concerned with the increment of physical product per unit of time due to the employment of one more physical unit of capital, or with the increment of value due to the employment of one more value unit of capital. The former involves difficulties as to the definition of the physical unit of capital, which I believe to be both insoluble and unnecessary (Keynes, 1936, p. 138).

Furthermore, in his "sundry observations on the nature of capital" he notes, "It is much preferable to speak of capital as having a yield over the course of its life in excess of its original cost, than as being *productive*" (Keynes, 1936, p. 213). His alternative to productivity theory, as noted above, was to fall back on the notion of "scarcity" as the fundamental reason for the ability of produced means of production to earn a return over cost. It was this view, no doubt, from which derive the comments concerning the euthanasia of the rentier and the secular decline of productive outlets for investment that are scattered throughout the *General Theory*. It is clear that these comments - politically naive about the possibilities of altering the class structure of capitalists societies, and historically wrong concerning the secular course of investment opportunities in a technologically vibrant world - reveal Keynes at his worst, as far as the *General Theory* goes. But they are merely obiter dicta, prognostications on the long-run about which his explicitly short-run theory could offer little guidance. This does not indict him of 'circular-reasoning,' or 'flawed logic,' just occasional lapses into bad judgement.

Thus while Keynes's *portmanteau* relation, the marginal efficiency of capital, appears to be free from the fatal logical flaws known to lie at the root of neoclassical capital theory, it would clearly be overpraise in the extreme to credit him with a complete alternative capital theoretic foundation for investment demand. But this of course is a fault shared by all of modern economic theory - including, and perhaps especially, the neo-Ricardianism spawned by Sraffa. As Colin Rogers (1989) argues persuasively, though, Keynes's interest in short-run "monetary analysis" - as opposed to the traditional focus of "real analysis" - frees Keynes to some extent from the need to seek a more "fundamental" grounding for the rate of return on capital. Especially when one considers the pervasive uncertainty of the world Keynes was contemplating, a case could surely be made for history and social psychology as the ultimate grounds upon which we might expect an answer to the question of the fundamental motivation to invest. But for now all that we need is the assumption that, over the course of the boom, the combinations of falling *expected* returns and rising supply prices for capital goods will eventually cause the marginal efficiency of capital, and so its own-rate of interest, to decline.

[15] In fact, Irving Fisher found a case of the effect on interest rates that uncertainty, not just over the stability of the monetary unit, but uncertainty over its actual *existence* has. He analyzes an example in his *The Rate of Interest* (1907, pp. 258-261) where two types of U.S. bonds existed simultaneously that were payable in gold and paper notes, respectively. The variations in the spread between the two over the years 1870 to 1896 are attributed by Fisher to the changing expectations of the future form of the standard of payment caused by the then active public debate over the various proposals of the "money doctors."

[16] Darity and Horn (1983) and Lawlor (1991) both argue for the irrelevance of fixed money-wages to Keynes' definition of unemployment equilibria.

[17] Keynes seems to have thought that most of the adjustments in the "a" terms would be accomplished by movements in the present spot prices. See the discussion in chapter 17 (p. 228) of an example of the quilibrium of own-rates. Also, in a protracted pre-publication correspondence with R. C. Hawtrey, Keynes defends his own-rate theory in the case of stocks

of liquid commodities from Hawtrey's criticism (on both theoretical and practical grounds). In the process, he makes the same point about the adjustment factor "normally" being the spot price (1973a, p. 629).

[18] In Keynes' collected works (1979, p. 235), Townshend is identified as follows: "Another discussant was Hugh Townshend (1890-1974), who, after taking a first in mathematics in Cambridge in 1912, had been a pupil of Keynes while preparing for Civil Service examinations in 1914. He had then entered the Post Office." Besides the note referred to in the text and a few scattered reviews in the *Economic Journal* in the late '30s, the only other work of his I have found is a co-authored book (Curtis and Townshend, 1938). This book is interesting in that it is an attempt to provide a layman's guide to the workings of a "monetary economy" via the views of two authors who "belong to the school of thought associated with the name of J.M. Keynes" (p. vi). That this self-identification is not idle (at least for Townshend) is attested to by Keynes' surviving correspondence with Townshend in which he credits him with even *more* than a complete understanding of his theory. For example, consider the following fragments from Keynes' letters to Townshend (in Keynes, 1979, pp. 235-247 and 255-259):

> "It is evident that you have a perfect comprehension of the matter: and indeed it may prove to be the case that, whilst the book is chiefly meant for my academic friends, it may sometimes get easier reception from those outside academic circles, whose ideas are not so crystallized" (p. 238).

> "Once more you have shown a complete comprehension of what I am driving at, and I am very grateful" (p. 239).

> "Once again I have to thank you for an acute and understanding criticism, with the whole of which, I think I may say, I agree" (p. 245).

> "Criticisms like yours are mainly useful in helping me to get more fully emancipated from what one has emerged out of" (p. 247).

This last fragment reinforces the view of Shackle that Townshend saw earlier and deeper than most writers into the depths of the departure from orthodoxy that Keynes' views on money and interest represent:

> "Townshend's brilliant paper, although thirteen pages long, appeared only under Notes and Memoranda. It leapt too far ahead for the mass of Keynes' critics, still tapping the wheels of his theory to see whether it would clank decently round like the sort of thing they were used to, and Townshend attracted no attention" (1967, p. 228).

[19]   "Moreover, it would seem to follow that there can be no such thing as long-period dynamic economic theory, failing the (most unlikely) discovery of a plausible long-term convention of price-stability. It is perhaps now being generally realized that such long-term dynamic theories as these are considered unplausible ones. It is not unnatural that those who forecast the future in algebra or geometry should be chastened by hard fact more slowly than those who have to forecast it in arithemetic. Nor is the conclusion that the search for laws to enable us to predict economic events far ahead, like eclipses, must be given up, so surprising--not to say nihilistic--as it may seem (to some economists) at first sight. For in the past, in long periods, prices have in fact moved all over the place. The inference that there is no reason to believe in the probably indefinite recurrence of a *regular* cycle of price-fluctuations is less generally accepted, but seems to follow from Mr. Keynes' conclusions" (Townshend, 1937, p. 166).

[20] There is an interesting parallel between Keynes' discussion of a liquidity standard in a nonmonetary economy and Menger's (1892; 1976, ch. 8) hypothetico-historical account of the origin of a medium of exchange. Both revolve around the concept of "marketability." I think a comparison of them would show a strong complementarity between the discussions. Menger explains the process and reasons for the evolution of a generally accepted means of payment. Keynes shows that this spontaneously evolved social institution has important externality effects--even in the most primitive monetary systems.

[21] There is an interesting parallel between Keynes' discussion of a liquidity standard in a nonmonetary economy and Menger's (1892; 1976, ch. 8) hypothetico-historical account of the origin of a medium of exchange. Both revolve around the concept of "marketability." I think a comparison of them would show a strong complementarity between the discussions. Menger explains the process and reasons for the evolution of a generally accepted means of payment. Keynes shows that this spontaneously evolved social institution has important externality effects--even in the most primitive monetary systems.

[22] That is, an economy in which land has the greatest excess of liquidity premium over carrying cost.

References

Adarkar, B. P. (1935) *The Theory of Monetary Policy*. London: P.S. King & Sons.

Bagehot. (1873) *Lombard Street: A Description of the Money Market*. London: P. S. King.

Boulding, K. E. (1950) *A Reconstruction of Economics*. New York: John Wiley & Sons.

Bridel, P. (1987) *Cambridge Monetary Thought: Development of Saving-Investment Analysis from Marshall to Keynes*. New York: St. Martins.

Clower, R. W. (1967) "A Reconsideration of the Microfoundations of Monetary Theory," *Western Economic Journal* 6: 1-8.

Conard, J. W. (1959) *An Introduction to the Theory of Interest*. Berkeley and Los Angeles: University of California Press.

Cottrell, A. (1993) "Keynes's Theory of Probability and Its Relevance to his Economics: Three Theses." *Economics and Philosophy, 9: 25-51.*

Cottrell, A. (1994) "Post Keynesian Monetary Economics: A Critical Survey." *Cambridge Journal of Economics*, forthcoming.

Cottrell, A and M. Lawlor. (1991) "'Natural Rate' Mutations: Keynes, Leijonhufvud and the Wicksell Connection." *History of Political Economy*, 23: 625-643.

Curtis, M., and H. Townshend. (1938) *Modern Money*. New York: Harcourt, Brace and Company.

Darity, William A., Jr., and Bobbie L. Horn. (1983) "Involuntary Unemployment Reconsidered." *Southern Economic Journal 49: 717-733.*

Eatwell, J. (1983) "Theories of Value, Output and Employment." *Keynes's Economics and the Theory of Value and Distribution,* J. Eatwell and M. Milgate, eds, pp. 93-128. London: Duckworth.

Fisher, I. (1907) *The Rate of Interest*. New York: Macmillan.

Fisher, I. (1930) *The Theory of Interest*. New York: Macmillan.

Frydman, R. (1982) "Towards an Understanding of Market Processes' Individual Expectations, Learning, and Convergence to Rational Expectations Equilibrium." *American Economic Review* 72: 652-668.

_____ , G. P. O'Driscoll, Jr., and A. Schotter. (1982) "Rational Expectations of Government Policy: An Application of Newcomb's Problem." *Southern Economic Journal* 49: 311-319.

Goodhart, C. A. E. (1989) *Money, Information and Uncertainty, 2nd. ed.* Cambridge: The MIT Press.

Hansen, A. (1953) *A Guide to Keynes*. New York: McGraw Hill.

Harrod, R. F. (1947) "Keynes, the Economist." In S.E. Harris, ed. *The New Economics*. New York: Alfred A. Knopf.

Hayek, F. A. (1932) "Dr. Hayek on Money and Capital: A Reply." *Economic Journal* 42: 237-249.

_____. (1935) (1931). *Prices and Production*. 2nd ed. London: Routledge and Kegan Paul.

Hazlitt, H. (1959) *The Failure of the "New Economics."* Princeton, NJ: D. Van Nostrand.

Hicks, J. R. (1946) *Value and Capital*. 2nd ed. Oxford: Oxford University Press.

Kahn, R. F. (1954) "Some Notes on Liquidity Preference." *Manchester School of Economics and Social Studies,* 22.3: 229-57.

Kaldor, N. (1939) "Speculation and Economic Stability." *Review of Economic Studies 7: 1-27.*

_____. (1960) "Keynes's Theory of the Own Rate of Interest." *Essays in Economic Stability and Growth*. London: Duckworth, pp. 59-74.

Keynes, J. M. (1921) *A Treatise on Probability*. Reprinted as Vol. VIII of Keynes's *Collected Writings*. London: Macmillan.

_____. (1930) *A Treatise on Money*. Reprinted in The *Collected Writings of John Maynard Keynes*, v. 5-6. London: Macmillan.

_____. (1933) "A Monetary Theory of Production." In Der Stand und die Nächste Zundkunft der Konjuncturforschung: *Festschrift für Arthur Spiethoff. Reprinted in The Collected Writings of John Maynard Keynes 13: 408-411. London: Macmillan.*

_____. (1936) *The General Theory of Employment, Interest and Money*. New York: Harcourt, Brace and World.

_____. (1937a) "The Theory of the Rate of Interest." In *The Lessons of Monetary Experience: Essays in Honour of Irving Fisher*. Reprinted in The Collected Writings of John Maynard Keynes 14: 101-108. London: Macmillan.

_____. (1937b) "Alternative Theories of the Rate of Interest." *Economic Journal* 47: 241-252. Reprinted in The *Collected Writings of John Maynard Keynes* 14: 201-215. London: Macmillan

_____. (1937c) "The General Theory of Employment." *Quarterly Journal of Economics* 51: 209-223. Reprinted in The *Collected Writings of John Maynard Keynes* 14: 109-123. London: Macmillan.

_____. (1937d) "The 'Ex Ante' Theory of the Rate of Interest." *Economic Journal* 47: 663-669. Reprinted in The *Collected Writings of John Maynard Keynes* 14: 215-223. London: Macmillan.

_____. (1972) (1933). *Essays in Biography*. Reprinted as The *Collected Writings of John Maynard Keynes*. 10. London: Macmillan.

_____. (1973a) *The Collected Writings of John Maynard Keynes* 13. London: Macmillan.

_____. (1973b) *The Collected Writings of John Maynard Keynes* 14. London: Macmillan.

_____. (1979) *The Collected Writings of John Maynard Keynes* 29. London: Macmillan.

Lawlor, M. S. (1991) "Keynes, Meltzer and Involuntary Unemployment: On the Intensional and Extensional Logic of Definitions." *Review of Social Economy,* xvlix: 317-338.

_____. (1993) "Keynes, Cambridge and the New Keynesian Economics." *Labor Economics: Problems in Analyzing Labor Markets*, W. A. Darity, ed., pp. 11-58. Boston: Kluwer Academic Press.

_____. Forthcoming. "On the Historical Origin of Keynes's Financial Market Views." *Higgling: Transactors and Their Markets in the History of Economics*, N. de Marchi and M. Morgan, eds. *History of Political Economy*, 26 (Supplement), forthcoming.

Lawlor, M. and B. Horn. (1992) "Notes on the Sraffa-Hayek Exchange." *Review of Political Economy*.

Laidler, D. (1991) *The Golden Age of the Quantity Theory*. Princeton, N.J.: Princeton University Press.

Leijonhufvud, A. (1981) "The Wicksell Connection: Variations on a Theme." In *Information and Coordination*. Oxford: Oxford University Press.

Lerner, A. P. (1952) "The Essential Properties of Interest and Money." *Quarterly Journal of Economics* 66: 172-193.

Marx, K. 1894. *Capital, Vol. III.* London: Allen and Wishart, 1977.

Menger, C. 1892. "On the Origin of Money." Trans. C.A. Foley. *Economic Journal* 2: 238-255.

Marshall, A. 1871. "Money." In J. Whittaker, ed., 1975. *The Early Writings of Alfred Marshall*, 2 vols. London: Macmillan.

O'Driscoll, G. P., Jr. (1977) *Economics as a Coordination Problem: The Contributions of Friedrich A. Hayek.* Mission, KS: Sheed Andrews and McNeel.

O'Driscoll, G. P., Jr., and M. J. Rizzo. (1985) *The Economics of Time and Ignorance.* Oxford: Basil Blackwell.

Pasinetti, L. L. (1974) *Growth and Income Distribution: Essays in Economic Theory.* Cambridge: Cambridge University Press.

Robertson, D. H. (1940) *Essays in Monetary Theory.* London: King and Sons.

Robinson, Joan. (1953-54) "The Production Function and the Theory of Capital." *Review of Economic Studies* 21: 81-106.

_____. (1961) "Own Rates of Interest." *Economic Journal* 71: 599-600.

_____. (1971) *Economic Heresies*. New York: Basic Books.

_____. (1981) *What Are the Questions? And Other Essays*. Armonk, NY: M.E. Sharpe.

Rogers, C. (1989) *Money, Interest and Capital: A Study in the Foundations of Monetary Theory*. Cambridge: Cambridge University Press.

Samuelson, P. A. (1947a) "The General Theory." In S.E. Harris, ed. *The New Economics*. New York: Alfred A. Knopf.

Shackle, G. L. S. (1967) *The Years of High Theory*. Cambridge: Cambridge University Press.

_____. (1972) *Epistemics and Economics*. Cambridge: Cambridge University Press.

_____. (1974) *Keynesian Kaleidics*. Edinburgh: Edinburgh University Press.

Sraffa, P. (1926) "The Laws of Returns Under Competitive Conditions." *Economic Journal* 36: 535-550.

_____. (1932a) "Dr. Hayek on Money and Capital." *Economic Journal* 42: 42-53.

_____. (1932b) "A Rejoinder." *Economic Journal 42: 249-51*

_____. (1960) *Production of Commodities by Means of Commodities*. Cambridge: Cambridge University Press.

Tobin, James. (1958) "Liquidity Preference as Behavior Towards Risk." *Review of Economic Studies* 67: 65-86. Reprinted in Tobin and Hester, 1967.

Tobin, James and Donald Hester, eds. *Risk Aversion and Portfolio Choice*. New York: Wiley.

Townshend, H. (1937) "Liquidity-Premium and the Theory of Value." *Economic Journal* 47: 157-169.

Veblen, T. B. (1909) "The Limitations of Marginal Utility." *Journal of Political Economy*. Reprinted in *The Place of Science in Modern Civilization*, pp. 231-251. New Brunswick, NJ: Transactions, 1990.

Weintraub, Sidney. (1982) "Information and Coordination: Essay in Macroeconomic Theory, A Review Essay on Leijonhufvud." *Journal of Money Credit and Banking 14: 420-424.*

White, M. V. (1982) "Reading and Rewriting: The Production of an Economic Robinson Crusoe." *Southern Review*, 15(2).

Wicksell, K. (1935) *Lectures on Political Economy*. 2 volumes. New York: Macmillan.

Wicksteed, P. H. (1914) "The Scope and Method of Political Economy in the Light of the 'Marginal' Theory of Value and Distribution." *Economic Journal* 24: 1-13.

MICHAEL LAWLOR'S OWN-RATES INTERPRETATION OF THE GENERAL THEORY

COMMENT BY COLIN ROGERS*

In his paper Michael Lawlor sets out to provide detailed textual support for the thesis that *"..Keynes' theoretical attempt to explain unemployment is fundamentally related to his views on money and interest."* Anyone who has read my own *Money, Interest and Capital* will recognize that I am in fundamental agreement with this thesis. In terms of this thesis Chapter 17 should not be read as a mere theoretical aside or curiosum but as a general statement of the analytical foundation for Keynes' monetary theory of production[1]. Furthermore, it provides an analytical framework within which to locate *all* the analysis of the *General Theory* (expectations and uncertainty included. On this see, in particular, O'Donnell, 1989, pp. 241-42). In other words, on these foundations rest all of the analytical innovations that distinguish Keynes' "monetary analysis" from the "real analysis" of the (neo)classical tradition[2].

Despite this general agreement with the thrust of Lawlor's thesis I will argue that Lawlor does not go as far as he might in establishing the theoretical claims made by Keynes. I believe that he does not go far enough because he follows Keynesian tradition and restricts Keynes' theoretical analysis to the short period. I will argue that this is a fundamental mistake made by Keynesians[3]. It is a mistake because anything less than the demonstration of the existence of *multiple long-period equilibria* does not provide an adequate *theoretical* counter to the (neo)classical vision. By the existence of multiple equilibria I mean that the set of long-period equilibrium positions envisaged by Keynes includes the full employment outcome as a special case which occurs only when the *optimum* rate of interest exists (Keynes, 1936, pp. 242-244). The long-period equilibrium position of a monetary economy is not uniquely determined at full employment; a long-period unemployment equilibrium can exist[4].

The short-period interpretation of Keynes misses the power of this point. For example, the short-period perspective offers no theoretical counter to Say's Law and the quantity theory of money; two key theoretical propositions about long-period equilibrium that apply in (neo)classical theory but which Keynes replaces with the principle of effective demand in his monetary theory of *long-period equilibrium*. In addition the short-period interpretation restricts the theoretical contribution of the *General Theory* to an analysis of the trade cycle; which is where most Keynesian interpretations leave it. Keynes offers *obiter dicta* on the trade cycle but the *General Theory* is more than another theory of the trade cycle[5]. Its major contribution is the demonstration that in a monetary economy long-period unemployment equilibrium is possible and that the unique full employment result of the non-monetary (neo)classical theory is at best a special case. In this sense Keynes's monetary theory is a generalization of classical non-monetary analysis of long-period equilibrium. This is the ultimate implication of Harrod's quote with which Lawlor opens his paper and the trail to this conclusion begins with Sraffa's critique of Hayek.

Origins of the Own-rates Framework; Sraffa

Lawlor begins his textual analysis by tracing the source of Keynes' own rates analysis of interest rates to the Hayek-Sraffa debate conducted in the *Economic Journal* of 1932. As Lawlor clearly shows, a key element of this debate was Sraffa's methodological criticism of Hayek's use of a barter economy to examine questions of monetary theory and policy. This is a key point because it exposes the sterility of attempts to build monetary theory on a barter or Robinson Crusoe foundation. The recognition of this fact in turn exposes the need for more institutional detail in the analytical foundations of monetary theory. Both of these themes were taken up by Keynes in the development of the *General Theory*.

In interpreting this debate, however, I would elaborate on Lawlor's argument in one respect. Lawlor interprets Hayek from a Wicksellian perspective while I believe that Sraffa's criticisms are most damaging when seen from a Walrasian perspective. In one sense this may be pedantic on my part because Hayek clearly saw himself as a follower of both Wicksell and Walras and may even have believed the analytical properties of their models to be identical. I don't wish to speculate about that[6]. There is both a Wicksellian and Walrasian connection in Hayek and my purpose here will be to spell out the implications of Hayek's Walrasian connection to complement Lawlor's discussion of the Wicksell connection.

The Walrasian Connection

In stressing the Walrasian connection I follow Milgate (1979), Desai (1982), and Lachmann (1986) who interpret the Hayek of *Prices and Production* as an exponent of (temporary equilibrium) Walrasian general equilibrium analysis rather than the Wicksellian. As noted above, from the textural perspective adopted by Lawlor this is not an issue but it does raise some analytical points which could be used to strengthen Lawlor's thesis. That is, the analytical distinction is important because it sheds additional light on Sraffa's critique of Hayek.

It is now generally realized that the temporary equilibrium version of the Walrasian general equilibrium system generates own rates of interest for each commodity. In an *n*-commodity world there are potentially *n* commodity rates of interest. It is also recognized that there is no mechanism in terms of which these rates can be equalized. That is, the temporary equilibrium Walrasian general equilibrium model cannot generate *a* natural rate of interest. As noted in Rogers (1989a, p.53) Wicksell seemed to apply the temporary equilibrium interpretation of Walras's model when he complained that Walras's general equilibrium system gave no information about *the* [natural] rate of interest because capital was treated narrowly as only durable goods (clay) and not financial capital (putty). From the Walrasian temporary equilibrium perspective it seems that both Sraffa and Wicksell would agree; there is no natural rate of interest in the general equilibrium system employed by Hayek.

But if Hayek has a Walrasian temporary equilibrium system in mind as the theoretical basis of the model in *Prices and Production* then Sraffa's critique displayed considerable prescience as his critique of Walrasian monetary theory re-emerged in the 1970s. As Desai(1982) noted, Frank Hahn (1973), without any reference to Sraffa, initiated a critique of Walrasian monetary theory which makes essential the same points as those raised by Sraffa against Hayek in the 1930s. Essentially Hahn's critique exposes the Walrasian general equilibrium model as a model of *perfect or costless barter to which "money" is always an inessential addition*. These properties are readily apparent in the most logically extreme form of the Walrasian general equilibrium system; the Arrow-Debreu version. On this score it is important to stress that the Walrasian model is not a model of primitive barter economy. It is a model of a highly sophisticated barter economy in which the costs associated with primitive barter, e.g., the double coincidence of wants, do not occur and in which the real rates of exchange between all known commodities are conveyed by a super computer (the auctioneer) to all agents. Such a world is a hypothetical fiction and no known economy has ever approximated its behavior. Clearly it is a hypothetical world in which no agents need nor want money (Hahn, 1982). Consequently, it is unlikely to shed much light on the behavior of a world which has evolved a social convention called money. This is the force of Sraffa's methodological critique of Hayek and it is as relevant today as it was in 1932.

For these reasons I think Lawlor is right to start with Sraffa's critique of Hayek's use of the barter model. I would add only that the criticism is strengthened when seen from the Walrasian perspective and draw attention to Desai's (1982) view that Sraffa's criticism of Hayek reappeared in the 1970s in the guise of Hahn's critique of Walrasian monetary theory. Since then the situation has deteriorated further with the realization that uniqueness and stability of aggregate Walrasian equilibrium cannot, in general, be established (Kirman, 1989). The important conclusion that follows from these developments is that there is no *theoretical basis* in Walrasian general equilibrium theory for the belief that the economy is inherently self-adjusting to *the* natural rate of output in the long run. Where does that leave the real balance effect?

As a corollary it should also be conceded that attempts, such as that by Patinkin, to interpret Keynes from a Walrasian general disequilibrium perspective miss the point. Keynes was not presenting a Walrasian general equilibrium model nor was his main objective the presentation of a new theory of the trade cycle which is what Patinkin's disequilibrium interpretation implies[7]. As Patinkin (1990, p. 226) himself points out, the trade cycle implications of Keynes' analysis are not part of the major theoretical innovations presented in the body of the *General Theory* which are, we can all agree: the principle [theory] of effective demand; the marginal efficiency of capital, and the theory of liquidity preference[8]. However, this should not be interpreted to mean that a disequilibrium or slow adjustment story is inconsistent with the monetary analysis of the *General Theory* (isn't that what chapter 19 is all about); just that it is not the fundamental theoretical point that Keynes was proposing; which, in my opinion, was the existence of long-period unemployment equilibria in a monetary economy.

The Wicksell Connection

Throughout his paper Lawlor uses the Wicksellian concept of the natural rate and loanable funds theory of the rate of interest as a foil against which to contrast Keynes' liquidity preference theory of the rate of interest. Keynes certainly made use of Wicksell's concept of *the* natural rate in the *Treatise* and it appears to have formed the basis of Robertson's interpretation of the loanable funds theory of the rate of interest to which Keynes objected in the *General Theory*. But from my perspective this theory is open to criticism on grounds different from that which Sraffa levelled against Hayek's Walrasian scheme in *Prices and Production* although there is some overlap on the methodological question of the relevance of a barter model as the basis for monetary theory. Both the Walrasian and Wicksellian models are barter models but they have different analytical properties as a result of the different treatment of "capital" in each.

In the Walrasian temporary equilibrium system "capital" is treated as part of the endowment: i.e., "clay" -a vector of capital goods; tractors, ploughs etc. As both Wicksell and Sraffa noted, in the Walrasian scheme clay cannot be molded to produce a uniform rate of interest on all forms of clay; hence the multitude of rates of interest in equilibrium. In Wicksellian general equilibrium, capital is putty. "Capital" is treated as putty so that any initial endowment can be re-arranged between sectors to generate a uniform rate of interest (*the* natural rate) on alternate uses of capital. It is the putty characteristic of Wicksellian analysis which is reflected in the savings-investment analysis of the natural rate of interest. For example, both Wicksell and Robertson saw saving and investment in physical terms as determining the natural rate of interest which acted as an attractor for the ephemeral movements of the money rate.

This "vision" of Wicksellian loanable funds theory is usually articulated in terms of saving and investment schedules in physical terms which determine the natural rate of interest. Reflecting these physical schedules but acting as a veil obscuring the real forces of productivity and thrift are financial flows in which bonds are exchanged for money. At times Hayek also appears to have this Wicksellian vision in mind when he talks about the banks inability to match the money rate of interest with *the* natural rate. From an analytical perspective, however, these observations on the natural rate by Hayek do not follow from the temporary equilibrium Walrasian properties of other parts of his analysis.

Keynes (1936, chapter 14) launched a sustained attack on what he called the classical theory of the rate of interest in the *General Theory*. The classical theory which he attacked was the loanable funds theory in which the natural rate plays a key role. That is, Keynes, in the *General Theory*, attacks what Lawlor calls the Wicksell connection. Most commentators have concluded that this critique was ineffectual. But Wicksell's analysis had in any event been subject to searching criticism by Swedish economists who reached conclusions remarkably similar to those presented by Keynes'[9]. Subsequently, the capital controversy has led to the general recognition that Wicksell's unique natural rate can be defined only in a one-commodity world.

Fortunately, as Lawlor suggests, Keynes' own rates framework provides a way around these Walrasian and Wicksellian dilemmas; it provides the analytical scaffolding for his monetary theory of production.

Keynes, Own Rates Framework

Having dispensed with the *cul de sac* into which "real analysis" leads, Lawlor traces how Keynes' adapted Sraffa's own rates analysis to the monetary theory of production presented in the *General Theory*. In tracing the development of Keynes' own rates framework Lawlor provides a rich textual embroidery to support his thesis that the own rates framework is central to Keynes' analysis in the *General Theory*. All of this is well done. However, I don't believe that Lawlor makes as strong a case as he might when spelling out the implications of Keynes' analysis.

The reason for my doubts about this stem from that fact that Lawlor restricts the own rates framework to a short-period perspective. I think this is a mistake and that extending the analysis to long-period equilibrium illuminates Keynes' powerful critique of (neo)classical economics in a way which is lost when the story is restricted to the short period. Furthermore, and to pre-empt any misgivings that some Keynesians have about the long period, let me also claim that this long-period analysis is quite compatible with all the other features of Keynes' analysis, in particular the existence of *irreducible* uncertainty and a role for expectations (O'Donnell, 1989). This leads to two interdependent issues raised by Lawlor which I believe require further elaboration by Keynesian theorists; the implications of money as a social convention and Townshend's proposal for the generalization of value theory. The two issues are interdependent and Townsend's position has recently received attention from Rotheim(1993). Consequently, I will concentrate on the implications of money as a social convention as they relate to Lawlor's paper.

Keynes' Own Rates and Long-period Equilibrium

Lawlor provides a comprehensive and clear analysis of Keynes' own rates framework as presented in chapter 17 of the *General Theory* and I have no quibbles with any of these details. My only concern with this story is that Lawlor follows Keynesian tradition by restricting his interpretation to the short period when I believe that everything Lawlor says applies equally well to the long period. I argue that restricting the analysis to the short period is a fundamental mistake which has seriously undermined the Keynesian position from its inception. In this respect Lawlor seems to misunderstand my own position when in footnote 14 he remarks that in *Money, Interest and Capital* I distinguish between Keynes' short-run "monetary analysis" as opposed to the traditional focus of "real analysis"[10]. This is not the distinction I wished to make. The point that I was trying to make was that Keynes' "monetary analysis" of *both* short *and* long period needed to be distinguished from traditional "real analysis" of these periods. A normal characteristic of the latter is uniqueness of long-period equilibrium while Keynes' "monetary analysis" is characterized by multiple long-period equilibria[11]. This distinction is, I believe, fundamental to Keynes' attack on Say's Law and the quantity theory of money; the twin flagships of (neo)classical economics.

The analytical basis for a long-period analysis using Keynes' own rates framework is noted by Lawlor in terms of Sraffa's view that equilibrium requires that all own-rates measured in quantity terms must be equal as all spot and futures prices coincide. As noted in the previous section the (neo)classical application of this idea was applied in the barter context by Wicksell, Robertson, and Keynes in the *Treatise*, to imply that long-period equilibrium was unique and determined when the "money" rate of interest had adjusted to the natural or barter rate of interest; all of this at full employment. I would argue that what Keynes abandoned in the *General Theory* was not this long-period perspective (in favor of a short-period perspective) but the non-monetary or "real analysis" of the relationship between the money rate of interest and commodity rates in an economy which money has evolved as a social convention. In short, I would argue that the *General Theory* represents a radical change in theoretical perspective but a conservative application of largely Marshallian analytical technique.

To illustrate my argument, Lawlor's presentation of the own rates framework will be applied to demonstrate the theoretical basis of Keynes' claim to have established the existence of a long-period unemployment equilibrium. If this proposition is established, Say's Law and the quantity theory of money fail and the principle of effective demand determines employment.

Lawlor writes asset market equilibrium as:

$$r_{w,m} = r_{h,m} = r_{m,m} \qquad (1)$$

where each of the own rates expressed in terms of money as the common standard are defined in his expressions (11) through (13) and $r_{w,m}$ = the wheat rate of interest expressed in money; $r_{h,m}$ = the house rate of interest expressed in money and $r_{m,m}$ = the money rate of interest in terms of itself. As Lawlor's expression (10) reveals, the wheat rate and the house rate both contain a terms that are not zero whenever the demand price is not equal to the supply price. That is, in Lawlor's expression (10) which appears as:

$$a^i = \frac{P_2^i - P_1^i}{P_1^i}(\frac{Q_2^i}{Q_1^i})$$

the a terms are non-zero whenever $P_2^i \neq P_1^i$ and I define P_2^i = the future or long-period supply price in the case of a reproducible commodity like wheat or housing and P_1^i = the demand or spot price. From a Marshallian perspective the equality of own rates in money terms presented in expression (1) above is not a position in which the economy is at rest because abnormal profits and/or losses will be made whenever the a terms are non zero. In other words, Lawlor's statement of asset market equilibrium may be interpreted as a Marshallian short-period equilibrium from which the economy will move away as entrepreneurs respond to the pattern of abnormal profits and/or losses[12]. Thus Lawlor's short-period asset market equilibrium condition could be interpreted as a snap-shot of the process of adjustment between long-period equilibria. But from the perspective of long-period equilibrium it is a *disequilibrium* position from which the economy will move away. The difficulty with this interpretation is that it specifies a short-period equilibrium from which the economy will move away in the next period; it is not a theory of unemployment equilibrium. In addition it appears to reduce the *General Theory* to a theory of the trade cycle only.

Relating this concept of asset market equilibrium to the quotation from Harrod at the beginning of Lawlor's paper which stresses the "natural" rigidity of the money rate of interest in a monetary economy it is also apparent that Lawlor's asset market equilibrium will collapse into Sraffa's long-period or stationary equilibrium as the demand prices of wheat and houses are driven to equality with their long-period supply prices. Once the economy is in this long-period asset market equilibrium it is natural to enquire whether full employment exists. Keynes' revolutionary insight was to realize that in an economy which had evolved the social convention of money the answer may be no. For reasons that Lawlor explains in convincing detail there is no automatic market mechanism in a monetary economy which will adjust the money rate of interest to the level which produces just the right level of investment to generate full employment.

This in essence is the static version of the principle of effective demand which overthrows Say's Law[13]. For, once in long-period monetary equilibrium, unless the money rate of interest falls, there is a limit to the profitable expansion of output and the short-run expansion of employment will come to a halt. This, as I understand it, is what the principle of effective demand is all about and I have outlined the argument at greater length elsewhere (Rogers 1989a, 1990). In this respect it must be stressed that the version of the principle of effective demand presented here is static and follows from an application of Marshallian comparative statics to a monetary economy in which the money rate of interest can determine long-period equilibrium[14]. In such a world Say's Law fails; a limit to the profitable expansion of output can be encountered before full employment is reached. Supply does not create its own demand as the increased output cannot be sold at even a normal profit and output contracts unless the money rate of interest falls *pari passu*. Lawlor provides extensive textual and analytical detail to explain why Keynes thought the latter outcome was unlikely.

In Lawlor's notation Keynes' long-period equilibrium appears as:

$$r_w = r_h = r_{m,m} \qquad (2)$$

where r_w and r_h are the commodity rates of interest. These are Wicksell's and Robertson's natural rates and in equilibrium the LHS of expression (2) can be described as *the* natural rate. It is my contention that Keynes has no difficulty with this part of the analysis. Where he differs from Wicksell and Robertson is in the realization that in a monetary economy $r_{m,m}$ may be the determinant of the equilibrium outcome in expression (2). In other words Keynes allows the money rate of interest to determine the natural rate; the direction of causation in "real analysis" may be reversed in a monetary economy[15]. Thus for every long-period equilibrium determined by the level of $r_{m,m}$ there is a different natural rate:
"..for every rate of interest there is a level of employment for which that rate is the 'natural' rate in the sense that the system will be in equilibrium..." (Keynes, 1936, chapter 17, p.242). The equality of the natural and money rates of interest has no particular claim to fame because it is true of all long-period equilibria, with or without full employment, in Keynes's monetary analysis. If, as Keynes believed, there was no mechanism for adjusting the money rate of interest to the optimum level consistent with full employment then a long-period equilibrium with unemployment could exist.

Consequently, the potential existence of *multiple long-period equilibria* is the message that I take from chapter 17 of the *General Theory*. The possibility arises because, as Lawlor documents convincingly, Keynes realized that a monetary economy has properties that distinguish it from the "real analysis" of Wicksell and Robertson. In an economy that has evolved the social convention of money there are numerous reasons for believing that the money rate of interest will not be driven by market forces to a level consistent with full employment. As Harrod puts it in Lawlor's opening quotation: "*But this wrong rate of interest, as we may call it, is not in itself a rigidity or inflexibility. It is natural, durable, and in a certain sense, in a free system inevitable.*" As I interpret Harrod, and Keynes in chapter 17, as a theoretical matter it is the money rate of interest that establishes the point of effective demand and the possible existence of a long-period unemployment equilibrium. The practical implications of this theoretical insight are that the economy may fluctuate for decades about an unemployment equilibrium because the money rate of interest is too high (Keynes, 1936, p204).

The demonstration of the potential existence of multiple long-period equilibria I interpret in the context of the Marshallian statical method employed by

Keynes[16]. The question of the stability of such equilibria is a separate question and it is dealt with by Keynes, particularly in chapter 19, when he discusses the question of wage flexibility. On these matters I am in agreement with Lawlor when he notes that Keynes argues that the question of stability cannot be explained purely on *a priori* grounds but requires some understanding of the existing conventions. In particular, as Lawlor stresses, stability of equilibrium is tied up with the stability of wages because wages tie down the long-period supply prices.

Concluding Remarks

The demonstration of the potential existence of multiple long-period equilibria is, in my view, the essence of Keynes' critique of the (neo)classical vision. It provides a strong *theoretical* counter to the (neo)classical vision of an economy that automatically adjusts to the natural full employment equilibrium in the long run. Furthermore, it provides the rationale for Keynes' policy proposals.

By comparison, most Keynesians failed to follow Keynes' use of "monetary analysis" and opted instead to remain within the confines of "real analysis." This meant that they effectively had no monetary theory and Keynesian analysis was restricted to a short-run story in the context of a (neo)classical model that adjusted (slowly) to *the* natural full employment equilibrium in the long run. All the sterile debates between Keynesians and representatives of the (neo)classical vision can be traced to the attempts by Keynesians to tell Keynes' story in the context of (neo)classical "real analysis"[17]. Not surprisingly, Keynesians have often come off second best in these theoretical jousts because the story they wish to tell has no theoretical basis in "real analysis." Lawlor does an admirable job in alerting Keynesians to the appropriate theoretical foundations but by stopping in the short period he also runs the risk of being absorbed into the tradition of "real analysis."[18] The latter strategy has a long history in terms of which monetary issues are relegated to the short period where their disruptive influences can be quarantined from the real forces that determine the natural long-period equilibrium with full employment. But as the Hayek-Sraffa debate attests, this strategy masks the fundamental methodological objection that monetary theory cannot be erected on the barter foundations of "real analysis" in any of its forms.

Lawlor clearly flags the road around this sterile *cul de sac* but I am concerned that he has not driven on. The work by Townshend to which he refers clearly illustrates the need to generalize the axioms of "real analysis" to include social conventions; money itself is one. Once this is recognized all of the other elements of Keynes' analysis fall naturally into place. I have in mind here the treatment of uncertainty and expectations which, I would argue, are quite compatible with Keynes' treatment of long-period equilibrium as outlined in chapter 17 in particular[19].

Thus although I find myself in strong agreement with the general thrust of Lawlor's thesis, and with most of the detail, I am concerned that he weakens his case by restricting his analytical perspective to the short period.

Notes

* I am grateful to T.K. Rymes for helpful comments. The usual disclaimer applies.

[1] For a dissenting view see Mongiovi (1990, p. 153) who concludes that: "... Chapter 17 is, in the end, redundant and ineffective: Redundant because its main assertion - that the marginal efficiency of capital is regulated by the money rate of interest - had already been made with greater clarity in chapters 11 and 13; and ineffective because it merely repeats the earlier arguments, without providing the critique of orthodox distribution theory necessary to render coherent a monetary theory of the interest rate."

[2] The distinction between "real" and "monetary analysis" is due to Schumpeter (1954).

[3] On this score I seem to be in fundamental disagreement with the majority of Keynesians who treat the *General Theory* as a short-period story. I believe that this is a fatal mistake which hands the theoretical debate to the (neo)classical position. Nevertheless, Keynesians have always been puzzled by the long-period character of chapter 17 which they perceive as inconsistent with the short-period perspective of the rest of the *General Theory*. It is my contention that the short-period interpretation of the *General Theory* is mistaken and I have discussed the issue in more detail elsewhere (Rogers, 1989 a,b, 1990, 1991). For interpretations of chapter 17 in a long-period context see Chick (1983) or Mongiovi (1990, p.132). It is also important to stress that the use of long-period equilibrium does not preclude a role for expectations and uncertainty as is sometimes suggested by neo-Ricardians.

[4] It may help to clarify this point by thinking about the long-period equilibrium outcomes of (neo)classical theory and Keynes' monetary theory as containing only one element in common; long-period equilibrium at full employment. In Keynes's monetary theory the set of long-period equilibria is enlarged to include equilibrium at less that full employment. However, long-period equilibrium in "monetary analysis" should always be distinguished from long-period equilibrium in "real analysis."

[5] In this respect I am in agreement with Meltzer's (1983, 1989) interpretation of Keynes' intentions.

[6] Milgate (1979, p.4) argues that Hayek was well aware that his [Walrasian] analysis would generate a multitude of [intertemporal] equilibrium rates of interest. Milgate also argues, convincingly, that the [Walrasian] intertemporal equilibrium concept used by Hayek constituted a fundamental break with the traditional concept of long-period equilibrium. Sraffa clearly had the latter concept in mind.

[7] Patinkin (1990, p. 215) justifies his disequilibrium interpretation of Keynes on the grounds that it avoids the need to assume rigid wages or invoke the liquidity trap. On the interpretation suggested here neither of these are central to Keynes' demonstration of the existence of a long-period unemployment equilibrium. Meltzer (1983, pp. 67-69, especially footnote 9) is baffled by Patinkin's inability to see the point of Keynes' claim that the economy's equilibrium remained stable at less that full employment. Meltzer attributes the difference between them on this score to the fact that Patinkin adopts a dynamic disequilibrium interpretation of the *General Theory*.

[8] Patinkin (1990) does not consider Keynes' treatment of uncertainty and expectations to be a fundamental theoretical contribution.

[9] This issue is discussed in greater detail in Rogers (1989a). See also Milgate (1979) p.7 for Lindahl's critique of Wicksell's concept of the natural rate.

[10] This is the interpretation of Keynes due to Meir Kohn (1986) which I think is simply incorrect. A comprehensive discussion is provided in Rogers (1989b)

[11] It is somewhat ironic that uniqueness of equilibrium has subsequently emerged as a fundamental problem for aggregate Walrasian general equilibrium theory (Kirman, 1989).

[12] Note that in Marshallian comparative statics demand price equals supply price in each period. For example, in market period equilibrium the spot demand price equals the supply price at a point on the perfectly inelastic supply curve. In short-period equilibrium the demand price again equals the short-period supply price as dictated by the short-period supply curve. Finally, in long-period equilibrium the same relationship holds. It is clear from Lawlor's discussion of Sraffa's interpretation of own rates equilibrium as a stationary or long-period equilibrium that Lawlor interprets asset market equilibrium as a short-period equilibrium. But in that case the future price must be the long-period supply price if the *a* term is to be non-zero.

[13] Note that my long-period interpretation of Keynes means that I also differ from Lawlor's interpretation of Keynes' shifting equilibrium as a short-period equilibrium. On my interpretation Keynes' shifting equilibrium results once the state of long-term expectations is revised. The model of shifting equilibrium represents a more advanced application of the insights obtained by the static analysis to a world in which those items held in the *ceteris paribus* compound are bound to change. All of this is quite consistent with the Marshallian method. For further discussion see (Rogers, 1990).

[14] Expression (2) embodies a static version of the principle of effective demand which asserts that a limit to the profitable expansion of output exists if condition (2) holds before full employment is reached. The thrust of Harrod's quote at the beginning of Lawlor's paper is that there is no reason why expression (2) should occur only at full employment. By contrast, most statements of the principle of effective demand are dynamic in form as they interpret the principle to mean that it is changes in income, rather than changes in the rate of interest, that bring saving and investment into equality.

[15] This does not exclude some reverse causality between the two sides of the equality as would be expected from a generalisation of the classical analysis.

[16] It should be stressed that the existence of multiple long-period equilibria in Keynes does not rest on the assumption of rigid money wages or the liquidity trap. Rigid wages impart a degree of stability to the system by pining down the long-period supply prices and the inability of the money rate of interest to adjust automatically to the optimum level consistent with full employment has nothing to do with the liquidity trap.

[17] To the extent that New Keynesians remain within the confines of "real analysis" their attempts to provide the microfoundations for Keynes' macroeconomics will suffer the same fate. But that is another story.

[18] Examples are too numerous to list but Patinkin (1990, p. 215) and Kohn (1986) illustrate the point.

[19] I have discussed this matter in greater detail elsewhere (Rogers, 1991). For a compatible view of Townshend's contribution see Rotheim (1993).

References

Chick, V. (1983) *Macroeconomics After Keynes*. London: Philip Allan.

Desai, M. (1982) The Task of Monetary Theory: The Hayek-Sraffa Debate in Modern Perspective, *Advances in Economic Theory*, M. Baranzini, ed. pp. 149-170, Oxford: Blackwell.

Hahn, F. H. (1973) On The Foundations of Monetary Theory, *Essays in Modern Economics*, M. Parkin, ed., pp. 230-242, London: Longman.

_____. (1982) *Money and Inflation*. Oxford: Blackwell.

Keynes, J. M. (1936) *The General Theory of Employment, Interest and Money*. London: Macmillan.

Kirman, A. (1989) The Intrinsic Limits of Modern Economic Theory: The Emperor Has No Clothes, *Economic Journal*, Supplement, pp. 126-139.

Kohn, M. (1986) Monetary Analysis, The Equilibrium Method and Keynes' General Theory, *Journal of Political Economy*, 94, pp. 1191-1224.

Lachmann, L. M. (1986) Austrian Economics Under Fire: The Hayek-Sraffa Duel in Retrospect, *Austrian Economics: Historical and Philosophical Background*, W. Grassl and B. Smiths eds, pp. 225-242, New York: New York University Press.

Meltzer, A. (1983) Interpreting Keynes, *Journal of Economic Literature*, XXI, pp. 66-78.

——————. (1989) *Keynes' Monetary Theory*. Cambridge: Cambridge University Press.

Milgate, M. (1979) On the Origin of the Notion of "Intertemporal Equilibrium," *Economica*, 46, pp. 1-10.

Mongiovi, G. (1990) Keynes, Hayek and Sraffa: On the Origins of Chapter 17 of The General Theory, *Economie Appliquee*, XLIII, pp. 131-156.

O'Donnell, R. (1989) *Keynes: Philosophy, Economics and Politics*. London: Mammalian

Patinkin, D. (1990) On Different Interpretations of the General Theory, *Journal of Monetary Economics*, 26, pp. 205-243.

Rogers, C. (1989a) *Money, Interest and Capital: A Study in the Foundations of Monetary Theory*. Cambridge: Cambridge University Press.

——————. (1989b) Monetary Analysis, The Equilibrium Method and Keynes' General Theory: A Comment, unpublished mimeo University of Adelaide.

——————. (1990) The Nature and Role of Equilibrium in Keynes' General Theory: An Alternative Perspective, unpublished mimeo University of Adelaide.

——————. (1991) Keynes' Monetary Theory of Employment: Expectations and Uncertainty in Long-period Equilibria, unpublished mimeo University of Adelaide.

Rotheim, R.J. (1993) On the indeterminacy of Keynes's monetary theory of value, *Review of Political Economy*, 5, pp. 197-216.

Schumpeter, J. (1954) *History of Economic Analysis*. New York: Oxford University Press.

4 RETHINKING THE KEYNESIAN REVOLUTION

Bradley W. Bateman

I. "You often say - 'It is nonsense to talk about confidence . . .'"

During the last 15 years, while economists and historians of economic thought have kept their gaze focused on Maynard Keynes's *theoretical work*, a host of other scholars has been trying to put him in a fuller, historical context. As historians, political scientists, sociologists, and economic historians have turned their attention to the question of how demand management became institutionalized in the Western democracies they have made some startling discoveries.[1]

They have discovered, for instance, that Keynes and *The General Theory* had little or no *direct* influence in most countries until well after the Second World War.[2] They have found that in countries (like Britain and the United States) where he did have some direct influence, that the structure of the state, the nature of political coalitions, and questions of political autonomy had a much larger role to play than the brilliance (or widespread academic acceptance) of Keynes's ideas.

When one reads this "new" Keynesian literature[3], one is struck by its novelty and by the historical complexity of the process by which economic ideas become embedded in the political sphere. Then, as this novelty and complexity sink in, one is struck by the fact that economists have a lot to learn. Economists are notoriously ahistorical in their analytical work, and one begins to wonder if this historical neglect may not be in line for a re-evaluation.[4] While economists have happily embraced the power of pure theory over historical description, one wonders if they will be able to neglect the historical truth about the limited power of their theoretical models in influencing the world. If "the greatest economist of the 20th century" had only a limited influence on economic policy, then what about the work of lesser mortals?

The point of this essay, however, is *not* to survey the whole of the interdisciplinary literature which re-evaluates the Keynesian Revolution[5]. This would be a task far beyond the bounds of a single essay. The task of this essay, rather, is to explain how we might gain a better understanding of Keynes's own work by placing it in the fuller historical context which the "new" Keynesian literature invites[6]. For while this new literature provides us with a de-mythologized Keynes, he is still an important historical figure. Keynes may not have been responsible for everything attributed to him in the traditional hagiographies, but he was a great economist who forged his theories in a fascinating environment in which the influences cut across many frontiers, academic and political.

Our point of departure will be Keynes's incorporation of expectations and uncertainty into *The General Theory*. This is a field which will perhaps seem worked over all too well. In fact, the burgeoning literature in the field has already earned a label for itself: New Fundamentalist.[7] But the name betrays the narrow approach which characterizes much of this literature; it is a literature largely predicated on the idea that there is a textual continuity between Keynes's *Treatise on Probability* and his *General Theory*. As such, the literature focuses on the purely *theoretical* connections to be drawn between the two books. Like all good fundamentalists, this tribe focuses its attentions on the truth(s) in the text(s); context and historical circumstance are of little interest to the cognoscenti.

This essay takes a different tack. Starting from a very different point, it attempts to take a closer look at Keynes's own policy recommendations in and after *The General Theory*. Beginning with the surprising fact that from mid-1930 until at least mid-1933 Keynes was a vociferous *critic* of the idea that business confidence and expectations were important to explanations of the trade cycle, this essay examines the sources for and implications of his change of heart. Why did Keynes switch from his strong opposition to confidence to a belief that it was central to an understanding of a capitalist economy? The fact of his original opposition to theories based on business confidence has been neatly hidden from scholars who attempt to compare *Probability* and *The General Theory* because they have been able to overlook everything in the interim between 1921 and 1936. Now, however, with the completion of the publication of Keynes's *Collected Writings* and the explosion in literature on the Keynesian Revolution, the rich historical background to Keynes's thought has been laid open for examination.

One of the most surprising things in this new historical trove is Keynes's early dismissal of the idea that confidence and expectations are important to the trade cycle. The earliest signs of this dismissal come in Keynes's work in the Macmillan Committee in the spring of 1930. In the transcripts of the Committee's hearings one finds Keynes arguing with Richard Hopkins, Dennis Robertson, and A.C. Pigou about the importance of confidence.[8] They think that it is important; he refuses to accept their arguments. This refusal surfaces repeatedly in his correspondence of that year and plays a part in the deliberations of the Committee of Economists that fall. One can track the argument straight through to the spring of 1933 when Hubert Henderson reports in a letter to Keynes, "You often say--'It's nonsense to talk about confidence . . .'"

How then did Keynes come to change his mind in the course of the next three years? How, by the spring of 1936, did he come to place expectations at the heart of *The General Theory*? As is the case with many of Keynes's volte faces, we still do not know the complete answer to this question. Scholars have yet to turn up the document(s) that provide a certain answer. What *has* been turned up is fairly clear cut evidence that the change in Keynes's outlook occurred late in 1933. Thomas Rymes's careful reconstruction of Keynes's lectures between

1932 and 1935 establishes that by the Michaelmas term of 1933, uncertainty and expectations were firmly in place in Keynes's emerging theoretical constellation.

But while nailing down the time frame for Keynes's change of heart still has not helped to locate all the document(s) which explain the change, the historical context of his thinking almost certainly *does* help us understand Keynes's original position. During the entire period that Keynes was arguing with others that confidence was unimportant to the business cycle, a large part of his disagreement stemmed from the fact that business confidence was being used as part of an argument *against* activist fiscal policy. This is most clear in his correspondence with Hubert Henderson. In 1929, Henderson had been Keynes's co-author in writing *Can Lloyd George Do It?*, the tract promoting the Liberal Party's proposals for large scale budget deficits to finance public works projects. Only a year later, Henderson's own position had changed and he was arguing *against* such programs on the grounds that they would cause a downturn in business confidence and so stymie any possible recovery. In all their correspondence, it is clear that Keynes is opposed to confidence arguments because they lead to a conclusion he could not countenance: public works and budget deficits will not help stimulate a recovery.[9]

It is at this point - the understanding of Keynes's original position on business confidence - that this essay begins. For a natural question arises at this point, "If Keynes originally opposed business confidence as an explanation of the trade cycle because this was the approach of opponents to debt-financed public works projects, then how did he escape coming to their conclusions when he later embraced business confidence as an important element in the trade cycle?" The simple answer is, "He didn't." It has become increasingly fashionable over the last ten years to argue that *The General Theory* is not really about *activist* fiscal policy, but the reason why this is the case is still not well understood. Indeed, one can say that the reason why Keynes came to this conclusion is largely *unexamined*.[10]

Looking more closely at the record of Keynes's writings from 1936 until his death, one finds clear evidence that his thinking on monetary and fiscal policy was underpinned by a concern for the effects of uncertainty. What officials could, and couldn't, do was limited by business confidence. Seen in the context of the *evolution* of his ideas, this concern makes perfect sense.

II. "The Socialization of Investment"

As Allan Meltzer has pointed out, first time readers of *The General Theory* are often struck by what is *not* in the book; most notably the lack of any strong argument in favor of activist fiscal policy.[11] For economists trained in the decades after the Second World War, the book's approach to monetary policy is also discombobulating. Raised to believe that Keynes had come to the position that "money doesn't matter" (i.e., that monetary policy is unimportant), it is odd to find that this is not his position at all. For while he argues that monetary policy *alone* cannot raise an economy out of a slump, he actually has a well-articulated stance as to the difference between good and bad monetary policy and a clear belief that good (stable) monetary policy is a necessary part of a well-functioning capitalist economy.[12]

Taken together, this asymmetrical treatment of fiscal and monetary policy is further disconcerting in that the explicit treatment of monetary policy undercuts the argument that the book was only meant as a theoretical tract. Granted that theoretical innovation was *one* of the book's primary purposes, it is impossible to argue that Keynes did not also mean to have the theory applied to policy problems given his argument for the importance of a stable policy of keeping long-run interest rates as low as possible.

Don Patinkin has tried to defend the more traditional interpretation of *The General Theory* as a book meant to promote activist fiscal policy by arguing that Keynes's frequent references to "the socialization of investment" are actually references to public works projects.[13] On this interpretation, these many references are calls for the activist policy which follow from Keynes's revolutionary new model. The large number of actions that Keynes subsumed under this rubric, however, taken together with the limitations he acknowledged to large scale public work projects, make Patinkin's interpretation questionable. In addition, one would expect that a person who had made a highly successful journalistic career by articulating the position for activist policies would have had *no* problem in making a similar argument in an academic tract (as is borne out by his arguments in *The General Theory* for a stable long-run policy of low interest rates). If Keynes had meant "the socialization of investment" as an analogue for "undertaking public works projects" it seems that he could, and would, have said exactly that.

There is, thus, more to Keynes's concept of the socialization of investment than debt-financed public works; seen in historical context, the idea has much broader implications than this traditional interpretation suggests. Following his acceptance of the position that confidence is an important element in the success of government policies, Keynes also became an advocate of the theory that the business cycle is the result of oscillations in business confidence.[14] "I suggest that the essential character of the Trade Cycle and, especially, the regularity of time-sequence and of duration which justifies us in calling it a *cycle*, is mainly due to the way in which the marginal efficiency of capital fluctuates."[15] And it was *this* position, that stabilizing business confidence would be necessary to mitigating the business cycle, that underlaid his concept of the socialization of investment.

The connection between the trade cycle and the socialization of investment is first made clear in Chapter 22 of *The General Theory*, Keynes's "Notes on the Trade Cycle".

> Thus with markets organized and influenced as they are at present, the market estimation of the marginal efficiency of capital may suffer such enormously wide fluctuations that it cannot be sufficiently offset by corresponding fluctuations in the rate of interest. Moreover, the corresponding movements in the stock-market may,

as we have seen above, depress the propensity to consume just when it is most needed. In conditions of *laissez-faire* the avoidance of wide fluctuations in employment may, therefore, prove impossible without a far-reaching change in the psychology of investment markets such as there is no reason to expect. I conclude that the duty of ordering the current volume of investment cannot safely be left in private hands.[16]

But as Keynes makes clear in his concluding chapter, he does not mean nationalization or state control of industry when he refers to the socialization of investment.

In some other respects the foregoing theory is moderately conservative in its implications. For whilst it indicates the vital importance of establishing certain central controls in matters which are now left in the main to individual initiative, there are wide fields of activity which are unaffected. The State will have to exercise a guiding influence on the propensity to consume partly through its scheme of taxation, partly by fixing the rate of interest, and partly, perhaps, in other ways. Furthermore, it seems unlikely that the influence of banking policy on the rate of interest will be sufficient by itself to determine an optimum rate of investment. I conceive, therefore, that a somewhat comprehensive socialization of investment will prove the only means of securing an approximation to full employment; though this need not exclude all manner of compromises and of devices by which public authority will co-operate with private initiative. But beyond this no obvious case is made out for a system of State Socialism which would embrace most of the economic life of the community. It is not the ownership of the instruments of production which it is important for the State to assume. If the State is able to determine the aggregate amount of resources devoted to augmenting the instruments and the basic rate of reward to those who own them, it will have accomplished all that is necessary. Moreover, the necessary measures of socialization can be introduced gradually and without a break in the general traditions of society.[17]

Taken together, these two statements demonstrate the apparent ambiguity in Keynes's proposal. On the one hand, the problem of "the psychology of the investment market" is so deep and intransigent in a laissez-faire economy that "ordering the current volume of investment cannot safely be left in private hands." On the other hand, he in no way intends for the State to take ownership or control of capital out of the private sector. What then does he intend? Just what is the "socialization of investment"?

There is clear evidence in the text that Keynes did not mean the *simple* substitution of public works projects for private investment. This answer would, of course, offer a way out of the apparent dilemma of leaving capital in private hands while at the same time arguing that the investment that resulted when private investors are left to their own devices is insufficient to maintain full employment; investment by the State could *replace* investment in the private sector. But by this time, Keynes was unable to see things in such a mechanical light.[18] Because the trade cycle was driven by expectations, it was impossible to ignore the effect of policy on businessmen's outlooks.

This means, unfortunately, not only that slumps and depressions are exaggerated in degree, but that economic prosperity is excessively dependent on a political and social atmosphere which is congenial to the average business man. If the fear of a Labour Government or a New Deal depresses enterprise, this need not be the result either of a reasonable calculation or of a plot with political intent; -- it is the mere consequence of upsetting the delicate balance of spontaneous optimism. In estimating the prospects of investment, we must have regard, therefore, to the nerves and hysteria and even the digestions and reactions to the weather of those upon whose spontaneous activity it largely depends.[19]

Keynes was now keenly aware of the possibility that public works might *displace* private investment and so whatever he meant by "the socialization of investment" it was *more* than the simple use of public works projects as a make-weight for private investment. His many years of work in economic policymaking had ultimately caused a change in his perspective.

III. "A Conventional Approach to Policy"

Thus, by the time Keynes had gotten to *The General Theory* he had a much more complex idea of what a good policy would be than he had in the period 1929-33 when he had been advocating large scale, loan-financed government work schemes. In the earlier period, he had dismissed the importance of confidence in the recovery saying that it would return *after* the programs he proposed had worked to stimulate profits and employment. Now, he was ready to admit that a lack of confidence could scotch even the best intentioned program.

But what, then, would constitute a good, effective policy to keep the economy at full employment? If it was not possible to simply adjust the volume of loan expenditure, then what *could* be done?

It helps, perhaps, in trying to answer these questions to look first at Keynes's proposals for monetary policy. His ideas here are straightforward and reveal a clear understanding of the problems posed by confidence and uncertainty. The key to Keynes's ideas about monetary policy was his new concept of liquidity preference; the amount of cash that people choose to hold is the crucial element in determining the rate of interest. When the demand for cash balances is high, *ceteris paribus*, interest rates will be, too, since the public's efforts to increase their cash holdings will cause interest rates to rise. Conversely, when the demand for cash balances is low, interest rates will be low.

Unfortunately, this means changes in liquidity preference may undercut efforts by the monetary authorities to stimulate the economy. If the central bank's actions *cause* changes in the public's desire to hold cash, then their efforts may be self-defeating. "Changes in the liquidity function itself, due to a change in the news which causes revision of expectations, will often be discontinuous, and will, therefore, give rise to a corresponding discontinuity of change in the rate of interest."[20] Should the authorities, for instance, try to increase the amount of money in circulation in hopes that its ready availability will cause interest rates to *fall*, the policy might backfire because the public's demand to hold cash will increase so much that interest rates will actually *rise*.

> It might be more accurate, perhaps, to say that the rate of interest is a highly conventional rather than a highly psychological, phenomenon. For its actual value is largely governed by the prevailing view as to what its value is expected to be. *Any* level of interest which is accepted with sufficient conviction as *likely* to be durable *will* be durable; subject, of course, in a changing society to fluctuations for all kinds of reasons round the expected normal. In particular, when M_l is increasing faster than M, the rate of interest will rise, and *vice versa*. But it may fluctuate for decades about a level which is chronically too high for full employment.[21]

The conundrum for the monetary authorities thus lies in fluctuating expectations. Fortunately, however, most people form their subjective expectations according to what they take to be the "conventional" view of the effects of policy. This means that if the authorities can foster a belief in their intention to keep interest rates low, the public's belief in this policy will be self-fulfilling; if the policy *convention* is one of keeping long-term interest rates low, then a *conventional outlook* will form among the public that this will be the case. One good convention leads to another.[22]

This answers, in part, the question of "What would constitute a good, effective policy to keep the economy at full employment?" As regards monetary policy, the answer is a (stable) policy of low long-term interest rates. Just as importantly, it points to the answer to the second question, "If it is not possible to simply adjust the volume of loan-expenditure, then what *could* be done?" As Keynes's vision of the possibilities for economic policy changed and matured after 1933, he came to see that maintaining the proper conventions was crucial to investment, too. Just as a well-established convention of low interest rates might be self-fulfilling, so, too, might be a well-established convention of stable, high levels of investment.

The essence, however, of this "socialization of investment" was more complex than in the case of monetary policy; decisions to make expenditures on capital outlay are vested in many places, rather than in one central authority, so there is no analogue to the central bank. It was not the case, as with monetary policy, that one agency could make a decision which then only needed to be accepted (with confidence) by the public. Whereas, in the case of monetary policy the public could be induced to hold (financial) assets by the reassurance that the authorities would keep their future yields at an appropriate level, in the case of investment in plant and equipment the future yield on these (physical) assets would be determined by many factors. Thus, the socialization of investment would necessarily involve something more than was involved with monetary policy; many kinds of good conventions would be necessary to obtain the high (and stable) levels of investment necessary to maintaining full-employment.[23]

The three most prominent ways in which Keynes meant to socialize investment by creating new conventions are each revealed in the years following the publication of *The General Theory*. Keynes did not ever actually use his ambiguous phrase again, but it is clear in his writings from 1937 to 1946 that he was trying to find practical manifestations for the ideas that flowed from his book: in particular, how effective demand could be stabilized by the stabilization of investment. In both his public writings (essays, articles, and letters to the editor) and his policy work (Commodity Policy, the Beveridge Plan, the White Paper on *Employment Policy*, the National Debt Inquiry), he developed various arguments and proposals aimed at stabilizing the aggregate level of investment. Not surprisingly, given the importance which he attached to expectations in his theory of investment, the three means to stabilization are closely interconnected.

Socializing Public Investment

One way in which Keynes hoped to socialize investment was through what he called the Public Corporations. He argued that two-thirds to three-fourths of Britain's capital stock was under the control of "corporations" which were regulated by the State or served a public function. He included the utilities, the port and dock authorities, the London County Council and building contractors in this category. This part of the capital stock, which "lie(s) half way between private and public control," seemed an obvious point of departure for developing a new convention. Keynes had written about the importance of the distinction between private and public corporations in the 1920's, especially during the Liberal Industrial Enquiry, but had dropped such talk from his policy repertoire with the publication of the *Treatise*. There are, however, important differences between his vision in the 1920's and his vision after 1936.

One difference is between the *purposes* of his argument in the two periods. In the 1920's he had been trying to argue that there were no grounds for nationalizing large scale industry. After *The General Theory*, on the other hand, he was trying to argue that these same industries could be made a part of a system of increasing and decreasing investment as was necessary for the society as a whole. These two arguments might not necessarily be so different, of course, if one just takes them to be two cases of arguing that public managers can be expected to do the 'right' thing, but there is more than this to the difference.

In arguing against nationalization in the '20's, Keynes was trying to make a point about the day-to-day operation of the public corporations. The issues at stake involved whether or not the corporations worked for the public good (rather than the stockholders' good) and whether they were managed efficiently. He argued that these corporations already attempted both to please their customers and to avoid public controversy because of their high public profile; thus, provided that more information was made public regarding their accounts, Keynes believed that adequate pressure would exist to insure that the public interest was served. Likewise, he argued that it would be possible to recruit top-notch managers to run the existing public corporations without nationalizing them.

His argument after *The General Theory* is quite different. Now instead of arguing that good men in the right position will do the right thing, Keynes argues that the control of investment by the public corporations should take place through the auspices of a "board of public investment." This board would encourage the public corporations to prepare "detailed plans" of the projects that they could profitably undertake. The board would then make financial (and design) critiques of these plans and give them back to the managers for reworking. In this way, "some large and useful projects, at least, can be launched at a few months' notice."

In stark contrast to his advice in the 1920's, however, Keynes took the last step in this process of controlling public investment to lie *outside* the corporations.[24] Rather than relying on an argument that the managers of the public corporations would undertake particular projects when the nation needed them to, he vested the responsibility for initiating the projects with the *monetary authorities*.

> There can be no justification for a rate of interest which impedes an adequate flow of new projects at a time when the national resources for production are not fully employed. The rate of interest must be reduced to the figure that the new projects can afford. In special cases subsidies may be justified; but in general it is the long-term rate of interest which should come down to the figure which the marginal project can earn. We have the power to achieve this. This Bank of England and the Treasury had a great success at the time of the conversion of the War Loan. But it is possible that they still underrate the extent of their powers. With the existing control over the exchanges which has revolutionized the technical position, and with the vast resources at the disposal of the authorities through the Bank of England, the Exchange Equalization Fund, and other funds under the control of the Treasury, it lies within their power, by the exercise of the moderation, the gradualness, and the discreet handling of the market of which they have shown themselves to be masters, to make the long-term rate of interest what they choose within reason. If we know what rate of interest is required to make profitable a flow of new projects at the proper pace, we have the power to make that rate prevail in the market.[25]

Keynes had suggested that the investment board should see that the public corporations rank their projects according to the interest rate which would make them profitable; it would then be the responsibility of the Bank of England and the Treasury to take the next step and trigger the projects ("at a few month's notice") by lowering interest rates.

This change in Keynes's approach to the public corporations may have been due to many causes. He may, for instance, have dropped his belief that good managers were likely to seek employment with such concerns. Or he may have ceased believing in the likelihood that *any* manager in such a position, left to his own, was likely to include the national interest in his firm's investment plans. The most likely reason, however, was the argument which he had first encountered in the Macmillan Committee that the planning horizon for new investment was too long to make countercyclical policy feasible.[26] These objections from the Treasury had focused on public works projects, but Keynes almost certainly came to see their general point after so many years of hearing the argument. In order to mobilize resources quickly enough to make a difference, it would require that the plans for new investment be ready to hand.

Public Works and a Balanced Budget

Just as Keynes's approach to the management of public investment changed over time, so too did his approach to public works projects. Whereas in 1929 and 1933 he had argued for discretionary, large scale projects which would lead to an unbalanced budget, he was arguing by 1944 for a regularly planned program of public works in the context of a *balanced budget*. Seen in historical context, as part of the evolution of his thinking, this change seems to have been motivated by his concern with business confidence.

His concern with confidence, however, was not *solely* about how businessmen viewed the budgetary situation. While he continued to be worried about this and recognized the potential for "upsetting the delicate balance of spontaneous optimism" (*JMK*, vii, p. 162) he was also worried about the problem of setting up mistaken expectations of a rapid expansion with poorly timed projects. This is most obvious in his collection of three short essays which appeared in *The Times* in January 1937. At this time, less than a year after the publication of *The General Theory*, Britain was experiencing a pick up in economic activity and Keynes was interested in how to sustain it. But with unemployment hovering between 10% and 11%, we find Keynes in the surprising position of arguing *against* any further stimulus from public works.

Part of Keynes's reluctance to increase loan expenditure was his belief that current expenditures could be better directed. He believed that refocusing the *direction* of the spending would yield important results which an outright increase in expenditure would not. "We are in more need today of a rightly distributed demand than of a greater aggregate demand; and the Treasury would be entitled to economize elsewhere to compensate for the cost of special assistance to the distressed areas."[27]

The real crux of his argument, however, was that continued loan expenditure at the time was likely to cause overexpansion through a sequence of mistaken expectations.

> The longer the recovery has lasted, the more difficult does it become to maintain the stability of new investment. Some of the investment which properly occurs during a recovery is, in the nature of things, non-recurrent; for example, the increase in working capital as output increases and the provision of additional equipment to keep pace with the improvement in consumption. Another part becomes less easy to sustain, not because saturation point has been reached, but because with each increase in our stock of wealth the profit to be expected from a

further increase declines. And, thirdly, the abnormal profits obtainable, during a too rapid recovery of demand, from equipment which is temporarily in short supply is likely to lead to exaggerated expectations from certain types of new investment, the disappointment of which will bring a subsequent reaction. Experience shows that this is sure to occur if aggregate investment is allowed to rise for a time above the normal proper proportion. We can also add that the rise in stock exchange values consequent on the recovery usually leads to a certain amount of expenditure paid for, not out of current income, but out of stock exchange profits, which will cease when values cease to rise further. It is evident, therefore, what a ticklish business it is to maintain stability. We have to be preparing the way for an increase in sound investments of the second type which have not yet reached saturation point, to take the place in due course of the investment of the first type which is necessarily non-current, while at the same time avoiding a temporary overlap of investments of the first and second types liable to increase aggregate investment to an excessive figure, which by inflating profits will induce unsound investment of the third type based on mistaken expectations.[28]

Thus, the state faced two problems in the use of public works: *killing* spontaneous optimism and *creating too much* of it. The right way to avoid a slump was to create a steady path to a higher level of aggregate investment. This concern was still evident a year later when, after the slump he feared had come, Keynes found himself arguing against the old saw that public projects could create no net gain in jobs.

Public loan expenditure is not, of course the only way, and not necessarily the best way, to increase employment. Nor is it always sufficiently effective to overcome other adverse influences. The state of confidence and of expectation about what will happen next, the conditions of credit, the rate of interest, the growth of population, the state of foreign trade, and the readiness of the public to spend are scarcely less important.[29]

Keynes clearly saw the proper use of public works as determined, in part, by its effect on *private* investment; instability in the one-quarter to one-third of new investment which lay in private hands possibly being enough to offset the effects of any government program.

But despite his consistent focus on expectations, Keynes's statements in 1937-38 are of an unsystematic nature. His heart attack in March 1937 kept him from his usual busy schedule and he made no attempt in the years following the publication of *The General Theory* to lay out his *general* conception of economic policymaking. Economic circumstances, too, undoubtedly kept him from focusing on the "normal" policymaking as rearmament and war planning were about to take centerstage.

The only really systematic statement of his views after *The General Theory* come from his pamphlet *How to Pay for the War* (1940) and in his work on postwar planning between 1942-45. Of these, it is his work on postwar policy that provides the clearest insights into his thinking on public works. First in 1942, and then again in 1945, Keynes advocated that the Budget be broken down into two parts, the Exchequer's Budget (ordinary government expenditure) and a Capital Budget (which would include loan financed public works which were self-liquidating). He argued strongly that the Government should always plan to balance the Exchequer's budget. "It is important to emphasize that it is no part of the purpose of the Exchequer or the Public Capital Budget to facilitate deficit financing, as I understand this term."[30] In fact, he argued that it could *best* be kept in balance by such a scheme as he advocated; if public capital expenditure was successfully undertaken so as to help dampen the trade cycle, then receipts and expenditures in the Exchequer's budget would be stabilized and so make it less likely that it would ever become unbalanced in the first place.

This focus on a balanced budget differentiates Keynes from traditional Keynesians in two senses. The first is his obvious emphasis on balanced budgets as against the normal type of Keynesian argument that unbalanced budgets can be used as a countercyclical tool. The second, related difference is his belief that consumption would make a poor countercyclical policy tool; the traditional Keynesian argument that a deficit, regardless of how incurred, will be stimulatory depends on the premise that the changes in tax receipts will cause changes in consumption.[31] This second difference is clear in his arguments as early as 1943 and he stressed it in correspondence with James Meade, one of the young economists in the Treasury's economic section who was more inclined at the time to activist policies.

> I have much less confidence than you have in off-setting proposals which aim at short-period changes in consumption. I agree with Henderson that one has to pay great attention to securing the right long-period trend in the propensity to consume. But the amount one can do in the short period is likely to be meager. I think it may be a tactical error to stress so much an unorthodox method, very difficult to put over, if, in addition to its unpopularity, it is not very likely to be efficacious.[32]

The more fully formed picture that emerges from this systematic treatment during the War is one of public works as a *preventative* tool rather than something that can be used as a short-term, discretionary policy tool. Used properly, Keynes seems to argue, they can help to alleviate the problems with expectations in both phases of the cycle. During the downturn, there need be no fear of a large-scale project which would lead to budgetary problems; on the upswing, there was no need to overstimulate expectations with unnecessary and poorly timed projects. Thus, the creation of a *balanced budget* approach to regular fluctuations in public works projects could be made a *new convention* which would yield more stability in the level of aggregate investment.

Stabilizing Private Investment

Keynes was never explicit about *exactly* what steps the government might take to insure the stability of private investment. That is, he never advocated a formal mechanism by which the volume of private investment could be adjusted to a particular level. The reason is not far to seek.

In *The General Theory*, Keynes had laid particular stress on the role of expectations in determining the amount of private investment and had attributed the trade cycle to the fluctuations in aggregate investment caused by changes in the expectations of investors. The key, then, to "controlling" private investment was to stabilize the "uncontrollable and disobedient psychology of the business world." No mechanical formula or easy state directive could accomplish this task, and Keynes had no intention of offering one.

Instead he offered his proposals for stable monetary policy and the socialization of *public* investment with the intention that they would both help to create more stable expectations among *private* investors. It is difficult to know, perhaps, what order of magnitude he placed on the relative importance of *private* investment given his idea that it constituted only a quarter to a third of *total* investment, but it was clearly enough that he was willing to acknowledge that the adverse effect on business confidence of ill-conceived public projects could undermine the State's efforts to stabilize the economy. Thus, private investment still had an important role to play in stabilizing a capitalist economy.

It took several more years, however, after the publication of *The General Theory*, to work out all the dimensions of his plan. Although he had a good idea in 1937 of how a national board of investment, together with the central bank, might influence the rate of investment of the Public Corporations (see above), it was not until he began work on postwar planning that he glimpsed the full possibility of using public works expenditure to help maintain a balanced (Exchequer's) budget.[33] With the (Exchequer's) budget constantly in balance, and with public works financed separately as self-liquidating projects, the type of shocks to confidence of which Henderson had so often complained would (he hoped) no longer be a problem. The construction and maintenance of the necessary infrastructure could be made a regular part of the State's work in such a way that it lent to the stability of employment.

Once he had developed his ideas for establishing new conventions to use monetary policy, the Public Corporations and public works to stabilize aggregate investment, his hope was that an *expectation* would form that full employment could and would be maintained. For instance, in his comments on the various documents that led up to the publication of the White Paper on *Employment Policy* he emphasized the importance of the *prevention* of cycles through the careful use of public investment, rather than short-period, discretionary efforts at counter-cyclical expenditure. And as the White Paper neared completion, his comments often turned to the overall effect of a full-employment policy on confidence.

> Such a procedure as this might give greatly increased confidence to the public that the maintenance of employment and national income was now an avowed and deliberate aim of financial and economic policy."[34]

I believe that the announcement by the Chancellor of a presentation on the above lines would have an enormous public success, since it would greatly increase confidence that the Full Employment policy is intended seriously.[35]

If a new conventional outlook could be established that the economy would run at full tilt, then Keynes's new policy conventions would be a (self-fulfilling) success.

IV. "Rules and Conventions Skillfully put across and Guilefully Preserved"

From the perspective of the late twentieth century, it is a fine irony that Maynard Keynes ended his career as the proponent of several "policy rules" which he believed could help to mitigate the trade cycle. The irony stems from the fact that macroeconomists today tend to advocate one of two mutually exclusive approaches to stabilization: one is either in favor of rules (e.g. constant money growth and a balanced budget) or of discretionary counter-cyclical policies (e.g. fluctuating interest rates and cyclically unbalanced budget). But while those who advocate rules come in many varieties (monetarists, rational expectationists, new classicals, and constitutional economists), those who advocate discretionary policies are invariably labelled as *Keynesians*.

Keynes's specific proposals do not fit neatly into either camp, however. Those today who want a rules based monetary policy believe in a money growth rule rather than an interest rate target; the experience of the great inflation in the 1970's has disabused everyone of the idea that the central bank can easily maintain a long-term policy of low interest rates. And few, if any, of the economists interested in balanced budgets see public works (and a separate capital budget) as the appropriate means of achieving their desideratum. Likewise, no school of thought comes readily to mind as the proponent of a national investment board to help lay the groundwork for the capital planning of Public Corporations: in fact, the widespread push for privatization (from both the left and the right), taken together with the corporate restructuring that has followed the increase in international competitiveness, seems to make the Public Corporation an antiquated idea.

The fact remains, however, that Keynes advocated rule based policies and that he did so for the same reasons that contemporary theorists do so; he realized that the use of short-term, discretionary policies as a *reaction* to the trade cycle is likely to set up adverse expectations that blunt their effectiveness. Repeatedly, after 1936, he backed away from the kind of grandiose policies he had advocated earlier in his life. Repeatedly he argued against the types of policies that we identify today as Keynesian. Keynes, after *The General Theory*, believed that stable, long run policies were the best route to successfully stabilizing the economy.[36]

There is another fine irony, of course, in Keynes becoming an advocate of the use of rules to help create a better world. When he was a young man he had devoted himself to the study of probability in order to disprove G.E. Moore's argument for the importance of established rules and conventions; now he found himself as an old man arguing in favor of rules and conventions as the necessary means to maintaining liberal civilization.[37] As a young man he had constructed an objective theory of probability to help establish the individual's right to ignore society's rules and make an independent judgment of the right course of action; as an old man he found it necessary to argue in favor of rules because of the "uncontrollable and disobedient" psychology of businessmen. The objective probabilities he had postulated in *A Treatise on Probability* had made it possible to ignore rules; the subjective probabilities he embraced in *The General Theory* made it necessary to follow rules.

Keynes himself was aware of the change in his outlook. In "My Early Beliefs" he reported, "We were not aware that civilization was a thin and precarious crust erected by the personality and the will of a very few, and only maintained by rules and conventions skillfully put across and guilefully preserved."[38] The change was not a bitter pill, however, for he was now able to see the sorts of rules he was advocating as the *means* to a good life. In many of the questions of *personal* morality which had driven him to his original quest for objective probability, Keynes still saw himself as an "immoralist," but he had come to the view that certain conventions were necessary to make possible the space and tolerance for what he called "personal liberty" and the "diversification of . . . fancy." Thus, in a final irony, we find Keynes concluding *The General Theory* with a defense of his policy proposals against the libertarians who might object that the proposals will lead to more State control of individual lives.

> Whilst, therefore, the enlargement of the functions of government, involved in the task of adjusting to one another the propensity to consume and the inducement to invest, would seem to a nineteenth-century publicist or to a contemporary American financier to be a terrific encroachment on individualism, I defend it, on the contrary, both as the only practicable means of avoiding the destruction of existing economic forms in their entirety and as the condition of the successful functioning of individual initiative.[39]

Keynes's realization that people would object to his ideas for many (different) reasons undoubtedly led him to the conclusion that their successful implementation would require 'skill and guile.' But while we can rightly wonder if his use of 'guile' is not a bit of playful hyperbole, he no doubt saw the very real, and delicate parameters of the problem of achieving his desired end. A nice example of this occurs in a well-known letter he wrote to Friedrich Hayek in 1944 to congratulate him on his new book, *The Road to Serfdom*. After beginning by telling Hayek that "morally and philosophically I find myself in agreement with virtually the whole of it; and not only in agreement with it, but in deeply moved agreement," Keynes goes on to discuss his practical disagreements with the book. In the process, he reveals the odd assortment of motivations and visions which lie behind opposition to and support for his own proposals.

I should therefore conclude your theme rather differently. I should say that what we want is not no planning, or even less planning, indeed I should say that we almost certainly want more. But the planning should take place in a community in which as many people as possible, both leaders and followers, wholly share your own moral position. Moderate planning will be safe if those carrying it out are rightly orientated in their own minds and hearts to the moral issue. This is in fact already true of some of them. But the curse is that there is also an important section who could almost be said to want planning not in order to enjoy its fruits but because morally they hold ideas exactly the opposite of yours, and wish to serve not God but the devil. Reading the *New Statesman & Nation* one sometimes feels that those who write there, while they cannot safely oppose moderate planning, are really hoping in their hearts that it will not succeed; and so prejudice more violent action. They fear that if moderate measures are sufficiently successful, this will allow a reaction in what you think the right and they think the wrong moral direction. Perhaps I do them an injustice; but perhaps I do not.[40]

Thus we find Keynes during the last ten years of life, as always, pushing with *unmatched* skill for the schemes and proposals he believed necessary for the solution to the economic problem. There were constant changes and innumerable compromises, but he never lost sight of his goal. In the context of the present story, he devised schemes to assuage business confidence and address the objections of Treasury mandarins, but he never lost hope that *something* could be done.[41]

Rethinking the Keynesian Revolution

Despite a quarter century of efforts to debunk the myths attached to Keynes's name, historians have been unsuccessful in producing a new public personae for him. For the general public, he is still the man who "saved capitalism" during the Great Depression. For economists, he is still the man to love, or hate, for fathering the theoretical revolution that fostered fine tuning.

If these myths are inescapable, it is because of the almost unimaginable changes in the last 60 years in the State's role in the economy. Despite the theoretical vogue among economists in the 1970's and 80's to demonstrate that economic policy is greatly limited in its effectiveness, the State *has* become involved in economic management in an irreversible fashion. While the totalitarian economies of Eastern Europe and Asia have crumbled in the last several years, the electorates in the West continue to clamor for policies of prosperity.[42] The idea that the government can (and should) manage aggregate demand to help achieve full employment is now so deeply ingrained that it requires a name. The name we have chosen--Keynesianism--also provides us with a (mythological) explanation of how we came to embrace this set of beliefs: hence the (mythological) idea of Keynes riding to the rescue to save the world from Depression with *The General Theory*.

Now, however, the scholarly revolution which has dethroned Keynes as the "saviour of capitalism" invites a re-evaluation of Keynes's own thinking. The work of the "new" Keynesian scholars has pointed to the fact that the process by which demand management became institutionalized had little (directly) to do with Keynes's ideas. But by extending their historical enquiry and considering how Keynes himself was influenced by his work in the policy process we come to another startling conclusion: by the time Keynes published *The General Theory*, he was no longer the vociferous advocate of activist fiscal policies that he once had been. Thus, it is not just that Keynes's ideas were not directly responsible for the Keynesian Revolution; his ideas are not what we have long taken them to be. Had Keynes's ideas been more influential, we might have had a different kind of Keynesian Revolution.

Notes

[1] The collection of essays edited by Peter Hall (1989) provides a rich interdisciplinary introduction to this literature.

[2] See the individual case studies in Hall (1989). There has also been an intense debate about the origins and extent of the Keynesian Revolution in Britain; this literature is reviewed in Peden (1988). Higgs (1992) questions whether the increase in economic activity in the U.S. during the Second World War is correctly described as a Keynesian stimulus.

[3] I use the phrase "new" Keynesian literature in this essay to refer to the work in several disciplines which seeks to place Keynes in historical context. I do not mean the "new Keynesian" literature of Gregory Mankiw and others who are attempting to re-introduce ideas of price rigidities into macroeconomics.

[4] Even leading economic theorists have begun to complain about the ahistorical nature of most economic theorizing. See Arrow (1985), Baumol (1991) and Solow (1985).

[5] I use the term Keynesian Revolution in this essay to refer to the widespread adaptation of demand management policies during the 20th century. I do *not* refer to the academic, theoretical Revolution that followed the publication of *The General Theory*. For more on this other sense of the Keynesian Revolution see Dimand (1988) and Patinkin (1993).

[6] See also Bateman (1994).

[7] The first reference I can find using this moniker is Gerrard (1991).

[8] Much of the relevant testimony is reprinted in *JMK*, xx. See also Clarke (1989). Following a now standard convention, citations to Keynes's *Collected Writings* are given as *JMK* followed by the volume number (and page number, where appropriate).

[9] The bulk of this correspondence is reproduced in *JMK*, xx, xxi.

[10] Notable exceptions are Meltzer (1989) and Skidelsky (1992).

[11] See Meltzer (1981, 1989).

[12] See Meltzer (1989) and Bateman (1991).

[13] Patinkin (1990).

[14] This marks a return for Keynes to an earlier adherence to Cambridge cycle theory.

[15] *JMK*, vii, p. 313.

[16] *JMK*, vii, pp. 320-21.

[17] Ibid, pp. 377-78.

[18] I owe the important insight that Keynes dropped his mechanical, magic formula mentality after 1931 to Patinkin (1976).

[19] *JMK*, vii, p. 162.

[20] Ibid, p. 198.

[21] Ibid., pp. 203-4.

[22] This argument adumbrates a part of Bateman (1991).

[23] Much of the argument here questions the more traditional interpretation of Patinkin (1976, 1982, 1990) that Keynes continued to be an advocate of activist fiscal policy.

[24] Robert Skidelsky's (1989) argument that Keynes's writings about "socialized firms" are consistent through the 1920s and 1930s is clearly mistaken. This undercuts his argument that the later Keynes was a Victorian advocate of public service.

[25] *JMK*, xxi, p. 395.

[26] See Clarke (1989) and Peden (1988).

[27] *JMK*, xxi, p. 385.

[28] *JMK*, xxi, pp. 387-8.

[29] *JMK*, xxi, pp. 429-30.

[30] *JMK*, xxvii, p. 406.

[31] It has also been frequently maintained by Keynesians that any government expenditure, rather for investment or consumption purposes, will have an equal effect on the economy.

[32] *JMK*, xxvii, p. 326.

[33] The best survey of Keynes's thinking (through time) on budgetary policy is in N.H. Dimsdale (1987).

[34] *JMK*, xxvii. p. 369.

[35] Ibid, p. 413.

[36] Contrast this conclusion with Patinkin's (1990, 225-33).

[37] See Bateman (1988) for a full account of Keynes's early argument against rules.

[38] Keynes (1938, p. 99)

[39] *JMK*, vii, p. 380.

[40] *JMK*, xxvii, p. 387.

[41] Dimand and Dimand (1990) contains an excellent explanation of Keynes's proposals (after *The General Theory*) to stabilize commodity prices using buffer stocks.

[42] The persistent belief that elected officials can affect the level of U.S. economic activity is documented nicely in Morris (1993).

References

Arrow, Kenneth J. (1985) "Maine and Texas," *American Economic Review*, 75, pp. 320-23.

Bateman, Bradley W. (1988) "G.E. Moore and J.M. Keynes: A Missing Chapter in the History of the Expected Utility Model," *American Economic Review*, 78, pp. 1098-1106.

_____. (1991) "The Rules of the Road," in Bradley W. Bateman and John B. Davis, eds. *Keynes and Philosophy: Essays on the Origin of Keynes's Thought*. Aldershot: Edward Elgar, pp. 55-68.

_____. (1994) "In the Realm of Concept and Circumstance," *History of Political Economy*, 26.

Baumol, William J. (1991) "Toward a Newer Economics: The Future Lies Ahead!" *Economic Journal*, 101, pp. 1-8.

Clarke, Peter F. (1989) *The Keynesian Revolution in the Making: 1924-1936*. Oxford University Press: Oxford.

Dimand, Robert W. (1988) *The Origins of the Keynesian Revolution*. Stanford: Stanford University Press.

_____ and Mary Ann Dimand (1990) "J.M. Keynes on Buffer Stocks and Commodity Price Stabilization," *History of Political Economy*, 23, pp. 113-24.

Dimsdale, N.H. (1987) "Keynes on British Budgetary Policy 1914-46," in Michael J. Boskin, John S. Flemming, and Stephan Gorini, eds. *Private Saving and Public Debt*. Oxford: Basil Blackwell, pp. 208-33.

Gerrard, Bill. (1991) "Keynes's *General Theory*: Interpreting the Interpretations," *Economic Journal*, 101, pp. 276-87.

Hall, Peter, ed. (1989) *The Political Power of Economic Ideas: Keynesianism Across Nations*. Princeton: Princeton University Press.

Higgs, Robert. (1992) "Wartime Prosperity? A Reassessment of the U.S. Economy in the 1940s," *The Journal of Economic History*, 52, pp. 41-60.

Keynes, John Maynard. (1938) "My Early Beliefs," *Two Memoirs*. London: Rupert Hart-Davis. Reprinted in *JMK*, ix.

───────────. (1981) *Activities 1929-31: Rethinking Employment and Unemployment Policies*, Donald Moggridge, ed. *The Collected Writings of J.M. Keynes*, Vol. XX. London: Macmillan.

───────────. (1982) *Activities 1931-39: World Crises and policies in Britain and America*, Donald Moggridge, ed. The Collected Writings of J.M. Keynes, Vol. XXI. London: Macmillan.

─────────── and Hubert Henderson. (1929) *Can Lloyd George Do It?: An Examination of the Liberal Pledge*. Reprinted in *JMK*, ix.

Meltzer, Allan H. (1981) "Keynes's *General Theory*: A Different Perspective," *Journal of Economic Literature*, 29, pp. 34-64.

───────────. (1989) *Keynes's Monetary Theory: A Different Interpretation*. Cambridge: Cambridge University Press.

Morris, Charles R. (1993) "It's Not the Economy, Stupid," *The Atlantic Monthly*, 272, pp. 49-62.

Patinkin, Don. (1976) *Keynes' Monetary Thought: A Study of its Development*. Durham, NC: Duke University Press.

───────────. (1982) Anticipations of the *General Theory*? And Other Essays on Keynes. Chicago: University of Chicago Press.

───────────.(1990) "On Different Interpretations of the *General Theory*," *Journal of Monetary Economics*, 26, pp. 205-43.

───────────. (1993) "On The Chronology of The *General Theory*," Economic *Journal*, 103, pp. 647-63.

Peden, G.C. (1988) *Keynes, the Treasury, and British Economic Policy*, London: Macmillan.

Rymes, Thomas K., ed. (1989) *Keynes's Lectures, 1932-35*: Notes of a Representative Student. London: Macmillan.

Skidelsky, Robert. (1989) "Keynes and the State," in Dieter Helm, ed. *The Economic Borders of the State*. Oxford University Press: Oxford.

───────────. (1992) *John Maynard Keynes, Vol. 2: The Economist As Savior, 1920-37*, London: Macmillan.

Solow, Robert M. (1985) "Economic History and Economics," *American Economic Review*, 75, pp. 328-31.

EXPECTATIONS, CONFIDENCE AND THE KEYNESIAN REVOLUTION

COMMENT BY ROBERT W. DIMAND

The relationship of Keynes's *Treatise on Probability* (1921) to his *General Theory of Employment, Interest and Money* (1936) has been the subject of intense discussion and controversy in recent years, with the appearance of books by Anna Carabelli, Rod O'Donnell, and Athol Fitzgibbons and volumes edited by O'Donnell, by Bateman and Davis, by Lawson and Pesaran, and by Gerrard and Hillard. Keynes's views about probability and reasonable ways to form expectations about an uncertain future have attracted so much attention because it is the dependence of liquidity preference and the marginal efficiency of capital on volatile long period expectations that accounts for the volatility of private investment in the *General Theory*. These investment fluctuations are the source of the failure of the economy to be remain in stable equilibrium at full employment without government stabilization. As Keynes remarked in his notes for his 1937 lectures (1973, XIV, 183), he was prepared to be more classical than the Swedes in assuming that short period expectations were always realized. Long period expectations, however, are subject to fundamental uncertainty and may be drastically revised in response to news or changes in animal spirits.

Bradley Bateman succeeds in his important and scholarly paper, "Rethinking the Keynesian Revolution," in saying something new on this subject, and in basing his argument on careful examination of the historical evidence. Other writers tracing the development of Keynes's thought on expectation and uncertainty from 1921 to 1936 have concentrated on his discussion of probability in his memorial article on Frank Ramsey. Bateman focuses instead on Keynes's attitude to the concept of business confidence, which Bateman identifies closely with the expectations of entrepreneurs. From his consideration of Keynes on confidence, Bateman proceeds to interpret Keynes's proposed "socialization of investment" in terms of creating policy conventions conducive to a stable aggregate level of effective demand, rather than discretionary, short run fiscal policy.

Bateman draws on Keynes's *Collected Writings* to show Keynes as critical of the importance of confidence from the Macmillan Committee hearings of 1930 to the spring of 1933, when Hubert Henderson, then joint secretary of the Economic Advisory Council, wrote to him that "You often say -- 'It's nonsense to talk about confidence; confidence depends on orders'" (Keynes 1981, XX, 166). Henderson, who had written *Can Lloyd George Do It?* with Keynes in 1929, had turned against public works as a remedy for unemployment, and subsequently denounced the *General Theory* before the Marshall Society at

Cambridge, as well as in a review. He argued that deficit-financed fiscal expansion would reduce private investment by weakening confidence.

Opponents of expansionary fiscal and monetary policy frequently warned of the effect of budget deficits or leaving the gold standard on business confidence. The need to restore Wall Street confidence in the fiscal soundness of the U. S. government contributed to the Revenue Act of 1932, which raised the maximum income tax rate from 24% to 63%. Even economists who favored reflation were deterred by the possible effect of deficits on business confidence. Sumner Slichter of the Harvard Business School, while "emphatically ... not in favor of attempting to balance the budget in the midst of depression," warned in 1933 that "*if the deficit is too large and excites too much alarm, its net effect may be deflationary*" (Garraty 1987, 19). Jacob Viner (1933, 18-19), then at the University of Chicago, held that "The outstanding though unintentional achievement of the Hoover Administration in counteracting the depression has in fact been its deficits of the last two years, and it was only its own alleged fears as to the ill effects of these deficits, and the panic which the big business world professed to foresee if these deficits should recur, which have made this method of depression finance seriously risky. Had the government and the business magnates retained their mental balance, there would have been less cause to fear net ill effects during a depression than during the war from even a ten billion dollar deficit." Despite considering business panic over budget deficits irrational, Viner remained sufficiently worried about the effect of deficits on confidence to resign as adviser to the Treasury Department in protest against deficit finance in response to the 1938 recession, objecting that "I believe that heavy deficit spending ... will involve serious dangers" (Garraty 1987, 159n). Sutton, Harris, Kaysen and Tobin (1962, 216, 223) provide noteworthy quotes from the Economic Principles Commission of the National Association of Manufacturers about the effect of activist government on business confidence.

It is highly plausible that Keynes was averse to the notion of confidence because the threat to business confidence was used as a bogeyman to ward off fiscal or monetary expansion in the depression. Even a committee of economists advising the British cabinet in November 1932, believing that deflation would reduce economic activity, felt able only to recommend that deflation "not be carried further in a time of depression than considerations of confidence really justify" (Howson and Winch 1977, 284). It is also clear, as Bateman notes, that the student notes assembled and edited by T. K. Rymes (1989) show uncertainty and expectations figuring prominently in Keynes's lectures in the Michaelmas term of 1933. This appearance of expectations in Keynes's lectures deserves closer attention than the single sentence that Bateman accords it before going on to consider the implications for Keynes's views on fiscal policy.

The expectations that appear in Keynes's lectures are not quite the same as the confidence cited by the opponents of budget deficits. The marginal efficiency of capital is an expectation in the minds of entrepreneurs, and reflects the optimism or pessimism with which they form their expectations. It involves, however, a subjective expectation about something in particular, being the rate of discount that would equate the present value of the expected stream of earnings from a capital asset to the replacement cost of the asset. Confidence, as the term was used in popular discussions of economic policy, came to refer to a general sense of well-being on the part of the business community, fed by traditional, familiar and pro-business policies. If the marginal efficiency of capital was what entrepreneurs expected would be the stream of earnings from an additional capital asset, there was no reason within Keynes's system why deficit-financed public works, raising the equilibrium level of income, should lower this expectation. The later Keynes was sensitive as a policy advisor to the effect of policies on expectations, just as in chapter 19 of the *General Theory* he considered the effect of wage deflation on expectations, but his concept of expectation was more of an expectation about something than was Henderson's deficit-shy, panic-prone confidence.

There is a striking feature of Keynes's lecture of 4 December 1933 (Rymes 1989, 125), relevant to his view of expectation, confidence, and their implications for fiscal policy. This was the concluding lecture of the series of that he gave that Michaelmas term. In that lecture, he summarized his new theory in equations and commentary. The variable W, "State of the News," appears as an argument in three functions: liquidity preference, investment, and consumption. (Keynes also used W for the money wage rate in the same lecture, at which point Lorie Tarshis, copying Robert Bryce's notes for the lecture, wrote "*why in hell?* See Bob!" Rymes 1989, 126n.) The dependence of liquidity preference and the marginal efficiency of capital on long period expectations (the state of the news), causing private investment to be volatile, was continued up to and in the *General Theory*. The state of the news vanished, however, from the consumption function after the December 1933 lecture. With the marginal propensity to consume and hence the multiplier known, the government could select the appropriate fiscal policy to offset observed fluctuations in private investment. In Keynes's Michaelmas 1933 formulation, however, the consumption function also depended on uncertain expectations and revision of expectations could change the value of the multiplier. Countercyclical fiscal policy would not be feasible with an unpredictable multiplier. In the Michaelmas terms of 1934 and 1935, Keynes discussed the motives to consume and save and used the marginal propensity to consume to derive the multiplier, but did not write down the consumption function.

A piece of the context for Keynes's attitude towards confidence, not cited by Bateman in the present version of his paper, is the psychological theory of the trade cycle presented by A. C. Pigou in *Industrial Fluctuations* (1927, 2nd ed. 1929). Pigou (1927, 66, 79) attributed economic fluctuations, at least in substantial part, to "variations in the tone of mind of persons whose action controls industry, emerging in errors of undue optimism or undue pessimism in their business forecasts" which spread contagiously through "a quasi-hypnotic system of mutual suggestion" (see Macfie 1934, chapter IX). The fluctuations would be rhythmic because "errors of either sort ... have the characteristic of generating, after a while, errors of the opposite sort" (Pigou 1927, 83). Pigou thus stressed animal spirits as a source of fluctuations, with the trade cycle driven by exogenous, random changes in tone of mind. A similar psychological account of the cycle had been offered by another Cambridge economist, Frederick Lavington, a former pupil of Keynes who succeeded Keynes as Girdlers' Lecturer in 1921 (Lavington 1922, Macfie 1934, 141), and the approach had strong Marshallian roots. Keynes was not impressed by *Industrial Fluctuations*, judging the book "rather miserable" and writing to Lydia that "Perhaps Mrs Marshall is right that [Pigou] should have married, his mind is dead, he just arranges in a logical order all the things we knew before" (letter of 21 February 1927, Moggridge 1992, 434n). Keynes was acquainted with confidence-based explanations of economic fluctuations from his Cambridge colleagues before 1930, but did not find them persuasive.

In his opening and concluding paragraphs, Bateman refers to recent scholarship showing how little direct influence Keynes and his ideas had on the institutionalization of demand management in most countries. Canada may be noted as an exception to this statement. While, as Scott Gordon (1965) observed on the twentieth anniversary of the 1945 White Paper on Employment and Income, Keynesian ideas did not penetrate deeply into Canada's journalistic and business communities, they were absorbed by the group of academics and senior bureaucrats who developed a symbiotic relationship with the governing party during the long Liberal administration of 1935-57 (Campbell 1987, Granatstein 1982, Owram 1986, Wolfe 1984). A. F. Wynne Plumptre of the University of Toronto, wartime financial attaché in Washington and at Bretton Woods and Assistant Deputy Minister of Finance from 1954 to 1965, studied with Keynes at Cambridge in the late 1920s. Robert Bryce attended Keynes's lectures for three years and was a member of Keynes's Political Economy Club, and presented Keynes's ideas at LSE and Harvard (Keynes 1979, XXIX, 132-50). Recruited into the Finance Department as a recognized Keynesian in October 1938, he rose rapidly to be assistant to the Deputy Minister, secretary to the Economic Advisory Committee from its formation in September 1939, Secretary to the Treasury Board 1947-54, Secretary to the Cabinet and Clerk of the Privy Council 1954-63, and Deputy Minister of Finance 1963-70. Bryce, who kept the minutes during Keynes's visits to Ottawa in August and November 1944, recalls that Keynes's "exercise of fluency and charm was so powerful that the Canadian ministers preferred to take their decisions after they had met with him rather than while they were still under his spell" (Bryce 1988, 150, LePan 1979, 70). The poet and diplomat Douglas LePan offers a vivid portrayal of Keynes's May 1945 discussions at King's College with a Canadian delegation led by W. A. Mackintosh of Queen's University, acting Deputy Minister of Finance and author of the April 1945 White Paper, meetings that "showed in a remarkable way Keynes' closeness to his friends in Ottawa and his trust in them" (LePan 1979, 96). Such consultations with Keynes began with a delegation in October 1942 led by Mackintosh (Mackintosh 1965, 9-10). Postwar Canadian demand management, following the 1945 White Paper committing Canada to a high employment policy, was strongly and directly influenced by contact with Keynes and his ideas, adapted to a natural resource-exporting small open economy.

In his subsection "Socializing public investment," Bateman states that Keynes changed his position after the *General Theory* to the "quite different" position that a "board of public investment" should control the volume of investment by public corporations. Keynes reached such a position several years earlier. In the Winter 1932-33 inaugural issue of the *Economic Forum*, Keynes proposed a National Investment Board to control the volume of capital spending by the central government, local authorities and public boards such as the Central Electricity Board, the Port of London, and the Metropolitan Water Board, as well as construction financed by the Building Societies, which Keynes regarded as semi-public (see Dimand 1991, 13-14). He offered this as an alternative to a resolution passed by the annual conference of the Labour Party, which proposed a National Investment Board designed to protect investors, rather like the Securities and Exchange Commission established in the United States in 1933. Keynes's proposed board would control the larger part of investment spending. He did not in 1932 extend his proposal, as in the later version discussed by Bateman, to having private businesses list their investment projects with the board, together with the interest rate which would trigger each project.

Bateman draws attention to Keynes's skepticism about tax-induced changes in consumption as a countercyclical policy tool, as reflected in Keynes's 1943 letter to James Meade (Keynes 1980, XXVII, 326), quoted by Bateman. Such countercyclical adjustment of consumption had been advocated by Meade in his book on *Consumers' Credits and Unemployment*, which Keynes had reviewed in the *Economic Journal* in 1938. I would also draw attention to a reason offered by Keynes for the inefficacy of short-term management of consumption: "A remission of taxation on which people could only rely for an indefinitely short period might have very limited effect in stimulating their consumption" (Keynes 1980, XXVII, 320). In contrast to the stereotypical Keynesian linkage of consumption only to current disposable income, Keynes, like the postwar consumption theorists, discounted the impact on current consumption of a change in disposable income that consumers expected to be temporary.

As Bateman reminds us, the *General Theory* is not a polemic for fiscal fine tuning, and Keynes was attentive to the effect of public policy on expectations and private investment. In his conclusion, however, Bateman appears to go further than this, and to dismiss as mythical the association of the name of Keynes with the notion that governments can and should manage aggregate demand to help achieve full employment: by 1936, Keynes "was no longer the vociferous advocate of activist fiscal policies that he had once been. Thus, it is not just that Keynes's ideas were not directly responsible for the Keynesian Revolution [in public policy]; his ideas are not what we have long taken them to be." This is a stronger conclusion than is supported by the evidence presented in the body of the paper. There is more to fiscal policy than fine tuning. Keynes's proposals in 1939 and 1940 about *How to Pay for the War* took a fiscal approach to managing aggregate demand to avoid wartime inflation, and in discussions leading to the White Paper on postwar economic policy he supported a commitment to maintaining a low level of unemployment. As for his earlier period as a "vociferous advocate of activist fiscal policies," it is noteworthy how in *A Treatise on Money* (1930), Keynes treated the sort of fiscal stimulus envisioned in the Lloyd George pledge endorsed by Keynes and Henderson the previous year. Keynes considered public works in 1930 as a second-best national alternative, to be resorted to in the absence of international cooperation for a concerted monetary expansion. As Bateman states in the lines immediately before his conclusion, "There were constant changes and innumerable compromises, but [Keynes] never lost sight of his goal ... he never lost hope that *something* could be done."

Keynes's central message to the economics profession and to policy makers was that decentralized market forces do not guarantee full employment in the absence of government intervention, and that government action can reduce involuntary unemployment by expanding effective demand. His concern appeared in his 1924 question, "Does Unemployment Need a Drastic Remedy?," well before he developed his theory of how involuntary unemployment can occur and persist and how it can be alleviated. Fluctuations in investment spending, due to revision of long period expectations, drove fluctuations in aggregate demand. Recent writers on Keynes's views on probability and uncertainty have extensively studied the basis of these volatile expectations. Other scholars, notably Don Patinkin, have considered the development of Keynes's theory of aggregate effective demand, which translates a change in investment into a change in the equilibrium level of income. As I have suggested elsewhere (e.g. *The Origins of the Keynesian Revolution*, 1988), I find another aspect of the *General Theory* at least as crucial as volatile expectations or the determination of aggregate demand, but not as thoroughly covered in the literature. This is Keynes's analysis of why market forces may be too weak to clear the labor market and how changes in aggregate demand affect real output. The term Keynesian is used in macroeconomics (as distinct from the "new Keynesian" historical scholarship noted by Bateman) to refer to approaches in which the labor market does not always clear and systematic aggregate demand policy affects output and employment. I find this usage to be appropriate in light of what I take to be Keynes's central message, and not a piece of mythmaking.

References

Bryce, R. B. (1988) "Keynes During the Great Depression and World War II," in O. F. Hamouda and J. N. Smithin, eds. *Keynes and Public Policy After Fifty Years*. Aldershot: Edward Elgar, pp. 146-50.

Campbell, R. M. (1987) *Grand Illusions: The Politics of the Keynesian Experience in Canada 1945-75*. Peterborough, ONT, and Lewiston, NY: Broadview Press.

Dimand, R. W. (1988) *The Origins of the Keynesian Revolution.* Aldershot: Edward Elgar and Stanford, CA: Stanford University Press.

_____. (1991) "Cranks, Heretics and Macroeconomics in the 1930s," *History of Economics Review.* No. 16, pp. 11-30.

Garraty, J. A. (1987) *The Great Depression.* Garden City, NY: Anchor Books.

Gordon, H. S. (1965) "A Twenty Year Perspective: Some Reflections on the Keynesian Revolution in Canada," in S. F. Kaliski, ed., *Canadian Economic Policy Since the War,* Canadian Trade Committee, no place [Montreal?], pp. 23-46.

Granatstein, J. L. (1982) *The Ottawa Men: The Civil Service Mandarins, 1935-57.* Toronto: Oxford University Press.

Howson, S., and D. Winch (1977) *The Economic Advisory Council.* Cambridge: Cambridge University Press.

Keynes, J. M. (1971-89) *Collected Writings,* ed. E. A. G. Robinson and D. E. Moggridge. 30 Vols., London: Macmillan and New York: Cambridge University Press for the Royal Economic Society.

Lavington, F. (1922) *The Trade Cycle.* London: P. S. King.

LePan, D. V. (1979) "Introduction to Economics: Lord Keynes and the Audit Room Meetings," in LePan, *Bright Glass of Memory.* Toronto: McGraw-Hill-Ryerson.

Macfie, A. L. (1934) *Theories of the Trade Cycle.* London: Macmillan.

Mackintosh, W. A. (1965) "The White Paper on Employment and Income in Its 1945 Setting," in S. F. Kaliski, ed., *Canadian Economic Policy Since the War.* Canadian Trade Committee, no place [Montreal?], pp. 9-21.

Moggridge, D. E. (1992) *Maynard Keynes, An Economist's Biography.* London and New York: Routledge.

Owram, D. (1986) *The Government Generation: Canadian Intellectuals and the State 1900-1945.* Toronto: University of Toronto Press.

Pigou, A. C. (1927) *Industrial Fluctuations.* London: Macmillan.

Rymes, T. K. (1989) *Keynes's Lectures, 1932-35: Notes of a Representative Student.* Ann Arbor: University of Michigan Press and London: Macmillan.

Sutton, F. X., S. E. Harris, C. Kaysen and J. Tobin (1962). *The American Business Creed.* New York: Schocken Books.

Viner, J. (1933) *Balanced Deflation, Inflation, or More Depression.* University of Minnesota Press, Minneapolis, as reprinted by Garland Publishing, New York and London, 1983.

Wolfe, D. A. (1984) "The Rise and Demise of the Keynesian Era in Canada: Economic Policy, 1930-1982," in M. S. Cross and G. S. Kealey, eds., *Modern Canada 1930-1980s,* Volume 5 of *Readings in Canadian Social History.* Toronto: McClelland and Stewart, pp. 46-78.

5 KEYNES'S VISION: METHOD, ANALYSIS AND "TACTICS"

G. C. Harcourt and C. Sardoni[*]

The "Keynesian revolution" is linked in an indissoluble way to the publication of *The General Theory* in 1936. This was the book that, for Keynes, was to "largely revolutionise (...) the way the world thinks about economic problems," and that had to "knock away" the Ricardian foundations of Marxism. *The General Theory* and its revolutionary impact can be best understood and appreciated only if we take into serious account all of Keynes's previous work.[1] Moreover, *The General Theory* has to be read and interpreted also by taking account of Keynes's tactics in dealing with the profession in the attempt to introduce his new ideas, and to persuade them of their correctness.

At the analytical and methodological levels, Keynes's contribution in *The General Theory* may perhaps be best appreciated and understood by considering two fundamental elements: his Marshallian legacy and his earlier work on philosophical issues, especially on probability and uncertainty. The next two sections of our paper are an attempt to reconstruct the "methodological core" of *The General Theory* in the light of these two elements. More specifically, section 2 deals with Keynes's Marshallian inheritance and its impact on his work from *A Treatise on Probability* to *The General Theory*. Section 3 is concerned with a reconstruction of the logical structure of the model underlying *The General Theory*. The nature of such a model is explained by taking into consideration Keynes's ideas concerning economics as a "moral science" and his unwillingness to get too far from the "real world," in which institutions and conventions naturally play crucial roles which cannot be ignored. In *The General Theory* there are, as it were, some "mysteries" concerning the reasons why Keynes chose not to deal with certain issues or why he chose to deal with them in particular ways. In the paper we discuss three of these "mysteries": why did Keynes decide to ignore the issue of market structures in *The General Theory* despite his knowledge of the debate which was going on at that time in Britain and US? Why did he take the supply of money as an exogenous variable despite his previous work, especially in *A Treatise on Money*, in which he had convincingly shown that the money supply is endogenous? Why did he choose to deal with a closed economy when he spent so much of his professional life studying and discussing international economic issues?

There can be various different reasons for such choices by Keynes but we feel that one particular reason may have been decisive. Keynes's main objective in writing *The General Theory* was to convince his "fellow economists" of what he felt was of fundamental importance: to get rid of the analytical strictures of Say's Law and the quantity theory of money, in order to show that there are no automatic mechanisms at work which necessarily bring the economy to full employment. Getting rid of these strictures meant recognizing the need for suitable policies to correct the spontaneous behaviour of the economy. From this point of view, it may well be that Keynes decided to avoid complications and unnecessary controversies which would have taken the emphasis away from his central and crucial message.

In section 4, we discuss Keynes's attitude towards these topics by pointing out that Keynes's tactics were neither necessarily wise nor successful. Quite the contrary, it is reasonable to hold that, in several cases, Keynes's choices might have been responsible for serious misinterpretations of his theory, and for lessening or blurring the impact on those he wished to convince.

FROM *A TREATISE ON PROBABILITY* TO *THE GENERAL THEORY* AND THE MARSHALLIAN LEGACY

In order to put Keynes's vision into perspective it is useful to start with his own legacy when he decided to become an economist in the early part of this century. Keynes himself (and others on his behalf, notably Joan Robinson) claimed that he tried to change our *method* of doing economics as well as our way of *seeing* how our economies work.[2]

To make the case for a change in method we must remind ourselves of two important facts: first, that Keynes came to economics through his own distinctive kind of philosophy, and concern with certain philosophical issues; secondly, that his earliest mentor in economics, and one by whose methods he was greatly influenced, was Alfred Marshall. As to the philosophical aspects, though Keynes read mathematics as an undergraduate, he seems to have spent as much time on philosophical issues and he was much influenced by the philosophers of his day at Cambridge - McTaggart, G. E. Moore, Bertrand Russell, Whitehead and, of course, Wittgenstein and Frank Ramsey.[3]

His first major research project, as we would say now, was his fellowship dissertation for King's College,[4] which eventually became *A Treatise on Probability* (1921; KCW/VIII). A key theme of the dissertation was Keynes's argument that in certain disciplines, the whole need not *only* be the sum of the parts. Keynes's realization of this, that overall systems could have separate lives of their own, that indeed the behaviour of parts could themselves be constrained by overall relationships, and that profound implications followed from this realization greatly influenced his subsequent work on economics. Here is a typical statement by Keynes of this view, in this instance in his 1926 biographical essay on Edgeworth, where he is discussing "the application of mathematical method to the measurement of economic value."

> Mathematical Psychics has not (...) fulfilled its early promise (...) When the young Edgeworth chose it, he may have looked to find secrets as wonderful as those which the physicists have found since those days (...) this has not happened (...) The atomic hypothesis which has worked so splendidly in physics breaks down in psychics. We are faced at every turn with the problems of organic unity, of

discreteness, of discontinuity - the whole is not equal to the sum of the parts, comparisons of quantity fail us, small changes produce large effects, the assumptions of a uniform and homogeneous continuum are not satisfied. (KCW/X: 262).

Keynes's full and mature realization of its significance came to fruition in *The General Theory*, not least in one of the meanings that he attached to the term "general" and his repeated stress on the need to avoid the fallacy of composition when the workings of the economy as a whole are considered. Thus, in the preface to the French edition (dated 20 February 1939), he wrote:

I have called my theory a *general* theory. I mean by this that I am chiefly concerned with the behaviour of the economic system as a whole - with aggregate incomes, aggregate profits, aggregate output, aggregate employment, aggregate investment, aggregate saving rather than with the incomes, profits, output, employment, investment and saving of particular industries, firms or individuals. And I argue that important mistakes have been made through extending to the system as a whole conclusions which have been correctly arrived at in respect of a part of it taken in isolation. (KCW/VII: xxxii)

And in the original preface (dated 13 December 1935) he wrote:

Our method of analysing the economic behaviour of the present under the influence of changing ideas about the future is one which depends on the interaction of supply and demand, and is in this way linked up with our fundamental theory of value. We are thus led to a more general theory, which includes the classical theory with which we are familiar, as a special case. (KCW/VII: xxii-xxiii)

Another issue which preoccupied Keynes in *A Treatise on Probability* and which was vitally relevant for his economics was his systematic pondering on the principles of reasonable behaviour in an uncertain environment. This major theme of *A Treatise on Probability* and the approach and conclusions which Keynes came to fitted very neatly with Marshall's stress, which runs through the *Principles*, on the nature of reasonable behaviour of businessmen in particular in their own uncertain environments.[5]

Keynes's philosophical reasoning discerned many different appropriate languages for different situations and areas. In effect, he believed there was a *spectrum* of appropriate languages which ran all the way from poetry to formal logic and all of which were consistent with arguments being possible and knowledge being acquired. This view clashed starkly with the views of Russell, the early Wittgenstein and Ramsey of his day.[6] In 1924, Keynes wrote:

The gradual perfection of the formal treatment [of logic] at the hands of [Russell], of Wittgenstein and of Ramsey had been, however, gradually to empty it of content and to reduce it more and more to mere dry bones, until finally it seemed to exclude not only all experience, but most of the principles, usually reckoned logical, of reasonable thought. (KCW/X: 338)

Keynes went on to ask, in effect, the rhetorical question: "Can these dry bones live?"[7]

Keynes's philosophical attitudes meant that in his economics he never liked to stray very far from actual happenings, from concrete situations and the use of language and concepts and practices which were grounded in them, though he was, of course, exceptionally careful about definitions and the appropriate choice of units for his actual theorizing. Thus, in *The General Theory* itself, he placed much emphasis on his chapter 4, "The choice of units," and he wrote: "In dealing with the theory of employment I propose (...) to make use of only two fundamental units of quantity, namely quantities of money-value and quantities of employment. The first of these is strictly homogeneous, and the second can be made so" (KCW/VII: 41). He felt that "perfect precision" was needed for causal analysis and for quantitative analysis, "whether or not our knowledge of the actual values of the relevant quantities is complete or exact" (KCW/VII: 40). Clearly such an attitude is consistent with Marshall's insistence on the use of empirical generalizations as the basis for "formal" theory, in contrast to the very rigorous, concise and precise axiomatic approach.

Keynes and Marshall often preferred to be "vaguely right rather than precisely wrong"[8] and they hoped, though their hopes were not always fulfilled, that people would look at their theories, their systems, generously and in the large, rather than nit pick about details.[9] Nevertheless, both were very careful to try to define the limitations of theory and clearly to demarcate where it left off and reality began, to ask how far structures could be true in their own domain and, a separate point, illuminate actual situations.

Keynes absorbed Marshall's careful definitions of the short period and of the long period, whereby what was and what was not impounded in the *cet. par.* pound was the crucial distinction. This implied that "period" referred to a logical, theoretical construction while "run" referred to historical situations and events, to actual stretches of calendar time.[10] It enabled him to adapt Marshall's static supply and demand analysis in a manner which allowed him both to tackle the dynamic problems of the trade cycle and to put content to the inherent tendency of capitalist economies to generate sustained and persistent forces which not only brought about prolonged slumps but also made full employment situations tend to be rare and unsustained occurrences. In doing so he shifted the principal emphasis from the long period, which Kahn (1929: 1) considered to be "the real business of the *Principles*," to the short period.

In making this step Keynes departed quite radically from Marshall, especially Marshall of the *Principles* with his emphasis on normal situations and the equilibrium of supply and demand, which implied an overall situation of full employment, but also Marshall of the, never satisfactorily written, volume II on money. Here, again, the shadowy world of a Say's Law full employment equilibrium position was still the essential backdrop. For in the "normal" world of volume I of the *Principles* monetary disturbances were absent, relative prices and their accompanying quantities were of central importance while the analysis itself was deliberately partial, for all of Marshall's well known reasons. There was, nevertheless, an underlying general equilibrium model of the whole economy, the long-period equilibrium positions of which were ones where supply and demand were equated in every market, including labour markets. The role of the (real) rate of interest was then to equate real saving and real investment and to bring about in effect the optimum saving programme of the community and its inhabitants.

The determination of the *overall* level of output and employment was not an interesting theoretical problem in itself, since in principle it only required a simple summation of the quantities and employments of individual markets. Thus, a properly constituted volume II on money would have included a discussion of the determinants of the general price level, of money prices overall, with which could be coupled the volume of overall output implied by volume I. This would provide in turn a backdrop to discussions of monetary and banking matters and policy, the appropriate institutional arrangements through which could be pursued both stable overall prices at the implied overall level of activity and which would help to guide the economy with a minimum of monetary dislocation to a new overall long-period equilibrium when either tastes, or techniques, or endowments, or all together, changed.

So Keynes took over Marshall's method and in *The General Theory* used much space to discuss the forces which determined the equilibrium level of employment, though he did sometimes discuss simultaneously how the equilibrium could be attained. He later came to regret this mode of exposition. For example, in his 1937 lectures, he wrote: "If I were writing the book again I should begin by setting forth my theory on the assumption that short-period expectations were always fulfilled; and then have a subsequent chapter showing what differences it makes when short-period expectations are disappointed" (KCW/XIV: 181). He seems to have had Hawtrey particularly in mind at this juncture for he mentions in a number of places (KCW/XIV: 27 and 182) that Hawtrey tended to confuse the forces which are responsible for how the equilibrium is found with those which are responsible for the equilibrium itself, his own prime concern.

Keynes thus adopted Marshall's methods for his own purposes, the determination of output and employment as a whole, the theory of effective demand, once he had convinced himself that Say's Law did not hold so that an underemployment rest state was a theoretical possibility just as it was obviously a practical possibility in the world around him at the time. To form his theory he amalgamated Marshall's method with his own insights and mode of reasoning, from *A Treatise on Probability*, on how reasonable people behave in an uncertain environment. It was not so much that, in the first instance anyway, he wished to reject Marshall's concept of the "normal" but rather that he wanted to adapt it, partly under the influence of Kahn's work on the sustained depression in the U. K. textile industries and especially his classic article on the multiplier (Kahn 1931), to the possibility of underemployment equilibrium situations.

In *A Treatise on Money* Keynes had felt inhibited, because of Marshall's influence, from straying very far into the intricate story of short-period output and employment because he felt that a volume on money should be concerned with a sophisticated development of the quantity theory which, at the time, he felt "his fundamental equations" provided. But once he realized that Marshall's dichotomy between volume I and volume II was a false one, that is to say, when he ceased to move "along the traditional lines of regarding the influence of money as something so to speak separate from the general theory of supply and demand" (KCW/VII: xxii), he was able to construct a theory of the overall activity of a money using production economy in which there would be appropriate roles for monetary matters, especially the rate of interest, and for 'those homely but intelligible concepts" of marginal cost and the elasticity of short-period supply in an integrated theory of employment, output, prices and interest rates. For Keynes now,

> the right dichotomy [was] between the theory of the individual industry or firm and of the rewards and the distribution between different uses of a *given* quantity of resources on the one hand, and the theory of output and employment *as a whole* on the other hand. [For the latter] we require the complete theory of a monetary economy. (KCW/VII: 293)

And in it we have to deal with how "changing views about the future are capable of influencing the present situation. *For the importance of money essentially flows from its being a link between the present and the future"* (KCW/XIV: 293). This was to be contrasted with the theory he was casting off which did not imply this importance for money because it tried "to deal with the present by abstracting from the fact that we know very little about the future" (KCW/XIV: 115).

With this change of view, and with the important proviso that his principal relationships are concerned with expected variables, especially the values expected by the decision-makers in the economy, so that a theory of expectation formation in an uncertain environment becomes necessary, Keynes was content to use the Marshallian tools of supply and demand to determine the point of effective demand in a situation which was recognizably a Marshallian short-period one (suitably modified, of course, for his purposes of aggregate analysis). Keynes spent much more space on the concept of aggregate demand because he thought, mistakenly as it turned out, that the aggregate supply function would be easily recognized as, again suitably modified for aggregative analysis, the Marshallian short-period supply function.

In his own thought - and in those of his acute pupils, for example, Lorie Tarshis (1979) - the aggregate supply function was nevertheless as important as the aggregate demand function.[11] Indeed it could be argued that it was even more important, for the starting point of any analysis of the determination of the level of employment at a moment in time is a point on the aggregate supply curve - the expected proceeds that will justify that level of employment, *i. e.* be expected to maximize the short-period profits of the business people concerned, where the expectations relate to the prices which all the business people currently expect for their products. Whether this point is in fact the equilibrium of aggregate demand and supply depends upon whether the resulting employment, production and income creation result in a level of spending on consumption goods which in conjunction with that on investment goods - taken together, these constitute the usual aggregate demand schedule of textbooks - fulfills the expectations that created the employment in the first place.

KEYNES'S MODELLING

It is at this point that we can conveniently sketch in Keynes's methodological approach to the modelling of behaviour under uncertainty. In chapter 18 of *The General Theory* (KCW/VII: 245-54), Keynes describes the structure of the model which underlies the whole book. He lists the factors which are considered as given, the independent variables and the dependent variables. The given factors are: the skill and quantity of labour; the quality and quantity of equipment; the technique; the degree of competition;[12] the tastes and habits of consumers; the disutility of different intensities of labour; the social structure (including the forces which determine the distribution of income).[13]

The *independent variables* are three: the propensity to consume; the schedule of the marginal efficiency of capital; the rate of interest.[14] The distinction between given factors and independent variables is quite arbitrary, in the sense that it has to correspond

> on the one hand to the factors in which the changes seem to be so slow or so little relevant as to have only a small and comparatively negligible short-term influence on our *quaesitum*; and on the other hand to those factors in which the changes are found in practice to exercise a dominant influence on our *quaesitum* (KCW/VII: 247).[15]

The *quaesitum* is the determination of the two *dependent variables*, which are the volume of employment and the national income.

In the second section of the chapter, Keynes depicts the working of the model. Physical conditions of supply in the capital goods industries, the state of confidence concerning the prospective yields, the attitude to liquidity, and the quantity of money determine the rate of new investment. Changes in the rate of investment determine changes in income and employment (the multiplier effect). Changes in income and employment affect the schedule of liquidity preference with a feedback on investment (see KCW/VII: 247-9). The interactions and repercussions of these factors, together with others, will influence the position of equilibrium of the economy and determine the general price level.[16]

Let us first deal with the issue of how Keynes referred to his model in order to offer an explanation of some characteristic features of the actual economic system. More precisely, we mainly refer to Keynes's explanation of the relative stability of capitalist market economies. Keynes believed that actual economies, though rarely experiencing full employment, are not violently unstable.[17]

Economic theory has to explain this relative stability of actual economic systems. However, if we look back to Keynes's theoretical model, we see that it is not such as to ensure any stable result or behaviour. It does not embody any mechanism which necessarily ensures either equilibrium or regular fluctuations around it. Since psychological factors -which crucially depend on expectations- play such an important role in the model and expectations are about a future which cannot be known with certainty, there is no logical reason why the factors determining the position of the economy should not change suddenly and substantially.[18] Therefore, Keynes's model, in its general form, is "open" to many possible solutions. In fact, at this stage, Keynes did not feel any need to introduce particular assumptions concerning the behaviour of his independent variables.

A model of this kind is, quite obviously, highly intractable. Therefore, it had to be "tamed."[19] Keynes tried to reduce the generality of his model by making some specific hypotheses on changes in expectations. Having distinguished between short-term and long-term expectations, Keynes made several different hypotheses concerning their behaviour. Kregel, who has provided an important contribution on Keynes's methodology in dealing with changes in expectations, has singled out three models: of *static*, *stationary*, and *shifting* equilibrium (Kregel 1976, pp. 214-7).[20] However, the three models, although characterized by three different levels of abstraction, are still purely logical structures. Each model can provide a certain range of results which, under its assumptions, are logically possible. It is not yet possible to say which results are more likely. A further step is required.

On the grounds of logic, the "ultimate independent variables" of the model could take on any value and therefore produce any level of income and employment. But, in the actual world, these variables tend to take on particular values.

> [T]he actual phenomena of the economic system are also coloured by certain special characteristics of the propensity to consume, the schedule of the marginal efficiency of capital and the rate of interest, about which *we can safely generalize from experience, but which are not logically necessary.* (KCW/VII: 249; emphasis added).

Although Keynes was convinced that the economy is not "violently unstable," "logical necessity" does not lend any support to this conviction and, therefore, the conclusion is that it is determined only by the specific values that the variables tend to take on in reality.

> Now, since these facts of experience *do not follow of logical necessity,* one must suppose that the environment and the psychological propensities of the modern world must be of such a character as to produce these results. (KCW/VII: 250; emphasis added)

Thus, the next step for Keynes is to consider the values that the variables actually take on to produce stable results. He identifies three main conditions of stability which are likely to be met by an actual economy. They are: (i) the marginal propensity to consume is such that the multiplier is > 1 but not very large; (ii) the schedule of marginal efficiency of capital is such that changes in investment are not in great disproportion to changes in the prospective yield of capital (a shift of the schedule) or in the rate of interest (a movement along the schedule); (iii) moderate changes in employment are not associated with very great changes in the money-wages.[21]

What is methodologically crucial is the relationship between the logical necessity of theory and the "safe generalizations from experience," and the conceptual difference between these two analytical levels. We can express this difference also by referring briefly to Keynes's arguments and definitions in *A Treatise on Probability*. The abstract model deals with demonstrative certainty. Given two propositions **a** and **b**, between them there is a certainty-relation: for example, if **a** is true it necessarily and logically follows that **b** is certainly either true or false. When we pass to the realm of "safe generalizations from experience," we must abandon demonstrative certainty and use probability-relations. It is no longer possible to argue demonstratively from one proposition to another.[22]

Keynes, in concluding chapter 18, stressed again the difference between the two planes of his analysis. After having repeated that actual economies tend to be relatively stable, Keynes pointed out that such behaviour is not "therefore established by laws of necessity. The unimpeded rule of the above conditions is *a fact of observation concerning the world as it is or has been, and not a necessary principle which cannot be changed*" (KCW/VII: 254; emphasis added).

Keynes's views on these topics were also expressed in correspondence with Harrod. In 1938, Keynes wrote two letters to Harrod (see KCW/XIV: 295-7 and 299-301; for Harrod's replies, see pp. 297-8 and p. 301) where Keynes dealt mainly with three issues: the nature of economics; the relationship between theory and facts; and, finally, the relationship between his model and the "classical" model; we shall only consider the first two here.

Keynes first pointed out that a model, being an abstract logical structure, cannot be filled with actual values of the studied variables. If this were done the model would lose its generality. Furthermore, economics has another fundamental characteristic (which makes it different from natural sciences): it is a *moral science*. In the second letter, Keynes explained what he meant by "moral science" in more detail.

... the art of thinking in terms of models is a difficult -largely because it is an unaccustomed- practice. The pseudo-analogy with the physical sciences leads directly counter to the habit of mind which is most important for an economist proper to acquire. I also want to emphasize strongly the point about economics being a moral science. I mentioned before that it deals with introspection and with values. I might have added that it deals with motives, expectations, psychological uncertainties. (KCW/XIV: 300).[23]

Since economics is a moral science, the model has to deal with introspection, values, expectations, etc. In other words, economics being a moral science implies that the variables chosen must be of a particular nature. The economist cannot avoid dealing with such variables in order to explain the working of the economic system.[24] Not all possible models, though logically consistent, are relevant. The economist has to choose a model which is useful for the comprehension and solution of relevant actual problems.

But all this is not sufficient to make an economic model a "good" model. How can we be sure that the logical structure which has been chosen and built is useful for such a purpose?[25] For Keynes, this dilemma has no easy solution. The choice of the "right" model is difficult, and to think in terms of models is an art.

> Economics is a science of thinking in terms of models joined to the art of choosing models which are relevant to the contemporary world. (...) The object of a model is to segregate the semi-permanent or relatively constant factors from those which are transitory or fluctuating so as to develop a logical way of thinking about the latter, and of understanding the time sequences to which they give rise in particular cases. (KCW/XIV: 296-7).

The choice of the relevant variables and their classification into dependent and independent variables must be made on the basis of experience. Thus, it is "vigilant observation" of reality which increases the chances for the economist to build the "right" model.[26] "Vigilant observation" produces more evidence and, hence, gives more "weight" to the economist's rational belief, from which the model will be developed.

The choice of the model cannot be made without strict and careful analysis and knowledge of reality. But, once the model has been chosen, its construction and development must be carried out in complete separation from reality, in a purely logical context. The economic model is an example of economics being a branch of logic, a way of thinking. The model will help the economist analyze actual phenomena in an easier and orderly way. But the final step -making hypotheses about the values which the independent variables are likely to take on in reality-is again crucially dependent on "vigilant observation," intuition, introspection.

Observation of reality also necessarily implies taking into serious consideration the role which institutions and conventions play, the rules of the game, as Joan Robinson put it. Keynes always had a sense of the importance of these elements.

In *The Economic Consequences of the Peace*, published in 1919, he has a startling passage on the role of the distribution of income in the accumulation process, of the tacit understanding between the classes concerning the distribution of the product and its respective use by each, which allowed pre-First World War European capitalism to function.

> Europe was so organised socially and economically as to secure the maximum accumulation of capital. (...) On the one hand the labouring classes accepted from ignorance or powerlessness, or were compelled, persuaded, or cajoled by custom, convention, authority, and the well-established order of society into accepting a situation in which they could call their own very little of the cake that they and nature and the capitalists were co-operating to produce. And on the other hand the capitalist classes were allowed to call the best part of the cake theirs and were theoretically free to consume it, on the tacit underlying condition that they consumed very little of it in practice. (...) And so the cake increased, but to what end was not clearly contemplated. (...) There were two pitfalls in this prospect: lest, population still outstripping accumulation, our self-denials promote not happiness but numbers; and lest the cake be after all consumed, prematurely, in war, the consumer of all such hopes. (KCW/II: 11-3)

Keynes recognized both the crucial role of such institutional arrangements and their fragility which the requirements of the Peace Treaty threatened to expose.

But Keynes had not yet in his own mind split saving from investment in the process of accumulation. That was to occur in the *Treatise on Money* and, especially, in *The General Theory*. Moreover, in *The General Theory*, with the emphasis laid on uncertainty, Keynes also stressed the importance of social conventions. Pervading and persistent uncertainty leads to the establishment of conventions which guide economic decisions, especially those associated with real and financial accumulation, as well as speculation in financial assets.

Within certain bounds, decisions guided by those conventions give stability if not optimality to the working of the system. Outside these bounds, their fragility is explicitly revealed and this may well sow the seeds of crisis. These phenomena are brilliantly analyzed in chapter 12 of *The General Theory*, where the role and pathology of stock markets are discussed.

Keynes's sense of the need to have or to design appropriate institutions for implementations of effective policy was never more in evidence than when, with events unfolding with the inevitability of a Greek tragedy, he literally killed himself, first, helping to guide the United Kingdom's economy through the Second World War; and then, throughout and after the war, helping to plan the institutions needed to make the post-war world a more just and efficient economic environment.

SOME "MYSTERIES" IN *THE GENERAL THEORY*

There are, in *The General Theory*, several highly controversial issues which, over the years since 1936, have given rise to long and wide ranging debates aimed at providing both an interpretation of what Keynes "really meant" and more satisfactory grounds for further analytical developments. In considering some of these topics, priority must be given to the issue of market forms in *The

General Theory, especially at a time when attempts to develop macro-models with hypotheses of non-perfect competition are becoming increasingly frequent.[27]

Amongst the participants in the debate on imperfect competition in 1930s, there was a virtually universal consensus on two aspects: most industries were characterized by imperfect competition and it was *at least possible* to have an industry in equilibrium with excess capacity. This being the "state of the art" at that time, it is apparently a mystery why Keynes, who knew about the imperfect competition revolution, nevertheless chose to use the short-period Marshallian pricing model for his chapter on prices and, more generally, wrote *The General Theory* usually ignoring imperfect competition.[28]

As we have seen, in chapter 18 of *The General Theory*, Keynes stated that the degree of competition was one of the givens in his analysis. This approach implies that Keynes thought that any hypotheses on market forms would have left his results fundamentally unaffected. However, Keynes usually stated his propositions as if he were assuming Marshallian competition with expected prices equal to marginal costs, though, when he stated the first classical postulate in such a form, he added provisos for the imperfect competition case.[29] The postulate, being in turn based on the assumption of short-period decreasing returns, implies an inverse correlation between the level of output (and employment) and real wages.[30]

Keynes's acceptance of the first postulate and its implications is surprising in view of what he knew about Kahn's work in 1929. Kahn, in his 1929 Fellowship dissertation for King's, analyzed the factors which determine the shape of prime cost curves by questioning the usual assumption of U-shaped cost curves (see Kahn 1929: 45-63). Kahn convincingly argued that, in many industries, short-period prime cost curves had a reverse-L shape: costs were constant up to full capacity and then became virtually vertical (Kahn 1929: 49-58). From this it follows that, in general, average prime cost is independent of the level of output and, therefore, that the marginal prime cost is equal to the (constant) average prime cost. This, for Kahn, implied the *collapse of the assumption of perfect competition*.[31]

The implications of Kahn's analysis for the first postulate are evident: if prime and marginal costs are constant up to capacity there is no reason why the real wage rate should decrease when output increases. On the other hand, as Harrod (1930 and 1931) also had pointed out, in the short period and in imperfect competition, an increase in output did not necessarily bring about an increase in prices because firms produce below capacity.[32] Keynes, however, ignored such implications in *The General Theory*. It was only in 1939 that he rather reluctantly took on board some of the imperfect competition arguments.

In 1938-39, Keynes's analysis of the behaviour of real wages was questioned by referring to empirical evidence. Dunlop, Tarshis, and Kalecki (Dunlop 1938, Tarshis 1939, Kalecki 1939) observed that, over the cycle, the real wage does not behave in the way predicted by the classical theory and by Keynes. They provided alternative explanations of the distributive shares which were based on the hypothesis of short-period constant returns and the introduction of some form of imperfect competition. In 1939, Keynes wrote a rejoinder to the articles mentioned above (KCW/VII: 394-412) where, though accepting the idea that it was sensible to suppose that some form of imperfect competition is prevailing in the economy,[33] he remained convinced that the hypothesis of short-period decreasing returns was the most reasonable.[34] Moreover, he argued that accepting the hypothesis of constant real wages would have not affected his general results in a negative way but, quite the contrary, it would have reinforced them by eliminating the inflationary implications of expansionary policies to increase employment.[35]

Nevertheless, Keynes remained quite hostile to the concept of imperfect competition and the surrounding debate.[36] The "mystery" of Keynes's attitude towards the "second revolution" of 1930s can perhaps be partly solved by taking into consideration two aspects. First, Keynes certainly was not helped by the protagonists of the "second revolution" to perceive the macro-implications of imperfect competition: they did not seem to be aware of any analytical connection between their microeconomic results and the analysis of the output as a whole.[37] It was Kalecki who, in the late 1930s, linked the analysis of market forms to the theory of effective demand.[38]

Secondly, there could be strong "tactical" reasons why Keynes chose to ignore imperfect competition in *The General Theory*: his desire to concede as much as possible to his adversaries. In the 1939 article, he recognized that in *The General Theory* he had simply accepted the then prevailing generalization that short-period increasing marginal costs substantially coincide with marginal wage costs and that, in *competitive conditions*, prices are governed by marginal costs (see KCW/VII: 400). Keynes may have felt that rejecting this prevailing assumption would have been strategically unwise. He was knocking over Say's Law and abandoning the quantity theory of money and so arguing that the system may settle at an underemployment equilibrium. To introduce the imperfect competition hypothesis could have weakened the strength of his critique. That is to say, it was as if he said to the orthodox of the time, I will grant you everything that Marshall and Pigou said about the formation of relative prices in terms of "those homely but intelligible concepts" of short-period elasticity of supply and marginal cost, and I will assume a competitive environment so that you cannot say that I have obtained my unemployment results by slipping in monopoly, in which situation everybody knows that unemployment can result, and *yet* I will get involuntary unemployment and an underemployment equilibrium. Such a demonstration, he may have thought, was more impressive than starting off with imperfect competition as the general case.[39]

Be as it may - for a similar interpretation see, for example, Kregel 1985 and Darity 1985 - there are a number of people, of whom Kaldor was one of the most prominent, who think that Keynes made a mistake:

> ... while [Keynes's] 1939 article was a laudable attempt to rectify erroneous statements (both empirical and theoretical) in *The General Theory*, it would be an exaggeration to say that Keynes even then showed full awareness of the critical

importance of increasing returns and imperfect competition to his general theory of employment. Had he done so, a great deal of the post-war controversy concerning the *nature* of Keynesian theory might have been avoided. And (...) by the time his 1939 article appeared the harm was done, and there were a number of influential writers who maintained, in line with Milton Friedman later, that the increase in employment associated with a Keynesian policy of demand management was both inflationary and temporary (Kaldor 1983: 181)[40]

Kaldor has also commented on Keynes's assumption of an exogenous supply of money in *The General Theory* whereas in most of his earlier and later work Keynes had usually regarded the money supply as endogenous, a theme which was dear to Kaldor's heart. Again, there may have been a "tactical" reason involved; for if the money supply could be regarded as given, at least from the viewpoint of the new theory, and yet the general price level could be shown to vary for other reasons, then this would be another blow against the quantity theory of money - though not a very telling one since the situation in which the quantity theory was traditionally argued to hold hardly coincided with the situation which Keynes was discussing in *The General Theory*. In any event, even from a tactical viewpoint, it was not a success for in subsequent years it allowed the monetarists to use the same assumption and to launch their counteract.[41]

The last "puzzle" which we want to raise here and which again may be associated with Keynes's tactical sense and which again with hindsight may appear as another example of faulty tactics, is why Keynes chose to develop the principal arguments of *The General Theory* within the confines of a closed economy model. This too was unusual for Keynes: practically all of his theoretical and policy work before and after 1936 was done in the context of an open economy model. Moreover, from the beginning of his career as an economist he had very definite views on the roles of international trade, and especially of international capital movements, in his discussion of price levels and their control in 1920s and activity levels and their control in 1930s and 1940s.[42]

It is true that Harrod and Joan Robinson among others soon extended the analysis of *The General Theory* to take account of the effects of openness on the level of activity and the size of the multiplier. But it was a strange omission by Keynes in view of his strong opinion on the importance of capital movements as well as of trade. Moreover, one of Keynes's last acts was, of course, his contribution at Bretton Woods to the setting up of the IMF and World Bank, international institutions and arrangements to complement those counterparts in individual countries which were designed to ensure full employment, in order to guard against the latter creating balance of payments problems that would require contractionary responses.

Hicks too (1985) was puzzled by *The General Theory* being apparently set within a "closed" framework and suggested that a reasonable guess was to think of Keynes's model in *The General Theory* as referring to the world economic system rather than to a single country.[43] There are, however, two other possible lines of explanation. On the one hand, it may be that at the level of abstraction at which the core of *The General Theory* was pitched Keynes thought that openness or otherwise of the economy would not make any essential difference in principle to the processes he was attempting to analyze. The practical consequences were, of course, very important indeed as Keynes himself pointed out in the chapter on the effects of changes in money-wages on employment and in some asides on the effect on the size of the multiplier of leakages into imports (see, *e.g.*, KCW/VII: 120).

The second possible explanation is based, in our view, on more solid grounds. It relies on Keynes's conviction that internal conditions should be of primary concern. Though Keynes was famous for changing his mind,[44] he consistently throughout his life argued that internal levels of output, activity, and prices should have precedence over external pressures and requirements. Thus, his commitment as a liberal to free trade was lower down on his list of priorities than was his desire to have and maintain decent levels of employment. James Meade has described this attitude well:

> Keynes was concerned with macroeconomic conditions, with getting people to design polices which would expand or maintain high levels of activity. He thought this was infinitely more important than the free allocation of resources. At the same time, he was a man who believed in the freedom of the human spirit, so that he did not believe in an economy that had to be excessively controlled, but in one where there was the necessary intervention in order to obtain a high level of activity. (...) [H]e was somebody who believed passionately in building a new, decent, liberal and effective international order which was based on conditions which would allow prosperity and expansion to be. (...) [W]hile Keynes [himself] was not working for the micro liberal part of the synthesis, he was saying that if you can get the rest to work you may do quite a bit of good by getting it in as well. (Meade 1983: 129-30)

Keynes was always consistent in his view that the wage-earning classes should not have to carry an unfair burden of the adjustments to the malfunctioning of the economy. *The Economic Consequences of Mr Churchill* (1925; KCW/IX: 207-30)[45] is a relatively early, passionate statement of this view. He did argue that if satisfactory levels of activity could be ensured world-wide an argument could be made whereby the benefits of the classical system, including those flowing from free trade, could be added as a bonus. But he would not make free trade, free movements of international capital, coupled with freely floating exchange rates, an over-riding priority, indeed quite the opposite.

This was Keynes's view still in 1946:

> I find myself moved, not for the first time, to remind contemporary economists that the classical teaching embodied some permanent truths of great significance, which we are liable to-day to overlook because we associate them with other doctrines which we cannot now accept without much qualification. (...) I do not suppose that the classical medicine will work by itself or that we can depend on it. We need quicker and less painful aids of which exchange variation and overall import control are the most important. But in the long run these expedients will work better and

we shall need them less, if the classical medicine is also at work. (KCW/XXVII: 444-5)

Notes

* This chapter is partly based on two previous articles: Harcourt 1987 and Sardoni 1989-90. The authors wish to thank John Davis, Sheila Dow, Alessandro Roncaglia and Mario Tonveronachi for their helpful comments.

[1] And, of course, his subsequent work. Keynes's three 1937 articles represent fundamental contributions: "The General Theory of Unemployment" (KCW/XIV: 109-23); "Alternative Theories of the Rate of Interest" (KCW/XIV: 201-15); "The *'Ex Ante'* Theory of the Rate of Interest" (KCW/XIV: 215-23). For Keynes's works, reference is to his *Collected Writings* in 30 volumes (KCW). Where necessary, the date of the first publication is also given.

[2] As to the latter, James Meade has put it succinctly: "Keynes's intellectual revolution was to shift economists from thinking normally in terms of a model of reality in which a dog called *savings* wagged his tail labelled *investment* to thinking in terms of a model in which a dog called *investment* wagged his tail labelled *savings*" (Meade 1975: 82).

[3] The literature on Keynes's philosophy and its relationship to his economics has greatly increased in the last few years. See, for example, Carabelli 1988, Fitzgibbons 1988, O'Donnell 1989. O'Donnell was the pioneer (his book grew out of his PhD dissertation of the late 1970s and early 1980s). The most lively and probably most incisive account of Keynes's interaction with the Cambridge philosophers and especially with Wittgenstein is Coates 1990. Although we have entitled our paper "Keynes's Vision," we have in mind the Schumpeterian sense of the term rather than the sense in which Fitzgibbons uses it as the title of his 1988 book.

[4] He was elected in 1909 after an earlier attempt had been unsuccessful.

[5] A theme taken up but later abandoned by Clower and Leijonhufvud. See Clower & Leijonhufvud 1975 and Leijonhufvud 1977.

[6] And it clashes with the attitudes of mathematical economists of our own day (see, *e.g.*, Debreu 1984), who sometimes argue as if truth in our subject may only be gained in the guise of a mathematical model. But see Frank Hahn's reconsideration of all this in the first issue of the second century of the *Economic Journal* (Hahn 1991).

[7] To this we should add Keynes's revealing aside in the original preface to *The General Theory*: "The writer of a book such as this, treading along unfamiliar grounds, is extremely dependent on criticism and conversation, if he is to avoid an undue proportion of mistakes. It is astonishing what foolish things one can temporarily believe if one thinks too long alone, particularly in economics (along with other moral sciences), where it is often impossible to bring one's ideas to a conclusive test either formal or experimental" (KCW/VII: xiii).

[8] This well known motto of Wildon Carr is quoted in Shove 1942: 323.

[9] In his answer to Hayek's review of *A Treatise on Money* Keynes regretted that Hayek did "pick over the precise words I have used with a view of discovering some verbal contradiction or insidious ambiguity" instead of trying "to step into a new pair of trousers," that is to say into a new and alternative theoretical approach. See KCW/XIII: 243-56.

[10] Although neither Marshall nor his pupils were always consistent in using such distinction. On this see Harcourt 1992a: 268.

[11] On Keynes's aggregate supply function, see also Asimakopulos 1991: 53-7.

[12] We return to the degree of competition as a given in Section 4.

[13] Of course, to regard these factors as given does not imply that they cannot change but only that, for the analytical purposes of the book, the effects of their changes are abstracted from. See KCW/VII: 245.

[14] The marginal efficiency of capital depends partly on given factors and partly on expected yields of capital assets, the rate of interest depends partly on liquidity preference and partly on the money supply. Therefore, ."... we can sometimes regard our ultimate independent variables as consisting of (1) the three fundamental psychological factors, namely, the psychological propensity to consume, the psychological attitude to liquidity and the psychological expectation of future yield from capital assets, (2) the wage-unit as determined by the bargains reached between employers and employed, and (3) the quantity of money as determined by the action of the central bank" (KCW/VII: 246-7).

[15] Moreover, the independent variables may also have to be chosen by taking into account their relevance from the point of view of policy. "Our final task might be to select those variables which can be deliberately controlled or managed by central authority in the kind of system in which we actually live" (KCW/VII: 247). In the first proof of *The General Theory*, Keynes pointed out that, in some cases, also the subjective factors which affect consumption decisions can be taken as given, so that we are left with two independent variables, the marginal efficiency of capital and the rate of interest (cf. KCW/XIV: 503). Under this assumption, the "ultimate independent variables" become the prospective yield of capital, the state of liquidity preference, the quantity of money, and the wage-unit (cf. KCW/XIV: 503-4).

[16] Here we do not analyze how Keynes dealt with the problems of the interaction among variables and of their time dimension. For a discussion of the problem of the logical interrelation among variables in Keynes's model, see Pasinetti 1975: 43-4. See also Hicks 1979: 73-86, where some of the difficulties associated with the different time dimension of the three independent variables are analyzed.

[17] "[I]t is an outstanding characteristic of the economic system in which we live that, whilst it is subject to severe fluctuations in respect of output and employment, it is not violently unstable" (KCW/VII: 249).

[18] Keynes pointed out: "there is not one of the above factors which is not liable to change without much warning, and sometimes substantially" (KCW/VII: 249).

[19] The term "tamed model" has been used by Kregel. See Kregel 1976: 213.

[20] In the static model, long-term expectations are given and constant and short-term expectations are realized; in the stationary model, short-term expectations may be disappointed while long-term expectations are still given and constant; in the shifting model (the most general), long-term expectations change over time and short-term expectations are disappointed. Moreover, there are feedbacks between the disappointment of short-term expectations and long-term expectations.

[21] There is, moreover, a fourth condition: on the presumption that capital goods are of different ages, do not last indefinitely and are not very long-lived, if the rate of investment falls below a certain minimum, the marginal efficiency of capital will rise sufficiently to bring investment above this minimum again. Analogously, if the rate of investment rises to a higher level than formerly, the marginal efficiency will fall sufficiently to cause a decline in investment and, hence, a recession (see KCW/VII: 251-4.) Finally, it is to be stressed also that the conventional element in behaviour, to which Keynes gave much importance, is a relevant factor in the explanation of the relative stability of actual variables. See, for example, Keynes's viewpoint on the conventional nature of the interest rate (KCW/VII: 203-4).

[22] A "safe generalization" is a rational belief of a certain degree of probability. This degree of probability depends on the available relevant evidence. As this evidence increases, the probability of an argument can either increase or decrease; in any case its weight has increased, that is the basis on which our conclusions rest has become more substantial. "As the relevant evidence at our disposal increase (...) we have a more substantial basis upon which to rest our conclusions (...) New evidence will sometimes decrease the probability of an argument, but it will always increase its 'weight'," (KCW/VIII: 77).

[23] "It is as though the fall of the apple to the ground depended on the apple's motives, on whether it is worth while falling to the ground, and whether the ground wanted the apple to

fall, and on mistaken calculations on the part of the apple as to how far it was from the centre of the earth" (KCW/XIV: 300).

[24] John Davis has suggested to us that Keynes was here criticizing the natural science view of economics of Lionel Robbins: "The 'motives, expectations, psychological uncertainties' remark seems to be meant to distance Keynes from Robbins's law-like behaviour view."

[25] Keynes's criticism of Hayek's *Prices and Production* is an example of his attitude towards an inadequate logical structure, a wrong model: "[*Prices and Production*] is an extraordinary example of how, starting with a mistake, a remorseless logician can end up in Bedlam" (KCW/XIII: 252).

[26] For Keynes, there are not many economists who have the gift of using "vigilant observation." "Good economists are scarce because the gift for using 'vigilant observation' to choose good models, although it does not require a highly specialized intellectual technique, appears to be a very rare one" (KCW/VII: 297).

[27] In recent years there has been a flourishing of models of imperfect (or monopolistic) competition which claim to yield "Keynesian results"; see, *e.g.*, Ng, 1980; Weitzman, 1982; Hart, 1982; Mankiw, 1987; Startz, 1989, Marris 1991. For a criticism of some of these models see Sardoni 1992. But see also Harcourt 1965.

[28] Not only was Keynes familiar with Sraffa's, Kahn's, and Shove's work in this area, he was also the reader for Macmillan of Joan Robinson's *The Economics of Imperfect Competition*.

[29] Chapter 2 of *The General Theory* (Keynes 1936: 4-22) is devoted to the discussion of the two postulates of classical economics. Keynes rejected the second postulate: the utility of the wage of a given amount of labour employed is equal to the marginal disutility of that amount of employment. But Keynes accepted the first under the hypothesis that competition is perfect: "The wage is equal to the marginal product of labour subject, however, to the qualification that the equality may be disturbed (...) if competition and markets are imperfect" (KCW/VII: 5).

[30] "Thus, if employment increases, then, in the short period, the reward per unit of labour in terms of wage-goods must, in general, decline and profit increase. This is simply the obverse of the familiar proposition that industry is normally working subject to decreasing returns in the short period during which equipment etc. is assumed to be constant; so that the marginal product in the wage-good industries (...) necessarily diminishes as employment is increased" (KCW/VII: 17-8)

[31] With prime costs perfectly elastic to the point of full capacity, only downward sloping individual demand curves, because of market imperfections, could explain the phenomenon of firms producing below capacity and still earning positive profits.

[32] On Harrod on imperfect competition see also Kregel 1985: 75-8.

[33] ".. it may be the case that the practical workings of the laws of imperfect competition in the modern quasi-competitive system are such that, when output increases and money wages rise, prices rise less than in proportion to the increase in marginal money cost" (KCW/VII: 406).

[34] "Even if one concedes that the course of the short-period marginal cost curve is downwards in its early reaches, Mr. Kahn's assumption that it eventually turns upwards is, on general common-sense grounds, surely beyond reasonable question; and that this happens, moreover, on a part of the curve which is highly relevant for practical purposes. Certainly it would require more convincing evidence than yet exists to persuade me to give up this presumption" (KCW/VII: 405). Here, Keynes was not referring to Kahn's 1929 work but, probably, to Kahn's 1931 article where, in fact, he had assumed slightly increasing supply functions. On the relationship between Kahn's 1929 dissertation and his 1931 article, see Marcuzzo 1988; Harcourt 1991; Marris 1991: 181-7).

[35] "If we can advance farther on the road towards full employment than I had previously supposed without seriously affecting real hourly wages or the rate of profits per unit of output, the warnings of the anti-expansionists need cause us less anxiety" (KCW/VII: 401).

[36] This emerges clearly from some letters to Joan Robinson in February and March 1941 (KCW/XII: 829-36). The correspondence was about an article by Kalecki originally submitted for publication in the *Economic Journal* ("A Theorem of Technical Progress," which eventually appeared in the *Review of Economic Studies* in May 1941). The topic in discussion was Kalecki's assumption that in the long period all firms produce under capacity, an assumption that "bewildered" Keynes. Joan Robinson replied by pointing out that such a hypothesis was "part of the usual bag of tricks of Imperfect Competition Theory" (in KCW/XII: 830).

[37] The only, partial, exception, may be Harrod who was always most interested in the connections between imperfect competition and the theory of the trade cycle. On this see Harrod 1934 and 1936 and also Kregel 1985.

[38] Joan Robinson, one of the most prominent participants in the debate on imperfect competition in 1930s, reminded us in 1969 that "It was Michal Kalecki rather than I who brought imperfect competition into touch with the theory of employment" (Robinson 1969: viii).

[39] As, for example, Kalecki did in his 1936 review of *the General Theory* (Kalecki 1990: 223-32).

[40] John Davis has pointed out to us that these issues were secondary to the primary issue of showing underemployment equilibria to be possible and Keynes himself did not have much to say about demand management in the sense made popular by subsequent Keynesians.

[41] On this, see, *e.g.*, Kaldor's lament in Kaldor 1983. Sheila Dow, though, has reminded us how conscious Keynes was of the importance of persuasion: See, *e.g.*, Dow 1988 for her cogent analysis and for several statements of Keynes's view on all this. She added that she feels "uncomfortable with Kaldor's criticism of Keynes. Certainly in many ways *The General Theory* misfired. But would it have fired at all if it had thrown out much more of the orthodoxy? It is *The General Theory* which spearheaded Keynes's lasting influence on the profession." In her view, "Kalecki's work has not attracted so much attention not just because Keynes stole the limelight but because his work was not so accessible to economists brought up on the orthodoxy."

[42] Moggridge (1986) has chronicled Keynes's contributions over his entire working life to the issues associated with the international monetary system. Moggridge uses a classification by Williamson (1977) as an organizing mechanism with which to discuss all the published writings by Keynes on the topic.

[43] Hicks observed: "If it [the model] was to be applied to the economy of a single nation, it could only have been to one where external trade was minimal, or to one (like Russia or the Germany of the date when he was writing) where it was tightly controlled. It is impossible to believe that such were the main applications that he had in mind. The only alternative is to suppose that it was meant to apply to the 'world economy'" (Hicks 1985, pp. 22).

[44] Joan Robinson's favourite story about Keynes was that when someone remonstrated with him for being inconsistent, he responded: "When someone persuades me that I am wrong, I change my mind. What do you do?"

[45] Which recently has been brilliantly re-interpreted by Wells (1986).

References

Asimakopulos, A. (1991) *Keynes's General Theory and Accumulation*. Cambridge: Cambridge University Press.

Boskin, M., J. (ed.) (1979) *Economics and Human Welfare. Essays in Honour of Tibor Scitovsky*. New York: Academic Press.

Carabelli, A. M. (1988) *On Keynes's Method*. London: Macmillan.

Clower, R. & Leijonhufvud, A. (1975) "The Coordination of Economic Activities: A Keynesian Perspective." *American Economic Review*, vol. 65, May, pp. 182-8.

Coates, J. (1990) *Ordinary Language Economics: Keynes and the Cambridge Philosophers*, unpublished Ph. D. thesis. University of Cambridge.

Cohen, J. S.& Harcourt, G. C. (eds.) (1986) *International Monetary Problems and Supply-Side Economics. Essays in Honour of Lorie Tarshis*. London: Macmillan.

Darity, Jr., W. (1985) "On Involuntary Unemployment and Increasing Returns," *Journal of Post Keynesian Economics*. Vol. 7, Spring, pp. 363-72.

Debreu, G. (1984) "Economic Theory in the Mathematical Mode." *American Economic Review*. Vol. 74, No. 3, pp. 267-78.

Dow, S. C. (1988) "What Happened to Keynes's Economics?," in Hamouda-Smithin, pp. 101-10.

Dunlop, J. T. (1938) "The Movement of Real and Money Wage Rates," *Economic Journal*. Vol. 48, September, pp. 413-34.

Fitzigibbons, A. (1988) *Keynes's Vision*. Oxford: Oxford University Press.

Hahn, F. H. (1991) "The Next Hundred Years." *Economic Journal*. Vol. 101, January, pp. 47-50.

Hamouda, O. F. & Smithin, J. N. (eds.) (1988) *Keynes and Public Policy after Fifty Years, Volume I: Economics and Policy*. Aldershot: Edward Elgar.

Harcourt, G. C. (1965) "A Two-Sector Model of the Distribution of Income and the Level of Employment in the Short Run," *Economic Record*. Vol. 41, pp. 103-17.

——————————. (ed.) (1977) *The Microeconomic Foundations of Macroeconomics*. London: Macmillan.

——————————. (ed.) (1985) *Keynes and His Contemporaries. The Sixth and Centennial Keynes Seminar held at the University of Kent at Canterbury, 1983*. London: Macmillan.

—————————— (1987) "Theoretical Methods and Unfinished Business." in Reese 1987, and Harcourt 1992, pp. 235-49.

——————————. (1991) "R. F. Kahn: A Tribute," in *Banca Nazionale del Lavoro Quarterly Review*. No. 176, March, pp. 15-30.

——————————. (1992a) "Marshall's *Principles* as seen at Cambridge through the eyes of Gerald Shove, Dennis Robertson and Joan Robinson," in Harcourt 1992b, pp. 265-77.

——————————. (1992b) *On Political Economists and Modern Political Economy. Selected Essays of G. C. Harcourt*, edited by C. Sardoni. London: Routledge.

Harrod, R. F. (1930) "Notes on Supply." *Economic Journal*. Reprinted in Harrod 1972, pp. 77-88.

——————————. (1931) "The Law of Decreasing Costs." *Economic Journal*. Reprinted in Harrod 1972, pp. 89-102.

——————————. (1934) "Doctrines of Imperfect Competition." *Quarterly Journal of Economics*. Reprinted in Harrod 1972, pp. 111-38.

_____. (1936) "Imperfect Competition and the Trade Cycle," *Review of Economics and Statistics*. Vol. 18, pp. 84-8.

_____. (1972) *Economic Essays*, 2nd ed. London: Macmillan.

Hart, O. (1982) "A Model of Imperfect Competition with Keynesian Features," *Quarterly Journal of Economics*. Vol. 97, February, pp. 109-38.

Hicks, John. (1979) *Causality in Economics*. Oxford: Basil Blackwell.

_____. (1985) "Keynes and the World Economy," in Vicarelli 1985, pp. 21-7.

Kahn, R. F. (1929) [1989] *The Economics of the Short Period*. London: Macmillan.

_____. (1931) "The Relation of Home Investment to Unemployment," *Economic Journal*. Vol. 41, No. 162, pp. 173-98.

Kaldor, N. (1983) "Keynesian Economics after Fifty Years" in Worswick-Trevithick 1983. Reprinted in Targetti & Thirlwall 1989, pp. 164-98.

_____. (1989) *The Essential Kaldor* (edited by F. Targetti and A. P. Thirlwall). London: Duckworth.

Kalecki M. (1938) "The Determinants of Distribution of the National Income," *Econometrica*. Vol. 6, pp. 97-112.

_____. (1990) *Collected Writings, Vol. I*. Oxford: Clarendon Press.

Keynes, J. M. (1971-89) *The Collected Writings of John Maynard Keynes*, Vols. I-XXX, edited by D. E. Moggridge for the Royal Economic Society. London: Macmillan.

_____, (ed.) (1975) *Essays on John Maynard Keynes*. Cambridge: Cambridge University Press.

Kregel, J. A. (1976) "Economic Methodology in the Face of Uncertainty: The Modelling Methods of Keynes and the Post-Keynesians," *Economic Journal*. Vol. 86, No. 342, pp. 209-25.

_____. (1985) "Harrod and Keynes: Increasing Returns, the Theory of Employment and Dynamic Economics," in Harcourt 1985, pp. 66-88.

Leijonhufvud, A. (1977) "Costs and Consequences of Inflation," in Harcourt 1977, pp. 265-312.

Mankiw, G. N. (1988) "Imperfect Competition and the Keynesian Cross," *Economics Letters*. 26, pp. 7-13.

Marcuzzo, C. (1988) *Richard F. Kahn: un discepolo di Keynes*. Milan: Garzanti.

Marris, R. (1991) *Reconstructing Keynesian Economics with Imperfect Competition*. Aldershot: Edward Elgar.

Meade, J. E. (1975) "The Keynesian Revolution," in Keynes, M. (1975), pp. 82-8.

_____. (1983) "Comment," in Worswick & Trevithick 1983, pp. 129-30.

Moggridge, D. E. (1986) "Keynes and the International Monetary System 1909-46," in Cohen-Harcourt 1986, pp. 56-83.

Ng, Y. K. (1980) "Macroeconomics with Non-perfect Competition," *Economic Journal*. 90, September, pp. 598-610.

O'Donnell, R. M. (1989) *Keynes: Philosophy, Economics and Politics*. London: Macmillan.

Pasinetti, L. L. (1975) *Growth and Income Distribution*. Cambridge: Cambridge University Press.

Reese, D. A. (ed.) (1987) *The Legacy of Keynes. Nobel Conference XXII*. San Francisco: Harper and Row.

Robinson, J. V. (1969) *The Economics of Imperfect Competition* 2nd ed. London: Macmillan.

Sardoni, C. (1989-90) "Chapter 18 of *The General Theory*: Its Methodological Importance," *Journal of Post Keynesian Economics*. Vol. 12, pp. 293-307.

_____. (1992) "Market forms and effective demand: Keynesian results with perfect competition," *Review of Political Economy*. Vol. 4, October.

Shove, G. F. (1942) "The Place of Marshall's Principles in the Development of Economic Theory," *Economic Journal*. Vol. 52, December, pp. 294-329.

Startz, R. (1989) "Monopolistic Competition as a Foundation for Keynesian Macroeconomic Models," *Quarterly Journal of Economics*. Vol. 104, November, pp. 737-52.

Targetti, F. & Thirlwall, A. P., (eds.) (1989) *The Essential Kaldor*. London: Duckworth.

Tarshis, L. (1939) "Changes in Real and Money Wages," *Economic Journal*. Vol. 49, March, pp. 150-4.

_____. (1979) "The Aggregate Supply Function in Keynes's *General Theory*." in Boskin 1979, pp. 361-92.

Vicarelli, F. (ed.) (1985) *Keynes's Relevance Today*. London: Macmillan.

Weitzman, M. L. (1982) "Increasing Returns and the Foundations of Unemployment Theory," *Economic Journal*. Vol. 92, December, pp. 787-804.

Wells, P. (1986) "'Mr Churchill' and *The General Theory*," in Cohen & Harcourt 1986, pp. 8-27.

Williamson, J. W. (1977) *The Failure of World Monetary Reform 1971-74*. Sunbury-on-Thames: Nelson.

Worswick, G. D. & Trevithick, J. A. (eds.) (1983) *Keynes and the Modern World*. Cambridge: Cambridge University Press.

KEYNES'S: VISION AND TACTICS

COMMENT BY ALLIN COTTRELL*

I. Introduction

Geoff Harcourt and Claudio Sardoni offer, as one might expect, a clear, balanced and informative account of both the intellectual background to, and the analytical substance of, Keynes's pathbreaking *General Theory*. Harcourt and Sardoni (henceforth HS) divide their contribution into three main sections, dealing respectively with Keynes's dual background in Marshallian economics and the philosophy of probability; his approach to modeling in *The General Theory*; and the "tactics" he employed in presenting his new macroeconomic arguments, with respect to which HS try to elucidate certain "mysteries."

By virtue of the breadth of their sweep, HS provide something of an *embarras de richesses* for the commentator. But I must, of course, be severely selective. I shall not say much about the first two sections of their paper. Here, HS work with a fairly broad brush, and I find little to disagree with. (For instance, while illuminating Keynes's concerns in *The General Theory* by reference to his earlier philosophical work, HS do not appear to commit themselves to any particular side in the recent debates on this subject among Rod O'Donnell, Anna Carabelli, Brad Bateman, John Davis and others.) On these sections, I might just add a few items to the HS bibliography--works which seem to me particularly illuminating on some of the topics they raise. Thus, when HS draw attention to Keynes's "repeated stress on the need to avoid the fallacy of composition when the workings of the economy as a whole are considered" (HS: 3), I would add that Peter Clarke (1988) is very good on this point. On Keynes's choice of units in *The General Theory* (HS: 4), Carabelli (1992) has an interesting and well-developed argument. And on the question of the stability or instability of investment, as it relates to Keynes's idea of a "convention" (HS: 8-9), I would chip in Runde (1991) and Littleboy (1990) as useful discussions. Among the questions I have chosen to pursue in more depth, the first concerns the connection between "vision" and "tactics" (two elements yoked together in HS's title). This then leads me into some specific points regarding the "mysteries" that HS discuss in relation to Keynes's tactics. Then finally, I chase a hare which pops up in the HS paper but which is not pursued there at all, namely, What does Keynes's attitude towards Marx and Marxism have to tell us about his "vision"?

II. Vision and tactics

At first sight, the juxtaposition of "vision" and "tactics" in the title chosen by HS appears somewhat incongruous. Aren't these chalk and cheese? One thinks of an author's "vision" as something relatively invariant, enduring and overarching, while tactics are mutable, contingent, sensitive to particular circumstances. On the other hand, following Einstein's dictum that "God is in the details," it may be that a writer's tactics have, on close examination, something important to tell us about his vision. I'm not sure that HS explore this angle as fully as they might; and I shall try to supplement them on this point. HS (p. 1) set out their three tactical "mysteries" as follows:

> [W]hy did Keynes decide to ignore the issue of market structures in *The General Theory* despite his knowledge of the debate which was going on at that time in Britain and the US? Why did he take the supply of money as an exogenous variable despite his previous work, especially in *A Treatise on Money*, in which he had convincingly shown that money supply is endogenous? Why did he choose to deal with a closed economy when he spent so much of his professional life studying and discussing international economic issues?

First of all, I wish to demur at the presumption that these *are* all matters of "tactics," faulty or otherwise (cf. HS: 15). Surely it only makes sense to speak of a writer adopting a certain assumption as an expositional tactic, if one supposes that he regards that assumption as substantively false. In that case he might nonetheless choose to grant the assumption because his dialectical opponents uphold it, and because he wishes to produce a critique *a fortiori* of their conclusions; or perhaps because he regards it as a useful heuristic simplification. But making an assumption one regards as essentially *correct* is not a "tactic" at all.

Let us consider in this light the three examples discussed by HS. I treat the third point--the assumption of a closed economy--first, since it seems to me to be on a different plane from the other two.

Closed and Open Economies

Why is the model of *The General Theory* essentially closed, with only a few comments here and there on the open case? Clearly, this particular assumption is not a matter of Keynes granting anything to his opponents. Pigou's *Theory of Unemployment* (1933) contains a more systematic treatment of open economy issues than *The General Theory*. And Keynes (along with everyone else) was well aware of the importance of international issues in relation to the UK policy debates of the 1930s (as HS remark).

I think that the answer hinted at by Hicks (cf. HS: 16) is on the right track, though it might be developed a bit further: the assumption has to do with the *generality* at which Keynes was aiming. At first sight this may appear paradoxical, since there is an obvious sense in which an open economy model is more "general" than a closed economy model: write down an open model, and you obtain the closed economy counterpart by deleting certain variables or setting certain parameters to zero. There is another sense, however, in which the tables are turned. A model of a single open economy is a *partial equilibrium* system, constructed on the basis of *ceteris paribus* clauses concerning "the rest of the world," while a closed model is capable of representing the (monetary, capitalist) system as a whole.[1]

It should be remembered that in *The General Theory*, Keynes self-consciously chose to operate at a quite different level from his practical policy-related writings: this was the book that was to provide a theoretical *foundation* for the latter. The object of his critique, therefore, was the "classical" theory of the macroeconomic working of the market mechanism as such, not as applied to any particular national economy. As Keynes (1936: 11) remarks:

> The classical conclusions are intended, it must be remembered, to apply to the whole body of labour and do not merely mean that a single individual can get employment by accepting a cut in money-wages which his fellows refuse. They are supposed to be equally applicable to a closed system as to an open system, and are not dependent on ... the effects of a reduction of money-wages in a single country on its foreign trade, which lie, of course, entirely outside the field of this discussion.

In this light, the assumption of a closed economy is not so much a convenient simplification as a principled *abstraction*, in order to get at the "essential" logic of the monetary capitalist economy. What moral can we extract from this, with regard to Keynes's "vision"? Well, while HS are doubtless correct to emphasize Keynes's "unwillingness to get too far from the 'real world'"--he was certainly not concerned to do theory for theory's sake--I think the above remarks show that Keynes was quite willing to move into the realm of abstraction when the occasion demanded.

Market Structure and Diminishing Returns

Unlike the assumption of a closed economy, there is a *prima facie* case for regarding Keynes's assumption of perfect competition and short-run diminishing returns (the "first classical postulate") as a tactical concession to his opponents--at least in the sense that this assumption makes for an argument *a fortiori*, as Keynes recognized in his 1939 response to the empirical work of Dunlop and Tarshis (KCW/VII: 394-412).[2] On the other hand, in the course of their own useful discussion HS (pp. 13-14) actually undermine the idea that Keynes's attachment to the first classical postulate was a "tactical" matter. There are three issues here. Although they are rather intricately intertwined, it may be illuminating to separate them as far as possible.

1. The question of short-period physical returns to the employment of labor: Are these diminishing, constant, or increasing?

2. The question of the structure of product markets: Is competition imperfect, in the sense that firms are constrained by downward sloping demand curves for their products?

3. The question of labor market structure: Are there significant elements of monopoly (trade unions) and/or monopsony?

The third question can be dismissed quite briefly. Of course there are both monopolistic and monopsonistic elements in the labor market, but there would have been nothing in the least "revolutionary" about a theory of unemployment couched in terms of such imperfections, even in 1936; such arguments were part of the Pigovian conventional wisdom.[3] Keynes himself explicitly placed unemployment due to the restrictive actions of the trade unions in the category of "voluntary unemployment"; he was angling for the bigger fish, namely the unemployment that would persist even if such imperfections were removed.

That leaves issues 1 and 2. Keynes's position on these questions is clear. He regarded the first question as relevant to his theory, but maintained a confident belief in short-period diminishing returns (and hence rising marginal cost).[4] If returns were constant (as might be the case in the depths of a severe depression) that would make the case for an expansion of aggregate demand in order to alleviate unemployment *easier* to defend; but such a policy was, he thought, readily defensible even when returns were diminishing. As for the second question, Keynes saw it as basically irrelevant to his theoretical project.[5] HS point out that if product markets are imperfectly competitive, firms may, even in long-run profit-maximizing equilibrium, produce "below capacity." That is true, of course (where "below capacity" means at a level of output that falls short of that which minimizes average cost), but it is not obvious what connection this has with Keynes's "involuntary unemployment." That firms are producing below capacity in the sense aforementioned is perfectly consistent with labor-market clearing and absence of involuntary unemployment. It is also, for that matter, quite consistent with rising marginal cost: look at the typical textbook diagram showing equilibrium for the monopolistically competitive firm.

I don't have space to develop the analysis from first principles here, but readers familiar with the aggregate demand price/aggregate supply price (D-Z) apparatus employed by Keynes in chapter 3 of *The General Theory* may find the following account helpful. Keynes held that equilibrium employment is given by the point of intersection of the D and Z schedules, *i.e.*, the point of "effective demand." Shifts in the level of employment are therefore to be explained in terms of shifts of one or both of these schedules. Now the degree of product-market imperfection, or "degree of monopoly," might be expected to play a role in fixing the positions of both the D and Z schedules. If an increase in the degree of monopoly shifts the distribution of income in favor of profits, and if the aggregate propensity to consume falls as a result, this will lower the aggregate demand associated with any given level of employment and aggregate income, *i.e.*, shift the D schedule downwards. At the same time, if an increase in the degree of monopoly raises the mark-up of price over marginal cost, this will raise the profit-maximizing sales proceeds associated with any given level of employment, hence shifting the Z schedule upwards. If, as Keynes argues, both D and Z are upward sloping, and Z cuts D from below, then both of these shifts will tend to push the point of effective demand to the left, *i.e.*, lower equilibrium employment.

It is evident, then, that the degree of monopoly *does*, in principle, play a role in Keynes's theory, at least as a "given factor" (cf. HS: 7). But it is a second-order issue for this reason: the hard theoretical work in *The General Theory* does not consist in determining the precise *location* of the point of effective demand, but rather in showing that there *is* a point of effective demand at all, that D and Z are not coincident (as in Say's law). Any argument to the effect that *this* task can be accomplished only on the assumption of imperfect competition is a straightforward repudiation of Keynes's core theoretical position, not merely a dispute over "tactics."

Indeed, in this light I would suggest that an egregious example of questionable tactics is found in some Keynesians' following the fashion of attempting to justify "Keynesian" results by reference to various microeconomic imperfections (in the manner, e.g., of Weitzman, 1982). This approach may make it easier to get a hearing from the mainstream of the profession--which is quite comfortable with the idea that actual markets are less than perfect--but at the cost of diverting attention from Keynes's novel (and apparently disturbing) mode of *macroeconomic* reasoning.[6]

At any rate, as regards the implications for our understanding of Keynes's vision, one thing we see in this case is that although Keynes certainly aimed to make a "revolution" in economic theory, he was no iconoclast. He held onto those elements of the Marshallian heritage that he regarded as sound, rejecting only those that he saw as definitively refuted by observation. He was, as he said of the social implications of *The General Theory*, "moderately conservative."

Exogenous Versus Endogenous Money

"Why," ask HS, "did [Keynes] take the supply of money as an exogenous variable [in *The General Theory*] despite his previous work, especially in *A Treatise on Money*, in which he had convincingly shown that money supply is endogenous?" My first comment is that it is not so clear that Keynes argued for the endogeneity of money in the *Treatise*. Basil Moore (1988, chapter 8) provides what is perhaps the most thorough survey of Keynes's writings as they bear on the question of exogeneity or endogeneity of the money stock. Moore's account is written on the basis of a *parti pris* in favor of a radical and uncompromising version of the endogenous money thesis,[7] but although he finds some formulations in the *Treatise* and elsewhere that seem to point in this direction, his investigations show that none of Keynes's writings exhibit consistent and whole-hearted advocacy of the endogenous money theory. The *Treatise* contains several passages where Keynes talks in terms of the ability of the authorities to control the supply of money (cf. Moore, 1988: 190-191).

I should like to back up this point by reference to one text that Moore does not consider, namely Keynes's entry on "Credit Control" for the 1931 *Encyclopaedia of the Social Sciences* (KCW/XI: 420-427). In this piece--from the same general period as the *Treatise*--Keynes distinguishes between the "old" and "new" systems of monetary management in these terms:

> The old-fashioned system was wont to regulate deliberately the price of credit, that is, the bank rate or discount rate, but to allow the quantity of credit to be determined partly by the movements of gold and partly by the amount of rediscounting at the central bank attracted by the official rate. ... The new fashioned system of credit control, on the other hand, employs not merely bank rate policy but every other weapon in the armoury of a central bank in order to regulate the quantity and price of credit. (KCW/XI: 421-422)

The "weapons" to which Keynes refers include open-market operations, "moral pressure or disciplinary action," and purchases and sales of foreign exchange. He further notes that "critics [of the "new system"] are prone to under-estimate the independent efficacy of open market policy as a means of credit control" (*ibid.*).

After discussing the operating procedures of the US Federal Reserve and the post-WW I Bank of England, Keynes states that a "central bank, which is free to govern the volume of cash and reserve money in its monetary system by the joint use of bank rate and open-market operations, is master of the situation and is in a position to control ... the volume of credit..." (*op. cit.*: 424). He further observes that credit control "depends not merely on the control of the basis of credit but also on there being some more or less rigid relationship between the reserve resources of the member banks and the aggregate of credit that each one of them is free to create." Keynes suggests that this condition was reasonably well satisfied in the USA and Britain, though less so in Germany.

Thus, whether or not one agrees with Moore (and Kaldor) that Keynes's position on money-supply determination reflects a failure to break sufficiently radically with previous modes of thought, it seems clear that Keynes did *not* first develop a definite endogenous money theory and then set this theory aside for tactical reasons in 1935-36. Or at least, if Keynes's choice of the assumption of exogenous money in *The General Theory* (with only a few passing nods towards the possibility of endogenous variation) was "tactical," I believe the tactic in question was primarily a matter of heuristic *simplification* of a complex issue, rather than concession to his opponents. He wanted to abstract from the details of monetary and banking arrangements;[8] and he could do this most concisely by adopting one or the other of two polar simplifications. He could assume that the monetary authority sets the supply of money, and the interest rate plays the role of equilibrating the demand for money with the given supply; or he could assume that the monetary authority sets the rate of interest, and the stock of money adjusts endogenously in line with money demand. It may simply be that faced with these polar options, Keynes regarded the former as the less misleading.[9]

One might argue that even if Keynes had regarded the exogenous interest rate simplification as the less misleading, he would still have had a tactical reason for granting exogenous money in The General Theory (cf. Joan Robinson, 1970: 507). Keynes wanted to show that the interest-rate mechanism was incapable of ensuring that investment equals full-employment saving, hence undercutting Say's law. If he had assumed, in the course of making this argument, that the rate of interest is directly under the control of the central bank, defenders of the "classical" theory would have had a ready reply. While the monetary authorities may be able to *prevent* the interest rate from performing its equilibrating role, the "classicist" might say, if only they fix the money supply and let the rate of interest do its proper job, then Say's law would be restored.[10]

But this hypothetical argument aside, if Keynes were really conceding exogenous money in order to meet his opponents on their own turf, why should he not have said as much? It is striking that in chapter 17 of The General Theory--surely one of parts of that book in which "tactical" considerations are *least* in evidence--Keynes asserts that the inelasticity of its production is one of money's "essential properties."

My conclusion here is rather similar to the point made above, concerning the assumption of decreasing returns in The General Theory. Once again, we see Keynes as "moderately conservative"--and apparently, more as a matter of conviction than of tactics. He was not, so to speak, a closet post Keynesian, harboring all kinds of heresies but suppressing them for the sake of perceived polemical advantage!

III. Keynes and Marx

As I said above, in this final section I wish to pursue one additional perspective on Keynes's vision--that afforded by consideration of his views on Marx. My excuse for broaching this issue is the fact that in opening their paper, HS quote a relevant passage from Keynes's famous letter to George Bernard Shaw of January 1935. The full paragraph is as follows:

> To understand my state of mind, however, you have to know that I believe myself to be writing a book on economic theory, which will largely revolutionize--not, I suppose, at once but in the course of the next ten years--the way the world thinks about economic problems. When my new theory has been duly assimilated and mixed with politics and feelings and passions, I can't predict what the final upshot will be in its effects on action and affairs. But there will be a great change, and, in particular, the Ricardian foundations of Marxism will be knocked away. (KCW/XXVIII: 42)

On the face of it, the claim concerning the "knocking away" of the Ricardian foundations of Marxism is very strange, particularly in the light of the completed text of *The General Theory*. One might suppose "the Ricardian foundations of Marxism" to mean those elements of Ricardo's theory that Marx took to be important and scientifically valid, and hence incorporated into his own theory, *i.e.*, first and foremost the labor theory of value, and secondarily the theory of differential rent. But *these* elements are not put in question in *The General Theory*. Indeed, Keynes (1936: 213-4) goes out of his way to put in a kind word for the labor theory of value.[11] The "Ricardian" propositions that *are* subverted by Keynes are, of course, those concerning the neutrality of money and the automaticity of convergence on full employment. As Keynes puts it (1936: 32), the fundamental idea of "the Ricardian economics"--which, despite Malthus's efforts to the contrary, "conquered England as completely as the Holy Inquisition conquered Spain"--was that "we can safely neglect the aggregate demand function" since "it was impossible for effective demand to be deficient." Elsewhere (*e.g.*, 1936: 18) Keynes effectively equates "the Ricardian economics" with adherence to Say's Law. Yet *this* "Ricardian" principle was, of course, bitterly attacked by Marx. Keynes himself recognized Marx (along with Gesell and Major Douglas) as a writer in whose work the "puzzle of Effective Demand" lived on "furtively" after its banishment from mainstream economic theorizing (1936: 32).

In short, *The General Theory* does *not* repudiate the ideas which Marx actually took from Ricardo, and built upon, while the Ricardian ideas it *does* repudiate are ones that Marx himself rejected. So what on earth are we to make of Keynes's pronouncement to Shaw?

It appears that Keynes meant by "the Ricardian foundations of Marxism" something much more oblique and ironic than simply those ideas of Ricardo's of which Marx approved and upon which he built. A clue to his meaning is found in a piece he wrote for *The New Statesman* in November 1934 (which gave rise to the correspondence with Shaw from which the above quotation is taken). The stimulus for this piece, in turn, was a comment that Shaw had appended to the text of an interview between Stalin and H. G. Wells, published in a previous edition of *The New Statesman*.[12] Sharply critical of Shaw, whom he bracketed with Stalin as a Marxian dogmatist, Keynes used this occasion to reflect broadly on the problems of the age, the historical evolution of capitalist society, and the basis of Communism's attraction.

Keynes was naturally sympathetic with Shaw's disparagement of the "standard system of the economists" (*i.e., laissez-faire* and all that), but he then immediately turned this point against its author:

> Shaw has forgotten that he and Stalin are just as completely under the intellectual dominance of that standard system as Asquith and Inge. The system bred two families--those who thought it true and inevitable, and those who thought it true and intolerable. There was no third school of thought in the nineteenth century. Nevertheless, there is a third possibility--that it is not true. A most upsetting idea

to the dogmatists--no one would be more annoyed than Stalin by that thought--but hugely exhilarating to the scientists. (KCW/XXVIII: 32)

Here is the key to Keynes's association of Marxism with "the Ricardian economics" or "the standard system": both maintain that there is no possibility of ameliorating the working of capitalism. For the system's apologists, this is because it is already the best of all possible worlds; while for the Marxists, who regard the outcomes of that system as intolerable, the impossibility if amelioration provides the rationale for revolution. But, says Keynes, "the standard system is based on intellectual error" (*ibid.*). If he can provide "a sounder economic theory" to guide the policy-makers, and if this leads to the elimination of mass unemployment without the necessity of a social revolution, then the doctrine of the Marxists will be exposed as outdated dogma.

Very similar claims are found in an article Keynes wrote for *The Listener*, also in November 1934 (KCW/XIII: 485-492). Keynes talks of the (long-dominant) "self-adjusting school" of economics, and says "The essential elements in it are fervently accepted by Marxists. Indeed, Marxism is a highly plausible inference from the Ricardian economics, that capitalistic individualism cannot possibly work in practice. So much so, that, if Ricardian economics were to fall, an essential prop to the intellectual foundations of Marxism would fall with it" (*op. cit.*: 488).[13]

In the *New Statesman* piece this sort of claim is supplemented by an account of the social transformation that Keynes saw as separating the world of the 1930s from that of the nineteenth century (when Marx's picture of capitalism "had much verisimilitude"). In the Victorian era, the capitalists really held power, and it was "plausible to say that the economic organisation of society, in spite of its glaring faults, suited them on the whole, and that, so long as they held the power, they would successfully resist major changes coming from other quarters" (KCW/XXVIII: 33). By the 1930s, however, "Time and the Joint Stock Company and the Civil Service [had] silently brought the salaried class into power. Not yet a Proletariat. But a Salariat, assuredly. And it makes a great difference" (*op. cit.*: 34). One could no longer maintain that the "standard system" was defended on the basis of vested interest and class power: "[T]o-day's muddle suits no one. The problem to-day is first to concert good advice and then to convince the well-intentioned that it is good" (*ibid.*).

Following up on this point later in the same month, in a letter to the editor of *The New Statesman*, Keynes wrote: "This is the essential point. Are changes for the better prevented by wicked men who know the changes to be advisable, but resist them out of self-interest? Or are they prevented by the difficulty of knowing for certain where wisdom lies?" (*op. cit.*: 36) He then proceeded to argue for the latter interpretation.

There followed an exchange of private letters between Shaw and Keynes. Aside from yielding the famous quotation already cited, Keynes's side of the correspondence gives us an insight into what Joan Robinson (1966: vi) described as his "allergic" reaction to Marx's writings. While willing to recognize the historical importance of Marx's *Capital*, Keynes placed it on the same footing

as the *Koran*: "I know that many people, not all of whom are idiots, find it a
sort of Rock of Ages and containing inspiration. Yet when I look into it, it is to
me inexplicable that it can have this effect. Its dreary, out-of-date, academic
controversialising seems so extraordinarily unsuitable as material for the
purpose." In addition, Keynes pronounced himself sure that the book's
"contemporary *economic* value (apart from occasional but inconstructive and
discontinuous flashes of insight) is *nil*" (KCW/XXVIII: 38). After receiving a
long and dignified letter from Shaw in defense of Marxism, Keynes returned to
the attack. He had, he said, "made another shot at old K.M. ... reading the
Marx-Engels correspondence just published, without making much progress."
Keynes credited Marx and Engels with inventing "a certain method of carrying
on and a vile manner of writing, both of which their successors have maintained
with fidelity. But if you tell me that they discovered a clue to the economic
riddle, still I am beaten--I can discover nothing but"--once again!--"out-of-date
controversialising" (KCW/XXVIII: 42).

I suggested above that investigation of Keynes's attitude towards Marx might
tell us something about his "vision." As we can see, Keynes evidently regarded
Marx as a theoretical nullity: Marx's system was a mere mirror-image of the
"Ricardian" *laissez-faire* orthodoxy, sharing the latter's premises while drawing
the opposite conclusion.[14] This judgment would seem to bespeak a substantial
blind field in Keynes's vision. Certainly, few of Keynes's modern admirers
would take anything like so dismissive a line towards Marx; and some have
suggested a fairly substantial commonality between the two.[15]

Apart from the fact that Keynes's whole cultural formation predisposed him
to find the Marxian rhetoric of "class war" repellent, his blind spot was an
understandable function of his own (highly productive) fixation on the problem
of effective demand. This made it appear that the only serious objection the
Marxists could have to capitalism, was that it generated mass unemployment,
so a demonstration that capitalism could be operated at full employment via the
exercise of intelligent policy would entirely knock the wind out of the Marxists'
sails.

Two responses can be made here. First, it is surely not the case that the
Marxian critique of capitalism is exhausted by the claim that capitalism tends to
give rise to unemployment;[16] and, second, it appears that even with regard to the
possibility of abolishing unemployment, Keynes was much too sanguine. One
doesn't have to follow Mattick (1969) in belittling Keynes's intellectual
achievement from a Marxian standpoint, to find some of his formulations
extraordinarily naive--in particular, perhaps, the idea that the "more or less
comprehensive socialisation of investment" (Keynes, 1936: 378) could be pushed
through by intellectual persuasion of the great and good, without any serious
resistance on the basis of class interest. There is a stark contrast between
Keynes's sunny optimism regarding the Good Society that could be achieved if
only the ruling class were persuaded of the validity of his ideas, and Michal
Kalecki's (1943) darker reflections on "political aspects of full employment."
With hindsight, the effective abandonment of full employment as a practical

policy goal in most advanced capitalist economies, following the inflation of the 1970s, seems to indicate that Kalecki's assessment was the more prescient. It is at least arguable that Keynesian "full-employment capitalism" represented a progressive but unstable formation, with a tendency either to proceed in the direction of fuller social regulation of the economy (in the form of statutory incomes policies to restrain the inflationary tendencies consequent upon full employment, for instance), or to regress towards the re-establishment of what Marx called the "reserve army of the unemployed" as guarantor of a sufficient rate of exploitation.

The points made in the various sections above are in some degree mutually reinforcing; their common drift may be summarized as follows. While I agree with Harcourt and Sardoni that Keynes was a true innovator in economic theory, I also think it is helpful, in getting his "vision" into focus, to emphasize his complementary conservatism. Keynes sought to rescue liberal capitalism from the malign effects of the intellectual errors of its "classical" apologists--to preempt a political revolution by enacting an intellectual revolution, while preserving as much of the "classical" (i.e., in fact, primarily neoclassical) system as he reasonably could. Whether or not this program is ultimately coherent, or to the taste of some of his more radical followers, I believe it epitomizes the vision of Maynard Keynes.

Notes

*I am grateful to Michael Lawlor for useful comments on an earlier draft.

[1] One might argue that the truly general macrotheory would be one that represents a closed system composed of interacting (open) national economies; but it would be unreasonable to suggest that Keynes ought to have developed his new theory in this highly elaborate form in the first instance.

[2] As in the Harcourt-Sardoni paper, KCW denotes Keynes's *Collected Writings* (Keynes, 1971-1989).

[3] For a trenchant account of why the "New Keynesian" analyses of unemployment along these lines might be more aptly described as "New Pigovian," see Lawlor (1993).

[4] Cf. Keynes's remark (of 1937, see KCW/XIV: 190) that he regarded short-period diminishing returns as "one of the very few incontrovertible propositions of our miserable subject." And as HS point out, even Keynes's later response to Dunlop and Tarshis was far from a whole-hearted recantation of diminishing returns. If there is a "mystery" here, it is not why Keynes made an over-generous tactical concession to orthodoxy, but rather why he was a true believer in the same. But I'm not sure this really is a mystery: Keynes thought he had a sound theoretical rationale, in terms of the heterogeneity of productive facilities (such that an expansion of employment in the short period would involve bringing into use less efficient means of production).

[5] Commenting on *The General Theory* in 1937, Bertil Ohlin said that "Keynes does not seem to me to have been radical enough in freeing himself from the conventional assumptions. When reading his book one sometimes wonders whether he never discussed imperfect competition with Mrs Robinson" (KCW/XIV: 196). Keynes reacted rather sharply: "I have not been able to work out here what you are driving at. The reference to imperfect competition is very perplexing. I cannot see on earth how it comes in. Mrs Robinson, I may mention, read my proofs without discovering any connection" (*op. cit.*: 190).

[6] Cf. Tobin's apposite response to Kaldor in Worswick and Trevithick (1983, chapter 1, esp. 31-32); also see Davidson (1985).

[7] Thus Keynes's various writings are scored according to whether they suggest endogeneity (bravo, fine insights, Keynes almost made it to a proper understanding) or exogeneity (booh, backsliding, failure to break with the quantity theory).

[8] Keynes (1936: vii) remarks that while money plays an essential role in the scheme of *The General Theory*, nonetheless "technical monetary detail falls into the background."

[9] Not all post Keynesians regard this as a case of poor judgment, or failure of nerve. See for instance Dow and Dow (1989: 149), who suggest that, with respect to some important issues at any rate, "Keynes's exogenous money assumption simplifies, without altering the result of, a more holistic analysis."

[10] Kaldor and Moore would want to take this bull by the horns, arguing that "fixing the money supply" is simply *not an option* in a credit-money system; but it seems very doubtful that Keynes would have been willing to make this move.

[11] In addition, Keynes's use of the "wage-unit," rather than a goods price index, as a means of deflating nominal magnitudes in *The General Theory*, means that he effectively works with social labor-time commanded as a unit of account.

[12] Bibliographical details on all this are supplied in KCW/XXVIII.

[13] Here is a genuine mystery, if you will: How could Keynes write off "Ricardian economics" (and by association, Marxian economics too) as little more than a footnote to Say's law, when he was a friend and colleague of Piero Sraffa, whose knowledge of and respect for Ricardo as a theorist need no elaboration?

[14] ...despite the brief, incongruous acknowledgment in *The General Theory* that Marx might be counted among the anti-Say's law heretics.

[15] See for instance Kenway (1983), Rogers (1989). For a contrary view, see Mattick (1969); and for a useful summary of Keynes's ideas on social justice, Elliott and Clark (1987).

[16] Keynes did think he had an answer to another Marxian concern, regarding the inequality of incomes under capitalism, and in particular the inequity associated with property incomes. He looked forward to a not-too-distant future in which the accumulation of capital would have proceeded to the point of saturation, hence driving the marginal efficiency of capital to a level low enough to ensure the famous "euthanasia of the rentier" (1936: 376). But this expectation was not rooted in the core theoretical propositions of *The General Theory*; rather, it falls into the category of speculative long-term social prediction (at which Keynes was no better than Marx).

References

Carabelli, A. (1992) "Organic interdependence and the choice of units in the *General Theory*," in B. Gerrard and J. Hillard (eds.), *The Philosophy and Economics of J. M. Keynes*. Aldershot: Edward Elgar.

Clarke, P. (1988) *The Keynesian Revolution in the Making 1924-1936*. Oxford: Clarendon.

Davidson, P. (ed.) (1985) "Symposium on increasing returns and unemployment theory," *Journal of Post Keynesian Economics*, Vol. VII, 350-409.

Dow, A. C. and Dow, S. C. (1989) "Endogenous money creation and idle balances," in J. Pheby (ed.), *New Directions in Post-Keynesian Economics*. Aldershot: Edward Elgar.

Elliott, J. S. and Clark, B. S. (1987) "Keynes's General Theory and social justice," *Journal of Post Keynesian Economics*, Vol. IX, 381-394.

Kalecki, M. (1943) "Political aspects of full employment," *Political Quarterly*, Vol. XIV.

Kenway, P. (1983) "Marx, Keynes, and the possibility of crisis," in Eatwell, J. and Milgate, M. (eds.) 1983. *Keynes's Economics and the Theory of Value and Distribution*. New York: Oxford University Press.

Keynes, J. M. (1936) *The General Theory of Employment, Interest and Money*. London: Macmillan.

——————. (1971-1989) *The Collected Writings of John Maynard Keynes*, Vols. I-XXX, edited by D. E. Moggridge for the Royal Economic Society. London: Macmillan.

Lawlor, M. S. (1993) "Keynes, Cambridge, and the New Keynesian economics," in W. A. Darity, Jr. (ed.) *Labor Economics: Problems in Analyzing Labor Markets*. Boston: Kluwer.

Littleboy, B. (1990) *On Interpreting Keynes: A Study in Reconciliation*. London: Routledge.

Mattick, P. (1969) *Marx and Keynes*. Boston, MA: Porter Sargent.

Moore, B. (1988) *Horizontalists and Verticalists: The macroeconomics of credit money*. Cambridge: Cambridge University Press.

Pigou, A. C. (1933) *The Theory of Unemployment*. London: Macmillan.

Robinson, J. (1966) *An Essay on Marxian Economics*, second edition. London: Macmillan.

——————. (1970) "Quantity theories old and new," *Journal of Money, Credit and Banking*, Vol. II, No. 4, November, 504-512.

Rogers, C. (1989) *Money, Interest and Capital*. Cambridge: Cambridge University Press.

Runde, J. (1991) "Keynesian uncertainty and the stability of beliefs," *Review of Political Economy*, Vol. 3, 125-145.

Weitzman, M. (1982) "Increasing returns and the foundations of unemployment theory," *Economic Journal*, Vol. 92, 787-804.

Worswick, D. and Trevithick, J. (eds.) (1983) *Keynes and the Modern World*. Cambridge: Cambridge University Press.

6 ASPECTS OF J. M. KEYNES'S VISION AND CONCEPTUALIZED REALITY

Hans E. Jensen[*]

As I read the history of economics, the development of the discipline has been propelled by the specialized contributions of two functionally distinguishable groups of economists. Following suggestions by Joseph A. Schumpeter and Thomas S. Kuhn (Schumpeter, 1964, pp. 62, 70. Kuhn, 1970, p. 24), I label these groups "innovating economists" and "articulating economists," respectively. By innovating economists, I mean that small band of trailblazing scholars who constructed those bodies of economic doctrine that became "paradigms" (Kuhn, 1970, p. viii) by virtue of their acceptance by identifiable groups of practitioners.[1] John Maynard Keynes was a towering member of this band.[2] By the term articulating economists, I refer to those numerous economists whose contributions have taken the form of further articulations, consolidations, extensions, and refinements of the analytic tools contained in the particular paradigms that they accepted as frameworks for their own research. In focusing their attention on the analytic apparatus of an innovator's body of doctrine, pacemaking articulators have frequently disregarded, even recast, the innovator's *raison d'etre* for constructing his analytic apparatus and, consequently, reached different conclusions concerning appropriate actions on the part of public authorities.[3] This kind of muffling of their master's voice seems to have been particularly pronounced in the case of those economists whom Joan Robinson labeled variously the "self-styled Keynesians" and the "bastard Keynesians" (J. Robinson, 1975, p. 131).

Keynes denied the neoclassical "thesis . . . that the economic system is a self-adjusting one, and that . . . there is no obstacle to full employment." He "consider[ed] it [so] important to deny" this thesis that he devoted five years of his life to "writing a book on economic theory, which," in his opinion, would "revolutionise . . . the way the world thinks about economic problems" (Keynes, 1936a, p. 26; and 1935, p. 42). Thus if it is accepted that Keynes of *The General Theory* (Keynes, 1936b) was "diagnosing an inherent defect in the laissez-faire system" (J. Robinson, 1976, p. 5), namely that massive "unemployment is . . . inevitably associated . . . with . . . capitalistic individualism" (Keynes, 1936b, p. 381), and that "the bastard Keynesians turned the argument back into being a defense of laissez-faire" (J.Robinson, 1976, p. 5), then it might be of some interest to inquire into the nature and causes of Keynes's diagnosis; a diagnosis that was unacceptable not only to Keynesians but even more so to Monetarists, and so-called New Classicists and New Keynesians. It is my purpose to attempt such an inquiry in which I shall take the following approach.

In the first place, I shall endeavor to explain the motivations that prompted Keynes to become an economist, with special reference to his authorship of *The*

General Theory. I shall discuss these motivations under the heading of "Keynes's Vision." Secondly, I shall strive to unearth the contours, structure, problems and processes of the particular universe that Keynes analyzed in model terms in *The General Theory.* This universe, I shall label "Keynes's Conceptualized Reality." Combined, his vision and reality constitute what may be called the "pre-analytic" foundation of those "scientific propositions" (Schumpeter, 1954, p. 42) that are embodied in Keynes's *magnum opus.*

KEYNES'S VISION: SOURCES AND PRINCIPAL FEATURES

I use the term "vision" in Alfred Marshall's sense of a "hopeful view of the possibilities of human progress" in the *future* (Marshall, 1961, p. 48) rather than in the Schumpeterian meaning of a "vision of economic reality" as it exists *today* (Schumpeter, 1949, p. 352).[4] As I see it, Keynes's vision was a blend of two closely related components. Firstly, it included a set of "wish-images" (Mannheim, 1955, p. 193) of a potential socioeconomic order of the future. Secondly, it encapsulated an historically conditioned view of the contemporary society as an organism that contained the scientific-technological and socio-cultural prerequisites for a future realization of those imagined "ideal conditions of social life" that were embedded in Keynes's "range of vision" (Marshall, 1961, p. 48). As this phraseology indicates, Keynes's vision was "ideological almost by definition" (Schumpeter, 1954, p. 42).[5]

In the interregnum between his completion of the *Treatise on Money* (Keynes, 1930a) and the beginning of his work on *The General Theory*,[6] Keynes expressed the essence of his wish-image thus: This "author . . . believes that the day is not far off when the economic problem will take the back seat where it belongs, and that the arena of the heart and head will be occupied . . . by our real problems - the problems of life and of human relations, of creation and behaviour and religion" (Keynes, 1931b, p. xviii). But what was the nature of that viewpoint from which Keynes viewed the ideal society of the future?[7] And what were the principal features of that future "destination of economic bliss" (Keynes, 1930b, p. 331) that Keynes viewed in the particular light that emanated from his point of view? In an attempt at answering these questions, I shall first turn to Keynes's viewpoint and related matters.

Keynes's Viewpoint

Keynes identified two essential aspects of his point of view when he declared that his envisioned blissful society of the future would be characterized by "social justice, and individual liberty." The former "needs . . . an unselfish and enthusiastic spirit, which loves the ordinary man." The latter needs "tolerance, breadth, appreciation of the excellencies of variety and independence" (Keynes, 1926a, p. 311). Thus, as he put it himself, Keynes looked at human affairs from the viewpoint of a "humanitarian" who worked for "an advance towards economic equality greater than any which we have had in recent times" and for the simultaneous development of a type of "individualism" that would be ideal by virtue of having been "purged of its [present] defects and abuses." Significantly, individualism would become the "best [possible] safeguard of personal liberty" and, in consequence thereof, the "most powerful instrument to better the future" (Keynes, 1940, pp. 428, 368; and 1936b, p. 380). In view of these observations of Keynes, there is no reason to doubt that he "himself said that he was possessed by 'the Verbesserungs malady'" (Hession, 1984, p. 203).

It appears, therefore, that Keynes was an ethically committed person whose moral sentiments formed the foundation of that point of view from which he saw a necessity, and a possibility, for an improvement of the human condition, a view that spurred him, qua economist, to work for a realization of his vision.

It seems that those who knew Keynes well concurred in this assessment. According to Sir Roy Harrod, Keynes "believed that distress in all its forms should not go unheeded. He believed that . . . all our social evils, distressed areas, unemployment and the rest, could [and should] be abolished" (Harrod, 1951, p. 192). Sir Austin Robinson opined that Keynes "was an idealist in the sense that it mattered to him deeply and immediately what was the fate of mankind." This "sense of moral purpose and obligation" made "truth and right . . . his objective." Hence Keynes "pursued . . . the solution of reparations, or currency reform, or full employment . . . with a powerful conviction that thus only could the evils of the world be mitigated" (A. Robinson, 1947, pp. 25, 66, 26). Sir Austin "would [therefore] claim for Keynes a true altruism"; a claim that moved him to declare that he could not "fail to see . . . [Keynes] as the perfect 'do-gooder,' identifying the things that the world most needs to have done and using all his brains and persuasion to get them done" (A. Robinson, 1972, p. 546; and 1975, pp. 21-22). Geoffrey C. Harcourt, a recognized authority on Keynes, his work and influence, summed it all up recently when he declared that "Keynes was a good man" (Harcourt, 1992).

Looking back in 1938, however, Keynes observed[8] that he and his fellow Apostles and Blomsburyians[9] grew up in the conviction that "[n]othing mattered except [good] states of mind . . . chiefly our own." Such states "were not associated with action or achievement or with consequences" but "consisted in communion with objects of love, beauty and truth" (Keynes, 1938a, pp. 436, 438).[10] Consequently, said Keynes, "we discarded . . . morals . . . meaning by . . . 'morals' one's attitude towards the outside world." We "repudiated entirely customary morals, conventions, and traditional wisdom" and "claimed the right to judge every individual case on its merits." The Apostolic Bloomsburyians were, therefore, "immoralists" in the sense that they "recognised no moral obligation on . . . [them], no inner sanction, to conform or obey." And Keynes concluded that in this sense, he "remain[ed], and always . . . [would] remain, an immoralist" (Keynes, 1938a, pp. 436, 446, 447).[11]

Keynes's confessions of 1938 seem to be at odds with his alleged "do-goodism" and with another profession that he made in 1938, namely that "economics is essentially a moral science and not a natural science. That is to say, it employs introspection and judgments of value" (Keynes, 1938b, p. 297).[12] Keynes provided some hints, however, as to a possible reconciliation of what appears to be his irreconcilable positions.

First of all, he ended his 1938 reminiscences with the admission "that there may have been just a grain of truth when . . . [a critic of Bloomsbury] said in 1914 that we were 'done for'" (Keynes, 1938a, p. 450). Thus it seems that the mature Keynes attempted to distance himself from the Apostolic and Bloomsburyian mainstream of the past.[13]

Secondly, as the following observation by Keynes indicates, he began such a disassociation already when he was a member of Bloomsbury in good standing: "In practice, of course, at least as far as I was concerned, the outside world was not forgotten or forsworn" (Keynes, 1938a, p. 445; emphasis added). This world, or "Universe," was populated, however, by individuals who, like Keynes et al., had states of mind. Thus although it was "the excellence of the state as a whole with which . . . [Keynes was] concerned," the Universe "regarded as a whole is not . . . capable of mental states." Consequently, said Keynes, in "ethical calculations each individual's momentary state of mind is our sole unit." It means that the excellence of the state as a whole is "equal to the sum of the goodness [of the states] of the persons composing . . . the Universe" (Keynes, 1905, in Davis, 1991a, p. 65).[14] As pointed out by John B. Davis, it seems, therefore, that Keynes deemed it his "duty to aim [at] . . . the greatest sum of good states of mind across individuals."[15] Moreover, as Keynes saw it, one's "duty in promoting the greatest good becomes clear, since promoting the well-being of the greatest number of individuals is tantamount to promoting the greatest number of good states of mind" (Davis, 1991a, pp. 65, 66).[16] Thirdly, as mentioned above, Keynes "claimed the right to judge every

> . . . case on its merits" (Keynes, 1938a, p. 446). He made such a judgment when he declared that the "outstanding faults of the economic society in which we live are its failure to provide for full employment and its arbitrary and inequitable distribution of wealth and income." It may be inferred from these various pronouncements by Keynes that he was of the opinion that successful efforts "to cure the [economic] disease whilst preserving efficiency and freedom" (Keynes, 1936b, pp. 372, 381) would be synonymous with an increase in the number of people who would experience expanded well-being and therefore tantamount to an augmentation of the sum of good states of mind.

What was the impetus that made it possible for Keynes to equate an expansion of the sum of good states of mind with an increase in the number of people experiencing a growth of their economically rooted well-being? In my opinion, the stimulus was twofold. In the first place, Keynes was inspired retrospectively by what Sir Roy Harrod called the "presuppositions of [Keynes's home at] 6 Harvey Road" in Cambridge (Harrod, 1951, p. 4).[17] It was an inspiration that had been lurking in the back of Keynes's mind, so to speak, and which surfaced post Bloomsbury to reinforce a conviction that he had formed in his Bloomsbury period, namely his above-quoted opinion that "the outside world was not [to be] forgotten or forsworn" (Keynes, 1938a, p. 445).[18] Secondly, he was influenced by the moral sentiments of Marshall, who in Keynes's own words, had passed "into economics" through the portals of ethics so that "it was only through Ethics that . . . [Marshall] first reached economics" (Keynes, 1924a, p. 171).

Presuppositions of Harvey Road

The origins of the presuppositions of Harvey Road must undoubtedly be sought in the values that Keynes's parents, Florence Ada, nee Brown, and John Neville Keynes, had inherited from their respective homes. Both parents came from families of dissenters and were, therefore, "brought up in fairly strict nonconformist principles" (G. Keynes, 1975, p. 27). These principles were broadened, concretized and increasingly secularized in the course of Miss Brown's and Neville Keynes's subsequent experiences in academe and, in the case of the former, among those poor and disfranchised fellow human beings who lived outside the walls of the ancient colleges of Cambridge.

After having been awarded an undergraduate degree in moral science by the University of Cambridge and an M. A. degree in political economy by University College, London, Neville Keynes became part of the University of Cambridge establishment in 1876.[19] He married Florence Brown in 1882 and the newly married couple moved into No. 6 Harvey Road in the same year. She had been a student in one of Cambridge's first women colleges and she passed a non-degree examination in 1880. After her marriage, Florence Keynes became heavily involved in charitable work and social services.[20] She did so, it is said, because her "instincts and family tradition alike moved her towards self-improvement and do-gooding" (Skidelsky, 1983, p. 57).

The presuppositions of Harvey Road were, therefore, a blend of impulses and sentiments that emanated from two worlds: the scholarly and intellectual world in which Neville Keynes moved and the political world of social reform and services on which Florence Keynes's duty-driven contributions left their marks.

The impulses from the world of the intellectuals were brought to 6 Harvey Road by a number of dons, scholars, and others with intellectual roots in Oxbridge who were entertained by the Keyneses.[21] As Keynes put it himself, the "circle" of Neville Keynes's friends and associates "was at its full strength in my boyhood, and, when I was first old enough to be asked . . . to luncheon or dinner . . . I remember a homely, intellectual atmosphere which it is harder to find in the swollen, heterogeneous Cambridge of to-day" (Keynes, 1924a, p. 213). It was in this atmosphere that one half, so to speak, of the presuppositions of Harvey Road sprouted. This part consisted of the proposition "that the government was and would continue to be in he hands of an intellectual aristocracy using the method of persuasion." Keynes absorbed the essence of the idea and "tended till the end [of his life] to think of the really important decisions being reached by a small group of intelligent people." In other words, the intellectually derived, but normatively tinted, portion of the presuppositions of Harvey Road instilled in Keynes a belief "that by rational discussion one could plan and achieve reform and carry forward the progress of mankind" (Harrod, 1951, pp. 192-193, 193, 5). But the notion of what progress means, what the content of progress is, came to a large extent from the other half of the presuppositions of Harvey Road, namely from an overtly humanistic and ethical part that emanated from Florence Keynes's "robust variety" of "Liberalism" (Skidelsky, 1983, p. 57). The influence of his mother's humanism made Keynes think of progress in terms of the reversal of a process in capitalism in the course of which "the labouring classes [had] accepted from ignorance or powerlessness, or were compelled, persuaded, or cajoled by custom, convention, authority, and the well-established order of society into accepting a situation in which they could call their own very little of the cake that they and nature and the capitalists were co-operating to produce" (Keynes, 1919, pp. 11-12). In other words, progress meant the abolition of "poverty" which had become of such a magnitude in the early 1930s that it "consume[d] the possibilities of life" with the result that "civilisation crumble[d]" (Keynes, 1933b, p. 189). Keynes was therefore highly critical of laissez faire and applauded any system of thought that "departs from laissez-faire" (Keynes, 1926b, p. 290). In view of the humanistic contents of Keynes's thinking, Sir Roy was of the opinion that it "may well be that . . . [Florence Keynes's] practical humanity made a deeper impression on Maynard's young mind than the abstract doctrines of the social philosophers" who gathered at No. 6 Harvey Road (Harrod, 1951, p. 12). As intimated above, it does not mean, however, that his father, and his father's associates, had no influence on Keynes's ethical viewpoint. A correct interpretation seems therefore to be that it was from both of "his parents [that] he inherited the late Victorian conformist belief in the necessity and possibility of the improvement of society by the application of reason and the sense of obligation to one's social inferiors that went with it" (Johnson, 1974, p. 106).

Marshall's Moral Sentiments[22]

Toward the end of his life, Marshall summarized the development of his moral sentiments thus: "About the year 1867 . . . [Henry L.] Mansel's Bampton Lectures came into my hands and caused me to think that man's own possibilities were the most important subject for his study. So I gave myself for a time to the study of Metaphysics." But metaphysics did not provide Marshall with a satisfactory answer to a question that Mansel's Lectures had placed uppermost in his mind, namely "how far do the conditions of life of the . . . working classes . . . suffice for fullness of life?" In a further search for an answer to this question, Marshall went from "Metaphysics . . . to Ethics, and thought the justification of the existing condition of society was not easy." Then a friend said to Marshall: "'Ah! if you understood Political Economy you would not say that'." So Marshall read John Stuart "Mill's Political Economy and got much excited about it" (Marshall in Keynes, 1924a, p. 171). For one thing, it seems that Mill's discussion of "The Probable Futurity of the Labouring

Classes" (Mill, 1909, pp. 752-794) caused Marshall to sharpen his question. Now he questioned, or had "doubts" about, the "propriety of inequalities of opportunity, rather than of material comfort." Stimulated by these doubts, he "visited the poorest quarters of several cities and walked through one street after another, looking at the faces of the poorest people." After that experience, he "resolved to make as thorough a study as . . . [he] could of Political Economy" in order to find an answer to his question (Marshall in Keynes, 1924a, p. 171). Thus when he was in the process of writing his Principles of 1890 (Marshall, 1961), Marshall claimed "in the vein of [Jeremy] Bentham" (Edgeworth, 1925, p. 71) that it was his aim to "prepare the armament of knowledge" (Pigou, 1925, p. 84) that would be needed to ensure that "all the . . . poor may be improved away" which, in his opinion, would be tantamount to bringing about "increases [in] the sum total of human happiness" (Marshall, 1893a, p. 199; and 1883, p. 208). Hence three years after the publication of the first edition of his magnum opus, it was with considerable pride that Marshall made the following declaration: "I have devoted myself for the last twenty-five years to the problem of poverty, and . . . very little of my work has been devoted to any inquiry which does not bear on that" (Marshall 1893b, p. 205).

As intimated above, Marshall argued (a la Smith [Smith, 1937, pp. 79, 81, 325-326]), that happiness is a function of income. Thus he spoke of "an income of happiness" by which he understood a "flow or stream of wellbeing [sic] as measured by the flow or stream of incoming wealth and the consequent power of using and consuming it." Hence he concluded (again a la Smith [Smith 1937, p. 625]) that "consumption is the end of production." According to Marshall, however, consumption involves more than ingestion of the "necessaries of life." As he saw it, true happiness is associated with the total satisfaction that is enjoyed through the attainment of creature comfort plus access to, and acquisition of, those "higher forms of enjoyment" that he subsumed under the heading of "culture" (Marshall, 1961, pp. 134. 67, 137).

Accepting the classical economists' moral dictum that "the well-being of the whole people should be the ultimate goal of all private effort and public policy," Marshall visioned a future in which free access to education had brought about a situation in which the "working classes have been abolished" (Marshall, 1961, p. 47; and 1873, p. 118). The material foundation for such a development would be laid by a continuous "mechanical progress" that would usher in expanded use of "automatic and other machinery" that, in its turn, would cause a continuous growth of the "national income." In Marshall's opinion, these achievements, in conjunction with policies envisioned to effect an ever "more equal distribution of [the growing] wealth" and income, would facilitate "the production of human lives that are joys in themselves and the sources of joy" (Marshall, 1961, pp. 716, 524, 41; and 1897, p. 311). In short, Marshall's ethically tinted and optimistically shaped outlook on the future took the form of a vision of achievable "ideal conditions of human life" in which happiness would reach hitherto unimagined heights because all the people had "become not only more efficient producers but also wiser consumers, with greater knowledge of all that is beautiful, and more care for it" (Marshall, 1961, p. 48; and 1885, p. 173).

When Keynes struggled to shed the Marshallian "theory on which . . . [he] was brought up" (Keynes, 1936c, p. 35), he did not attempt to slough off Marshall's normative vision of the good society of the future. On the contrary, the society that Keynes envisioned has the appearance of a magnified replica of Marshall's vision, but one that is even more utopian than Marshall's.

Keynes's Vision as a Product of Ethics and History[23]

Keynes's vision was conditioned not only by those ethical preconceptions that he inherited from his home and mentors, but also by his interpretative use of historical works and compilations of contemporary statistical data. As a user of history,[24] Keynes was much influenced by Marshall's dictum that it is "from . . . history," including "contemporary history," that "all guidance for the future . . . proceeds" (Marshall, 1897, pp. 300, 310, 300).[25] Thus when he described Marshall as being "conspicuously historian" (Keynes, 1924a, p. 174), this characterization fitted Keynes himself. His reading of history, especially contemporary history, made him even more optimistic than Marshall, if possible, concerning the future. Keynes found, for example, that there was "evidence that the revolutionary technical changes, which have so far chiefly affected industry, may soon be attacking agriculture." These and other signs moved him to make the following prediction just when the Western economies were descending to the abyss of the Great Depression: "In quite a few years - in our own lifetimes I mean - we may be able to perform all the operations of agriculture, mining and manufacture with a quarter of the human effort to which we have become accustomed." When that comes to pass, "[t]hree-hour shifts or a fifteen-hour week" will become standard. Keynes was therefore confident that "a hundred years hence," i.e., 2030 a.d., the power of "science and compound interest" would make "all of us, on the average, eight times better off in the economic sense than we are" in 1930. Consequently, he drew the "conclusion that . . . the economic problem may be solved, or be at least within sight of solution, within a hundred years. This means that the economic problem is not - if we look into the future - the permanent problem of the human race" (Keynes, 1930b, pp. 325, 329, 326, 328, 326). By the economic problem, Keynes meant the "problem of want and poverty and the economic struggle between classes and nations," a problem that he viewed as "nothing but a frightful muddle" and a "transitory and . . . unnecessary muddle" at that (Keynes 1931b, p. xviii).

In other words, when he viewed the contemporary state of science and technology from his ethical standpoint and saw how it revealed itself in the light of his interpretation of recent historical trends, Keynes became convinced that it would only be a matter of a century before humankind would be capable of relieving itself "of its traditional purpose," namely that of "solving the economic problem" (Keynes, 1930b, p. 327).

When that ancient yoke has been lifted from the shoulders of the inhabitants of the future society envisioned by Keynes, "the accumulation of wealth is no longer of high social importance." He predicted, therefore, that "there will be great changes in the code of morals" (Keynes, 1930b, p. 329).

> We shall [then, said Keynes] be able to rid ourselves of many of the pseu-domoral principles which have hag-ridden us for two hundred years, by which we have exalted some of the most distasteful of human qualities into the position of the highest virtues. We shall be able to afford to dare to assess the money-motive at its true value. The love of money as a possession - as distinguished from the love of money as a means to the enjoyments and realities of life - will be recognised for what it is, a somewhat disgusting morbidity, one of those semi-criminal, semi-pathological propensities which one hands over with a shudder to the specialists in mental disease. All kinds of social customs and economic practices, affecting the distribution of wealth and of economic rewards and penalties, which we now maintain at all costs, however distasteful and unjust they may be in themselves, because they are tremendously useful in promoting the accumulation of capital, we shall then be free, at last, to discard (Keynes, 1930b, p. 329).

When humankind's "destination of economic bliss" has been reached, its members will "value ends above means and prefer the good to the useful," because by then "avarice" will be viewed as "a vice . . . the exaction of usury . . . [as] a misdemeanour, and the love of money . . . [as] detestable." When, "in days not so very remote," the "greatest change which has ever occurred in the material environment of life for human beings" is an accomplished fact, we "shall honour those who can teach us how to pluck the hour and the day virtuously and well, the delightful people who are capable of taking direct enjoyment in things, the lilies of the field who toil not, neither do they spin" (Keynes, 1930b, p. 331).

In 1930, Keynes was convinced that the movement toward this idyllic "destiny" of the future "ha[d] already begun" in the countries of Christendom (Keynes, 1930b, pp. 332, 331). It had also become clear to him in the very same year, however, that this movement was decelerating rapidly. Hence Keynes's vision of an achievable future society in which "man will be faced with his real, his permanent problem - how to use his freedom from pressing economic cares" now seemed to take on the mocking appearance of a mirage on the horizon of a faltering economy beset by a deep "depression" and hence plagued by an "enormous anomaly of unemployment in a world full of wants" (Keynes, 1930b, pp. 328, 322).

Keynes's realization that the economy's "magneto trouble" had thrown it into "one of the greatest economic catastrophes of modern history" did not persuade him that it would never again be prudent to "take wings into the future." But he did admit that he had to disembarrass himself temporarily of his long view of "economic life . . . a hundred years hence" (Keynes 1930c, pp. 129, 126; and 1930b, p. 322). The immediate challenge facing Keynes was that of devising "a right analysis of the problem [of depression and unemployment in order] to cure the disease whilst preserving efficiency and freedom" (Keynes, 1936b, p. 381). He was confident, however, that the journey toward the promised land could be resumed once he had laid bare the "originating causes of the slump," found its "cure," and convinced those "in authority" what they should "choose" to do in order to make society "emerge from . . . [the] semi-slump . . . which may be expected to succeed the acute phase" of the slump (Keynes, 1931c, p. 344).

In other words, in order to find an answer to the question of "How, then, can we start [the economy] up again" for a continuation of the journey toward the future state of bliss?, Keynes had to begin with a "correct . . . diagnosis" of the depression. For unless that be done, said he, "I do not see how we can hope to find the cure" (Keynes, 1930c, p. 129; and 1931c, p. 344). But a diagnosis of a slump, or any other socioeconomic malady, is a function of the diagnostician's conceptualization of the body economic that is afflicted with the malaise. Thus of necessity, it was a conceptualized socioeconomic order that Keynes analyzed in model terms in his General Theory. And to repeat, he did so for the purpose of showing how the great depression of the 1930s might be dislodged as an obstruction on the road to the ideal society of the future.

KEYNES'S CONCEPTUALIZED REALITY: MEANING AND SOURCES

The socioeconomic actuality in which Keynes lived could not "be 'known'" to him, or anybody else, "in the same way as natural objects get to be 'known'" (Kecskemeti, 1952, p. 31). Consequently, he was forced to substitute something knowable for the essentially unknowable actuality. This surrogate, I have become accustomed to label "conceptualized reality."[26] By Keynes's reality, therefore, I understand his conceptually formulated and mentally designed approximation to, or image of, the actual socioeconomic order and thus a proxy for that order.[27] Keynes's reality may therefore be viewed as the output of an intellectual process of conceptualization in which he used a variety of inputs. As I see it, these ingredients may be divided into three broad categories: Philosophical-theoretical elements, historical components, and data pertaining to the current economic scene.

Philosophical-Theoretical Inputs

The philosophical-theoretical inputs employed by Keynes when he constructed his reality originated largely, but not completely, in those sources that underpinned the viewpoint from which he viewed the ideal society of the future. The added inputs came from the works of Edmund Burke. Thus although he considered "their arguments preposterous" when Burke and Rousseau" et al. preached the gospel of "individualism and laissez-faire," Keynes referred approvingly to "what Burke termed 'one of the finest problems in legislation, namely to determine what the State ought to take upon itself to direct by the public wisdom, and what it ought to leave . . . to individual exertion'" (Keynes, 1926b, pp. 277, 276, 277, 288). Burke's influence upon Keynes was, therefore, especially pronounced when the latter constructed those state institutions that he included in his conceptualized reality.[28]

When he molded the character of those economic actors that he implanted in his reality, Keynes started from a position that was a reflection of his canon that it is desirable for people to experience good states of mind through the attainment of economically generated well-being. He posited, however, that the perception of such states, and of the means for their attainment and of the extent to which they are achievable, is a function of the perceptors' human nature. Under the impact of the "development of new ideas" in philosophical discourse in Cambridge in the 1920s and early 1930s (Davis, 1991b, p. 409), Keynes became convinced that human nature is multidimensional. Thus he argued that it is characterized by "spontaneous, volcanic and even wicked impulses." This does not mean that Keynes was of the opinion that human behavior is governed solely by "animal spirits." He confessed in 1938, for example, that he "still suffer[ed] incurably from attributing an unreal rationality to . . . people's feelings and behaviour" (Keynes, 1938a, p. 449; 1936b, p. 161; and 1938a, p. 448).

From this behavioral menu, Keynes sorted out those class-specific behavioral "propensities and habits" (Keynes, 1936b, p. 91) that he implanted in the principal actors in his conceptualized reality. It is my contention that in so doing, Keynes was influenced by the theory of human nature that was espoused by Marshall.[29]

Marshall conceived of human nature from two points of view: Utilitarianism[30] and evolutionism.[31] He maintained, therefore, that, "the whole of man's nature" is dichotomous because "though there is a kernel of man's nature that has scarcely changed, yet many elements of his character, that are most effective for economic uses, are of modern growth." Hence the kernel constitutes "the statics of human nature" whereas the elements form the "dynamics" of that selfsame nature (Marshall, 1897, p. 299; 1898, p. 44; and 1897, p. 299; emphasis added). The kernel is static because it harbors man's unchanging, innate "instincts" and a complement of "faculties" that includes "intelligence." Prominent among the instinctive proclivities is a "capacity for pleasure or pain." Moreover, each individual is capable of balancing pleasure and pain and of "measuring . . . [the] mental state[s]" that are caused by different pleasures (Marshall, 1961, pp. 752, 2, 236, 18, 16). The other "side of human nature," i.e., the elements, is dynamic in the sense that it is capable not only of redefining the individual's conception of how his innate "wants and desires" may be satisfied in a dynamically evolving society but also of adding new wants to a person's collection of wants. In Marshall's words, "each new step upwards is to be regarded as the development of new activities giving rise to new wants." As "history shows," said he, the "new methods of action" that power these activities "may alter . . . human nature . . . very much even in a few generations." In short, the interaction of the kernel and the elements produces a pronounced "pliability of human nature" (Marshall, 1897, p. 299; and 1961, pp. 86, 89, 752, 764).[32]

Keynes "was brought up" on Marshall's nature-cum-nurture theory of behavior at the same time as he was "taught" his analytical "stuff" (Keynes, 1936c, p. 35). By virtue of his employment of the former as an input when he constructed the human nature of the economic actors in his reality, Keynes was enabled to endow these actors with predictable behavior in terms of their responses to those stimuli that emanate from their milieu. As will be discussed below, the responses in question are those of liquidity-seeking "rentiers," profit-expecting "entrepreneurs" in "enterprises" characterized by a "separation between ownership and management," public-spirited managers of "big [self-socializing] undertakings," and propertyless "working classes" (Keynes, 1936b, pp. 92, 150; 1926b, p. 290; and 1923, p. 27). The stimuli that trigger the actors' responses are rooted in the facts of Keynes's reality. These facts are the particular forms that socioeconomic data assumed when Keynes viewed them through the "selecting grid" (Stark, 1958, p. 108) of his Marshallesque theory of behavior. A substantial portion of these data originated in Keynes's interpretative study of history.

Historical Inputs

As indicated in my discussion of his vision, Keynes was skillful in his "use [of] history" as narrated by historians (Wilson, 1975, p. 235). In my view, when Keynes made his selections from this recorded history, he was again influenced by Marshall who had "selected and traced out . . . a few prominent threads . . . from [that] tangled complex which constitutes the history of man" (Marshall, 1897, p. 300). Among these strands, Keynes chose Marshall's account of the development of capitalism's productive powers and his explanation of the impact of these powers upon the formation and modification of socioeconomic institutions.

According to Marshall, society's productive powers were rooted in "innumerable inventions" that had been applied economically by a small band of innovating "undertakers" and by those imitators who "follow[ed] . . . [the] tracks . . . beaten" by the former. Because of the resultant, and growing, "use of expensive appliances in manufacture," it became increasingly difficult for the undertakers to autofinance such equipment. Hence a rentier class of "owners of [financial] capital" split off from, and henceforth provided funds for, the class of formerly self-financing entrepreneurs. This bifurcation of property was followed by another division when it became impossible for the proprietary firms to pool sufficient fund for the acquisition of "new appliances" the use of which would be tantamount to the introduction of "powerful economies of production on a large scale" (Marshall 1961, pp. 712, 597, 746, 544, 287). To remedy this situation, the "joint stock company," or business corporation, was instituted. But when "a private firm is thrown into joint stock form," said Marshall, there occurs a "wholesale transference of authority and responsibility from the owners . . . to salaried managers" who do "not bring any capital into it." Thus the adoption of the corporate form of business was tantamount to a second bifurcation of the institution of property because it meant that "the ownership of capital . . . [was] effectively divorced from its control" (Marshall, 1919, pp. 317, 323; 1961, p. 302; and 1919, p. 317). Marshall also pointed out that in addition to the proprietary and managerial classes, there had emerged a group of "working classes," or "'lower classes'" as he put it, who sold their productive services to employers in "free markets for labour" (Marshall, 1873, p. 103; and 1961, pp. 3,747).

Marshall's historical inquiry into the causes of technological development and its subsequent impact upon the institutions of property and labor markets, was not lost upon Keynes. In 1930, for example, he paid the following Marshallesque tribute[33] to the scientific-technological development of the West:

> From the sixteenth century, with a cumulative crescendo after the eighteenth, the great age of science and technical invention began, which since the beginning of the nineteenth century has been in full flood - coal, steam, electricity, petrol, steel, rubber, cotton, the chemical industries, automatic machinery and the methods of mass production, wireless, printing . . . and thousands of other things . . . too . . . familiar to catalogue (Keynes, 1930b, p. 324).

Because of these dramatic events, more and more investable inventions had appeared on the scene. And, significantly, investments were actually made therein. Consequently, the "growth of [real] capital" in the latter part of the nineteenth century and the opening decade of the twentieth had "been on a scale which . . . [was] far beyond a hundred-fold of what any previous age had known." Keynes estimated, therefore, that "the average standard of life in Europe and the United States ha[d] been raised . . . about fourfold" (Keynes 1930b, pp. 324-325, 324). But that was not the whole story. In the process of industrial growth, each of the major national communities in the West had been transformed "into a vast and complicated industrial machine" that effected "a far-reaching transformation of the economic structure" of society (Keynes, 1919, p. 7). The transformed structure was the one that Marshall had seen unfolding and which, as intimated above, Keynes characterized as a division of society "into the investing class, the business class, and the earning class" of propertyless workers (Keynes, 1923, p. 4). These historically derived notions and insights on the part of Keynes were reinforced, strengthened and expanded in the course of his analysis of current data.

Current Factual Data

From the outbreak of the First World War till the end of his life, Keynes was frequently totally immersed in interpretative analyses of data pertaining to the contemporary economic scene. For example, referring to European trends in population, production and foreign trade in the two or three decades that came to an end in August 1914, Keynes concluded in 1919 that the European body economic was suffering from arteriosclerosis well before the onset of war in the former year. The malady manifested itself in the form of a multidimensional instability: "instability of an excessive population dependent for its livelihood on a complicated and artificial organization, the psychological instability of its labouring and capitalist classes, and the instability of Europe's claim, coupled with the completeness of her dependence, on the food supplies of the New World" (Keynes, 1919, p. 15). The British restoration of the gold standard in 1924 at sterling's prewar par rate was viewed by Keynes as a fifth kind of instability. That was so, he said, because from now on "whenever we sell anything abroad . . . we have to reduce the sterling price . . . by 10 per cent in order to be on a competitive level" (Keynes, 1925a, p. 208). Referring to the resultant difference between cost and export prices, the "colliery owners propose[d] that the gap should be bridged by a reduction of wages, irrespective of a reduction in the cost of living - that is to say, by a lowering in the standard of life of the miners." That "this should seem to anyone to be a reasonable proposal . . . is a grave criticism of our way of managing our economic affairs," said Keynes. And he predicted that the result of the mine owners' demand would "be war, until those who are economically weakest are beaten to the ground" (Keynes, 1925a, pp. 222, 211). Keynes was correct. When the miners refused to accept a cut in wages, they were locked out by the owners in the spring of 1926 whereupon the "Trades Union Council . . . supported them with a General Strike." When the strike collapsed after nine days, Keynes, whose "feelings . . . [were] with the workers," was "not very cheerful about the future" (Keynes, 1926c, p. 530; 1926d, p. 532; and 1926e, p. 543).

The more Keynes spent his "thought on these matters, the more alarmed . . . [he became] at seeing . . . [people] in authority attacking the problems of the changed post-war world with . . . unmodified pre-war views and ideas" which, he warned, was tantamount "to sow[ing] the seeds of the downfall of individualistic capitalism" (Keynes, 1924b, p. 271-272, 272). Keynes's alarm intensified in the closing years of the 1920s when his inspection of unemployment statistics revealed that unemployment had "never been less than one million since" 1923, and that in April of 1929 "1,140,000 workpeople . . . [were] unemployed" (Keynes, 1929, p. 92).

At first, Keynes attributed this development to what he called the "imbecility" of governmental and semi-governmental institutions, especially the Bank of England and the Treasury (Keynes, 1928a, p. 750); an imbecility that was exhibited in the return to gold and in fiscal actions based on the so-called "Treasury view" that "money raised by the state for financing productive schemes must diminish pro tanto the supply of capital available for private industry" (Keynes, 1931d, p. 147; and 1929, p. 115). Keynes rejected this view because when "we have unemployed men and unemployed plant and more savings than we are using at home, it is utterly imbecile to say that we cannot afford . . . roads, bridges, ports, buildings, slum clearances, electrification, telephones, etc. etc." (Keynes, 1928b, p. 765).

As he studied the recent economic record and listened to testimonies before committees of inquiry in the late 1920s and early 1930s, Keynes felt compelled to return to the concept of the economic order that he had portrayed in 1919. Hence he now maintained that imbecile governmental institutions had not caused the "collapse of private investment" that ushered in the depression. These institutions had merely failed to "mitigate the consequences of the collapse"

(Keynes, 1931d, p. 147; emphasis added). Rather, Keynes argued, the "severe decline in the volume of investment" had its origin in the capitalist order itself. Thus whereas he had earlier censured the businessmen for being "narrow and ignorant" and for making wrong decisions on the basis of old-fashioned "orthodoxies" a la governmental institutions, (Keynes, 1931c, p. 352; and 1926e, p. 545), Keynes now viewed the entrepreneurs as victims of a flawed economic system. To put it differently, the principal consequence of his digestion of economic information in the late 1920s and early 1930s was that Keynes was moved to resuscitate his 1919 concept of "the entrepreneur class of capitalists . . . [as] the active and constructive element in the whole capitalist society" (Keynes, 1919, p. 149). At the same time as he hailed the entrepreneurs anew as the heroes of capitalism, Keynes cast "the rentiers," who "represent[ed] on the whole the richer section of the community," in the role of the villains of the system (Keynes, 1936b, p. 262). He did so because these financiers had strangulated the economy by refusing to reduce their lending rates sufficiently to enable the increasingly pessimistic entrepreneurs "to call to the aid of their enterprises" those financial resources on which they depended as undertakers of new investments (Keynes, 1923, p. 5).

KEYNES'S CONCEPTUALIZED REALITY: COMPOSITION, PROBLEMS, AND STRUCTURES[34]

In his endeavor to conceptualize reality, Keynes viewed historical and contemporary socioeconomic data in the triparted light of his ethics, his nature-cum-nurture theory of human motivations and behavior, and Burke's theory of the state.[35] The output of this mental process of transforming data into facts took the form of a dual reality. One part consists of what Keynes termed the "domestic [economic] system of laissez-faire" and the other part is composed of the institutions of the "State" (Keynes, 1936b, pp. 382, 378).

The Economic System

According to Keynes, the "outstanding fault of the economic society" of his reality was its "failure to provide for full employment and its arbitrary and inequitable distribution of wealth and incomes." As a result, a distressingly large number of citizens had become immersed in "poverty in the midst of plenty," but idle, capacity to produce (Keynes, 1936b, pp. 372, 30). Hence poverty was not due to a lack of "material things and [of] the resources to produce them." Rather, workers and plants were unemployed because of "some failure in the immaterial devices of the mind, in the working of the motives which should lead to the decisions and acts of will, necessary to put in movement the resources and technical means" already in existence (Keynes, 1933c, p. 335).

The lack of motives and will had emerged, at first slowly and then with increasing rapidity in recent years, in the course of intertwined technological and institutional processes in which the actors in an increasingly productive economic society had become divided into three major classes: A "rentier" class of "professional [financial] investor[s] and speculator[s]" who own, "but do not manage," business enterprises; an "active business class" of "entrepreneurs" who manage, but do not own, the enterprises; and an "earning class" of "labour" whose members sell their "personal services" to the entrepreneurs (Keynes 1936b, pp. 221, 154, 153; 1923, p. 5; 1936b, p. 8; 1923, pp. 4, 26; and 1936b, p. 213).

The members of each of these classes live in households. Consequently, every economic actor plays a dual role: as a procurer of income and as a consumer who manages the disposition of that income. In performing these two activities, the behavior exhibited by each individual was shaped by Keynes in accordance with his dynamic theory of economic psychology. Hence he depicted each actor's instinctive desire for "utility" and innate aversion to "disutility" as having been molded functionally by the subculture in which the individual lives because, as Keynes put it, the "power to become habituated to his surroundings is a marked characteristic of mankind" (Keynes, 1936b, p. 128; and 1919, p. 1). Thus the income-procuring activities of the rentiers are governed by a socially conditioned "psychological attitude toward liquidity"; those of the entrepreneurs by a "psychological expectation of future yield from capital-assets"; and those of the workers by a socio-psychological submissiveness that makes them accept unquestioningly "a situation in which they . . . [can] call their own very little of the cake" in the production of which they participate (Keynes, 1936b, p. 247; and 1919, p. 12; emphasis added). The income-dispensing activities of the members of the three classes are regulated by a fourth historically and culturally conditioned "fundamental psychological law," namely a socio-psychological "propensity to consume" and, hence, to save (Keynes, 1936b, pp. 96, 247). It follows, therefore, that as an acquisitor of income and as a manager of the household, the individual's behavior is influenced deterministically by "his appointed place" in society (Johnson, 1974, p. 106).

The place of the rentiers is particularly important because under laissez faire, society has become "so framed as to throw a great part of . . . [an] increased income into the control of the class least likely to consume it," namely that of the rentiers. Consequently, to "save . . . became at once the duty and the delight" of this "large" and "richer section of the community." It is, therefore, to the rentiers as "lenders" that the entrepreneurs must turn as "borrowers" in order to obtain those investable funds on which their, and society's, welfare depends (Keynes, 1919, p. 11; 1923, p. 6; and 1936b, pp. 262, 219). The transmission belt that connects rentiers and entrepreneurs has ground to a nearly complete halt, however.

As intimated above, the cause of this calamity is rooted in a laissez-faire spawned and ever-growing, "inequality of the distribution of wealth" and income. The maldistribution has engendered a rise of the "savings propensities" of those "wealthier members" of society who dwell in the homes of the rentiers at the same time as it has occasioned a fall of the propensity to consume on the part of the multitude of "wage-earners" and, consequently, reduced the "collective propensity" to consume for the "community as a whole" (Keynes, 1919, p. 11; 1936b, pp. 31, 362; and 1939a, p. 271). One fateful consequence of these developments was that unsold goods piled up at an accelerating rate in the inventories of the entrepreneurs. Basing their profit "expectations on the assumption that the most recently realized [dismal] results . . . [would] continue" in the foreseeable future (Keynes, 1936b, p. 51), the entrepreneurs cut their expenditures for new equipment and reduced their work force drastically.

In other words, Keynes's economic reality is stuck "in a chronic condition of sub-normal activity" because the entrepreneurs' "inducement to invest is [so] weak" that they have felt compelled "to reduce . . . actual output" so that, "in spite of its . . . wealth," the reality "has become so poor that its surplus over its consumption is sufficiently diminished to correspond to the weakness of the inducement to invest" (Keynes, 1936b, pp. 249, 31).

Investments might pick up if the rate of interest were to fall at a "sufficiently rapid rate" to bring it below the currently low rate of expected future entrepreneurial profits, a rate that Keynes dubbed the "marginal efficiency of capital." Unfortunately, under laissez faire, "institutional and psychological factors" in the community of rentiers "set a limit [so] much above zero to the practicable decline in the rate of interest" that it exceeds the current marginal efficiency of capital (Keynes, 1936b, pp. 31, 135, 218). The rentiers refuse to lower the rate of interest below its current level because they "prefer the control of liquid cash to parting with it in exchange for debts on the terms indicated by the market rate of interest." In other words, there has been "a mass movement into cash" on the part of the rentiers because their "liquidity preference" has become "virtually absolute in the sense that almost everyone [in that tribe] prefers cash to holding a debt which yields so low a rate of interest" (Keynes, 1936b, pp. 205-206, 172, 207).

Because of these "outrageous defects of the economic system," the entrepreneurs are prevented by their low expectations from calling "to the aid of their enterprises" those funds that are controlled by the rentiers (Keynes, 1936b, p. 31; and 1923, p. 5). But that is not the end of the story. Entrepreneurial expectations are falling because of the pernicious influence of the maldistribution of income upon aggregate demand. As Keynes put it, his reality finds itself in a situation in which, "owing to its accumulation of capital being already larger" than warranted by aggregate demand, the entrepreneurs' marginal efficiency of capital is plummeting so rapidly that the day is not far off when it will have reached zero. Inasmuch as the aforementioned "institutional factor . . . prevents the rate of interest from being negative . . . . in conditions mainly of laissez-faire," the economy has exhausted nearly all of its investment opportunities. Hence it suffers from stagnation in the sense that it has descended to a "resting-place [well] below full employment" (Keynes, 1936b, pp. 31, 218, 219, 304).

Recovery of the stagnant economy is therefore a virtual impossibility because the volume of investment required to achieve full employment would have to be so large that it would cause a "growth of capital up to the point where it ceases to be scarce" (Keynes 1936b, p. 376). Keynes hardly needed to point out that such an expansion of investment would not occur in a laissez-faire setting in which the rate of interest is positive and sticky. He emphasized, however, that the "unimpeded rule of the above conditions is a fact of observation concerning the world as it is or has been, and not a necessary principle which cannot be changed" (Keynes 1936b, p. 254). But if the observed conditions were to be changed, said Keynes, they would have to be changed by the state. It may be asked, however, why Keynes was so confident that the "State is able to determine the aggregate amount of resources devoted to augmenting the instruments" of production and thereby "securing an approximation to full employment" (Keynes, 1936b, pp. 376, 378)? An answer to that question has to be sought in the way in which Keynes conceptualized the state and its institutions.

The State

As mentioned above, Keynes was much influenced by Burke when he, Keynes, formulated his concept of the state. Thus he referred approvingly to "what Burke termed 'one of the finest problems in legislation, namely, to determine what the State ought to take upon itself to direct by public wisdom, and what it ought to leave . . . to individual exertion'" (Keynes, 1926b, p. 288). Keynes recommended, therefore, that, like himself, the "[s]tatesmen . . . learn wisdom in the school of Burke" (Keynes in Skidelsky, 1983, p. 157). And Keynes believed that there were people in public and semi-public institutions who not only would seek such wisdom, perhaps with the aid of Keynes himself, but who already were in possession thereof. Hence in response to the question as to from "whence are we to draw the forces which are to 'change the laws, customs, rules, and institutions of the world'?" Keynes answered: "We must recruit our revolutionaries from . . . amongst the scientists and the great modern business men" (Keynes, 1927, pp. 318, 319). They and the "intelligentsia" in general are the once who "carry the seeds of all human advancement" (Keynes, 1925b, p. 258).

This conviction of Keynes was one of the cornerstones of what might be called his concept of the **extended state** of which the **nuclear state** of Parliament, cabinet, civil service and the judiciary was only a part, but an important one. Keynes described the non-governmental institutions of the extended state thus:

> I suggest . . . that progress lies in the growth and the recognition of semi-autonomous bodies within the State -bodies whose criterion of action within their own field is solely the public good . . . and from which deliberations motives of private advantage are excluded . . . bodies which. . . are mainly autonomous within their prescribed limitations, but are subject in the last resort to the sovereignty of the democracy expressed through Parliament (Keynes, 1926b, pp. 288-289).

What Keynes had in mind was something like "a return towards medieval conceptions of separate autonomies" of which the ancient "universities, [and] the Bank of England" were present-day manifestations. For the purpose of economic reforms, however, Keynes observed that "more interesting than these is the trend of joint stock institutions" (Keynes, 1926b, p. 289); and he continued:

> [W]hen they have reached a certain age and size, [they]. . . approximate to the status of public corporations rather than that of individualistic enterprise. One of the most interesting and unnoticed developments of recent decades has been the tendency of big enterprise to socialise itself. A point arrives in the growth of a big institution. . . at which the owners of the capital, i.e. the shareholders, are almost entirely dissociated from the management, with the result that the direct personal interest of the latter in the making of great profit becomes quite secondary. When this stage is reached, the general stability and reputation of the institution are the more considered by the management than the maximum of profit for the shareholders (Keynes, 1926b, p. 289).

In Keynes's opinion, it was fortunate that this institutional evolution had taken place because the state would "have to take on many duties" for which "Ministers and Parliament will be unserviceable" (Keynes, 1925c, pp. 301, 302). Therefore, said he,

> [o]ur task must be to decentralise and devolve wherever we can, and in particular to establish semi-independent corporations and organs of administration to which duties of government, new and old, will be entrusted - without, however, impairing the democratic principle or the ultimate sovereignty of Parliament (Keynes, 1925c, p. 302).

Unless guided and coordinated in some fashion, however, the growing propensity of large business corporations to promote the common good might be abortive. Furthermore, without coordination, the agencies of the nuclear state might work at cross purpose with unguided semi-autonomous corporations. **Planning** was the instrument that Keynes included in his concept of the extended state as the method of coordination and guidance. As he saw it, the "essence of state planning [is] to do those things which . . . lie outside the scope of the individual" and its "object is to take hold of the central controls and to govern them with deliberate foresight and thus modify and condition the environment within which the individual freely operates" (Keynes, 1932b, p. 88). And, said he in 1939, "we need, if we are to enjoy prosperity and profits, so much more central planning than we have at present that the reform of the economic system needs as much urgent attention if we have war as if we avoid it" (Keynes, 1939b, p. 492). For the institutionalization of such a "scheme of collective planning," Keynes implanted a "National Investment Board" in his conceptualization of the extended state, a board that works "in close collaboration with a Board for the location of industry. But the functions of the former body . . . go . . . very far beyond those of the latter," he observed (Keynes, 1930d, p. 475; and 1939c, p. 591).

All indications are, therefore, that Keynes was convinced that if an extended state cum planning were established, men of reason and good would be capable of banning slumps and unemployment from the economic system. He selected the label "liberal socialism" for the socioeconomic order that would come into being subsequent to the introduction of such a state. By liberal socialism, he meant "a system where we can act as an organized community for common purposes and . . . promote social and economic justice, whilst respecting and protecting the individual - his freedom of choice, his faith, his mind and its expression, his enterprise and his property" (Keynes, 1939b, p. 500; emphasis added).

If, however, they were to accomplish this goal, the managers of the extended state must have in their hands "new instruments to . . . control the working of economic forces." Keynes proffered the requisite instruments in The General Theory in the form of means to the end of drastically "reform[ing] . . . the economic system" (Keynes, 1925c, p. 306; and 1939b, p. 492). He formed his suggestions on the basis of his concepts of the extended state and the economic order, and in consequence of those conclusions that he reached after his formal analysis of the behavior of that order. In advancing his proposals, Keynes hoped to contribute to an abolition of unemployment and thereby to the removal of what he viewed as the major obstacle on the road toward "our destination of economic bliss" and ultimate abolition of the ancient "economic problem" of scarcity and poverty (Keynes, 1930b, pp. 331, 326).

KEYNES'S RECOMMENDATIONS

In the 1930s, Keynes was convinced that what has become known as "Keynesian policies" would not be of any use as a means of lifting the economy out of the depression. In the first place, he was "now somewhat sceptical of a merely monetary policy directed towards influencing the rate of interest." This was a logical position in view of his opinion that "due to [the fact that] the liquidity function [was] flattening out," the monetary authority was on the verge of loosing "effective control over the rate of interest" (Keynes 1936b, pp. 164, 207). Hence the rate would remain above the falling marginal efficiency of capital. Secondly, as pointed out by Peter Clarke, there is "nothing" in The General Theory "on fiscal methods of demand management, nor on deficit budgeting" (Clarke, 1988, p. 305). It seems that Keynes was of the opinion that deficit-financed public works would have only a temporary effect. They would be in the nature of pump-priming, but the pump would go dry again after all the public works had been completed because there would be no self-sustaining spread effect from the public to the private sector. Hence the multiplier would shift into reverse gear. It also seems that Keynes was of the opinion that the argument that a public debt could "keep on growing" was "humbug" (Abba Lerner in Colander, n.d., p. 26). He might have taken this position because he was of the opinion that interest payments on the debt would make an already unacceptable maldistribution of income worse at the same time as the creation of the debt would give the rentiers a new lease on life by providing them with an essentially unearned "bonus" while they remained "functionless" as far as the private sector was concerned (Keynes, 1936b, p. 376). Keynes concluded, therefore, that "the duty of ordering the current volume of investment cannot safely be left in [the] private hands" of rentiers (Keynes, 1936b, pp. 376, 320). This duty would have to be lodged in a new partnership of the state and the firms of the "Entrepreneur Economy" (Keynes, 1933d, p. 83). Keynes was confident that such a partnership would be capable of shifting the multiplier into a high-speed forward gear.

As far as the entrepreneurial firms are concerned, when in operation, none of these "seriously misemploys the factors of production which are [actually] in use" because Keynes's economic reality behaves as if it were competitive. The trouble is, of course, that an uncomfortably large number of firms is not producing. Thus it "is in determining the volume, not the direction, of actual employment that the existing system has broken down." In order to correct the situation, large volumes of affordable funds for investment would have to be injected into the economy in order to arouse the latent energies of idle entrepreneurs who would finally be freed of the "cumulative oppressive power" of the rentiers. Under the given circumstances, the "only means of" restarting the entrepreneur economy and thereby "securing an approximation to full employment," Keynes called "a somewhat comprehensive socialisation of investment" (Keynes, 1936b, pp. 379, 376, 378). As he saw it, such an approach would have to consist of two parts.

In the first place, he recommended that "the State" establish a system of "communal saving . . . to be maintained at a level which will allow for the growth of capital up to the point where it ceases to be scarce" (Keynes, 1936b, p. 376). With regard to the fiscal tools to be employed in such a program, it seems that Keynes was thinking in terms of "instrument[s] of direct taxation" in the form of "income tax and surtax and death duties." These levies could be imposed at progressive rates and thereby contribute to a "redistribution of incomes in a way likely to raise the propensity to consume." This would be economically beneficial, said Keynes, because "the growth of capital depends not at all on a low propensity to consume but is, on the contrary, held back by it" because of the underconsumption that it occasions (Keynes, 1936b, pp. 372, 373, 272-273).[36]

The mere raising of funds by the state could not, of course, bring about the necessary economic mobilization of idle entrepreneurs. The communal savings had to be channeled into the hands of potentially productive entrepreneurs. The second part of Keynes's proposal for a socialization of investment consists, therefore, of a system of political economy in which the state has taken "an ever greater responsibility for directly organizing investment." According to Keynes, the state "is in a position" to do so because it has the capacity "to calculate the marginal efficiency of capital-goods on long views and on the basis of the general social advantage" (Keynes, 1936b, p. 164). What Keynes seems to have had in mind was something like the following. The agencies of the extended state would collect the necessary data for a calculation of the marginal efficiencies in various industries. The resultant estimated efficiencies would then provide criteria for the distribution of the social savings among industries and among individual entrepreneurs in each industry. Decisions about intra-industry distribution would be made relatively easy for the above-mentioned reason that none of the operating firms in Keynes's reality "seriously misemploys the factors of production" (Keynes, 1936b, p. 379. Hence it could be assumed that the marginal efficiency of each firm is represented by the marginal efficiency calculated for the industry in which it is located. Inter-industry distribution, on the other hand, would presumably be made on the basis of a weighing of the importance of two factors: The relative marginal efficiencies of different industries and the priorities for industrial development contained in a program of "planning" formulated and implemented by the "National Planning Board" (Keynes, 1939c, p. 591). It is conceivable, therefore, that an industry with a relatively low marginal efficiency of capital might be targeted for infusion of funds because the planners deemed it to be in the national interest to accelerate the growth of the industry in question.

As Keynes emphasized again and again, growing investments would gradually reduce the scarcity of capital. Hence rising prosperity would be accompanied by an equally gradual lowering of the "schedule of the marginal efficiency of capital." It may be surmised, therefore, that Keynes was of the opinion that the government would have to make communal savings available to the entrepreneurs at lower and lower costs; perhaps ultimately at that "negative . . . rate of interest" that could not come into being in the old laissez-faire system because the then existing "institutional and psychological factors . . . set a limit much above zero to the practicable decline in the rate of interest" (Keynes, 1936b, pp. 308, 218).

Although Keynes might have been vague with regard to the details of his program for the socialization of investment and hence having failed to develop "it into a policy blueprint" (Clarke, 1988, p. 305), he displayed no vagueness when it came to an explanation of the purpose of furnishing the state with the "central controls necessary to ensure full employment." It must be "the policy of the state," said he, to channel communal savings to the entrepreneurs in such a volume that "our aim of depriving capital of its scarcity-value" will be achieved "within one or two generations." Inasmuch as the rentier "can obtain interest [only] because capital is scarce," such a development would result in the evanescence of interest as a property income which, of course, "would mean the euthanasia of the rentier" (Keynes, 1936b, pp. 379, 377, 376).

Keynes insisted, however, that his proposals should not be construed to mean that he advocated "a system of State Socialism which would embrace most of the economic life of the community" (Keynes, 1936b, p. 378).

> It is not the ownership of the instruments of production, which it is important for the State to assume [said he]. If the State is able to determine the aggregate amount of resources devoted to augmenting the instruments and the basic rate of reward to those who own them, it will have accomplished all that is necessary. Moreover, the

necessary measures of socialisation can be introduced gradually and without a break in the general traditions of society (Keynes, 1936b, p. 378).

It may be asked how it would be possible for the state to fix the basic rate of return to those who own the instruments of production, namely the rentiers, when their incomes disappear together with their own now "functionless" selves! Keynes's answer was that only the unearned "bonus" of "pure . . . interest" would vanish (Keynes, 1936b, pp. 376, 221). Thus although "the rentier would disappear" as a receiver of a rent-like rate of pure interest, "there would still be room" for such a person to exercise "skill in the estimation of prospective yields about which opinions differ." That is to say, the rentier turned his own portfolio manager would under favorable circumstances earn an "allowance for risk and the like" that would be equal to the "gross yield" minus the pure rate of interest. Keynes admitted that "it is not unlikely that . . . the eagerness to obtain a yield from doubtful investments might be such that they would show in the aggregate a negative net yield" (Keynes, 1936b, p. 221). Society might find the services of the portfolio managers so valuable, however, that a "scheme of direct taxation" would be devised for the support of the former rentiers. This would make it possible for the "intelligence and determination and executive skill of the financier . . . to be harnessed to the service of the community on reasonable terms of reward" (Keynes, 1936b, pp. 376, 376-377). Such an institutional reformation would "result . . . [in] a gradual disappearance of the rate of return on accumulated wealth" and with it the principal cause of the present economics system's "outrageous . . . defects" in the form of depression and unemployment (Keynes, 1936b, pp. 221, 31).

In 1943, Keynes reiterated his conviction that socialization of investment would pave the way for society's travel to the "golden age" of his vision. Along this road, "two-thirds or three-quarters of total investment is carried out or can be influenced by public or semi-public bodies" (Keynes, 1943, pp. 323, 322). It seems, however, that Keynes was of the opinion that state-directed investments would take place in a setting of continuous technological advance. Thus after he in 1942 had familiarized himself with studies that showed that "technical progress between 1938 and 1946 will amount to 10 per cent," Keynes was confident that "improvement in technical production . . . will not cease to take place" in the future. On the contrary, he was certain that "technical progress" would result in growing annual outputs that could be produced by a work force whose members worked shorter and "shorter hours" (Keynes, 1942, p. 272; and 1943, p. 323).

Keynes had presented a similar argument when he was in the process of gearing up for the project of writing The General Theory. He observed then that "science and compound interest" would make it possible to increase future outputs in a setting in which "[t]hree-hour shifts or a fifteen-hour week" were the rule rather than the exception. He even hinted at the possibility that working hours might be reduced still further once "the old Adam in most of us" has been acculturated to be content with an even shorter work week (Keynes, 1930b, pp. 328, 329).

Citizens of the future would not only have to adjust to spending less time on the job. In the face of growing outputs, they would also have to "change [their] social practices" in the realm of consumption and saving. "It becomes necessary," said Keynes, "to encourage wise consumption and discourage saving" and, he reiterated, "to absorb some part of" what he called an "unwanted surplus" by means of "increased leisure, more holidays . . . and shorter hours." In Keynes's opinion, the surplus would become unwanted in the sense that it would not be needed for investment. "Eventually depreciation funds should be almost sufficient to provide the gross investment that is required" (Keynes, 1943, p. 323). When that comes to pass, the state can relax its activities as a collector and transmitter of communal saving for the purpose of net investment. A largely unchanged capital stock will be made increasingly productive through replacement investments that embody the latest and most sophisticated technologies.

Keynes's grand scenario may be summarized as follows. If the stagnation of investment in the laissez-faire economy of his reality is ameliorated through socialization of investment, society will gradually take on the appearance of his envisioned ideal society. In the process of this transformation, scientific and technological progress continues to occur. Hence entrepreneurial investments, financed by the extended state, will embody state-of-the-art technology. Thus unlike the unguided economy that Keynes analyzed in The General Theory, the planned economy of the future will be capable of exploiting "the possibilities for economic wealth afforded by the progress of . . . technique" (Keynes, 1933a, p. 765). Consequently, the social surplus will grow in a setting in which it is gradually released from its ancient function of sustaining net investment because growing technology has made it possible to reduce gross investment to replacement investment financed from depreciation funds. Instead, the surplus will be available for consumption in the broadest sense of the word. The consequences will be revolutionary. There "will be ever larger and larger classes and groups of people from whom problems of economic necessity have been practically removed." Keynes's envisioned ideal society will be reached "when this condition has become so general that the nature of one's duty to one's neighbour is changed." That is to say, given the pliability of human nature, "there will be great changes in the code of morals" because it will "remain reasonable to be economically purposive for others after it has ceased to be reasonable for oneself" (Keynes, 1930b, pp. 331, 329, 331).

Thus whereas Keynes's laissez-faire reality was faltering because of a vicious stagnation of net investment, his proposed planned economy of the future would grow, prosper and become increasingly humane and just because it would be propelled by forces that would ultimately cause a virtuous stagnation of net investment.

Of course, Keynes's predictions of the future leave many questions to be answered, especially with regard to the motives for, and nature of, the entrepreneurs' decisions after net investment has become obsolete. Maybe he expected that he would himself be able to fill in the lacunae at a later date or, perhaps, he might have hoped that potential disciples would take up the challenge. Neither of these hopes was fulfilled. Keynes was prevented from assuming the task by illness and advisory activities during the Second World War. And those economists who adopted Keynes's analytical apparatus merged his techniques with the principal preconceptions of orthodox normal economic science. The idealistic, some would say utopian, features of Keynes's work were therefore eliminated from the corpus of twentieth-century economics. Hence Keynes may have been the last of those visionary economists, including Adam Smith, Karl Marx, John Stuart Mill, and Alfred Marshall, who fashioned economic theories for the purpose of showing the way to the good life of our species, theories that were undergirded by a conception of a pliable human nature that, in its turn, led to the conviction that the human beast is improvable, if not perfectible.

CONCLUSION

Keynes's proposal for a socialization of investment is therefore not a mere aside, or inconsequential digression, in The General Theory. On the contrary, it is a logical conclusion that follows inexorably from the merger of his conceptualization of the economic order with his conceptualization of the extended state. From the former he obtained the elements of which he constructed his economic model as well as the assumptions for those economic theories that he forged in order to explain and predict the behavior of his model. His concept of the extended state provided Keynes with the ingredients that he needed in order to explain how to mobilize those spending propensities that his analysis told him that society had to arouse if the body economic were to be cured of the twin diseases of depression and unemployment. In other words, once he had placed the money-starved entrepreneur in the center of an economic order that had been derailed by the rentiers and once he had conceived of an extended state governed by reasonable men of good will, it was well nigh unavoidable that Keynes should hit upon the idea of the socialization of investment as the instrument to be employed in an effort to rescue the economy from self-destruction and thereby save society from all the consequences for the travel to the promised land that would follow from such a catastrophe.

Notes

* I should like to thank John B. Davis and James P. Henderson for valuable comments on, and suggestions for improvement of, earlier versions of this chapter. I alone am responsible for any errors of fact and interpretation.

[1] Among the several definitions of a paradigm that have been offered by Thomas S. Kuhn, Joseph A. Schumpeter and others, the following seem to be appropriate when dealing with economics: A paradigm, which Schumpeter called "a classical situation," may be viewed as "a recognized field" in a given discipline. The characteristic of such a field is that it "contains tooled knowledge" (Schumpeter, 1954, pp. 51, 143) that is directed toward the solution of selected problems. A paradigm may therefore be said to consist of a set of "scientific

achievements that for a time provide model problems and solutions to a community of practitioners" (Kuhn, 1970, p. viii).

[2] In the text, John Maynard Keynes will be identified as "Keynes." When references are made to other members of the Keynes family, their full names will be given. In addition to Keynes, the tribe of innovators includes Adam Smith, W. Stanley Jevons, Alfred Marshall, Carl Menger and Leon Walras. Inasmuch as all the innovators were of the male sex, and for the sake of simplicity, I shall use the pronouns "he" and "his" throughout when referring to an innovator.

[3] A comparison of the economics of Marshall with Marshallian economics will illustrate this phenomenon. See Jensen (1987, pp. 34-35; and 1990, pp. 33-34).

[4] Joseph A. Schumpeter's concept of vision is similar to that which I call a "conceptualized reality." I conceive of a vision as a mental picture of a desired future state of affairs, rather than as an intuition of an existing state of affairs. Hence I prefer the term "conceptualized reality" as a label for the latter.

[5] It is frequently asserted that ideology is a concept that has received such a "wide range of definitions" (Minar, 1961, p. 320) that the meaning of the term has become "thoroughly muddied" (Converse, 1964, p. 207). A definition that seems useful in connection with Keynes's work, however, is simply that ideology is a cluster of values. As used here, a value, or a set of values, connotes notions of what is good or bad, desirable or undesirable, and so on. As I see it, such notions are formed in a process of assessment in the course of which a "judgment [is made] on the goodness or otherwise" of a particular object, proposition, act, or outcome of an act (Collini, 1985, p. 33). In other words, a process of valuation leads to the formation of value judgements that fuel pronouncements of what ought to be.

[6] Referring to the Treatise on Money, Keynes observed in the closing month of 1931 that he was "now endeavouring to express the whole thing over again more clearly and from a different angle; and in two years' time I may feel able to publish a revised and complete version" (Keynes, 1931a, p. 243). It took five years, rather than two, to complete what proved to be an entirely new work, namely The General Theory of Employment, Interest and Money.

[7] As Gunnar Myrdal never tired of reminding his readers, a "view presupposes a viewpoint" (Myrdal, 1968, p. 32).

[8] Keynes did so in a memoir that he read in September, 1938 to a group of friends who met at Tilton, his country home in Sussex. "They were members of the Memoir Club, founded in 1920 to read memoirs of an earlier age" (Moggridge, 1992, p. 116). Keynes and most of the audience had belonged to the so-called Bloomsbury Group that owed its name to a "particular kind of social and cultural life which grew up among a group of friends in a couple of adjacent Georgian squares" in the Bloomsbury district of London. In 1913, the group consisted of 20 members of whom "ten were Apostles" (Skidelsky, 1983, pp. 243, 247). They were so called because in their student days, these individuals belonged to the Conversazione Society, a secret organization of Cambridge undergraduates that was known as the Apostles because its active membership was restricted to twelve undergraduate students. As an Apostle, Keynes read several papers at meetings of the Society.

[9] See the following works for discussions of how Keynes's experience as an Apostle and Bloomsburyian influenced his philosophic and ethical preconceptions: Harrod (1951, pp. 69-81, 172-194), Keynes (1938a), Paul Levy (1975), Piero V. Mini (1991), Moggridge (1992, pp. 112-142, 213-232), and Skidelsky (1983, pp. 115-132, 242-251). For an account of what Bloomsbury was all about and of how it came to be, see Leon Edel (1979).

[10] Keynes traced the origins of this outlook to a work on philosophy, Principia Ethica, by the Cambridge philosopher George E. Moore (Moore, 1903), that was published at the end of Keynes's first academic year as an undergraduate in the University of Cambridge. Moore was a former Apostle who attended some of the meetings of their Society where his philosophy was debated. The effect of the Principia "on us, and the talk which preceded and followed it, dominated, and perhaps still dominate, everything else," said Keynes (Keynes, 1938a, p. 435).

[11] Thus, said Keynes, "what we got from Moore was by no means entirely what he offered us. . . . There was one chapter in the Principia [Chapter 5, "Ethics in Relation to Conduct," pp. 142-182] of which we took not the slightest notice. We accepted Moore's religion . . . [but] discarded his his morals." By religion Keynes et al. meant "one's attitude towards one self and the ultimate." This attitude manifested itself in the form of a preoccupation with states of mind that, in turn, "consisted in timeless, passionate states of contemplation and communion, largely unattached to 'before' and 'after'" (Keynes, 1938a, p. 436). John B. Davis has pointed out to me that rational egoism, or ethical egoism, was a widely shared doctrine at the time when the Bloomsburyians' intellectual fervor was at its peak. Doubtless, Keynes was influenced by this principle when he declared himself an "immoralist." For example, said Davis, Henry Sidgwick thought that this kind of egoism was defensible, Moore, who was a student of Sidgwick, denied it, and Keynes, a student of Moore, rejected Moore's position and accepted that of Sidgwick. Moreover, Davis observed that Keynes's early ethical position influenced his interpretation of economic history in The Economic Consequences of the Peace where he found that self-interest had been a propellant of a salutary economic development in the late nineteenth and early twentieth century (Davis 1993). As Keynes put it in the Consequences: "Europe was so organized socially and economically as to secure the maximum accumulation of capital." Although he was critical of certain aspects of the culture of capitalism as it existed before the outbreak of war in 1914, Keynes did "not necessarily disparage the practices" of the prewar generation. "Society was working not for the small pleasures of today but for the future security and improvement of the race - in fact for 'progress'" (Keynes 1919, pp. 11, 12). It might be added, so would the entrepreneurs in The General Theory if they were not frustrated by the antisocial behavior of the rentiers (see the sections on "Keynes's Conceptualized Reality," infra).

[12] For different, and sometimes conflicting, explanations cum interpretations of the origins, nature and development of Keynes's moral sentiments and philosophic outlook, see R.B. Braithwaite (1972 and, especially, 1975), Anna M. Carabelli (1988), John B. Davis (1991a, 1991b, and 1991c), Athol Fitzgibbons (1988, pp. 34-52, 92-106 and 1992), Harrod (1951, pp. 133-141, 651-656), Suzanne W. Helburn (1991a and 1992), R.M. O'Donnell (1989, especially pp. 106-137), Yuichi Shionoya (1991), and Skidelsky (1983, especially pp. 133-160).

[13] This impression is reinforced by the following statements by Keynes that preceded the above quotation: "Indeed it is only states of mind that matter, provided we agree to take account of the pattern of life through time and give up regarding it as a series of independent, instantaneous flashes, but the ways in which states of mind can be valuable, and the objects of them, are more various, and also much richer, than we allowed for. . . . If, therefore, I altogether ignore our merits - our charm, our intelligence, our unworldliness, our affection - I can see us as water-spiders, gracefully skimming, as light and reasonable as air, the surface of the stream without any contact at all with the eddies and currents underneath" (Keynes, 1938a, pp. 449-450, 450).

[14] Davis's quotations are from pages 21 and 22 of "Miscellanea Ethica," an unpublished paper written by Keynes in 1905 and deposited in the Library of King's College, Cambridge.

[15] Davis statement reads: "The greatest good at which it is our duty to aim . . . is . . . the greatest sum of good states of mind across individuals" (Davis, 1991a, p. 65; emphasis added). Given Keynes's use of the word "our" in the text quoted by Davis, it is clear that he, Keynes, included himself when he used that term.

[16] And this in spite of the fact that Keynes argued that he had "escaped from the Benthamite tradition" which he now (1938) "regard[ed] . . . as the worm which has been gnawing at the insides of modern civilisation and is responsible for its present moral decay." It was in consequence of their critical reading of the Principia that Keynes et al. "had thrown hedonism out of the window and, discard[ed] Moore's so highly problematic calculus" (Keynes, 1938a, p. 445). At a first blush, R.B. Braithwaite was puzzled by the apparent contradiction between

Keynes's statements quoted in the text above, on the one hand, and the just quoted anti-Utilitarian statements by the same Keynes, on the other hand. Braithwaite solved the puzzle by arguing that "Moore's influence made . . . [Keynes] spew out the hedonism, but left the consequentialism intact." Braithwaite concluded, therefore, that "Keynes was brought up in, and never departed from, a consequentialist moral philosophy" (Braithwaite, 1975, pp. 244, 245). Based on his reading of Keynes's work on probability (Keynes, 1921), R.M. O'Donnell maintained that Keynes's ethical philosophy was in the nature of "act-consequentialism" by which O'Donnell understood the proposition that a "right action consists in that action which is judged to produce the greatest amount of probable goodness on the whole" (O'Donnell, 1989, p. 107). Suzanne W. Helburn "disagree[d] with O'Donnell's description of the philosophy [of Keynes] . . . as a form of act-consequentialism." She did so because, in her opinion, "Keynes rejected consequentialism as usually defined and practiced - basing judgments on a summing-up of mathematical expectations" (Helburn, 1992, pp. 44, 43). I would tend to agree with Helburn in this respect. Nevertheless, it seems to me that Keynes did entertain some sort of consequentialist notions. Thus when he was in an early stage of his work on The General Theory, Keynes observed that he sympathized with the view "that in one's behaviour one ought to consider the total effect of one's action on the situation taken as a whole" (Keynes, 1932a, p. 407). Perhaps Keynes's consequentialism could be called pragmatic, instrumental, or "ends-in-view" consequentialism a la John Dewey's instrumentalism. Thus because "'there . . . [was] something the matter' . . . because there was some 'trouble' in . . . [the] existing situation" Keynes "desire[d]" particular "[e]nds-in-view as anticipated results" that were to be realized through actions that would "produce specified consequences" (Dewey, 1939, pp. 25, 33, 17, 52, 17). In other words, ends-in-view are instrumental in that "they are re-directing pivots in action" (Dewey, 1957, p. 209).

[17] Harrod has been censured for his failure to make any reference to Keynes's homosexuality in his Life of John Maynard Keynes. Skidelsky has observed, for example, that the "result is a severely impoverished account of Keynes's feelings, his values,, his friendships, and his cultural milieu" (Skidelsky, 1983, p. xvii). In this respect, Charles H. Hession's biography of Keynes is the polar opposite of Harrod's. Hession traced Keynes's "intellectual capacity" and "creativity" to the fact that he was an "androgyne" in consequence of his homosexuality. Hession also argued that Keynes's sexual orientation made him skeptical "of conventional belief and practice . . . [which] contributed to his questioning attitude toward the respectable and accepted in the economic and political realms" (Hession, 1984, pp. 110, 111, 112, 219). Whether or not one accepts Hession's interpretation, there is no doubt that Keynes's experience as an Apostle and Bloomsburyian provided significant inputs for that mental process in which he formed an ethically tinted critical attitude toward accepted norms and institutions. The intellectual milieu of Harvey Road predisposed Keynes, however, to be receptive to the unconventional ideas that engulfed him in the Apostles and in the Bloomsbury Group. It was largely because of the impact of these intertwined intellectual climates that he was enabled to "escape from [those] habitual modes of [economic] thought and expression" on which he was "brought up" and which constituted the "stuff" on which he "lectured [himself] . . . for many years" (Keynes 1936b, p. viii; and 1936c, p. 35). But it was not only from the intellectual system of neoclassicism that Keynes struggled to escape. He was engaged in an equally intense struggle to escape from conventional attitudes toward the economic system which, in his opinion, the neoclassicists interpreted so faultily that they could not "solve the economic problems of the actual world" of capitalism. Consequently, Keynes was "beginning to despise" this world in the early 1930s (Keynes, 1936b, p. 378; and 1933a, p. 761. He escaped from his twin struggles with an entirely new economic theory in his possession.

[18] It may very well be, of course, that this judgment was itself conditioned by the presuppositions of 6 Harvey Road. Peter Clarke has gone so far as to argue that Keynes's Apostolic and Bloomsburyian beliefs may be construed as a "fight" against his Harvey Road "heritage" that "bears some marks of being a put-up fight" (Clarke, 1988, p. 10).

[19] Neville Keynes entered the ancient institution as a fellow in one of its colleges and for some years, he lectured on economics and logic in a number of colleges and in the University's moral science program. Soon, however, he moved from the world of scholarship into the world of administration and he ended his career as a university administrator of some repute (Moggridge, 1992, pp. 8-12. Skidelsky, 1983, pp. 7-14). Neville Keynes did produce some scholarly work. In 1884, he published Studies and Exercises in Formal Logic that in the 1960's was declared to be "'still one of the best and most technical expositions of syllogistic logic'" (John Passmore as quoted in Moggridge, 1992, p. 17). In 1891 he published The Scope and Method of Political Economy (J.N. Keynes, 1955) that became a classic but one that is seldom read today, except by a small band of students of the history of economics and its methods.

[20] Florence Keynes was prominent in the establishment and leadership of local service organizations and she worked for governmental assumptions of the delivery of social services. She held the office of President of the British National Council of Women in 1930-1931. She was elected town councillor and alderman in Cambridge and she topped her political career by being elected Cambridge's first woman mayor for the 1932-1933 term (Harrod, 1951, pp. 11-12. Moggridge, 1992, pp. 12-14, 18-19; Skidelsky, 1983, pp. 15-25).

[21] Keynes's brother, Geoffrey Keynes, remembered that when "distinguished guests came to luncheon" and dinner, or, as in the case of Marshall, for "discussion," Keynes "was ready from an early age to join learned discussions." Especially clear in Geoffrey Keynes's memory were "the exchanges with the philosopher, W.E. Johnson" with Keynes "joining in whenever he saw an opening" (G. Keynes, 1975, p. 29; Skidelsky, 1983, p. 69. G. Keynes, 1975, p. 29). Other prominent guests included the philosopher and psychologist James Ward, the economists Herbert S. Foxwell, Sir Robert Giffin, R.H.Inglis Palgrave and Philip H. Wicksteed, and the diplomat and author Harold G. Nicolson (Moggridge, 1992, p. 20. Skidelsky, 1983, p. 69).

[22] This section covers some of the same material as Jensen (1987, and 1990).

[23] This section covers some of the same material as Jensen (1983, and 1984).

[24] See Keynes's use of the economic histories written by Earl J. Hamilton and others plus his subsequent references to latter-day statistical series and reports on monetary affairs (Keynes, 1930a, Vol. 2, pp. 132-186). Also see Keynes's use of the economic history cum doctrinal history written by Eli Heckscher as well as Keynes's own exercise in doctrinal history (Keynes, 1936b, pp. 333-371). Because of Keynes's imaginative "use [of] history," Charles Wilson called him an "historical amateur in the best and original meaning of the word" (Wilson, 1975, p. 235).

[25] Keynes was receptive to Marshall's message because of his prior exposure to history. "In King's College it was [in] the air that Keynes breathed as an undergraduate." Among the scholars who aroused Keynes's early interest in history was "John Clapham" who had been put "on to the path of economic history . . . [by] the great economist Alfred Marshall" (Wilson, 1975, p. 230). Thus when Marshall "called on [future generations of economists] to apply . . . [their] knowledge of history" (Marshall 1897, p. 310), his exhortation exercised a direct influence upon Keynes that came on top of the indirect influence of the sage that he, Keynes, had received via Clapham. Keynes Marshallesque interpretation of history is explained in more details below under the heading of "Historical Inputs" in the section on "Keynes's Conceptualized Reality: Meaning and Sources."

[26] In formulating this concept in the 1970s (Jensen, 1976), I was influenced not only by Schumpeter but also by Joseph J. Spengler who observed that an economist's universe "consists of the mental constructs . . . [that he] built . . . out of his percepts and concepts of the real realm" (Spengler, 1960, p. 7).

[27] Elsewhere I have given the following more elaborate explanation of what I mean by the term: As "I view it, a conceptualized reality is an experientially conditioned, subjectively conceived, factually structured, and mentally formulated approximation to, or image of (and

a proxy for), the actual socioeconomic order of the contemporary society" (Jensen, 1983, p. 70).

[28] For a discussion of Burke's influence upon Keynes when he formulated his political philosophy, see Helburn (1991b).

[29] For fuller discussions of Marshall's theory of human nature and of his influence on Keynes when the latter formulated his theory of the same nature, see Jensen (1987, pp. 17-20; and 1983, pp. 74-78).

[30] Marshall accepted Jeremy Bentham's dictum that it is for "pain and pleasure . . . to determine what we shall do" (Bentham, 1876, p. 1). In following Bentham, however, Marshall confined himself to the economic realm when he endeavored to prove that "pleasure and pain" act as "powerful incentives to action" (Marshall, 1961, pp. 18, 17).

[31] Reiterating his frequently expressed belief that the "Mecca of the economist is economic biology," Marshall asserted that "changes [occur] in man" in a process of "evolution" or "organic life growth" (Marshall, 1898, pp. 43, 44, 42, 44). Marshall's evolutionism had its origin in two strands in Western thought. In the first place, it was rooted in "biology, as represented by the writings of Herbert Spencer" and, especially, as exhibited in Charles "Darwin's profound discussions" of the "laws of struggle and survival" (Marshall, 1961, pp. ix, 50; and 1897, p. 298). Secondly, in taking an evolutionary approach, Marshall was influenced by Continental "history and philosophy, as represented by [G.W.F.] Hegel's Philosophy of History" and by the "careful and profound analyses" of the members of the German historical school (Marshall, 1961, pp. ix, 768).

[32] Although Marshall was vague about the precise relationship between the kernel and the elements, he had no doubt about the outcome of their interaction. Man's basic instincts are reshaped and attuned to the opportunities, incentives and socioeconomic phenomena in their cultural environment. The marketers play an important role in this regard. Thus Marshall observed that "a characteristic task of the modern manufacturer" has emerged in capitalism, namely "that of creating new wants by showing people something which they had never thought of having before; but which they want to have as soon as the notion is suggested to them" (Marshall, 1961, p. 280).

[33] According to Marshall, technological development started in earnest with a series of events that included "the invention of the printing press, the Revival of Learning, the Reformation, and the discoveries of the ocean routes to the New World and to India," discoveries that were made possible by the "growth of knowledge" in the arts and sciences of shipbuilding and navigation. "Any one of these events alone would have been sufficient to make an epoch in history," said Marshall. But "coming together as they did, and working all in the same direction, they effected a complete revolution" (Marshall, 1961, p. 738; 1885, p. 154; and 1961, p. 738; emphasis added).

[34] This section covers some of the same material as Jensen (1991b).

[35] Keynes thought that "Burke [was] one of the great political thinkers of all time." Robert Skidelsky observed, therefore, that "Burke may lay strong claim to be his political hero. Certainly he was the only one he ever acknowledged as such" (Skidelsky, 1983, p. 154).

[36] Keynes emphasized the importance of increasing the propensity to consume in the following words: "Whilst aiming at a socially controlled rate of investment with a view to a progressive decline in the marginal efficiency of capital, I should support at the same time all sorts of policies for increasing the propensity to consume. For it is unlikely that full employment can be maintained, whatever we may do about investment, with the existing propensity to consume" (Keynes, 1936b, p. 225).

References

Bentham, Jeremy. (1876) An Introduction to the Principles of Morals and Legislation. Oxford: Clarendon Press.

Braithwaite, R. B. (1972) "Editorial Foreword." In *A Treatise on Probability*, by John Maynard Keynes, pp. xv- xxii. Vol. 8 of *The Collected Writings of John Maynard Keynes*. New York: St. Martin's Press, 1973.

_____. (1975) "Keynes as a philosopher." In *Essays on John Maynard Keynes*, edited by Milo Keynes, pp. 237-246. Cambridge: Cambridge University Press.

Carabelli, Anna M. (1988) *On Keynes's Method*. New York: St. Martin's Press.

Clarke, Peter. (1988) *The Keynesian Revolution in the Making 1924-1936*. Oxford: Clarendon Press.

Colander, David C. N.D. "The Development of Keynesian Economics: An Interview with Abba Lerner and Alvin Hansen." Unpublished Manuscript, pp. 1-30.

Collini, S. (1985) "The Idea of 'Character' in Victorian Political Thought." *Transactions of the Royal Historical Society 35* (5th Series): 29-50.

Converse, Philip E. (1964) "The Nature of Belief Systems in Mass Publics." In *Ideology and Discontent*, edited by David E. Apter, pp. 206-261. Glencoe, IL: The Free Press of Glencoe.

Davis, John B. (1991a) "Keynes's critique of Moore: philosophic foundations of Keynes's economics." *Cambridge Journal of Economics 15* (March): 61-77.

_____. (1991b) "Review Essay: *Keynes: Philosophy, Economics and Politics.*" *Review of Social Economy 49* (Fall): 405-413.

_____. (1991c) "Keynes's View of Economics as a Moral Science." In *Keynes and Philosophy: Essays on the Origin of Keynes's Thought*, edited by Bradley W. Bateman and John B. Davis, pp. 89-103. Aldershot: Edward Elgar.

_____. (1993) Letter to author of April 28.

Dewey, John. (1939) *Theory of Valuation*. Vol. II, No. 4 of the *International Encyclopedia of Unified Science*. Chicago: The University of Chicago Press.

_____. (1957) *Human Nature and Conduct*. New York: The Modern Library of Random House.

Edel, Leon. (1979) *Bloomsbury: A House of Lions*. Philadelphia: J. B. Lippincott Co.

Edgeworth, F. Y. (1925) "Reminiscences." In *Memorials of Alfred Marshall*, edited by A. C. Pigou, pp. 66-73. London: Macmillan and Co.

Fitzgibbons, Athol. (1988) *Keynes's Vision: A New Political Economy*. Oxford: Clarendon Press.

_____. (1992) "From Keynes's Vision to Keynesian Economics." In *Recent Developments in Post-Keynesian Economics*, edited by Philip Arestis and Victoria Chick, pp. 17-26. Aldershot: Edward Elgar.

Harcourt, Geoffrey C. (1992) In a Lecture at The University of Tennessee, Knoxville in the Spring Semester of 1992.

Harrod, Roy. (1951) *The Life of John Maynard Keynes*. London: Macmillan and Co.

Helburn, Suzanne W. (1991a) "Keynes's Idealism: A Critical Evaluation of Athol Fitzgibbons's *Keynes's Vision: A New Political Economy.*" *Review of Social Economy* 49 (Fall): 414-425.

_____. (1991b) "Burke and Keynes." In *Keynes and Philosophy: Essays on the Origin of Keynes's Thought*, edited by Bradley W. Bateman and John B. Davis, pp. 30-54. Aldershot: Edward Elgar.

_____. (1992) "On Keynes's Ethics." In *Recent Developments in Post-Keynesian Economics,* edited by Philip Arestis and Victoria Chick, pp. 27-46. Aldershot: Edward Elgar.

Hession, Charles H. (1984) *John Maynard Keynes: A Personal Biography of the Man who Revolutionized Capitalism and the Way we Live.* New York: Macmillan Publishing Co.

Jensen, Hans E. (1976) "Sources and Contours of Adam Smith's Conceptualized Reality in the *Wealth of Nations.*" *Review of Social Economy* 34 (December): 259-274.

_____. (1983) "J.M. Keynes as a Marshallian." *Journal of Economic Issues* 17 (March): 67-94.

_____. (1984) "Some Aspects of the Social Economics of John Maynard Keynes." *International Journal of Social Economics* 11 (Number 3/4): 72-91.

_____. (1987) "Alfred Marshall as a Social Economist." *Review of Social Economy* 45 (April): 14-36.

_____. (1990) "Value Premises in the Economic Thought of Alfred Marshall." *Economie Appliquee* 43 (No. 1): 19-35.

_____. (1991a) "The Role of Values in the Economics of Joan Robinson." In *The Joan Robinson Legacy*, edited by Ingrid H. Rima, pp. 20-33. Armonk, NY: M. E. Sharpe.

_____. (1991b) "J. M. Keynes's Theory of the State as a Path to His Social Economics of Reform in *The General Theory.*" *Review of Social Economy* 49 (Fall): 292-316.

Johnson, Elizabeth. (1974) "John Maynard Keynes: Scientist or Politician?" *Journal of Political Economy* 82 (January/February): 99-111.

Kecskemeti, Paul. (1952) "Introduction." In *Essays on the Sociology of Knowledge*, by Karl Mannheim and edited by Paul Kecskemeti, pp. 1-32. London: Routledge and Kegan Paul.

Keynes Geoffrey. (1975) "The early years." In *Essays on John Maynard Keynes*, edited by Milo Keynes, pp. 26-35. Cambridge: Cambridge University Press.

Keynes, John Maynard. (1919) *The Economic Consequences of the Peace.* Reprinted as Vol. 2 of *The Collected Writings of John Maynard Keynes.* London: Macmillan and Co., 1971.

_____. (1921) *A Treatise on Probability*. Reprinted as Vol. 8 of *The Collected Writings of John Maynard Keynes*. New York: St. Martin's Press, 1973.

_____. (1923) *A Tract on Monetary Reform*. Reprinted as Vol. 4 of *The Collected Writings of John Maynard Keynes*. London: The Macmillan Press, 1971.

_____. (1924a) "Alfred Marshall." In *Essays in Biography*, by John Maynard Keynes, pp. 161-231. Vol. 10 of *The Collected Writings of John Maynard Keynes*. London: The Macmillan Press, 1972.

_____. (1924b) Letter to Sir Charles Addis of July 25. In *Activities 1922-1929*, by John Maynard Keynes, edited by Donald Moggridge, pp. 270-272. Vol. 19, Part 1 of *The Collected Writings of John Maynard Keynes*. New York: Cambridge University Press, 1981.

_____. (1925a) "The Economic Consequences of Mr Churchill." In *Essays in Persuasion*, by John Maynard Keynes, pp. 207-230. Vol. 9 of *The Collected Writings of John Maynard Keynes*. London: The Macmillan Press, 1972.

_____. (1925b) "A Short View of Russia." In *Essays in Persuasion*, by John Maynard Keynes, pp. 253-271. Vol. 9 of *The Collected Writings of John Maynard Keynes*. London: The Macmillan Press, 1972.

_____. (1925c) "Am I a Liberal?" In *Essays in Persuasion*, by John Maynard Keynes, pp. 295-306. Vol. 9 of *The Collected Writings of John Maynard Keynes*. London: The Macmillan Press, 1972.

_____. (1926a) "Liberalism and Labour." In *Essays in Persuasion*, by John Maynard Keynes, pp. 307-311. Vol. 9 of *The Collected Writings of John Maynard Keynes*. London: The Macmillan Press, 1972.

_____. (1926b) "The End of Laissez-Faire." In *Essays in Persuasion*, by John Maynard Keynes, pp. 272-294. Vol. 9 of *The Collected Writings of John Maynard Keynes*. London: The Macmillan Press, 1972.

_____. (1926c) Letter to the *Chicago Daily News* of May 6. In *Activities 1922-1929*, by John Maynard Keynes, edited by Donald Moggridge, pp. 530-531. Vol. 19, Part 2 of *The Collected Writings of John Maynard Keynes*. New York: Cambridge University Press, 1981.

_____. (1926d) "Reflections on the Strike." In *Activities 1922-1929*, by John Maynard Keynes, edited by Donald Moggridge, pp. 531-534. Vol. 19, Part 2 of *The Collected Writings of John Maynard Keynes*. New York: Cambridge University Press, 1981.

_____. (1926e) "The General Strike." In *Activities 1922-1929*, by John Maynard Keynes, edited by Donald Moggridge, pp. 543-546. Vol. 19, Part 2 of *The Collected Writings of John Maynard Keynes*. New York: Cambridge University Press, 1981.

_____. (1927) "Clissold." In *Essays in Persuasion*, by John Maynard Keynes, pp. 315-320. Vol. 9 of *The Collected Writings of John Maynard Keynes*. London: The Macmillan Press, 1972.

_____. (1928a) Letter to Winston Churchill of May 13. In *Activities 1922-1929*, by John Maynard Keynes, edited by Donald Moggridge, pp. 749-750. Vol. 19, Part 2 of *The Collected Writings of John Maynard Keynes*. New York: Cambridge University Press, 1981.

_____. (1928b) "How to Organize a Wave of Prosperity." In *Activities 1922-1929*, by John Maynard Keynes, edited by Donald Moggridge, pp. 761-766. Vol. 19, Part 2 of *The Collected Writings of John Maynard Keynes*. New York: Cambridge University Press, 1981.

_____. (1929) "Can Lloyd George Do It?" In Essays in Persuasion, by John Maynard Keynes with the Assistance of Hubert Henderson, pp. 86-185. Vol. 9 of *The Collected Writings of John Maynard Keynes*. London: The Macmillan Press, 1972.

_____. (1930a) *A Treatise on Money. 1 The Pure Theory of Money* and *2 The Applied Theory of Money*. Vols. 5 and 6 of *The Collected Writings of John Maynard Keynes*. London: The Macmillan Press, 1971.

_____. (1930b) "Economic Possibilities for our Grand-children." In *Essays in Persuasion*, by John Maynard Keynes, pp. 321-332. Vol. 9 of *The Collected Writings of John Maynard Keynes*. London: The Macmillan Press, 1972.

_____. (1930c) "The Great Slump of 1930." In *Essays in Persuasion*, by John Maynard Keynes, pp. 126-134. Vol. 9 of *The Collected Writings of John Maynard Keynes*. London: The Macmillan Press, 1972.

_____. (1930d) "Sir Oswald Mosley's Manifesto." In *Activities 1929-1931*, by John Maynard Keynes, edited by Donald Moggridge, pp. 473-476. Vol. 20 of *The Collected Writings of John Maynard Keynes*. New York: Cambridge University Press, 1981.

_____. (1931a) Letter to Nicholas Kaldor of December 9. In *The General Theory and After. Part I: Preparation*, edited by Donald Moggridge, p. 243. Vol. 13 of *The Collected Writings of John Maynard Keynes*. London: The Macmillan Press, 1973.

_____. (1931b) "Preface." In *Essays in Persuasion*, by John Maynard Keynes, pp. xvii-xix. Vol. 9 of *The Collected Writings of John Maynard Keynes*. London: The Macmillan Press, 1972.

_____. (1931c) "An Economic Analysis of Unemployment." In *The General Theory and After. Part I: Preparation*, edited by Donald Moggridge, pp. 343-367. Vol. 13 of *The Collected Writings of John Maynard Keynes*. London: The Macmillan Press, 1973.

_____. (1931d) "The Economy Bill." In *Essays in Persuasion*, by John Maynard Keynes, pp. 145-149. Vol. 9 of *The Collected Writings of John Maynard Keynes*. London: The Macmillan Press, 1972.

_____. (1932a) Evidence submitted on December 15 to the Royal Commission on Lotteries and Betting. In *Social, Political and Literary Writings*, by John Maynard Keynes, edited by Donald Moggridge, pp. 398-412. Vol. 28 of *The Collected Writings of John Maynard Keynes*. New York: Cambridge University Press, 1982.

_____. (1932b) Broadcast on March 14. In *Activities 1931-1939*, by John Maynard Keynes, edited by Donald Moggridge, pp. 84-92. Vol. 21 of *The Collected Writings of John Maynard Keynes*. New York: Cambridge University Press, 1982.

_____. (1933a) "National Self-Sufficiency." *The Yale Review* N.S. 22 (June): 755-769.

_____. (1933b) Letter to the Editor of *The Times* of April 7. In *Activities 1931-1939*, by John Maynard Keynes, edited by Donald Moggridge, pp. 187-189. Vol. 21 of *The Collected Writings of John Maynard Keynes*. New York: Cambridge University Press, 1982.

_____. (1933c) "The Means to Prosperity." In *Essays in Persuasion*, by John Maynard Keynes, pp. 335-366. Vol. 9 of *The Collected Writings of John Maynard Keynes*. London: The Macmillan Press, 1972.

_____. (1933d) "The Distinction Between a Co-Operative Economy and an Entrepreneur Economy." In *The General Theory and After: A Supplement*, edited by Donald Moggridge, pp. 76-87. Vol. 29 of *The Collected Writings of John Maynard Keynes*. New York: Cambridge University Press, 1979.

_____. (1935) Letter to George Bernard Shaw of January 1. In *Social, Political and Literary Writings of John Maynard Keynes*, edited by Donald Moggridge, p. 42. Vol. 28 of *The Collected Writings of John Maynard Keynes*. New York: Cambridge University Press, 1982.

_____. (1936a) Letter to Ralph G. Hawtrey of April 15. In *The General Theory and After. Part II: Defence and Development*, edited by Donald Moggridge, pp. 23-28. Vol. 14 of *The Collected Writings of John Maynard Keynes*. London: The Macmillan Press, 1973.

_____. (1936b) *The General Theory of Employment, Interest and Money*. New York: Harcourt, Brace and Co.

_____. (1936c) Letter to Ralph G. Hawtrey of May 28. In *The General Theory and After. Part II: Defence and Development*, edited by Donald Moggridge, pp. 35-37. Vol. 14 of *The Collected Writings of John Maynard Keynes*. London: The Macmillan Press, 1973.

_____. (1938a) "My Early Beliefs." In *Essays in Biography*, by John Maynard Keynes, pp. 433-450. Vol. 10 of *The Collected Writings of John Maynard Keynes*. London: The Macmillan Press, 1972.

_____. (1938b) Letter to Roy Harrod of July 4. In *The General Theory and After. Part II: Defence and Development*, edited by Donald Moggridge, pp. 295-297. Vol. 14 of *The Collected Writings of John Maynard Keynes*. London: The Macmillan Press, 1973.

_____. (1939a) "Mr. Keynes on the Distribution of Income and 'Propensity to Consume': A Reply." In *The General Theory and After. Part II: Defence and Development*, edited by Donald Moggridge, pp. 270-271. Vol. 14 of *The Collected Writings of John Maynard Keynes*. London: The Macmillan Press, 1973.

_____. (1939b) "Democracy and Efficiency." In *Activities 1931-1939*, by John Maynard Keynes, edited by Donald Moggridge, pp. 491-500. Vol. 21 of *The Collected Writings of John Maynard Keynes*. New York: Cambridge University Press, 1982.

_____. (1939c) Letter to Margaret Hill of June 20. In *Activities 1931-1939*, by John Maynard Keynes, edited by Donald Moggridge, pp. 590-592. Vol. 21 of *The Collected Writings of John Maynard Keynes*. New York: Cambridge University Press, 1982.

_____. (1940) "How to Pay for the War?" In *Essays in Persuasion*, by John Maynard Keynes, pp. 367-439. Vol. 9 of *The Collected Writings of John Maynard Keynes*. London: The Macmillan Press, 1972.

_____. (1942) "Memorandum on the Post-War Relations Between Purchasing Power and Consumers' Goods." In *Activities 1940-1946*, by John Maynard Keynes, edited by Donald Moggridge, pp. 271-274. Vol. 27 of *The Collected Writings of John Maynard Keynes*. New York: Cambridge University Press, 1980.

_____. (1943) "The Long-Term Problem of Full Employment." In *Activities 1940-1946*, by John Maynard Keynes, edited by Donald Moggridge, pp. 320-325. Vol. 27 of *The Collected Writings of John Maynard Keynes*. New York: Cambridge University Press, 1980.

Keynes, John Neville. (1955) *The Scope and Method of Political Economy*. 4th ed. New York: Kelley and Millman.

Kuhn, Thomas S. (1970) *The Structure of Scientific Revolutions*. 2nd ed. Chicago: University of Chicago Press.

Levy, Paul. (1975) "The Bloomsbury Group." In *Essays on John Maynard Keynes*, edited by Milo Keynes, pp. 60-72. Cambridge: Cambridge University Press.

Mannheim, Karl. (1955) *Ideology and Utopia*. A Harvest Book. New York: Harcourt, Brace and World.

Marshall, Alfred. (1873) "The Future of the Working Classes." In *Memorials of Alfred Marshall*, edited by A. C. Pigou, pp. 101-118. London: Macmillan and Co., 1925.

_____. (1883) "Lecture 3. Remedies for Poverty: Is Nation-alisation a Remedy?" In "Alfred Marshall's Lectures on Progress and Poverty," by George J. Stigler, pp. 200-210. *The Journal of Law & Economics* 12 (April 1969): 181-226.

_____. (1885) "The Present Position of Economics." In *Memorials of Alfred Marshall*, edited by A.C. Pigou, pp. 152-174. London: Macmillan and Co., 1925.

_____. (1893a) "Preliminary Memorandum" submitted to the Royal Commission on the Aged Poor. In *Official Papers by Alfred Marshall*, edited by J.M. Keynes, pp. 200-210. London: Macmillan and Co., 1926.

_____. (1893b) "Minutes of Evidence Taken Before the Royal Commission on the Aged Poor, June 5." In *Official Papers by Alfred Marshall*, edited by J.M. Keynes, pp. 205-262. London: Macmillan and Co., 1926.

_____. (1897) "The Old Generation of Economists and the New." In *Memorials of Alfred Marshall*, edited by A. C. Pigou, pp. 295-311. London: Macmillan and Co., 1925.

_____. (1898) "Distribution and Exchange." *The Economic Journal* 8 (March): 37-59.

_____. (1919) *Industry and Trade*. London: Macmillan and Co.

_____. (1961) *Principles of Economics*. Vol. 1. *Text*. With Annotations by C.W. Guillebaud. 9th (Variorum) ed. London: Macmillan and Co.

Mill, John Stuart. (1909) *Principles of Political Economy*. New ed. Edited by W.J. Asley. London: Longmans, Green and Co.

Minar, David W. (1961) "Ideology and Political Behavior." *Midwest Journal of Political Science* 5 (November): 317- 331.

Mini, Piero V. (1991) *Keynes, Bloomsbury and The General Theory*. Houndsmills: Macmillan Academic and Professional.

Moggridge, D.E. (1992) *Maynard Keynes: An economist's biography*. London and New York: Routledge.

Moore, George Edward. (1903) *Principia Ethica*. Cambridge: Cambridge University Press.

Myrdal, Gunnar. (1968) *Asian Drama: An Inquiry Into the Poverty of Nations*. Vol. 1. New York: Pantheon of Random House.

O'Donnell, R. M. (1989) *Keynes: Philosophy, Economics and Politics: The Philosophic Foundations of Keynes's Thought and their Influence on his Economics and Politics*. New York: St. Martin's Press.

Pigou, A. C. (1924) "In Memoriam: Alfred Marshall." In *Memorials of Alfred Marshall*, edited by A.C. Pigou, pp. 81-90. London: Macmillan and Co., 1925.

Robinson, Austin. (1947) "John Maynard Keynes 1883-1946." *The Economic Journal* 57 (March): 1-68.

_____. (1972) "John Maynard Keynes: Economist, Author, Statesman." *The Economic Journal* 82 (June): 531-546.

_____. (1975) "A personal view." In *Essays on John Maynard Keynes*, edited by Milo Keynes, pp. 9-23. Cambridge: Cambridge University Press.

Robinson, Joan. (1975) "What has become of the Keynesian Revolution?" In *Essays on John Maynard Keynes*, edited by Milo Keynes, pp. 123-131. Cambridge: Cambridge University Press.

_____. (1976) "The Age of Growth." *Challenge* 19 (May/June): 4-9.

Schumpeter, Joseph A. (1949) "Science and Ideology." *The American Economic Review* 39 (March): 345-359.

_____. (1954) *History of Economic Analysis*. New York: Oxford University Press.

_____. (1964) *Business Cycles*. Abridged by Rendigs Fels. New York: McGraw-Hill.

Shionoya, Yuichi. (1991) "Sidgwick, Moore and Keynes: a Philosophical Analysis of Keynes's 'My Early Beliefs'." In *Keynes and Philosophy: Essays on the Origin of Keynes's Thought*, edited by Bradley W. Bateman and John B. Davis, pp. 6-29. Aldershot: Edward Elgar.

Skidelsky, Robert. (1983) *Hopes Betrayed 1883-1920*. Vol. 1 of *John Maynard Keynes*. London: Macmillan.

Smith, Adam. (1937) *An Inquiry into the Nature and Causes of the Wealth of Nations*. Edited by Edwin Cannan. New York: The Modern Library of Random House.

Spengler, Joseph J. (1960) "The Problem of Order in Economic Affairs." In *Essays in Economic Thought*, edited by Joseph J. Spengler and William R. Allen, pp. 6-34. Chicago: Rand McNally.

Stark, Werner. (1958) *The Sociology of Knowledge*. London: Routledge and Kegan Paul.

Wilson, Charles. (1975) "Keynes and economic history." In *Essays on John Maynard Keynes*, edited by Milo Keynes, pp. 230-236. Cambridge: Cambridge University Press.

J. M. KEYNES'S VISION AND CONCEPTUALIZED REALITY: WHAT ENDURES?

COMMENT BY JOHN E. ELLIOTT

Hans Jensen had provided an informed and valuable interpretative essay on leading elements in the "nature and causes" of Keynes's diagnosis of involuntary unemployment. By casting the scope of his intellectual net broadly, Jensen focuses on fundamental and enduring issues and minimizes technical details. His discussion of Keynes's long run "vision" of potential economic and moral progress, the social class bases of Keynes's theory of unemployment, the connecting linkages between "vision" and "conceptualized reality," and such underlying influences on Keynes's thought as those of Alfred Marshall, on the one hand, and Keynes's parents, John Neville and Florence Ada Keynes, on the other, enrich our understanding of Keynes's particular contributions and help to differentiate them from both neoclassical and standard "Keynesian" analyses.

The following commentary retains Jensen's useful organizational structure. Given that structure and associated insights he has developed, I shall endeavor to amplify, illustrate, fill in additional remarks, and generally clarify or extend some of Jensen's argumentarium. Space constraints dictate (brief) discussion of a limited number of issues. These include: the "utopian" character of Keynes's vision; Keynes's views on social classes, democracy, and the state; and Keynes versus the standard (or "Bastard") Keynesian explanations of unemployment and public policies to combat it. Throughout, parallels or contrasts are drawn between Keynes and other leading figures in economic thought.

Keynes's Long Run Vision of the Future Society

As Jensen aptly observes, Keynes's critique of neoclassical (notably Marshallian) theories of money, unemployment, and depression, which expanded over time and culminated in *The General Theory of Employment, Interest and Money* [hereinafter GT] and other works of the 1930s, did not carry with it a rejection of the "moral sentiments" or "normative vision" of the wealthier, more egalitarian, and liberally paternalist future society envisaged by Marshall and Keynes's parents. Specifically comparing Keynes and Marshall, Jensen observes that Keynes's long run vision was, if anything, more "optimistic," indeed, "utopian," than Marshall's.

Now, the term "utopian" requires a little clarification.[1] First, Keynes's vision of the future society, like utopias in general, incorporated powerful normative elements or, as Jensen puts it (following Mannheim), "wish-images." For some, like Joseph Schumpeter and other early twentieth century logical positivists, this indiscriminately mixes explanatory and normative components and renders a strictly scientific, *wertfrei* account virtually impossible. But in the words of Alexander Pope, loosely paraphrased here, "if man's reach did not exceed his grasp, then what is heaven for?" The normative components of Keynes's "wish-images" need to be assessed in their own right. One suspects that a certain amount of negative reaction to Keynes's long run vision, from both Left and Right, is rooted in contending normative assumptions rather than in what Jensen summarizes as the technological and sociocultural bases emerging in contemporary society for the potential realization of those norms.

Next, a "utopia," technically speaking, is a vision of a radically different future society. Because much social change is gradual and organic, building on what has evolved before, such images of the future are probably doomed to being characterized as "utopian" in the popular sense of impracticability or lack of realism. But were Keynes's hopeful expectations concerning "revolutionary technical changes" any more impracticable than, for example, Schumpeter's open-ended declaration (in 1950, p. 118) that "technological possibilities are an uncharted sea?" Similarly, did Keynes's (and Marshall's) views on the malleability of human nature impose any more exacting demands upon socio-cultural requisites for enhanced human virtue, social cooperativeness, and democratic participation than those which John Stuart Mill associated with the spread of representative government (1948) and worker-owned enterprises (1920, Pt. IV, chap. VII) or which Karl Marx identified as germinal potentialities within the Paris Commune (in Elliott, 1981, chap. 9)?[2] Keynes was one of the last of a long list of economists beginning with Adam Smith and extending through J.S. Mill and Marx to Alfred Marshall, Thorstein Veblen, and John Kenneth Galbraith, who considered the long run prospects for human progress to lie within the jurisdiction of their intellectual projects. His utopian excesses were less idiosyncratic than reflective of an entire body of thought extending over two centuries or so.

Finally, the perceived impracticability of Keynes's long run vision is muted if we consider his conceptualization of its relatively modest economic content, namely, the abolition of the "economic problem," defined not, in Robbinsian (1932) fashion, as supersession of the scarcity of resources relative to (all conceivable) human wants, but, more simply, as J.S. Mill, Marx, and Marshall understood it, the abolition of "want and poverty ..." in terms of the standards of the nineteenth/early twentieth century.[3]

This point is reinforced by noting briefly parallels with Schumpeter's assessment. Quantitatively, Keynes presupposes an eightfold expansion in real per capita income over one hundred years, beginning in 1930, whereas Schumpeter assumes a doubling in that statistic over a fifty year period, beginning in 1928. But qualitatively, Schumpeter reaches essentially the same conclusion, namely, that economic progress, by the end of the hypothesized period, "would do away with anything that according to present standards could be called poverty, even in the lowest strata of the population, pathological cases alone excepted" (1950, p. 66). Moreover, the process of economic progress could also be expected to improve substantially the quality of products, expand leisure time, increase the relative share of national income going to lower income groups, and underwrite generous social legislation. Thus, again, Keynes was not alone in envisioning dramatic and impelling "possibilities" in the process of economic and human progress.

Keynes's Views on Social Class, Democracy, and the State

Jensen's essay is also to be commended for its recognition and incorporation of such sociopolitical foundations of Keynes's economic theories as class and state. Although Keynes did not explicate the complexities of a class-based analysis in the manner, let us say, of a Marx, or those of a developed power or state-centered theory of political economy (as adumbrated, for example, in Caporaso and Levine 1992, chaps. 5, 7-8), social class, power, and state play integral roles in his conceptualization of both the sources of depression and unemployment and the policies and institutions needed to overcome them.

As Jensen observes, Keynes, like David Ricardo and Marx before him, basically employed a tripartite structure of social class relationships, that is, workers (primarily in the form of hired wage-laborers), entrepreneurs (including therein managers), and rentier (including landowners, money lenders, and financial speculators).[4] Unlike Marx, but to some extent like Ricardo, Keynes did not identify major class struggles or even tensions between workers and entrepreneurs in the domain of production. When he declared his sympathies for the view that "everything is produced by labour, ... as the sole factor of production, operating in a given environment of technique, natural resources, capital equipment and effective demand," he qualifies his statement by adding immediately that "labour" includes, "of course, the personal services of the entrepreneur (and their managerial agents), conceptualized as "active" members of the production process, every bit as contributive (or more) to profit creation as non-managerial workers. Even the "financier" is characterized as exercising "an intelligence and determination and executive skill," especially concerning risky ventures or "individual assets having a doubtful prospective yield" (Keynes, 1936, pp. 221, 376), that are supportive of the processes of production and profit-making.

Consequently, Keynes's view of conflicts between entrepreneurs and workers is essentially distributive. In Keynes's argument, resolution of distributive conflicts and their associated "inequitable distribution of wealth and income" are subject to remedy without radical modifications of the property and power relations embedded in intra-enterprise domination, as propounded by J.S. Mill, or in labor exploitation, as envisioned by Marx (Elliott 1987). Although the provisioning of (highly talented) entrepreneurial labor may justify "significant inequalities of incomes and wealth," it is "not necessary ... that the game should be played" with such "large disparities" and "for such high stakes as at present. Much lower stakes will serve the purpose equally well, as soon as the players are accustomed to them" (Keynes, 1936, pp. 372, 374). Moreover, egalitarian social justice, economic progress, and abolition of depression and massive unemployment, for Keynes, are congruent policy objectives. Keynes believed, for example, that progressive income and inheritance taxation can reduce disparities in wealth and income and thereby raise the propensity to consume and thus aggregate demand. Higher aggregate demand can stimulate enlarged production and lower unemployment and thereby "may prove positively favorable to the growth of capital" (Keynes, 1936, p. 373) and the economy generally. Similarly, an aggressively expansionary monetary policy, if successful in reducing interest rates, may simultaneously redistribute wealth and income from (generally more wealthy) rentier to (generally less wealthy) entrepreneurs and workers, expand investment and thereby aggregate demand, reduce unemployment, and foster a higher rate of capital accumulation and rate of economic growth. Thus, the goal of full employment (or at least an approximation thereof) and the instruments of expansionary state economic policy may potentially function as a basis for an economic and political alliance between entrepreneurs and workers.

By contrast, Keynes perceived the class-based propensities and habits of liquidity-oriented rentier as directly inimical to the interests of both entrepreneurs and workers, as Jensen nicely elaborates. It is not necessary here to recount the several reasons why the interest rate "rules the roost" and, by falling more slowly than the marginal efficiency of capital, "sets a limit to output" (Keynes, 1936, pp. 223, 229). It will suffice to observe that, for Keynes, the paramount perceived class conflict occurs between the rentier, whose psychological and institutional characteristics foster high and sticky interest rates, and the active, profit-seeking and creating entrepreneurial stratum of capitalist society.

Keynes differs from such classical predecessors as J.S. Mill, of course, by extending the anti-rentier argument from land to capital. According to Keynes, aside from the "special case" of full employment, "interest today rewards no genuine sacrifice, any more than does the rent of land. The owner of capital can obtain interest because capital is scarce, just as the owner of land can obtain rent because land is scarce." Consequently, making capital goods more abundant until they cease "to be scarce, so that the functionless investor will no longer receive a bonus" "may be the most sensible way of gradually getting rid of many of the most objectionable features of capitalism." Notably, Keynes identified the "euthanasia of the cumulative oppressive power of the capitalist to exploit the scarcity-value of capital," the excessive and "great inequality of wealth" justified prior to Keynes by his orthodox predecessors in economic theory by the perceived need for powerful inducements to elicit the "savings of the rich out of their superfluity" provided through the phenomenon of high interest rates, and the impetus to expanded investment and capital accumulation, reduced unemployment, and gradual movement toward "economic bliss" stimulated by low interest rates (Keynes, 1936, 3, 221, 372-73, 376).[5]

In contrast to many purely economic analyses, Keynes's confidence that the contemporary democratic state could approximate full employment (or at least could have a better chance of doing so than a regime of laissez-faire capitalism),[6] was based, as Jensen insightfully explains, on an express, albeit rudimentary, theory of the state and its institutions. The following remarks are intended to complement Jensen's discussion. First, in *The End of Laissez-Faire*, in a manner reminiscent of Edmund Burke, Keynes writes: "Perhaps the chief task of Economists at this hour is to distinguish afresh the *Agenda* of Government from the *non-Agenda*" (1926, p. 20). He then adds: "We must aim at separating those services which are *technically social* from those which are *technically individual*. The most important Agenda of the State relate to those functions which fall outside the sphere of the individual" (1926, p. 26). What Keynes here adds to Burke's sagacious counsel is the notion, later elaborated in the GT, that certain governmental functions are "technically social" in the sense that individual behavior is unable (not merely disinclined) to yield desirable social results.

For example, workers bargain for money, not real, wages. At the level of the individual firm, it may be reasonably assumed that money wage reductions may occur without adversely affecting prices and the overall level of demand. At the aggregate level, however, money wage cuts may very well elicit reductions in prices, income, and aggregate demand. Consequently, there may exist "*no* method" whereby "labour as a whole can reduce its real wage to a given figure by revising its money bargains with the entrepreneurs." It is thus "invalid" to "transfer the argument" that money wage cuts will stimulate higher employment from the level of the individual firm "to industry as a whole" (Keynes, 1936, pp. 13, 259) if (as is the case) the level of aggregate demand cannot plausibly be taken as fixed. By contrast, expansionary state policies can raise demand, output, and employment directly, thereby circumventing the roundabout, unjust, and uncertain method of wage and price reductions through the market system. Such policies, for Keynes, in effect function as public goods. They enable attainment of desired results through collective action which the disaggregated results of individual behavior are unlikely to be able to achieve.

After declaring that the central task of economics is to distinguish the Agenda from the non-Agenda of government on the basis of differentiation of "technically social" from "technically individual" functions, Keynes states that the "companion task of politics is to devise forms of Government within a *Democracy* which shall be capable of accomplishing the Agenda" (1926, p. 40). In his paper, Jensen has elaborated clearly some of the institutional bases, purposes, and content of Keynes's prescriptions, notably his notion of the "socialization of investment." I comment here on Keynes's conceptualization of democracy.

First, as Paul Streeten persuasively argued forty years ago, Keynes's view of government policy and democratic social reform lies "unmistakably in the classical liberal-utilitarian tradition" (1) in the specific *utilitarian* sense, "which Keynes shared with Bentham and Mill, that the economic welfare of a nation is something that the government can and should discover and promote;" (2) in the specific *liberal* sense that "the promotion of economic welfare requires only a little tampering here and there," leaving the rest to "the automatic play of self-interest;" and (3) in the specific *harmony* sense that "he looked upon the economic activities of a nation ... as if they had a common purpose, which properly understood, is also the purpose of each individual" (Streeten, 1954, pp. 356, 363).

Second, both positively and normatively, Keynes's view of democratic government was essentially "elitist" (although liberal and paternalist). On the one hand, Keynesian-style democracy is representative rather than populist or participatory. Members of parliament are elected by citizens, who hold and covet the full array of democratic rights and liberties to protect themselves from potential tyranny and rapacity by their political leaders. But, between elections, it is the function, indeed duty, of an "extended state," in Jensen's useful phrasing, to provide creative leadership in the interest of the nation as a collective entity, and not merely to passively record, transmit, and respond to the specific popular sentiments, notions, and pressures from below.[7]

Keynesian-style democracy is elitist in yet another sense. Although Parliament is the locus of political sovereignty, that sovereignty, for Keynes, is "ultimate," and is not properly operative on an intricate or day-to-day basis. Keynes presupposes that most of the real, complex, technical work of government, notably that pertaining to the planning for and provisioning of public infrastructure investment, is managed by technically skilled, paternalist, and accountable (to parliament) civil servants, working in the kinds of public and public/private institutions which Jensen has identified.[8] This group, led by an "educated bourgeoisie," of which Keynes considered himself a part and "whose ideas are more powerful than is commonly understood" (Keynes, 1936, p. 383), plays a strategic role, not only in analyzing technical issues, but in the "moral" function of balancing class interests so as to sustain democracy and individual liberties in a context in which collective action and government planning is significantly extended.[9]

Finally, as a corollary to his analysis of a reformed democratic capitalist (or "liberal socialist") system of political economy, Keynes, in the GT, makes two very important observations about authoritarian systems. The first of these is that a policy of downward wage (and price) flexibility as an antidepressionary strategy (Elliott, 1992) is typically perceived as a component of a competitive, laissez-faire system. But this is "the opposite of the truth." If a program of wage cuts were adopted during a period of falling aggregate demand, its greatest likelihood of success would occur if the cuts were sudden, large, and once-and-for-all, so as to have the maximum favorable effect on raising the marginal efficiency of capital (and reducing interest rates via reductions in the transactionary demand for money associated with once-and-for-all price cuts). "But this could only be accomplished by administrative decree and is scarcely practical politics under a system of free wage-bargaining. ...It is only in a highly authoritarian society, where sudden, substantial changes could be decreed that a flexible wage policy could function with success" (Keynes, 1936, 265, 269). Thus, for Keynes, expansionary state policy is preferable to wage and price austerity not only on grounds of efficacy and social justice, but because of its closer fit with the institutional realities and social values of liberal capitalist democracy.[10]

Keynes's second observation concerning the "authoritarian state systems" of the interwar period in the GT is that although their institutions and policies tend to sacrifice efficiency and freedom, they do "solve the problem of unemployment ... It is certain the world will not much longer tolerate the unemployment ... inevitably associated with capitalistic individualism." If this is true, then failure to at least approximate full employment under democratic auspices could trigger adoption of authoritarian solutions. Therefore, whereas "enlargement of the functions of government, involved in the task of adjusting to one another the propensity to consume and the inducement to invest" might be objectionable to a "nineteenth century publicist" or a "contemporary American financier," Keynes defended it, "on the contrary, both as the only practicable means of avoiding the destruction of existing economic forms in their entirety and as the condition of the successful functioning of individual initiative" (Keynes, 1936, pp. 380-81).

Keynes and/versus the Keynesians

In his explication of Keynes's analysis of the basic causes of involuntary unemployment, Jensen focuses on two main points: inequality in the distribution of wealth and income and high and sticky interest rates. Both, of course, are central to Keynes's argument, notably in the GT, and both help to differentiate Keynes's more radical interpretation of the causes and cures of unemployment from those of his contemporaries and successors, especially the so-called "Bastard Keynesians." Each deserves some additional commentary.

Keynes did not subject the causes of inequality to probing analysis. Even his discussion of inequality's effects in the GT are postponed largely to the book's final chapter. But from the *Economic Consequences of the Peace*, in 1919, to the GT and after, there is no question but that "capitalistic individualism" is understood as highly inegalitarian, and problematically sc. Indeed, in the GT, "inequality is in a very fundamental sense the root cause of unemployment and the greatest barrier to economic progress ..." (Dillard, 1948, p. 316). First, the greater the extent of inequality, the lower the propensity to consume and the higher the propensity to save. Second, the lower the propensity to consume, the lower the volume of investment. It is the negative implications of these effects of inequality for aggregate demand which undergird the potentiality for what came to be characterized as "economic stagnation" (Hansen, 1938), that is, an overall, long-run level of less-than-full employment, around which a laissez-faire capitalist economy would presumably exhibit its proclivities for short run cyclical fluctuations.

Under special circumstances, such as the nineteenth century, underlying growth factors, such as "the growth of population and of invention, the opening-up of new lands, the state of confidence and the frequency of war" were apparently sufficiently robust to permit a combination of reasonably high schedules of the marginal efficiencies of capital, a "rate of interest high enough to be psychologically acceptable to wealth-owners," and a level of ensuing investment high enough to keep unemployment not so "intolerably below" full employment as to "provoke revolutionary changes." In the twentieth century, by contrast, this fortuitous "balance of forces," in Keynes's view, was crumbling, "for a variety of reasons," some of which Keynes identifies in chapter 21 of the GT. *One* of the major consequences of this view was that, for Keynes, "capitalistic individualism" had reached a great historical divide beyond which it could no longer tolerate the unusually large inequalities of the nineteenth century. Egalitarian social reform, as described briefly in the preceding section of this paper, had become essential not only for social justice, but for fuller employment and economic progress. Second, in principle, downward shifts in the marginal efficiency of capital could be offset by reductions in interest rates. This brings us, by a different route, to the issue of high and sticky interest rates.

Keynes's explanation of this phenomenon is actually composed of a set of propositions which need to be unpacked. First, Keynes considers the level of and rapidity of reduction in interest rates *relative to* the positions of and proclivity toward downward shifts in marginal efficiency of capital schedules. These, in turn, exhibit both long run stagnationist tendencies, as noted above, and short run contractions subsequent, and organically linked, to over-expansion during preceding cyclical booms. Thus, from a secular perspective, interest rates may not fall sufficiently below low-level profit expectations to elicit adequate investment to match saving out of full-employment income. From a cyclical viewpoint, interest rates may not be able to fall as rapidly as do marginal efficiencies of capital.

Second, substantial reductions in aggregate demand, caused by downward shifts in profit expectations, are not plausibly accompanied by a reduced propensity to hoard and thereby decreases in interest rates. To the contrary, "the circumstances which lead to pessimistic views about future yields are apt to increase the propensity to hoard" (Keynes, 1937, p. 218). The "dismay and uncertainty" associated with a "collapse in the marginal efficiency of capital naturally precipitates a sharp increase in liquidity-preference -- and hence a rise in the rate of interest," thereby dealing investment a doubly depressive blow (Keynes, 1936, p. 316).

Moreover, because money "has an elasticity of substitution equal, or nearly equal, to zero," demand, during moments of uncertainty and crisis, "may be predominantly directed to money." And because money "has a very small elasticity of production," it "cannot be readily produced; -- labour cannot be turned on at will by entrepreneurs to produce money in increasing quantities as its price rises in terms of the wage-unit" (Keynes, 1936, pp. 230, 234). Indeed, because bankers are confronted, at moments of economic crisis, by increased "lenders' risk" and are afflicted by the same increased desire for liquidity that other owners of financial assets are, they tend to reduce credit creation and thereby the money supply more or less along with the general increase in the propensity to hold money. The tendency for bankers to curb credit and reduce the money supply below its potential gathers momentum, in Keynes's argument, as cyclical downturns turn into recessions. Consequently, the length and severity of contractions are greater than they otherwise would be and interest rates behave to some extent counter-cyclically, at first rising as the economy falls and subsequently failing to fall as rapidly as wages and prices do.

Third, money's importance, Keynes states, "*essentially flows from its being a link between the present and the future.*" Now, the single most important thing to be said about the future is that it is uncertain. For Keynes, "*uncertainty* about the future is the sole intelligible explanation" of the very existence of that "type of liquidity preference" designated as the "speculative" demand for money and a paramount reason for the special character of the inverse relationship between the interest rate and the amount of money demanded for speculative purposes. Because of uncertainty, purchasing a financial asset and later selling it for cash (rather than simply holding cash) runs the risk of a capital loss. Uncertainty also leads individuals to differ in their estimates of the future. "Anyone who differs from the predominant opinion ... may have a good reason for keeping liquid resources in order to profit, if he is right," from higher interest rates (and low asset prices) later. Given the overall position of the propensity to hold money for these reasons, every decrease in the interest rate "reduces the market rate relatively to the 'safe' rate and therefore increases the risk of liquidity; and [also] reduces the current earnings form illiquidity," which function as "a sort of insurance premium to offset the risk of loss on capital account," thereby making money more attractive and the parting with money in exchange for debt less so. A low rate of interest thus "leaves more to fear than to hope, and offers, at the same time, a running yield which is only sufficient to offset a small measure of fear." This, according to Keynes, "is perhaps the chief obstacle to a fall in the rate of interest to a very low level" (Keynes, 1936, pp. 169, 201-02, 293).[12] Last, as observed earlier, Keynes differentiates between the gross rate of interest, which includes "the intermediate costs of bringing the borrower and the ultimate lender together" and a risk allowance, and the pure rate of interest. "As the pure rate of interest declines, it does not follow that the allowances for expense and risk decline *pari passu*." Insofar as this is true, the gross interest rate, "which the typical borrower has to pay," is not only higher than but "may decline more slowly than the pure rate of interest, and may be incapable of being brought, by the methods of the existing banking and financial organization, below a certain minimum figure ... even if the pure rate of interest to the lender is nil" (Keynes, 1936, p. 208).

Such long run considerations as inequality in the distribution of wealth and power and historical changes in marginal efficiencies of capital, dynamic shifts in propensities to invest, consume, and hoard, fundamental uncertainty, the endogeneity of money, and institutional factors which depart from the assumption of perfect competition are all significant elements in Keynes's crude but powerful theoretical conceptualization of involuntary unemployment. They also serve to differentiate Keynes's analysis of unemployment from various versions of "Keynesian" economics.

The simplest version of "Keynesian" analysis (Samuelson, 1948) is a truncated model of "equilibrium at less that full employment" based on a relatively stable propensity to consume and an autonomous level of investment. Involuntary unemployment is explained by a level of aggregate demand insufficient to absorb all the output forthcoming under full employment conditions or, alternatively, a volume of investment insufficient to match full employment saving.

A second version, the standard neo-Keynesian LM-IS model first formulated by J.R. Hicks (1937) and Alvin Hansen (1949), provides an integrated, simultaneous explanation of national income and the interest rate. This model typically presupposes an exogenously given supply of money, a combination of a transactionary demand for money and a rather tame asset demand for money, a saving function dependent on income, and an investment function (given autonomous investment), dependent inversely on the rate of interest. On the basis of these presuppositions, unemployment is explained by the *shapes* of the various functions, notably a very flat, indeed horizontal, LM curve, caught in the vise of a "liquidity trap," and a very steep, perhaps vertical, IS curve, rooted in the insensitivity of investment to small changes in the rate of interest, resulting in an "inconsistency between investment and full employment saving" (Ackley, 1961).

A third, "neoclassical-Keynesian," model adds standard neo-classical labor supply and demand functions, the assumption that competition is "perfect" in its consequences for downward wage and price flexibility, and a "Pigou Effect," wherein a decrease in the price level (and thereby an increase in real money balances, M/P) causes the IS (as well as LM) curve to shift upward to the right. In this highly neoclassical version of Keynesian theory, even if the LM curve is perfectly elastic and the IS curve is perfectly inelastic, "automatic market forces," in the form of money wage and price reductions in the event of excess supplies of labor and of goods, "to push real income up from the unemployment level ... not only exist, but even succeed eventually in raising income to the full employment level" (Patinkin, 1965, p. 339). From this perspective, the unemployment conclusion can be restored *within the framework of a comparative static methodology*, but only by incorporating an assumption of downward wage and price rigidity (Modigliani, 1944).

Are these various "Keynesian" explanations of unemployment authentic interpretations or extensions of Keynes's own arguments or are the formulators of such theories, as Joan Robinson insouciently characterizes them, simply "bastard Keynesians [who have] turned the argument back into being a defense of laissez-faire?" (1976, p. 5). A reasonable answer is both "Yes *and* No." The GT is an ambiguous book, containing surviving vestiges of neoclassical argument and anticipations of standard Keynesianism[13] as well as more intellectually radical elements, such as those emphasized herein and in Jensen's essay. In assessing the relative merit or relevance of each in Keynes's thought, it is important to note that one major advantage of adopting a looser methodological approach, as Keynes does, for example, in chapters 12, 19 and 22 of the GT, is that historical, institutional, dynamic, and distributive dimensions may be incorporated into the analytical argument making it possible to retain the diagnosis of (perhaps severe and extended) unemployment without the need for the extreme assumptions of standard or neoclassical versions of "Keynesian" analysis.[14,15]

By going beyond the perspectives of standard Keynesian interpretations of Keynes, Jensen also clarifies and enhances our understanding of Keynes's more radical policy recommendations, such as those pertaining to the "socialization of investment" and the "euthanasia of the rentier." As in the instance of diagnosis, however, Keynes's views on policy in the mid 1930s and after also demonstrate a mixture of continuity and discontinuity. In this context, it would appear to be an (unnecessary) overstatement to say that Keynes became convinced in the 1930s that what is now known as "Keynesian policies" "would *not* be of *any use* in lifting the economy out of the depression" (emphasis added). First, Keynes differentiated between avoiding a "slump" (that is, a deep depression) and recovering from one once it has occurred. Unless we are to restrict Keynes's policy recommendations to the case of severe depressions, we must recognize that he believed a robustly expansionary monetary policy could play an indispensable, not merely a salutary, role in preventing deep depressions in the first place (Keynes, 1937a).

Second, even in the case of deep depressions, Keynes's reservations about monetary policy are typically expressed by stating that full employment "cannot be readily established *merely* by manipulating the quantity of money" (emphasis added). During a severe contraction into a deep depression, the "collapse" in profit expectations "may be so complete that no practicable reduction in the rate of interest will be enough." However, although expansionary monetary policy, taken by itself, is insufficient, it remains necessary, partly to help offset the rise in liquidity preference (and reduction in bank credit) which occurs "*after* the collapse in the marginal efficiency of capital," partly to provide "a great aid to recovery and, probably, a necessary condition of it" through a reduction in the rate of interest, and partly to serve as the most expansionary (and hence most appropriate) means of financing the public works expenditures which constitute a paramount component of the "socialization of investment" (Keynes, 1936, pp. 309, 316).[16]

Third, although it is true that Keynes says little in the GT (or elsewhere) about the methods of financing public expenditures, specifically, to deficit spending, it is also a bit of an exaggeration to permit Peter Clarke (1988, p. 305) to say there is "nothing" on the subject there. In his discussion of the multiplier, for example, Keynes designates "increased public works" as a means of fostering economic expansion. In this context, he specifically recommends "loan expenditures" as a means of financing government spending to recover from depression. Keynes defines loan expenditures as "the net borrowings of public authorities on all accounts, whether on capital account or to meet a budgetary deficit." Thus, Keynes uses the expression "deficit" not to encompass all instances of debt financing, but only those public expenditures on current account, such as "unemployment relief financed by loans," or, tongue-in-check, to take an extreme example, the Treasury's burying of banknotes in disused coal mines. These loan expenditures raise aggregate demand and hence employment by "increasing the propensity to consume." Loan expenditures also include public and public-private capital expenditures, which operate by "increasing investment" (Keynes, 1936, pp. 119, 128-29).

Prior to the early 1930s Keynes, like many economists, including Pigou, supported public works spending as a means of fostering economic recovery and reduced unemployment, but believed that the multiplier effects of expended public investment, coupled with savings from decreased unemployment relief, could permit this to occur with little, if not any, increased government borrowing. By the mid 1930s, however, Keynes again like many economists,[17] believed that the magnitude of public infrastructure expenditure required to recover from deep depression was substantial and that$_o$ in this context at least, an annually balanced budget constituted an impediment to economic recovery. Thus, "loan expenditure" is superior to taxation as a means of financing public works, at least during depressions.[18, 19] Indeed, as noted in the preceding paragraph, Keynes declines to characterize capital account public investment as "deficit" spending, just as capital expansion by private businesses financed by bank credit is not typically so characterized. Thus, Keynes's more radical arguments concerning the expansion of public investment and the regulation of private investment go substantially beyond the rather tame policy recommendations of the standard Keynesian proposals -- of expansionary monetary and fiscal policy, including government borrowing -- but do not reject those ideas per se. Conversely, although most "Keynesian" policy analyses after Keynes maintain a certain continuity with the ideas and policy recommendations of the founder of the paradigm, there is no question, as reinforced by Jensen's admirable exposition, that the "tiger" represented by Keynes's more radical views concerning such matters as socialization of investment and the euthanasia of the rentier was largely "defanged" by his successors. As in our earlier discussion, these remarks are intended to complement Jensen's persuasive account of Keynes, notably concerning expansion of public investment and public regulation of private investment, rather than to substitute for it.

Notes

[1] Some interpreters, for instance, characterize Keynes's 1930 essay on "The Economic Possibilities of our Grandchildren" as an example of "millenialist" thought. (See Salerno, 1992.)

[2] Political philosopher C.B. Macpherson (1977, p. 4) comments persuasively that the practicability of a model of a future society, that is, its functionality "over a fairly long run," requires assessment of the nature and capabilities of human beings, not only now, but as they potentially could become "in any attainable social circumstances." This potentialist stipulation is important because we "are not necessarily limited to the way people behave politically [or

economically or morally] now. We are not limited to that if we can show reasons for expecting that that could change with changes in, for instance, the technological possibilities or the economic relations of their society."

[3] It is not my purpose here to exonerate each detail of Keynes's long run vision. From the perspective of the late twentieth century, Keynes's stimulating 1930 essay ignores environmental and ecological issues, focuses on already highly industrialized societies rather than want and poverty in an international context, and naively assumes that "revolutionary technical changes" will more or less automatically translate into a fifteen hour work week and transcendence of the "economic struggle between classes and nations."

[4] For Ricardo, the basic class division emphasized was that among capitalists, landlords, and workers. For Marx, an analogous tripartite model would focus upon those who provide surplus labor and thereby create surplus value (workers), those who appropriate surplus value (industrial capitalists), and all those who provide requisite conditions for the functioning and continuity of surplus value creation and appropriation (including, among others, managers, money lenders, landlords, and state functionaries). (See Resnick and Wolff, 1987, chaps. 3-5.)

[5] Keynes's analysis of the character and consequences of conflicts between rentier and entrepreneurs is also reminiscent of Marx's explication of the "struggle between the moneyed and industrial capitalists [which] is simply a struggle over the division of the profit" (1958, Vol. III, p. 509). For Marx, unlike Keynes, conflicts between capitalists and workers are the paramount focus of his general argument, in Volume I of *Capital*. But in his elaborations, elsewhere, he observes that in the instance of "a general crisis of over-production the contradiction is not between the different kinds of productive capital, but between industrial and loanable capital -- between capital as directly involved in the production process and capital as money existing (relatively) outside of it" (Marx, 1975, p. 413). In a capitalist, money-using economy, "the supply of all commodities can be greater than the demand for all commodities, since the demand for the general commodity, money, exchange-value, is greater than the demand for all particular commodities ..." (Marx, 1968, Vol. II, p. 505.)

[6] Keynes was not invariably optimistic about the political feasibility of his proposals. For example, at one point after the GT (1940, p. 159), he wrote that "The conclusion is that in recent times investment expenditures have been on a scale which was hopelessly inadequate to the problem. ... It appears to be politically impossible for a capitalist democracy to organize expenditure on a scale necessary to make the grand experiment which would prove my case except in war conditions."

[7] As in other instances, Keynes's understanding of parliamentary democracy bears a striking resemblance to the ideas of Edmund Burke. In his famous speech to the citizens of Bristol (in 1774), Burke maintained that although an elected representative owes his constituents "communication," "respect," and "attention," he also has the duty of exercising his "mature judgment" in the interest of the nation. This, he declares, is inconsistent with "*authoritative* instructions [and] *mandates*," which the parliamentarian is "bound blindly" to obey. "Parliament," he continued, "is not a *congress* of ambassadors from different and hostile interests ... [but] a *deliberative* assembly of *one* nation, with one interest, that of the whole. You choose a member indeed; but when you have chosen him, he is not a member of Bristol, but he is a member of Parliament" (Cf, Cohen, 1972, pp. 436-37). (It should be noted that Burke was elected.)

[8] Keynesian-style democracy, interestingly, is in a sense more elitist on this issue than Ricardo's and roughly parallels the position of J.S. Mill. For Ricardo, one of Parliament's major functions was to serve as a forum for voicing contending perceived needs and interests, debating, and adjudicating divergent class interests, assuming a commonality of interest in prosperity and economic progress (Milgate and Stimson, 1991). In his *Representative Government*, the heavy weight that "Mill gave to knowledge and skill led him to recommend that Parliament should not itself initiate any legislation but should be confined to approving or

rejecting, or sending back for reconsideration but not itself amending, legislative proposals all of which would be sent up to it by a non-elected commission" (Macpherson, 1977, pp. 59-60).

[9] In his book, *The Road to Serfdom* (1944), Friedrich Hayek argued that government planning and collective action generally poses an overpowering threat to individual freedoms. In a letter to Hayek (cited in Harrod, 1951, pp. 436-37), Keynes argues that "we almost certainly want more," not no or even less, planning. "But the planning should take place in a community in which as many people as possible, both leaders and followers, wholly share your own moral position," that is, a deep commitment to individual freedoms. "Moderate planning will be safe if those carrying it out are rightly oriented in their own minds to the moral issue. ... Dangerous acts can be done safely in a community which thinks and feels rightly, which would be the way to hell if they were executed by those who think and feel wrongly."

[10] The primary cause of the cyclical crisis, Keynes believes, is "a sudden collapse of the marginal efficiency of capital." When "disillusion falls on an over-optimistic and over-bought market, it should fall with sudden and even catastrophic force" (Keynes, 1936, pp. 315-16).

[11] Reductions in the money supply, accompanying and succeeding reductions in aggregate demand associated with downward shifts in profit expectations and upward shifts in the "propensity to hoard," tend to nullify the potentially corrective effects (through decreases in the transactionary demand for money and thereby interest rates) of wage and price reductions on investment and aggregate demand generally. In Keynes's words, "If the quantity of money is itself a function of the wage- and price- level, there is nothing to hope in [the] direction" of increasing the real value of money (and hence decreasing interest rates) by reducing wages and prices during contraction (Keynes, 1936, p. 266).

[12] As a limiting case," Keynes describes a situation wherein, for these reasons, "after the rate of interest has fallen to a certain level, liquidity-preference may become virtually absolute in the sense that almost everyone prefers cash to holding a debt which yields so low a rate of interest." In light of Keynes's qualificatory language, it is reasonably open to debate as to whether this literally constitutes a "liquidity trap" or not. Because, in any event, "institutional and psychological factors ... set a limit much above zero to the practicable decline in the rate of interest," notably in the context of low and/or rapidly falling profit expectations, a liquidity trap in the strict sense is not necessary for Keynes's argument.

[13] As observed in footnote 12, Keynes presents something approximating a liquidity trap in chapter 15 of the GT. In chapter 18, Keynes describes briefly certain "special characteristics" of his analytical instrumentarium "about which we can safely generalize from experience, but which are not logically necessary," including the stylized fact that "moderate changes ... in the rate of interest will not be associated with very great changes in the rate of investment." In his basic model of the GT, summarized in chapter 3 and adumbrated in Books III and IV, Keynes assumes constant money wage costs, but as a "simplification," dispensed with later (in chapter 19), "introduced solely to facilitate the exposition" (Keynes, 1936, pp. 27, 250). Keynes also incorporates into the GT what is now called the "Pigou Effect," as well as the "Keynes Effect" and wage and price flexibility (1936, 92-93, 262-66).

[14] In a recent essay (Elliott, 1994), I characterize the intellectually conservative and radical elements coexisting in the GT and in Keynes's diagnosis of involuntary unemployment as "Keynes I" versus "Keynes II," respectively. The essay provides a rationale for *not* privileging Keynes I and elaborates the contributions of Keynes II to the content and integrity of Keynes's analysis of unemployment.

[15] Departure from a narrow and strict interpretation of comparative static methodology also permits Keynesians to retain (varying degrees of) continuity with Keynes's policy recommendations. Admitting the potential expansionary effect of wage and price cuts "does not imply indifference toward the amount or rate of price fall necessary to achieve full employment equilibrium" (Blaug, 1985, p. 667). Moreover, "though the real balance effect must be taken into consideration in our theoretical analysis, it is too weak -- and in some cases

(due to adverse expectations) too perverse -- to fulfill a significant role in our policy considerations" (Patinkin, 1965, p. 339).

[16] The "method of financing" increased public works "and the increased working cash, required by the increased employment and the rise in prices, may have the effect of increasing the rate of interest and so retarding investment in other directions, unless the monetary authorities take steps to the contrary; ... the increased cost of capital goods will reduce their marginal efficiency to the private investor, and this will require an actual fall in the rate of interest to offset it" (Keynes, 1936, pp. 119-20). Thus, for Keynes, expansionary monetary policy presumably accompanies and complements expansionary fiscal policy.

[17] Blaug (1985, p. 674) mentions "Slichter, Taussig, Schultz, Yntema, Simons, Gayer, Knight, Viner, Douglas, and J.M. Clark," in the United States, and "Pigou, Layton, Stamp, Harrod, Gaitskell, Meade, E.A.G. Robinson, and J. Robinson," in England, as economists who "joined Keynes in coming out publicly in support of public spending" in the early and mid 1930s.

[18] Thus, in his *Means to Prosperity* (1933, pp. 15-16), Keynes warned that the expansionary consequences of enlarged public works expenditures could be dissipated by reduced government spending in other areas (or increased taxation). The maximum benefit from expanded government expenditures on public works would occur from "*additional* expenditures made, not in substitution for other expenditure, but out of savings or out of borrowed money, either by private persons or by public authorities, whether for capital purposes or for consumption made possible by a relief of taxation or in some other way." In this context, "the contrary policy of endeavoring to balance the Budget by impositions, restrictions, and precautions will surely fail, because it must have the effect of diminishing the national spending power, and hence the national income."

[19] As indicated in footnote 16, this does not constitute an argument that public borrowing is superior to an expanded money supply. To the contrary, Keynes believed that loan expenditures should be accompanied by a vigorous expansion in the quantity of money so that, in effect, public borrowing occurs together with an increase in the money supply as a means of financing expanded public investment. As noted in the body of the text, above, he also believed expansionary monetary policy was essential in combatting the possibility that recovery from depression could be aborted through higher interest rates caused by higher income and prices fostered by expansionary fiscal policy and in reducing the likelihood that economic expansion could turn into a "slump."

References

Ackley, Gardner. (1961) *Macroeconomic Theory*. New York: Macmillan.

Blaug, Marc. (1985) *Economic Theory in Retrospect*. New York: Cambridge University Press.

Burke, Edmund. (1774/1972) "Speech to the Citizens of Bristol." *In Communism, Fascism and Democracy*, edited by Carl Cohen. New York: Random House.

Caparaso, James A. and David P. Levine. (1992) *Theories of Political Economy*. New York: Cambridge University Press.

Clarke, Peter. (1988) *The Keynesian Revolution in the Making*. Oxford: The Clarendon Press.

Dillard, Dudley. (1948) *The Economics of John Maynard Keynes*. New York: Prentice-Hall.

Elliott, John E. (1994) "Keynes's Two Perspectives in the General Theory and After." In *Recent Contributions to the History of Economic Thought*, edited by Karen Vaughn. Brookfield, Vt.: Edward Elgar.

_____. (1992) "Keynes' Critique of Wage Cutting as Antidepressionary Strategy." In *History of Economic Thought and Methodology*, edited by Warren A. Samuels. 9: 129-69. Greenwich: JAI Press.

_____. (1987) "Marx's Moral Critique of Capitalism." In *History of Economic Thought and Methodology*, edited by Warren A. Samuels. 4. Greenwich: JAI Press.

_____. (1981) *Marx and Engels on Economics, Politics, and Society*. Santa Monica: Goodyear.

_____ and Barry S. Clark. (1987) "Keynes' General Theory and Social Justice." *Journal of Post Keynesian Economics*. (Spring):

Hansen, Alvin. (1949) *A Guide to Keynes*. New York: McGraw-Hill.

_____. (1938) *Full Recovery or Stagnation?* New York: Norton.

Harrod, Roy. (1951) *The Life of John Maynard Keynes*. New York: Harcourt, Brace.

Hayek, Friedrich A. (1944) *The Road to Serfdom*. Chicago: University of Chicago Press.

Hicks, John R. (1937) "Mr. Keynes and the Classics: A Suggested Interpretation." *Econometrica 5* (April): 147-59.

Keynes, John Maynard. (1940) "The United States and the Keynes Plan." *The New Republic*. CIII (July 29): 156-159.

_____. (1937) "The General Theory of Employment." *Quarterly Journal of Economics*. LI (February): 212-23.

_____. (1937a) "How to Avoid a Slump." *The Times* (London). January 12, 13, 14: 13f, 13f, 13f.

_____. (1936) *The General Theory of Employment, Interest and Money*. New York: Harcourt, Brace.

_____. (1933) *The Means to Prosperity*. New York: Harcourt, Brace.

_____. (1926/1963) *The End of Laissez-Faire*. In *Essays in Persuasion*. New York: Norton.

Marx, Karl. (1975) *Grundrisse*. New York: Random House.

_____. (1968) *Theories of Surplus Value*, Vol. II, Vol. III. Moscow: Progress Publishers.

Macpherson, C.B. (1977) *The Life and Times of Liberal Democracy*. New York: Oxford.

Milgate, Murray and Shannon Stimson. (1991) *Ricardian Politics*. Princeton: Princeton University Press.

Mill, John Stuart. (1926) *Principles of Political Economy*. New York: Longsman.

_____. (1948) *Representative Government*. Chicago: University of Chicago Press.

Modigliani, Franco. (1944) "Liquidity Preference and the Theory of Interest and Money." *Econometrica 12* (January): 45-88.

Patinkin, Don. (1965) *Money, Interest and Prices*. New York: Harper.

Resnick, Stephen A. and Richard D. Wolff. (1987) *Knowledge and Class*. Chicago: University of Chicago Press.

Robbins, Lionel. (1932) *The Nature and Significance of Economic Science*. London: Macmillian.

Robinson, Joan. (1976) "The Age of Growth." *Challenge 19* (May/June): 4-9.

Salerno, Joseph T. (1992) "The Development of Keynes's Economics: From Marshall to Millenialism." *The Review of Austrian Economics*. 6 (1): 3-64.

Samuelson, Paul A. (1948) *Economics*. New York: McGraw-Hill.

Schumpeter, Joseph A. (1950) *Capitalism, Socialism and Democracy*. New York: Harper.

Streeten, Paul. (1954) "Keynes and the Classical Tradition." *In Post-Keynesian Economics*, edited by Kenneth Kurihara. New Brunswick: Rutgers University Press: 345-64.

7 KEYNES'S PHILOSOPHICAL THINKING *

John B. Davis

Introduction

The interpretation of John Maynard Keynes's philosophical thinking involves significant methodological difficulties which ought to be identified and understood prior to any attempt to explain that philosophy. These difficulties chiefly stem from the fact that Keynes's philosophical and economic work were carried out during almost entirely different periods of Keynes's life and intellectual career. When he was first an undergraduate at Cambridge, Keynes thought that his important scholarly efforts were likely to be made in contributions to the philosophy of logic only recently initiated in Bertrand Russell and Alfred North Whitehead's *Principia Mathematica*.[1] Yet when Keynes completed his undergraduate study, his interests had shifted more economics, politics, and economic policy, and philosophy had come to be more of an avocation than a vocation for him. Indeed by the time his *Treatise on Probability* was essentially finished (around the beginning of the first World War), he had all but put aside the sort of systematic discussion of philosophical ideas he had pursued in his undergraduate and immediate postgraduate years at Cambridge with the result that philosophical ideas are either altogether absent from the language and thought of Keynes's economics, or such philosophical themes as do appear in Keynes's economics appear at such significant remove from the contexts in which they originally functioned that we must wonder whether their meanings and roles have been subtly changed by their re-location to economics.

The first and perhaps most difficult problem confronting interpreters of the role of philosophy in Keynes's thought, then, is to determine how far one ought to go in reading Keynes's early philosophical ideas into his subsequent economics. Keynes, we know, developed his first philosophical ideas almost entirely before he had begun to think seriously about economics. One cannot simply assume, then, that those early ideas were instrumental to the development of his subsequent abstract thinking in economics. If Keynes had troubled himself over abstract economic questions at an earlier date, and should these abstract speculations have been clearly at issue in his early philosophical reasoning, then it could readily be argued that Keynes's early philosophical commitments were in some degree motivated by his theoretical concerns in economics. But this did not occur. Indeed, Keynes drew few connections between these two spheres of ideas after he turned to economics, suggesting rather that he found his early philosophical views only marginally valuable for the deeper theoretical issues of economics. This of course would not imply that Keynes's early philosophical ideas were of no value whatsoever to his thinking in economics. One certainly would not expect any philosophically accomplished thinker to engage in

223

wholesale abandonment of hard-won ideas upon turning to another field, and it should be emphasized that early philosophical themes do indeed appear in Keynes's economics. Rather the point here is that because the role of Keynes's early philosophical ideas in his subsequent economic thinking is not clear, one cannot assume that those ideas were foundational to Keynes's economics, or even rule out the possibility that other abstract ideas beyond the purview of philosophy formed the deeper conceptual roots of Keynes's economics.

But there is a second, independent problem involved in interpreting the place of philosophy in Keynes's economics. This stems from the fact that Keynes's economic thinking itself changed substantially over his later career, something Keynes himself was most emphatic about. Scholars of course dispute the manner and degree to which Keynes departed from his early economic thinking in *The General Theory*, but none deny that there were important changes in his later theoretical commitments, nor dispute the fact that Keynes himself believed these later commitments involved a change in his thinking at the deepest level. Thus, while abstract commitments in economic reasoning can generally be treated independently of traditional philosophical questions, there is no doubting the fact that change in one sphere often has implications for the other. It would be a mistake, then, to assume without argument that the changes in Keynes's theoretical commitments in economics occurred without concomitant changes or adjustments in his philosophical thinking, and indeed on the surface it would be more natural to think that changes in the foundations of Keynes's economic thinking were also accompanied by changes in his philosophical thinking.

This second problem adds significantly to the difficulties associated with our first problem. In the case of the first, we should be prepared to find that the functioning of philosophical ideas in the non-philosophical context of economic theorizing may have the effect of transforming the significance and meaning of these ideas relative to their original meaning and significance in pure philosophy. Thus, the interpreter of philosophy in Keynes's economics, who is already working with philosophical materials in somewhat transformed guise due to their embedding in a logic of economic discourse, now also finds that a change in economics paradigms requires that we further attempt to identify philosophical ideas not easily discernable as *per se* philosophical in a language of economics that has itself evolved since this initial embedding of philosophical ideas. The second problem of interpretation, then, compounds the difficulties associated with the first, leaving us, as it were, to locate Keynes's philosophy in his later economics at two removes from its original elaboration - removed from its original location in pure philosophical discourse and removed from its original point of entry into Keynes's economics. Twice so removed, such philosophical thinking would not only lack the clear outlines of Keynes's pre-economics philosophy, but also raise unavoidable questions concerning the path of development of Keynes's philosophical thinking.

Because of these two connected problems, it seems that interpreters of Keynes's philosophical thinking as it operates in his economics must consciously adopt and employ some theory of reading or strategy of interpretation regarding how ideas developed in one discursive framework should be thought to function in that of another, where the modes of inference, conceptual contents, and goals of analysis of the two frameworks possess significant differences. Having such a theory would provide the methodological basis for the claims made in the interpreter's analysis about the meaning and role of philosophy in Keynes's economics in that all an analysis' substantive claims would depend upon the system of translation adopted between different conceptual frameworks. In effect, interpreters of Keynes's philosophical thinking must respond to what has been explained in more philosophical-linguistic terms as a fundamental indeterminacy of translation across languages (Quine, 1969), that is, the inherent difficulty involved in explaining notions from different equally viable, self-contained languages or conceptual frameworks in terms of one another, when there exists no third medium or base language into which each might be adequately translated. From this perspective, a theory of reading or strategy of interpretation regarding Keynes and philosophy, like a theory of translation between any two languages, must be prescriptive in nature in that just as there cannot be definitive translations from one language into another, so there cannot be any last word on how Keynes's early philosophical concepts are to be seen at work in the very different world of his economics. This is not to say, it should be emphasized, that all theories of reading are equally adequate and acceptable, so that all opinions about Keynes and philosophy are equally acceptable. Rather, theories of reading must themselves be evaluated according to how well they appear to address the essential problems of interpretation involved in the literature in question, so that on the view here a theory of reading for Keynes and philosophy must be evaluated according to how well it addresses the two chief problems noted above.[2]

From this perspective, a naive theory of reading of Keynes on philosophy and economics (whether conscious or unconscious) would claim that Keynes's early philosophical ideas slipped unchanged and unaffected into his subsequent economics, and that his economics was thereby more surely constituted upon the foundation of these added notions. On this Panglossian view, not only is the fit between these two different systems of ideas essentially smooth and frictionless, but the incorporation of philosophical concepts in economics is also assumed to be conducive to straightforward progress in economic thought. Such a view, it needs to be emphasized, has as a central assumption the notion that philosophical ideas are relatively uncontroversial and convincing once grasped and appreciated, so that the chief question facing the interpreter is to see whether, and perhaps how, such ideas can be seen to find a foothold in non-philosophical disciplines. Philosophers, however, are more inclined to believe that philosophical ideas are complex and often problematical, in that they typically amount to shorthand for entire philosophical theories which themselves possess strengths and weakness relative to competing theories and the philosophical ideas that summarize them. But if philosophical ideas are inherently complex and problematical, then the view that they can easily constitute secure foundations for economic theory is mistaken. Moreover, since their incorporation in non-philosophical disciplines is likely to bring to light different dimensions of these ideas, or better theories, clearly their manner of incorporation and the different disciplines themselves into which they are incorporated are likely to affect their very meaning and interpretation. Thus, the incorporation of philosophical ideas in economic theory almost certainly transforms those ideas while at the same time injecting complex philosophical agendas into economics.

To avoid the errors of a naive reading of Keynes and philosophy, a more reasonable principle of interpretation would seem to be that Keynes's philosophical and economic thinking should each be seen to have had important effects upon one another. A first implication of this idea is that Keynes's philosophical thinking as it can be found in Keynes's early, pre-economics work should be seen to have been transformed in important respects by the development of his economic thinking, especially as it later developed itself in *The General Theory*, partly on account of the problematical character of a number of Keynes's early philosophical ideas, and partly on account of Keynes's stronger commitment to the logic of economic explanation to which his philosophical ideas increasingly adjusted. Most importantly, the central philosophical concept of Keynes's early thinking in both his early Apostles papers[3] and his *Treatise on Probability*, namely, the concept of intuitive judgment or intuition, can be seen to have altered with the development of Keynes's later economic thinking in such a manner that it ceased to have the meaning and role it possessed in these early works, becoming in *The General Theory* the very different idea of individual expectation. Significantly, this change in meaning was accompanied by a change in Keynes's view of the very nature of individual judgment in social life, whereby Keynes's early view of judgment as an individual's autonomous insight into the underlying nature of reality was supplanted by one of judgment as socially embedded and contingent.

A second implication of this view that both Keynes's philosophy and economics had important effects upon one another is that the development of Keynes's later economics also depended upon developments in Keynes's philosophical thinking. An important dimension of *The General Theory* is its emphasis upon conventions and the dispositional nature of behavior. Keynes speaks of his independent variables achieving states or levels of activity, and explains this in terms of the role conventions play in structuring the varying degrees to which psychological propensities and attitudes are manifest in different individuals. But this vision of interdependent individual judgment did not achieve prominence in Keynes's thinking until Keynes was struggling with the 1930s drafts of *The General Theory* and shortly after he had published an account of how Frank Ramsey's questions about his early philosophy had caused him doubts about his original concept of intuition.[4] Thus Keynes's later philosophical understanding of individual judgment represented both a response to difficulties he had encountered in attempting to use his old view of intuition in economics, and at the same time a means to the development of his new economic thinking with its emphasis upon the concept of convention. In this way, an overall intellectual development having transformative effects on both economics and philosophy concepts ended up creating a conceptual structure with reciprocal and mutual influences across its different theoretical domains.

Here, in order to give special attention to the transformative effects the development of Keynes's economic thinking had upon his philosophical ideas - a theme that seems underrepresented in the existing literature on Keynes and philosophy - it will be argued that an important task associated with explaining Keynes's new philosophical ideas is to account for their appearance in the non-philosophical discourse of his later economics. The methodological view here, it should be emphasized, is not that Keynes's involvement with economic reasoning caused him to re-select among available traditional philosophical concepts and theories, and that this arose from an intention to alter his traditional philosophical affiliations. Rather the view here is more radical in supposing that Keynes's changing concerns and increasing allegiance to economic thinking *per se* disrupted the integrity of philosophical reasoning itself for Keynes, so that his philosophical concepts, as they operated in transformed guise in the language of his economics, came to possess different roles than was customary for philosophical concepts in pure philosophy.

On this view, traditional philosophical questions appropriate to the early philosophical Keynes, such as whether judgment is objective or subjective, or whether Keynes continued to operate with a concept of rational belief in his later work, can only be posed for the later Keynes by interpreters intent upon disregarding the philosophical commitments implicit in Keynes's later economic reasoning. There Keynes operated with a view of individual judgment more properly characterized as intersubjective, and though it can indeed be argued by philosophers that elements of both objectivity and subjectivity inhabit such a notion, or that it is possible to regard individual judgments so understood as being consistent with rational belief, the view here is that a preoccupation with sorting out the balance between these pre-eminently traditional philosophical notions - paradigmatically the project of philosophers - chiefly serves to obscure the original philosophical issues at work in Keynes's later economics from the point of view of economics. That is, on the view here, a proper philosophy of economics arises more out of issues and questions internal to the abstract concerns of economics, and less out of effort to apply standard philosophical positions to economics. This particular view of the philosophy of economics is relatively recent, emerging historically, as did a similarly distinctive view of the philosophy of social science, with the discipline's recent maturity, and signaled most recently by methodologists' realization that the philosophy of economics is not the philosophy of science applied to economics.

The task called for here, then, is to distil the philosophical views from Keynes's later economics, where the traditional philosophical apparatus of concepts and principles of Keynes's early work is an imperfect guide for the analysis, where non-philosophical reasoning is the chief source of material for analysis, and where the result must be set forth as philosophy! Unavoidably this would require an effort that is at times speculative in nature, so that it will not be surprising should many interpreters of Keynes and philosophy, who prefer to take the ready-made, well-formed philosophical materials of Keynes's early years as their chief resource, dismiss such an approach. They do so, however, at the risk of ignoring the two principal problems involved in the interpretation of Keynes and philosophy described above, as well as running the risk, it should be emphasized, of making *The General Theory* the logical descendent of the *Treatise on Probability* by fitting the arguments of *The General Theory* into the pre-given conceptual layout of the *Treatise*. Indeed put this way, the matter is analogous to the problems of interpretation or reading associated with explaining Keynes's development from the *Treatise on Money* to *The General Theory*, where different interpretations emerge according to whether one sees the latter work as a essentially the final step in a generally continuous development of Keynes's ideas on monetary theory, or rather sees *The General Theory* as a significant departure from earlier ideas and a step forward in a discontinuous development of thinking.

Ironically, though the principal interest of the recent literature on the subject of Keynes and philosophy is to explain the contribution of Keynes's philosophical thinking to his later economics, most scholars have begun their research with the *Treatise on Probability*, as if Keynes's chronological intellectual development betokened a parallel conceptual or logical development, that is, as if later ideas depend upon earlier ones just as they follow earlier ones. Rather, then, than make *The General Theory* the starting point of their philosophical investigation, that book becomes the investigation's last step in a search to determine how the earlier book's themes came to be represented in the latter. This all implies, however, that the ideas of *The General Theory* tend to end up being evaluated according to conceptual requirements of the *Treatise*, a work completed before Keynes even began serious study of economics, and even longer before he began to revise his economic thinking. Ruled out is the notion that the *Treatise* might itself be evaluated by the standard of *The General Theory*, or, in the extreme, be regarded as an immature, fundamentally flawed conceptual structure that Keynes later found to be of little use as a whole upon turning to the problems of the social world. Of course, to represent the issue of the relationship between the *Treatise* and *The General Theory* dichotomously as a choice between only two approaches is to over-simplify the matter. The point emphasized here is that it is now necessary to explore how the *Treatise* measures up to *The General Theory*, in part because scholars have been so much favored the *Treatise*, and in part to find what is philosophically distinctive in *The General Theory*.

Practically speaking, then, what does this alternative emphasis imply? To argue that *The General Theory* should in important respects be taken as the measure of the *Treatise* is not to see the former as the teleological end-point in a march of progress toward some right economic philosophy. It is rather to show that Keynes's early philosophical thinking bore various contradictions and deficiencies, some of which he attempted to resolve while also working upon a number of relatively independent problems in economic theory. The philosophy of *The General Theory*, from this perspective, represents something of a temporary equilibrium in this process - one not necessarily free of its own difficulties, but nonetheless a comparatively settled state of affairs for a mature Keynes given the degree of accomplishment in the book. As an active thinker who was famously not reluctant to change his mind, Keynes thus continually reconstituted the structure of philosophical ideas that backed up his practical-theoretical affairs outside of philosophy, ever in search for what would assist him in accomplishing his goals. To tell the story of this process one must necessarily involve oneself in producing a rational reconstruction of what may be termed Keynes's philosophical development.

The Cambridge Interpretation and its Difficulties

The recent revival of interest in Keynes's philosophical thinking, however, has given little attention to the methodological issues described here.[5] Beginning in the 1980s largely in Cambridge, a number of scholars have argued that Keynes's early philosophical thinking is an important, overlooked source of understanding for his later economics, and that an examination of the ideas of his *Treatise on Probability* in particular provides firm foundations for explanation of Keynes's later arguments in *The General Theory*. In part this was stimulated by the breakup of the neoclassical Keynesian consensus among economists, and the conviction on the part of those still committed to Keynes's original vision that Keynes's thinking was somehow distinct at a deeper level from the Keynesianism that had become dominant in the postwar period. One way of explicating Keynes's unique vision was thus to link Keynes's economics to a distinct set of philosophical views concerning probabilistic argument. Whereas neoclassical thinking was attached to subjective utility theory of Ramsey and L. J. Savage, Keynes's views about uncertainty clearly had entirely different foundations in the objectivist view of probability in the *Treatise*.

Thus Tony Lawson argued in two influential papers (1985, 1987) that underlying Keynes's thinking about uncertainty in *The General Theory* was a view of rational behavior derived from Keynes's conception of objective or logical probability in the *Treatise*. At issue here was an earlier claim by Alan Coddington (1982) that Keynes's view of uncertainty was nihilistic in that it implied economic agents were ultimately irrational and thus beyond analysis.[6] The effect of Lawson's arguments was to demonstrate that, contrary to Coddington's view, Keynes had an entirely different, non-subjectivistic understanding of the capacities of economic decision-makers which was based on an early philosophical account of knowledge and belief. An especially important component of this early view was the idea that it was possible to speak about rational belief for Keynes in those epistemic contexts in which certainty was not available. The *Treatise*, then, provided the chief philosophical antecedents of *The General Theory*. At the same time, Lawson allowed and emphasized in later papers (1988, 1991, 1993) that Keynes's subsequent emphasis upon rule-following and the role conventions played in economic life required one also discuss rational belief within the context of enabling (and constraining) conditions that facilitated actual courses of action. The broad categories of agency and structure, that is, were both part of Keynes's later philosophical scheme, though it seemed that this balance and comparative emphasis were latent or missing in the *Treatise*.

Keynes, it should be emphasized, registered a number of hesitations over his early ideas. This was most apparent in the much commented-upon statements he made explicitly critical of his earlier philosophical views on two occasions: first, in 1930 in response to Ramsey's 1922 review of the *Treatise* (1978) immediately after its publication, Keynes asserted that Ramsey was in important respects correct in his criticisms of the principal philosophical claim of the book regarding the centrality of intuition (X, pp. 338-9); second, in his post-*General Theory* 1938 memoir of his first years at Cambridge, "My Early Beliefs," Keynes also asserted that his early pre-*Treatise* views had unduly emphasized intuition at the expense of the concept of convention (X, pp. 437, 446). To this might be added Keynes's comments regarding the change in his economic thinking in the Preface to *The General Theory*. There he said that the "composition of this book has been for the author a long struggle of escape ... from habitual modes of thought and expression" due to a "difficulty [that] lies, not in the new ideas, but in escaping from the old ones" (VII, p. viii).

These episodes suggest the possibility of significant discontinuities in Keynes's philosophical development, and we might thus emphasize them to set out a number of challenges to the Cambridge interpretation of Keynes and philosophy. First, given the clear, confident statement of his early views in the *Treatise*, Keynes's response to Ramsey indicating strong misgivings about his early positions seems to imply that there were indeed certain important respects in which Keynes's philosophical thinking changed and developed after he turned his attention to economics. Second, given that Keynes also thought it necessary to distance himself from important aspects of his pre-*Treatise* Apostles papers thinking in his 1938 "My Early Beliefs" memoir, that the *Treatise* made uses of many of these same ideas (especially the idea of intuitive judgment) suggests Keynes's doubts similarly applied to that work as well. Third, given that the *Treatise* and the Apostles papers are not easily reconciled, and that Keynes's early philosophical views are apparently less systematic and cohesive than they seemed prior to the recent discovery of the Apostles papers suggests that Keynes's early views subsumed fundamental dilemmas and divisions that may well have operated upon the development of his later thinking. Finally, it seems Keynes meant to signal in his Preface to *The General Theory* that his ideas had changed philosophically as well as in an economic sense, though he chose not to emphasize this.

Two major works of interpretation of Keynes's philosophy to come out of Cambridge, however, do not appear to have adequately addressed these issues. Indeed, Anna Carabelli's *On Keynes's Method* (1988) and Rod O'Donnell's *Keynes: Philosophy, Economics and Politics* (1989) present, in combination, a quite interesting puzzle of exegesis. Despite the evidence above, both works assume that Keynes's philosophical thinking did not change in significant respects, and thus argue that to make sense of Keynes's philosophical thinking, both across Keynes's career and in *The General Theory*, one must operate from the vantage point of the *Treatise on Probability*. Each in effect, then, takes on the double task of translating philosophical ideas into economic ones, and of inferring Keynes's later ideas from his earlier ones. Each also, interestingly, relate Keynes's philosophical thinking to the philosophy at Cambridge during his time there - a philosophy that developed from the beginning of the century analytic approach of Russell, Moore, and the young Wittgenstein to the very different forms of life philosophy of the later Wittgenstein (cf. Passmore, 1966).

Yet while Carabelli and O'Donnell share the opinion that Keynes's philosophy did not change and has its essential repository in the *Treatise*, they also differ in important respects from one another in just what they believe this philosophy to be. O'Donnell argues that Keynes's *Treatise* ideas were faithful to the early Cambridge philosophy of Russell, Moore, and the early Wittgenstein, while Carabelli argues that Keynes's thinking in the *Treatise* reflected an early, prescient attachment to themes characteristic of Wittgenstein's later philosophy. Further, operating from these dramatically different visions of how the *Treatise* underlies *The General Theory*, Carabelli argues that Keynes's later views were ultimately to represent an ordinary language philosophy reaction to early Cambridge neo-positivism, while O'Donnell argues that Keynes's later thinking was focused upon an explication of the intuitionist rational belief logic of early analytic philosophy. In effect, then, Carabelli and O'Donnell each seize upon different periods in Cambridge philosophy during Keynes's life there while agreeing that Keynes's views went unchanged. Carabelli locates this philosophy in a framework more suited to Keynes's later years and concerns, while O'Donnell locates it in a framework more reminiscent of his earliest preoccupations. If Keynes's views were thought to have developed, each might be said to have correctly captured a part of the story about Keynes's philosophical development, though each, on account of a common commitment to the notion that Keynes's views did not significantly change, has it seems at the same time failed to investigate the logic of development of Keynes's thinking that culminated in *The General Theory*.

Carabelli's approach, perhaps, suffers under the greatest strain of interpretation, since, in attempting to link Keynes's ideas in the *Treatise* to those of the later Wittgenstein, she needs to be able to explain the themes of the *Treatise* in terms of a philosophical thinking that did not receive expression at Cambridge until a decade and a half after the *Treatise*'s completion (in 1914 despite its publication in 1921). Wittgenstein did not return to Cambridge until 1929, and did not begin to seriously question his early views (and those of Russell and Moore) until shortly thereafter (Davis, 1988; Monk, 1990). Thus Carabelli's case requires that one believe that Keynes was extraordinarily prescient about future developments in philosophy at Cambridge (indeed more so than Wittgenstein), despite the fact that historians of philosophy almost universally reject this thesis. It also requires that one read the *Treatise* in an unusually creative way, since the imprint of the early Cambridge analytic philosophy of Russell and Moore on Keynes's ideas about intuition and indefinability is quite clear (Davis, 1991). Accordingly, though one might well want to investigate connections between Wittgenstein's later thinking and Keynes's later thinking, it seems highly unlikely a persuasive case can be made for linking the former and Keynes's views in the *Treatise*.

Perhaps because this case is such a difficult one to make, then, Carabelli chooses to explain the connection between Keynes and Wittgenstein in terms of a supposed shared commitment to ordinary language forms of expression. Keynes, she argues, can be seen to have had a preference for ordinary language forms of expression in the *Treatise*, and this orientation, she claims, is characteristic of Wittgenstein's later approach. However, most historians of philosophy (e.g., Passmore, 1966, pp. 440-2) would regard this as a mis-classification of Wittgenstein's later thinking, associating the ordinary language movement in philosophy principally with Oxford philosophers in the nineteen fifties (especially J.L. Austin and Gilbert Ryle). Though Wittgenstein was certainly attentive to the properties of our ordinary forms of linguistic expression, most would argue that his deeper concerns went substantially beyond those of the Oxford movement, and that to restrict his preoccupations to a preference for ordinary language seriously diminishes their importance. Whether these deeper concerns (such as what it means to follow a rule, or what is involved in describing a private mental experience) can be said to have connections to Keynes's later thinking remains an open question. There seems, however, to be little reason to think that they were foreshadowed by the arguments of the *Treatise*.

Despite such deficiencies in her argument, Carabelli is still to be commended for exploring possible linkages between Keynes's thinking and later developments in Cambridge philosophy. Indeed, though evidence of intellectual exchange between Keynes and Wittgenstein in the late nineteen twenties and early nineteen thirties is limited (Coates, 1990), a case can nonetheless be made for saying that Keynes's later thinking shared in a climate of ideas at Cambridge that characterized Wittgenstein's later views. Particularly important here is the central role of the concept of convention in the thinking of both men, a connection which Carabelli notes (pp. 224, 300), but does not pursue. Keynes, of course, emphasized the importance of conventions in his account of the formation of long-term investment expectations and the rate of interest (Keynes, VII, pp. 152-3, 203-4). Wittgenstein devoted much thinking to the analysis of conventional behavior and the institutions in which it operated, asserting at one point for example, that, "An intention is embedded in its situation, in human customs and institutions" (Wittgenstein, 1953, para. 337). For both men, moreover, this particular emphasis upon conventions and institutions represents an important departure from their earlier thinking.

Yet if Keynes in his later economics can be thought to share ideas with the philosophy of the later Wittgenstein, which by all accounts departs in significant respects from early, beginning of the century Cambridge philosophy, then it seems to follow that Keynes also must have given up some part of his early views in the transition to his later ones. As Carabelli well demonstrates in her discussion of Keynes's economics, there do indeed remain strong linkages between the *Treatise on Probability* and Keynes's later economics, especially in relation to such themes as the interdependence and complexity of relationships, belief and action, and the nature of theoretical investigation (pp. 151ff). But if this picture of continuity in Keynes's thinking is to be supplemented by the idea that this thinking also developed in a direction taken by the later Wittgenstein's thinking, then it is fair to ask what it is that Carabelli fails to see that Keynes must have given up from his early views to have ultimately adopted a form of thinking more like the later Wittgenstein's.

Here let it be briefly recalled that in his "My Early Beliefs" appraisal of his early views Keynes faulted his early thinking for its having made intuition of intrinsic qualities central to the business of establishing how individuals determine what they say they know (Keynes, X, pp. 437ff). On this view, individuals possessing particularly strong powers of intuition simply perceive the essential qualities or relations underlying the matters under investigation, and, when two individuals' intuitions are in conflict, there is little more to be said than that one must not have properly focused on the issue at hand. This doctrine, moreover, was central to *Treatise* where Keynes referred to the probability relation as that "type of objective relation between sets of propositions - the type which we claim to be correctly perceiving when me make [probability judgments] - to which the reader's attention must be directed" (Keynes, VIII, p. 6). On Keynes's own later statement, however, this sort of thinking was mistaken and naive. Indeed, were one to assert straightforwardly in a study of Keynes's philosophical thinking that *The General Theory* presupposes a metaphysics of "neo-platonism" (as Keynes termed his early thinking [Keynes, VIII, p. 438]), combined with an unacknowledged epistemology of the Cartesian subject (as he implicitly characterized it), it would be clear to most that the philosophical underpinnings of Keynes's later economics had probably not been properly addressed.

Carabelli, unfortunately, fails to see what Keynes's critique of his early rationalism amounted to, since she takes her discussion of "My Early Beliefs" to be an opportunity to deny Keynes became anti-rationalist or irrationalist (Carabelli, pp. 99-100). A more valuable task would have been to ask what Keynes's admission several years after the publication of *The General Theory* implied about the philosophical assumptions of that work. Did Keynes develop a new understanding of economic agents' cognitive behavior (as, for example, in his discussion of speculation and the 'beauty contest' [Keynes, VII, p. 156])? Did his abandonment of essential qualities and relations as the underpinnings of judgment transform his view of the objectivity of probability judgments (as, for example, in his later discussions of uncertainty)? Questions such as these, it seems, cannot be raised in an interpretive framework that takes Keynes's *Treatise on Probability* to possess all of the conceptual resources needed to explain Keynes's philosophical and economic thinking. At the very least, then, some analysis of the continuities and discontinuities in Keynes's philosophical thinking seems required if one is to explain both what persists and what is new in Keynes's philosophy across his career.

O'Donnell's book also suffers under the strain of its specific strategy of interpretation. Like Carabelli, O'Donnell makes Keynes's *Treatise* the essential repository of his philosophical thinking and argues that Keynes's views did not change in any essential respects. Unlike Carabelli, however, O'Donnell is altogether insensitive to both the development of philosophical thinking at Cambridge during Keynes's time there and its possible impact upon him. The tension this oversight imposes upon O'Donnell's book is perhaps most manifest in O'Donnell's discussions of Keynes's critical self-appraisals in the response to Ramsey and in his "My Early Beliefs," where rather than address the possibility that Keynes's remarks signaled a real change in thinking, O'Donnell first denies that Keynes was serious about these statements, and then argues that what we see in these two instances is merely a change in emphasis in Keynes's original thinking that enabled Keynes to accommodate such matters as uncertainty and confidence. Drawing upon Keynes's classification of different types of probability judgments (numerical and non-numerical, comparable and non-comparable, known and unknown) and discussion of weight in the *Treatise*, O'Donnell argues that Keynes first elaborated a theory of "*strong rationality*, based on known probabilities and referring to weight when appropriate," and then adopted a theory of "*weak rationality* [for] when reason in the strong sense has reached its limits and can proceed no further" for *The General Theory* (O'Donnell, p. 78).

Yet Keynes himself never made such a distinction anywhere in his published or unpublished works, and one must thus wonder whether this division adequately represents Keynes's own thinking or is rather the most ready conceptualization that O'Donnell was able to bring to bear to defend the continuity thesis. Indeed, the fact that Keynes's thinking in the *Treatise* operated on two distinct levels that O'Donnell does not clearly distinguish - that of the substantive apparatus of the probability calculus and that of the epistemological and ontological principles of the work - suggests that O'Donnell's description of changes in emphasis in Keynes's thinking may be confused. Specifically, since elements of Keynes's early probability calculus re-appeared in his later work (e.g., the reference to weight in connection with long-term expectations [Keynes, VII, p. 148]) without apparent accompaniment by their earlier philosophical elaboration (e.g., the early theory of intuition), it is quite possible that O'Donnell's view, as an interpretation of Keynes's philosophy, mistakes continuities in Keynes's substantive probability theory preoccupations for continuities in his philosophical concerns. This view gains further support from the fact that O'Donnell's description of Keynes's philosophical thinking in the *Treatise* as "a general theory of rational belief and action under uncertainty" (O'Donnell, p. 6) makes uncertainty - properly speaking, a substantive concern of the probability calculus in connection with unknown probabilities - a characteristic of Keynes's philosophy, though the latter should concern the form and character of knowledge irrespective of the certainty conditions under which it is exercised.

At the same time, care should also be exercised in arguing that significant continuity existed in Keynes's thinking about the substantive apparatus of the probability calculus. While a number of Keynes's early positions do make reappearance in his later thinking, that questions have been raised regarding the extent of continuity in even this domain, for example in connection with the Principle of Indifference (see, Gillies, 1988), gives us reason to wonder whether Keynes felt the same about his probability calculus at the time of the writing of *The General Theory* as he had in the *Treatise*. O'Donnell, if anything, only obscures these issues, in part because of his unhesitating commitment to the continuity thesis, and in part because his characterization of the *Treatise* as "a general theory of rational belief and action under uncertainty" improperly implants in the early Keynes a concern with the type of uncertainty issues that he really only turned to much later (perhaps most clearly after *The General Theory* in his 1937 *Quarterly Journal of Economics* response to reviews of *The General Theory* [Keynes, XIV, pp. 113-4]). While uncertainty and unknown probabilities may well be correlates of a sort that permit us to make rough comparisons between Keynes's early and later thinking, to say that Keynes in the *Treatise* was concerned with just the same matters surrounding uncertainty he investigated later on seems overbold.

For O'Donnell, then, Keynes's philosophy is essentially a theory of rationality, and we can at most detect changes in emphasis on this basic theme. Does this interpretation, one that seems to need to account for behavior in the world of *The General Theory* in terms of boundaries and limitations upon decision-making (reminiscent of the disequilibrium school interpretation of Keynes), adequately capture the revolutionary impact of that work on economic thinking? Certainly one thing central to *The General Theory* is its charge that traditional or Classical theory commits a fallacy of composition, or the idea that the economy in the aggregate functions quite differently than it does at the level of its units. Indeed, Keynes's critique of the Say's Law view of savings might be said to depend crucially on the notion that the rationality of the system is altogether different nature from the sort of rationality traditionally associated with agents' behavior. Alternatively, one might fairly say that there exist principles of organization operating at the level of the macroeconomy that altogether transcend rationality. Conventions, in particular, have a key role in Keynes's historical, shifting equilibrium method that has become increasingly central to scholars' characterization of Keynes's understanding of the economy (e.g., Rogers, 1989; Asimakopoulos, 1991), and whether or not conventional individual behavior may be regarded as rational seems less important than explaining just how conventions create structures of socio-economic interaction.

It is difficult, however, to make conventions a central focus should one's fundamental vision of Keynes's philosophy be Platonist, as it is in O'Donnell. On O'Donnell's view, Keynes never really abandons the "neo-platonism" of his early views that supposes that behind the play of everyday phenomena there exist timeless qualities and relations that are the proper objects of judgment in economics and ethics (though Keynes clearly disparages his early attachment to this thinking in "My Early Beliefs" [Keynes, X, p. 438]). Conventions, that is, are by their very nature *ad hoc* and indelibly historical in character, reflecting for Keynes past configurations of the economy that possess no deeper rationale than their fact of existence. Thus when one identifies the reigning conventions regarding long-term investment expectations or the rate of interest, it is hardly some underlying relation or quality one makes the object of one's judgment, as it was for Keynes in the *Treatise*; rather the investor or speculator is specifically concerned with transitory, historical objects of judgment. To term this a "weak rationality" on the model of a somewhat impaired "strong rationality" thus seems to wrongfully impose Plato's epistemology and ontology Keynes employed in the *Treatise* on a fundamentally different kind of thinking Keynes developed by the time of *The General Theory*.

In O'Donnell's case, then, it might well be said that it is less the particular difficulties of interpreting Keynes's later thinking in terms of his early philosophy than an essentially inadequate vision of what *The General Theory* was all about that raises questions. As has been made clear by Skidelsky (1983), the first World War inalterably transformed Keynes's early world. Except, perhaps, for a continuing utopian spirit regarding reform politics, Keynes found little of what had made up the conceptual approaches of his early years that could be brought to bear upon the deep problems of the then-modern age. There is no doubt that he did appropriate important elements of the logical apparatus of his probability calculus of the *Treatise* to employ in his later thinking, just as important components of the *Treatise on Money* found their way into new contexts in *The General Theory*. But the philosophical basis of Keynes's later thinking has its foundation in a different set of conceptual needs that Keynes faced in the nineteen thirties.

O'Donnell's work can be contrasted in these respects to the work of a last interpreter of Keynes and philosophy at Cambridge, Jochen Runde. Recognizing the need to show specific connections between the different but related concepts of the *Treatise* and *The General Theory*, Runde has argued in a number of careful papers that Keynes's later concerns re-shaped some of his earlier ones. In a discussion of the relationship between Keynes's earlier concept of weight and later concept of confidence, Runde distinguishes a conception of weight for Keynes as the degree of completeness of the information on which a decision is based, then argues that though this conception received little attention in the *Treatise*, it nonetheless can be seen to have links to Keynes's later concept of confidence (Runde, 1990). Similarly, in another discussion of Coddington's critique of Keynes on uncertainty, Runde maps out the connections between Keynes's early view of probability and later understanding of uncertainty, and then points out that any discussion of the instability of investment demand for Keynes also requires one distinguish both epistemic and institutional factors (Runde, 1991, pp. 142-3). Coddington's nihilistic view of Keynes, Runde argues, turns on a failure to appreciate the emphasis Keynes placed on conventions in observed decision-making practices - a view that requires one pay more attention to what Keynes brought to *The General Theory* after the *Treatise*.

This theme of the pattern of connection and disconnection between Keynes's two books, in fact, receives illuminating explication in a further paper by Runde (1994). Arguing in terms of the impact of Ramsey's criticisms of the *Treatise* on Keynes's subsequent thinking, Runde describes the effect of Ramsey's influence on Keynes as having driven Keynes from his early neo-Platonist metaphysics, while leaving him relatively convinced of the adequacy of his probability calculus. That re-tailoring of his views left Keynes's theory being better described as what Runde characterizes as a theory of comparative probability, or a theory of rules for the derivation of comparisons of probabilities from comparisons of probabilities already given, without Keynes's earlier attendant claims about the existence of probability relations. The impact of Ramsey's arguments, then, was to cause Keynes to abandon his early philosophical claims about the meaning or nature of probability for a greater emphasis upon the conditions that pertained to the kinds of judgments individuals make. In a not unrelated discussion (1993), Runde explains liquidity preference in *The General Theory* in terms of the extent of incompleteness of information agents face and the scope available for responding to this incompleteness. As Keynes's philosophical thinking developed, then, his acquaintance with the dilemmas of decision-making facing economic agents led him to focus more on the probability calculus of the *Treatise* and less on his earlier epistemological claims.

Surveying the line of interpretation recently developed at Cambridge, then, it seems that the underlying problems of interpretation involved in explaining Keynes's intellectual career have always been close to the surface. Beginning with the initial insights of Lawson, moving through the difficulties that emerge in the attempts at more complete statements of Keynes's philosophy on the part of Carabelli and O'Donnell, and then considering the later arguments of Runde, one finds efforts to reconcile the very different conceptual structures of two works Keynes wrote many years apart from one another always seem to raise issues of continuity and discontinuity. The Cambridge interpretation has emphasized an essential continuity in Keynes's theoretical development. The discussion that follows builds upon the methodological arguments concerning the need for a motivated theory of reading to emphasize discontinuities in Keynes's philosophical development.

Keynes's Changing Conception of Philosophy

Here I only set out in outline the elements of a view I have developed at length elsewhere (Davis, 1994a) to present one view of how the methodological issues addressed above may be confronted. The discussion is thus inevitably summary in nature, and its purpose is only to provide a general account of how the two problems of interpretation discussed above might be addressed. There, recall, it was argued that both Keynes's philosophical and economic thinking should be seen to have had important effects upon one another in Keynes's intellectual development. On the one hand, this meant that Keynes's philosophical thinking changed as his economic thinking developed and changed, and on the other hand, this meant that Keynes's economic thinking was influenced by his changing philosophical views. I will briefly treat each of these aspects of this development in the discussion that follows, and then close with general comments on the character of Keynes's later philosophical thinking.

First, there is the question of how the development in Keynes's economic thinking affected his philosophical views. The change in Keynes's philosophical thinking that is both most significant and which Keynes was most emphatic about was his abandonment of his early concept of intuition or pure insight into the underlying nature of reality. In his response to Ramsey and in his assertions in "My Early Beliefs," Keynes tells us that his early view of intuitive judgment was naive and that a society's conventions deserved greater attention. Another important source for Keynes's later views, however, is his exchange with Roy Harrod over the nature of economics as a moral science. Focusing on the "motives, expectations, [and] psychological uncertainties" of economic decision-makers (Keynes, XIV, p. 300), Keynes portrayed individual judgment in distinctly interactionist terms, such that the manner in which a single individual came to any given conclusion depended upon that individual's having some acquaintance with other individuals' thinking on like subjects in like contexts. Judgment seen in this light, it seems, is better characterized as a form of interdependent judgment, and thus when we emphasize the concern Keynes had with judgments about future, uncertain state of affairs, we may describe the pattern of judgments a variety of individuals exercise in interrelated circumstances as a system of interdependent individual expectations.

Keynes's thinking about economics, then, both in his methodological pronouncements to Harrod and in his efforts to explain the economic agents' motives, expectations, and psychological uncertainties in *The General Theory* appeared to exhibit a different understanding of what was involved in individual judgment from what Keynes had assumed in his earliest philosophical speculations through to the publication of the *Treatise on Probability*. There may well have been other influences on Keynes's thinking about intuition besides his confrontation with decision-making practices of economic agents in actual economies. The doctrine of pure unmediated insight Keynes had inherited from his teacher G.E. Moore was subjected to critical analysis by a variety philosophers and commentators in the nineteen twenties and thirties (Hudson, 1970), and it is unlikely Keynes was completely unaware of this. But Keynes clearly found the need to explain a society's conventions especially important in his analyses of the financial and investment dimensions of modern economies. Since he had employed the idea of a pure unmediated intuition in his early arguments to criticize the notion that individuals ought to follow general rules of conduct, his later conviction that a society's conventions and rules were important in the financial and economic world required him to re-evaluate that earlier critique of rule following. This in turn required that he re-consider the nature of individual judgment itself, since it seemed indisputable that individuals were reliant upon one another in their recourse to rules and conventions in economic life in ways that had not seemed significant to Keynes in his early reflections on ethics and aesthetics.

Keynes's later view of judgment as more socially embedded, however, also arguably affected deeper views he held regarding the nature of individuality and sociality. In his early work he had found himself unable to resolve a dilemma he encountered in his thinking between observing a responsibility to be good to oneself and a responsibility to do good to others. Indeed in his 1906 unpublished paper, "Egoism," Keynes despaired at ever being able to reconcile individuals' social responsibilities and individual interests, precisely because his original theory of intuition provided no means of linking different judgments that conflicted with one another. This situation was changed by his later experience with economic policy-making and reasoning about the need for social-economic institutions that would stabilize investment practices. Arguing on a number of occasions that semi-private, semi-public institutions such as the universities, port authorities, and Bank of England combined public purpose with private conception in an unique way, Keynes urged there be a general socialization of investment in shifting a greater proportion of total investment to such institutions. Such recommendations, clearly, were inspired by the practical exigencies of a national planning meant to erase unemployment. But attendant upon the call for such measures was a changed conception of the nature and capacities of individuals and the forms of interaction between them. It hardly made sense to say that economic agents were fully autonomous individuals when the idea of semi-private, semi-public institutions envisioned them relying upon one another in acting for the public good. Thus the movement away from Keynes's early philosophical thinking about intuition and judgment had broader implications for Keynes's social philosophy as well.

To argue, however, that both Keynes's philosophical thinking and economic thinking had effects upon one another also requires, secondly, that one be able to say how Keynes's later philosophical thinking assisted the development of his economic thinking. As suggested above, this is in many ways the more difficult and interesting argument to make, since the case in this instance rests on saying how a philosophical thinking no longer recognizable in its original outlines - one indeed removed from the language of traditional philosophy - came to operate in an economic thinking whose categories preoccupied Keynes. Nonetheless, Keynes provides good guidance for us here in signaling the importance to him of the concept of convention. That concept appeared only marginally in Keynes's earlier thinking, and on account of Keynes's early critique of general rules lacked the normative force he later attributed to it. To see how the notion later came to underlie Keynes's subsequent philosophical thinking, we must determine what its philosophical content is in the framework of the economic ideas in which it is elaborated, and then establish how the notion is employed in the economic argument of *The General Theory*.

Generally in *The General Theory* Keynes may be said to hold that an economy's conventions are responsible for determining the levels or states of activity displayed by the psychological propensities and attitudes at work in the economy. These psychological propensities and attitudes, however, manifest themselves in varying degrees in different individuals, so that it might be said that an economy's conventions ultimately act to structure different individuals' psychological propensities in relation to one another. In Keynes's most developed treatment of convention, in his twelfth chapter treatment of long-term expectations, this becomes a matter of understanding the relationship between average expectation and the set individual expectations surrounding a given investment. Keynes emphasizes that the convention governing investment is that "the existing state of affairs will continue indefinitely, except in so far as we have specific reasons to expect a change" (Keynes, VII, p. 152). He also tells us that what makes an investment good or bad is governed by the average expectation of those who buy and sell on the Stock Exchange. We may thus explain the convention operating in connection with investment as a structure of expectations having average expectation as a central tendency for a diverse collection of bulls and bears' individual expectations.

Treating convention as a structure of expectations enables us to combine both the inertial quality of a practice with that practice's potential volatility - something required in light of Keynes's seemingly paradoxical assertion regarding the investment convention that an existing state of affairs will endure unless people come to expect a change. That is, when we regard a convention as a structure of expectations, individual judgments both take consensus judgments (or average expectation) into account, yet also take them as points of departure as efforts are made to beat the market and make a profit. This means that there is a tendency for reigning prices for investments to prevail, but also a tendency for these prices to change as average expectation is changed by the judgments individuals make as bulls and bears. Investment understood in these terms might be volatile or relatively steady depending upon the willingness of individuals to gamble on changes in average expectation. The degree of willingness or unwillingness to gamble on changes in average expectation further depended for Keynes upon the state of confidence as it affected individual investors. Thus Keynes's understanding of investment as conventional in the sense here enabled him to estimate the path this important component of total expenditure might take as confidence among investors ebbed and grew.

Familiar though he had been for many years with finance and investment, then, it was not until *The General Theory* that Keynes produced this particular account of investment spending. We may attribute this in part to his development of a deeper understanding of the investment process brought on by a greater appreciation of the role conventions played in investment decisions. That deeper understanding itself, it is fair to say, only emerged with changes in Keynes's thinking about the nature of individual judgment. Looking upon individual judgment as individual expectation in a system of interdependent individual expectations, rather than as pure insight into the underlying nature of things,

Keynes acquired a fundamentally different view of how individuals responded to the radical uncertainty he emphasized in his discussion of long-term expectations. In particular, though uncertainty was an inescapable fact of life, the degree to which it affected investment depended upon the state the system of interdependent expectations affecting investment achieved. In this way, uncertainty over investment was for Keynes more of a social relation than a metaphysical dilemma, so that the nihilism of Coddington and others rather indicated a failure to grasp how Keynes's vision left open the possibility (and promise) of a social reform response to investment uncertainty.

The working of this new philosophical conception of interdependent judgment in Keynes's economics, however, lacked the clear outlines and familiar language of the traditional philosophical themes that had occupied Keynes in his first years at Cambridge. Perhaps most obviously the question of whether judgment should be termed objective or subjective did not naturally arise in this new context. Indeed, understood in essentially an intersubjective manner judgment can be said to be both objective and subjective with average expectation capturing elements of the former quality and individual expectation reflecting more of the latter. From this perspective, it is not clear that it makes good sense to debate whether Keynes remained wedded to the objectivist conception of judgment he began with in his *Treatise* (O'Donnell, 1989), or reversed himself after Ramsey's critique to adopt a subjectivist understanding of judgment (Bateman, 1987). Relatedly, it may also be beside the point to contest whether Keynes can be said to have thought conduct rational in *The General Theory*, when his earlier view of rational belief depended on a neo-Platonism he clearly had abandoned after Ramsey.

Admittedly, this view of how the original philosophical issues confronting Keynes ceased to be significant in his later work will strike some as inadequate. Yet should we suppose that Keynes's philosophical thinking went through a process of development as he moved to the theoretical domain of economics and then also within that domain, we must be prepared to find the nature of his philosophical concerns affected by that development. Thus to argue that convention is a philosophical concept is to argue that *The General Theory* involves fundamental philosophical concerns unique to the particular theorization of the economy its attempts. And, such philosophical concerns must, as it were, be read off that theorization or seen to be implicit in the underlying commitments the book's arguments presuppose if we are to grasp the issues and concerns that beset Keynes - more or less consciously or unconsciously - as he worked to produce an alternative understanding of the functioning of the economy.

Another way of getting at the theory of reading recommended here is to focus on what is involved in premising *The General Theory* in one's interpretation of Keynes's philosophy. All of the recent interpreters of Keynes's philosophical thinking discussed above (and others not discussed) have hoped to provide a better account of Keynes's later economics through their analysis of the arguments of the *Treatise on Probability*. Yet going to the *Treatise* for this purpose runs the risk of importing the *Treatise*'s organization of concepts into a conceptual structure that likely includes different materials and a different conceptual organization. Thus to avoid the danger of reading *The General Theory* in terms of the *Treatise* one needs to begin with the system of concepts in the later work. This is arguably not what is done when the chosen axis of analysis is probability-uncertainty, since the latter notion in this pair represents an aspect of the forms of social interaction Keynes investigates in economic life rather than a conceptual representation of that interaction itself. To premise the conceptual structure of *The General Theory*, then, is to begin with the principal social relationships at issue, and then link the philosophical notions involved there with earlier like notions. On the argument here, then, the preferred axis of analysis is autonomy-social interaction, especially as this is associated with intuition-interdependent expectations.

Keynes in many ways was much like the other two great philosopher-economists, Adam Smith and Karl Marx. All three developed philosophical views first, and then turned almost exclusively to economics and political economy. All three gave comparatively little indication of their later philosophical views, and especially how these corresponded to their earlier ones. And all three, arguably, were less concerned with the philosophical implications of their later work than with its more immediate significance. Scholars, of course, have for some time disputed the relationships between the Smith of the *Moral Sentiments* and the Smith of the *Wealth of Nations* and the Marx of the *1844 Economic and Philosophical Manuscripts* and the Marx of *Capital*. But few have been persuaded to think that the earlier works of these authors contained the essence of the latter works. Indeed few have been persuaded to think that the conceptual structure of those earlier works carried over unaffected into the frameworks of the latter works. This work takes it that the same opinions will ultimately prevail in regard to Keynes's intellectual career, and that the *Treatise* will be then seen as a work distinct in purpose and much removed from the goals and ambitions of *The General Theory*.

Notes

* Sections one and two of this paper draw upon Davis 1994a and 1994b.

[1] For a discussion of early Cambridge analytic philosophy and how Russell and Whitehead's work fit into it, see Urmson (1956). For Keynes's early history, see Skidelsky (1983) and Moggridge (1992).

[2] In this respect, the view here differs from the less restrictive view of interpretation strategies advanced in Gerrard (1991).

[3] For discussions of these early unpublished papers located in the King's College Modern Archive at Cambridge University, see Skidelsky (1983), Davis (1991), and Lawson (1993).

[4] See Rymes (1989) for the early drafts of The General Theory. For Keynes's reaction to Ramsey, see Bateman (1987), Cottrell (1993), and Runde (1994).

[5] For an overview, see Skidelsky (1992, pp. 56-89). Also see Lawson and Pesaran (1985), Bateman and Davis (1991), and Gerrard and Hillard (1992) for collections of papers on Keynes and philosophy.

[6] The view had its origins in Shackle (1974).

References

Ambrose, Alice. (1979) *Wittgenstein's Lectures, Cambridge, 1932-35*, Totowa, New Jersey: Rowman and Littlefield.

Asimakopoulos, Athanasios. (1991) *Keynes's General Theory and Accumulation*. Cambridge: Cambridge University Press.

Bateman, Bradley W. (1987) Keynes's Changing Conception of Probability. *Economics and Philosophy*, 3: 97-120.

_____. (1991) *Das Maynard Keynes Problem. Cambridge Journal of Economics*, 15: 101-111.

_____ and John B. Davis, eds. (1991) *Keynes and Philosophy*. Aldershot: Edward Elgar.

Carabelli, Anna. (1988) *On Keynes's Method*. New York: St. Martins.

Coates, John. (1990) *Ordinary Language Economics: Keynes and the Cambridge Philosophers*. Ph.D. dissertation, University of Cambridge.

Coddington, A. (1982) "Deficient foresight: a troublesome theme in Keynesian economics." *American Economic Review*, Vol. 72, No. 3, pp. 480-7.

Cottrell, Allin. (1993) "Keynes's Theory of Probability and Its Relevance to His Economics: Three Theses." *Economics and Philosophy*, Vol. 9, No. 1, pp. 25-52.

Davis, John B. (1988) "Sraffa, Wittgenstein and neoclassical economics." *Cambridge Journal of Economics*, Vol. 12, No. 1, pp. 29-37.

_____. (1991) Keynes's critiques of Moore: philosophical foundations of Keynes's economics. *Cambridge Journal of Economics*, 15: 61-77.

_____. (1994a) *Keynes's Philosophical Development*. Cambridge: Cambridge University Press.

_____. (1994b) "On Interpreting Keynes's Philosophical Thinking: *On Keynes's Method* by Carabelli, and *Keynes: Philosophy, Economics and Politics* by O'Donnell." *Research in the History of Economic Thought and Methodology*, Vol. 12.

Gerrard, Bill. (1991) "Keynes's *General Theory*: Interpreting the Interpretations." *Economic Journal*, Vol. 101, pp. 276-287.

_____ and John Hillard, eds. *The Philosophy and Economics of J.M. Keynes*. Aldershot: Edward Elgar.

Gillies, Donald A. (1988) Probability and Induction. In G.H.R. Parkinson(ed.), *Encyclopedia Of Philosophy*. London: Croom Helm.

Hudson, W.D. (1983) *Modern Moral Philosophy*. New York: St. Martin's.

Keynes, John Maynard. (1906) "Egoism." Unpublished manuscript, King's College Library, Cambridge University.

_____. (1971-1989) *The Collected Writings of John Maynard Keynes*, I-XXX. London: Macmillan.

Lawson, Tony. (1985) "Uncertainty and Economic Analysis." *Economic Journal*, Vol. 95, pp. 909-927.

_____. (1987) "The Relative/Absolute Nature of Knowledge and Economic Analysis," *Economic Journal*, Vol. 97, pp. 951-970.

_____. (1988) "Probability and uncertainty in economic analysis." *Journal of Post Keynesian Economics*, Vol. 11, No. 1, pp. 38-65.

_____. (1991) "Keynes and the Analysis of Rational Behavior." In *Keynes as philosopher-economist*, ed. R.M. O'Donnell. London: Macmillan.

_____. (1993) "Keynes and Conventions." *Review of Social Economy*, Vol. 51, No. 2, pp. 174-200.

_____. and Hashem Pesaran. (1985) *Keynes' Economics: Methodological Issues*. London: Croom Helm.

Moggridge, Donald E. (1992) *Maynard Keynes*. London: Routledge.

Monk, Ray. (1990) *Ludwig Wittgenstein*. New York: Free Press.

O'Donnell, R. M. (1989) *Keynes: Philosophy, Economics and Politics*. New York: St. Martins.

Passmore, John. (1968) *A Hundred Years of Philosophy*. Middlesex: Penguin.

Quine, W.V.O. (1969) *Ontological Relativity and Other Essays*. New York: Columbia.

Ramsey, Frank. (1978) *Foundations of Mathematics*. London: Routledge & Kegan Paul.

Rogers, Colin. (1989) *Money, Interest and Capital*. Cambridge: Cambridge University Press.

Runde, Jochen. (1990) "Keynesian Uncertainty and the Weight of Arguments." *Economics and Philosophy*, Vol. 6, No. 2, pp. 275-292.

_____. (1991) "Keynesian uncertainty and the instability of beliefs." *Review of Political Economy*, Vol. 3, No. 2, pp. 125-145.

_____. (1993) "Keynesian Uncertainty and Liquidity Preference." *Cambridge Journal of Economics*.

_____. (1994) "Keynes After Ramsey." *Studies in History and Philosophy of Science*.

Rymes, T.K., ed. (1989) *Keynes's Lectures, 1932-1935: Notes of a Representative Student*. London: Macmillan.

Savage, L.J. (1954) *The Foundations of Statistics*. New York: John Wiley.

Skidelsky, Robert. (1983) *John Maynard Keynes*, Vol. I, Hopes Betrayed, 1883-1920. London: Macmillan.

Urmson, J.O. (1956) *Philosophical Analysis*. Oxford: Oxford University Press.

Wittgenstein, Ludwig. (1953) *Philosophical Investigations*, 2nd ed. Oxford: Basil Blackwell.

THE KEYNESIAN PROBABILITY-RELATION:
IN SEARCH OF A SUBSTITUTE

COMMENT BY JOCHEN RUNDE

John Davis argues that many of the earlier contributions to the literature on Keynes's philosophy do not pay enough attention to the possibility that Keynes's philosophical commitments changed over time. This is an important point. It is not sufficient, as Davis puts it, merely to read the arguments of *The General Theory* into the pre-given conceptual layout of the *Treatise on Probablity*. The task of coming to grips with the philosophical underpinnings of Keynes's economics requires sensitivity, not only to the question of how his earlier philosophical thinking colored his later work, but also to how his economic thinking developed over time and how this process might have affected his later philosophical thinking.

That said, it is perhaps understandable in retrospect that the earlier contributions concentrated on elaborating continuities between the Treatise on Probability and The General Theory. The original impetus for much of this work sprang from the view that the Neoclassical Synthesis left out much that was central to Keynes's message. High on the list of omissions, one that received particular emphasis in the Post Keynesian literature, was the impact of uncertainty in economic life. The fact that the Master himself had produced a systematic and highly distinctive study of probability and rational conduct under uncertainty was therefore something of a godsend to heterodox Keynesians looking for alternatives to the expected utility model and the rational expectations hypothesis. The result, however, was that much of the early work that touched on Keynes's theory of probability was conducted by people whose primary interests were in areas other than pure history of economic thought.[1] In concentrating on providing rational reconstructions of Keynes's approach to economic analysis on the basis of his position in the *Treatise on Probability*, they were perhaps less sensitive than they might have been to the development and change that his philosophical ideas might have undergone.

Davis's paper and forthcoming (1994) book (and Brad Bateman's) aim to redress the balance and are therefore much to be welcomed. There is no doubt that these contributions will go a long way in providing us with a richer and more penetrating insight into Keynes's philosophical ideas. However, care should be taken to avoid having the pendulum swing too far in the opposite direction. This note argues that the differences between the *Treatise on Probability* and chapter 12 of *The General Theory* are in some respects smaller than Davis suggests and makes some observations on his reconstruction of Keynes's later philosophical views.

The main substantive point that Davis makes about Keynes's philosophical development is that he later abandoned his earlier commitment to "intuitionism". I now agree with this,[2] although I am not sure that the practical consequences for Keynes's economic analysis of behavior under uncertainty are quite so dramatic as Davis suggests. By intuitionism Davis means Keynes's view in the *Treatise on Probability* that a rational degree of belief in a proposition arises out of the apprehension (intuition) of a logical relation of partial implication (RPI) between that proposition and some set of evidential propositions. The RPI is written h/e, in Keynes's notation, and reads "hypothesis relative to the evidence."

Keynes's ontology of RPIs and his claim that we can come to know them have come under skeptical attack before. But it turns out that the *Treatise on Probability* does not enquire into the nature of the RPI itself, which is presented as an indefinable not analyzable in terms of simpler ideas (CW VIII, p. 8), nor, other than in rough outline, into how propositions and RPIs come to be known. What it does offer, in my view, is a theory of comparative probability that builds on given binary comparisons of the form $h^1/e^1 >* h^2/e^2$ (where $\geq*$ is the qualitative probability relation "at least as probable as"). That is to say, Keynes *assumes* a knowledge of RPIs in order to develop the structure of the relation $\geq*$, to show how further comparisons of probability and perhaps real-valued probabilities may be derived from other comparisons already given. As this particular enterprise requires no more of RPIs than that they are (sometimes) comparable by $\geq*$,[3] it does not turn on any particular interpretation of whatever it is that links conclusions and evidence in nondemonstrative arguments (Runde, 1994). Ramseyian doubts about the existence of RPIs are not as damaging as they may seem, since these do not entail anything about the formal structure of Keynes's theory of comparative probability.

It is therefore quite possible for Keynes to retain important elements of his earlier system while accepting Ramsey's view that "the basis of our degrees of belief - or the a priori probabilities as they used to be called - is part of our human outfit, perhaps given us merely by natural selection, analogous to our perceptions and to our memories rather than to formal logic" (CW X, p. 339). This position is quite compatible with the three key themes from the *Treatise on Probability* that reemerge in Keynes's economic writings on uncertainty, i) that probability is fundamentally comparative, even though many pairs of probability judgments are not even comparable, ii) that it will only be possible to assign unique real-valued probabilities in a highly restricted class of cases and iii) that differences in the amount, weight or completeness of the evidence on which estimates of probabilities are based may matter. I believe that Davis would be largely in agreement with this point.[4]

Clearly all of this leaves considerable scope for proposing an alternative theory of what provides the basis of our partial beliefs (if not directly intuited RPIs). Davis's positive contribution, both in the preceding chapter and his forthcoming book, is to reconstruct what he regards as Keynes's later position on this matter, implicit in his economic writings. He argues that "the central philosophical concept of Keynes's early thinking in both of his early Apostles papers and his *Treatise on Probability*, namely, the concept of intuitive judgment or intuition, can be seen to have altered with the development of Keynes's later economic thinking in such a manner that it ceased to have the meaning and role it possessed in these early works, becoming in the *General Theory* the very different idea of individual expectation" (1993, p. 5). Davis's aim is to establish a shift to a view of judgment as socially or conventionally based in this transition.

The suggestion that Keynes replaces the notion of intuition in the *Treatise on Probability* with the notion of an expectation in *The General Theory* is an important one, as it provides the locus of the "discontinuity" Davis identifies. I am however not convinced that there is any major change here. Keynes provides the following definition of "expectation" in *The General Theory*, which applies to both producer (short-term) expectations of sales-proceeds and investor (long-term) expectations of investment returns (CW VII, p. 46, n. 1).

> An entrepreneur, who has to reach a practical decision as to his scale of production [nature and level of investment], does not, of course, entertain a single undoubting expectation of what the sales-proceeds of [returns on] a given output [investment] will be, but several hypothetical expectations held with varying degrees of probability or definiteness. By his expectations of proceeds [returns] I mean, therefore, that expectation of proceeds [returns] which, if it were held with certainty, would lead to the same behavior as does the bundle of vague and more various possibilities which actually makes up his state of expectation when he reaches his decision (CW VII, p. 24, n. 3).

Keynes conceives of an expectation as some composite of a list of outcomes imagined possible, following some course of action, each of them weighted by some rough judgment of its probability. This is of course not to say that he is assuming precise mathematical expectations, or that his "certainty equivalent" assumption is equivalent to a calculated expected value. What he has in mind, in my view, is an abstract representation of the more ambiguous and partial real-world counterpart of what an expected utility calculation is typically taken to be an idealization of. His definition is compatible with some adjustment for risk (which appears implicitly in chapter 12) and evidential weight (which appears explicitly).[5]

This conception of expectation is more or less identical to that which appears in chapter 26 of the *Treatise on Probability*, where the same four kinds of judgment are introduced (probability, the "good" of possible outcomes, risk and weight). The position Keynes adopts on the definiteness of these judgments, moreover, is exactly the same as in his later writings: he is extremely skeptical, both about their numerical measurement and about weighing the good associated with each outcome by some more complicated function of its probability (that is, by one which includes some measure of weight and risk as arguments). I would therefore suggest that it is not right to say that Keynes substitutes the notion of expectation for the of notion intuition in his later writings. His conception of expectation in *The General Theory* is the same as in the *Treatise on Probability*. What he does substitute, and here I am in agreement with Davis, is his theory of what provides the basis of our partial beliefs.

Davis's emphasis, with respect to this last question, is on what he describes as Keynes's later view of judgment as "socially embedded":

> ... Keynes portrayed individual judgment in distinctly interactionist terms, such that the manner in which a single individual came to any given conclusion depended upon that individual's having some acquaintance with other individuals' thinking on like subjects in like contexts. Judgment seen in this light, it seems, is better characterised as a form of interdependent judgment, and thus when we emphasize the concern Keynes had with judgments about future, uncertain states of affairs, we may describe the pattern of judgments a variety of individuals exercise in interrelated circumstances as a system of interdependent individual expectations (Davis, 1994, p. 238).

Davis argues that these patterns or "structures' of individuals" (interdependent) judgments correspond to what Keynes calls "conventions" in his later economic writings. A key theme, here, is what Dupuy (1989) and Orléan (1989) call "specular behavior," that agents form beliefs by putting themselves into each others' shoes in attempt to "see" the situation from the others' perspective. Davis interprets Keynes later chapter 12 remarks on this theme as evidence of a departure from the notion of judgment as unmediated intuition in the *Treatise on Probability* to a notion of judgment as "socially-based."

There is clearly a case to be made along these lines and Davis has many good things to say here (not least in his parallel between Keynes's emerging views on the social nature of judgment and increasing interest in and involvement with public institutions). I would nevertheless urge that although specularity may be important, especially in situations of extreme uncertainty, that it cannot provide the basis for a general theory of partial belief in Keynes's later writings. The issue turns in part on what a "convention" is taken to be, which Davis defines very broadly as a "structure of expectations." I shall use the narrower definition of a convention as a self-sustaining regularity in the behavior of agents in a social group that has the following property: given that each agent expects the other members of the group to conform to it, it is in each agent's own interest to conform to it.[6]

Let us see how Keynes's "conventions" fit with this definition. In his 1937 QJE article, he distinguishes between three:

(1) We assume that the present is a much more serviceable guide to the future than a candid examination of past experience would show it to have been hitherto. In other words we largely ignore the prospects of future changes about the actual character of which we know nothing.

(2) We assume that the *existing* state of opinion as expressed in prices and the character of existing output is based on a *correct* summing up of future prospects, so that we can accept it as such unless and until something new and relevant comes into the picture.

(3) Knowing that our own individual judgment is worthless, we endeavor to fall back on the judgment of the rest of the world which is perhaps better informed. The psychology of a society of individuals each of whom is endeavoring to copy the others leads to what we may strictly term a *conventional* judgment (CW XIV, p. 114).

As stated, (1) is no more than an inductive rule of thumb that agents employ to get by when they are highly uncertain about the future outcomes of their current actions. Nothing in (1) entails that it will only be in the interest of an agent to conform to it if he or she expects the other agents to conform to it. It may be just as effective in "games against nature" as in social situations, and therefore does not qualify as a convention in the sense defined above. (2) is a special case of (1), namely (1) applied in the context of asset markets (where the "existing" situation is in large part given by the ruling configuration of asset prices). Here, of course, it is necessary that the other agents conform to (2) in order for it to be in the interests of the individual agent to conform to it. Clearly, the reflective market participant will realize this and may use this knowledge to his or her advantage. But (2) may usefully be adopted even by unreflective agents. Keynes remarks that it "will be compatible with a considerable measure of continuity and stability of our affairs, so long as we can rely on the maintenance of the convention" (CW VII, p. 152). The point is that this reliance need not be specularly-based.

(3) differs from (1) and (2) in that it involves each agent actively attempting to "see" the situation from the others' perspective, each recognizing that the others will be doing the same thing with respect to him or her. This process of following the others' leads, everyone doing the same thing, leads to Keynes's "conventional judgment." Specular behavior is clearly a necessary part of the story here, qualifying (3) as a convention in the narrower sense. The interesting thing here is that the object of agents' beliefs in asset markets may be dependent on those beliefs. Specularly-based beliefs may not only confirm stable asset prices or asset prices that are rising or falling over some period, but provide the basis for the behavior which leads to such price behavior. The trouble is that these beliefs will be disconfirmed the moment that some agents depart from the conventional judgment. And this may easily occur.

My point, then, is that specularly-based beliefs may be more of a special case in Keynes's later writings than Davis suggests, albeit an extremely interesting and important one. Further, it seems that Keynes seems to regard specular behavior as becoming important when agents find it impossible to make judgments of probability, even if only qualitative ones. This leads me to my final thought. Might specular behavior not be better interpreted as complementary to rather than a substitute for any particular theory of probable belief? The Keynesian beauty contest, after all, makes its first appearance in the *Treatise on Probability* in a long section on the numerical indeterminacy (and possible non-comparability) of probability. Even the orthodox personalist interpretation of probability, widely regarded as non-permissive than Keynes's in <u>Treatise on Probability</u>, runs into difficult questions about the existence of subjective probabilities in situations of strategic interaction (Sugden, 1991).

Notes

[1] See especially Shackle (1972, 1974a, 1974b, 1979), Minsky (1975), Rutherford (1984), Lawson (1985, 1987), Lawson and Pesaran (1985).

[2] My two earlier papers (Runde, 1990, 1991) make precisely the mistake identified by Davis.

[3] Keynes insists in the *Treatise on Probability* that some probability relations may not be comparable by $\geq*$, that is that for some h^1/e^1 and h^2/e^2, neither $h^1/e^1 \geq* h^2/e^2$ nor $h^2/e^2 \geq* h^1/e^1$.

[4] The basic notions of comparative probability and evidential weight are quite compatible with subjectivist interpretations of probability (see, for example, Koopman, 1940; Fishburn, 1983 and Gärdenfors and Sahlin, 1982). Of course the possibility that some propositions or events may not be comparable by $\geq*$ or that preferences over lotteries may be affected by differences in evidential weight raise severe difficulties for the orthodox Bayesian (and Ramseyian) view that subjective degrees of belief should always be regarded as corresponding to point probabilities.

[5] Keynes describes the entrepreneur's or borrower's risk in chapter 11 of *The General Theory* as arising "out of doubts in his own mind as to the probability of his actually earning the prospective yield for which he hopes" (CW VIII, p. 144). The considerations which go into the assessment of the expected "own-rate" of interest of an asset, moreover, also include judgments of good (returns), probability, risk and weight (CW VII, p. 240).

[6] This definition is similar to that proposed by Lewis (1969).

References

Davis, J.B. (1994) Keynes's Philosophical Thinking.
_____ (1994) *Keynes's Philosophical Development*. Cambridge: Cambridge University Press.

Dupuy, J.P. (1989) Common Knowledge, Common Sense. *Theory and Decision* 27, 37-62.

Fishburn, P.C. (1983) Ellsberg Revisited: A New Look at Comparative Probability. *The Annals of Statistics* 11, 1047-1059.

Gärdenfors, P. and Sahlin, N.-E. 1982) Unreliable probabilities, risk taking, and decision making. *Synthese* 53, 361-386.

Keynes, J.M. (1973) A Treatise on Probability. *The Collected Writings of J.M. Keynes* VIII. London: Macmillan.

_____ (1972) Essays in Biography. *The Collected Writings of J.M. Keynes* X. London: Macmillan.

Koopman, B.C. (1940) The Axioms and Algebra of Intuitive Probability. *Annals of Mathematics* 41, 269-292.

Lawson, T. (1985) Uncertainty and Economic Analysis. *Economic Journal* 95, 909-927.

_____ (1987) The Relative/Absolute Nature of Knowledge and Economic Analysis. *Economic Journal* 97, 951-970.

Lewis, D.K. (1969) *Convention: A Philosophical Study*. Cambridge, MA: Harvard University Press.

Minsky, H.P. (1975) *John Maynard Keynes*. New York: Macmillan.

Orlèan, A. (1989) Mimetic Contagion and Speculative Bubbles. *Theory and Decision* 27, 63-92.

Runde, J.H. (1990) Keynesian Uncertainty and the Weight of Arguments. *Economics and Philosophy* 6, 275-292.

_____ (1991) Keynesian uncertainty and the instability of beliefs. *Review of Political Economy* 3, 125-145.

_____ (1994) Keynes After Ramsey: In Defence of A Treatise on Probability. *Studies in History and Philosophy of Science*, forthcoming.

Rutherford, M. (1984) Rational Expectations and Keynesian Uncertainty. *Journal of Post Keynesian Economics* 6, 377-387.

Shackle, G.L.S. (1972) *Epistemics and Economics: A Critique of Economic Doctrines*. Cambridge: Cambridge University Press.

_____ (1974a) *Keynesian Kaleidics*. Edinburgh: Edinburgh University Press.

_____ (1974b) Decision: The Human Predicament. *The Annals of the American Academy of Political and Social Science* 412, 1-10.

_____ (1979) *Imagination and Choice*. Edinburgh: Edinburgh University Press.

Sugden, R. (1991) Rational Choice: A Survey of Contributions from Economics and Philosophy. *Economic Journal* 101, 751-785.

INDEX